INTRODUCING SPECIFI(

A Practical Ca

THE McGRAW-HILL INTERNATIONAL SERIES IN SOFTWARE ENGINEERING

Consulting Editor

Professor D. Ince
The Open University

Titles in this Series

INTRODUCING SPECIFICATION USING Z: A Practical Case Study Approach

Bryan Ratcliff

Aston University
Birmingham

McGRAW-HILL BOOK COMPANY

London · New York · St Louis · San Francisco · Auckland
Bogotá · Caracas · Lisbon · Madrid · Mexico
Milan · Montreal · New Delhi · Panama · Paris · San Juan
São Paulo · Singapore · Sydney · Tokyo · Toronto

Published by
McGRAW-HILL Book Company Europe
SHOPPENHANGERS ROAD, MAIDENHEAD, BERKSHIRE, SL6 2QL, ENGLAND
TELEPHONE 0628 23432   FAX 0628 770224

British Library Cataloguing in Publication Data
Ratcliff, B.
    Introducing Specification Using Z:
    Practical Case Study Approach. –
    (McGraw-Hill International Series in
    Software Engineering)
I. Title II. Series
005.1

ISBN 0–07–707965–5

Library of Congress Cataloging–in–Publication Data
Ratcliff, B.
    Introducing specification using Z : a practical case study
approach/Bryan Ratcliff.
        p. cm. —(The McGraw-Hill international series in software
engineering)
    Includes bibliographical references and index.
    ISBN 0–07–707965–5
    1. Z (Computer program language) I. Title. II. Series.
QA76.73.Z2R38 1994
005.1'2—dc20
                                                            93–33831
                                                               CIP

12345 CUP 97654

Typeset by Bryan Ratcliff
and printed and bound in Great Britain at the University Press, Cambridge

For my only child
Amy
(from the French 'aimée': beloved)

CONTENTS

PREFACE

The topic of formal methods, with varying degrees of rigour and depth, now finds a slot in most undergraduate and postgraduate computing degree programmes. Largely, it is to students on such courses that this introductory text is aimed. However, the book is also suitable for any software practitioner who wants to know more and is seeking a thorough introduction to the discipline. There are no particular prerequisites, although familiarity with programming in at least one high-level language is recommended; some broad understanding of what constitutes 'software engineering' would also be useful. No prior knowledge of discrete mathematics is assumed.

As the book's title indicates, the text focuses on specification using the Z notation. Originally, it was intended that the text should cover all of formal methods using Z, from specification through refinement to code. However, the size of the text became uncomfortably large, and so the decision was made to draw a boundary round specification (mainly).

First and foremost, the book is meant to be a teaching, even self-learning, text that provides a *practical* rather than theoretical treatment. To that end, the bulk of the material 'hangs off' a sequence of three system case studies of increasing complexity (firstly Chapter 3, then Chapters 5 and 6, and lastly Chapter 8). All the important mathematical basics are covered but are made somewhat subservient to the case studies, rather than vice versa. The vast majority of Z is described, with *bags* being the only topic that has been omitted.

Via the case studies, I have also tried to place some emphasis on technique, both as regards the construction of state models and also in respect of structuring specifications. Attention is paid to how state modelling relates to real-world problem domains—the choices available, the factors to consider, and the criteria that can be used to arrive at a good, valid state model. The book also devotes somewhat more space than is usual (Chapter 7) to the topic of data type construction, emphasizing the importance of axiomatic description in its role of supporting other, particularly system-level, specification work.

The text is not solely about constructing specifications, however. At a contextual level, the importance and potential impact of formal methods within the framework of software engineering is stressed. Although proof is not dealt with as a separate topic anywhere in the book, most of the final chapter is devoted to an overview of theorem proving and refinement. This is intended as a 'kickstart' to encourage the reader to find out more about these important topics in subsequent study. All the main consistency theorems are discussed and illustrated with simple examples. Data refinement and its concomitant theorems are also covered.

The practical orientation of the book manifests itself in other ways. The nine chapters are liberally infused with a large number of exercises which, to have maximum effect, should be treated as an integral part of the text and attempted as much as time and motivation permit. In a few cases, a whole exercise or (part-)question within an exercise carries a comment flagged by an initial '§' character. The comment indicates that the answer can be found *in the subsequent body of the text* and tells the reader where. This device has been used to avoid 'inadvertent cheating' on the part of the reader.

Example solutions to *all* non-§ exercises and questions (except the final exercise in the book) are given in Appendix II.

The text, prepared as camera-ready copy by the author (in retrospect, a supreme act of masochism), is the culmination of a rather exhausting four-year solo project. Along the way, many people have made the task easier in different ways or provided contributions which have resulted in significant improvements to the end product. In no particular order, but with equal conviction, I would like to thank the following.

Firstly, several referees at various junctures provided valuable criticism of the emerging text. Not quite every comment has been taken on board, but then I suppose that is author's prerogative. Nevertheless, I hope they will feel that their suggestions have been acted upon to good effect. At home base, I would like to thank various colleagues. Many useful conversations were had with Paul Golder and Hanifa Shah concerning E–R modelling. Peter Coxhead, always unruffled despite my persistent intrusions, was a constant, valuable source of some of the more arcane (and golden!) features of the word processor I was using. I am also grateful to Neil Toye who, whenever I bothered him, never failed to produce the necessary updates to an evolving prototype font containing all the Z symbols I needed. In later stages, Graeme Walters and John Aspinall uncomplainingly stuck to the task of picking up bugs as I bombarded them with chapter after chapter of a precursor to the final version.

I am particularly indebted to John Aspinall, without whose assistance achieving any sensible deadline would have been impossible. Firstly, John built on Neil's earlier work by enhancing the Z symbol font to publication standard. Secondly, John also carried out the necessary, though tedious, task of checking the syntax of virtually all Z paragraphs occurring in the book, including those in the exercise answers. This was achieved by retyping the Z text into the CADIZ™ tool available from York Software Engineering Ltd. Only fragments of Z—mainly those occurring below the paragraph level where checking with CADIZ would be impractical—have been bypassed. To facilitate the checking, minor adjustments had to be made in a small number of instances to make the syntax conform to the essentially pre-Spivey (1992) syntax expected by the version of the tool used. Where differences have arisen, the book uses syntax conforming to Spivey (1992), *not* to the tool.

Thanks must also go to various staff, past and present, at Shoppenhangers Lane who have been involved at various stages of the project. They have all managed to deal effectively with a slightly mad author and his awkward, sometimes complaining ways. I would particularly like to thank Liz Nemecek for her amazing calm and patience in dealing with a stream of (sometimes panic) phone calls near the final deadline.

Finally, whilst there is considerable freedom attached to being sole author and typesetter, the price one pays is that there is nobody else who can be blamed for mistakes. 'Bugs' in the text are naturally my responsibility, though if there are any, I trust they will be few and innocuous. My main hope is that the reader will find the approach, orientation, and content sufficiently refreshing amongst a burgeoning Z literature to give the book a real go.

Bryan Ratcliff
Aston University

1

SOFTWARE ENGINEERING: WHY FORMAL METHODS?

Key Topics   The life cycle: requirements, specification, design, implementation; quality: reviews, testing; problems. Formal methods: objectives, specification, proof; main benefits.

1.1   A SOFTWARE ENGINEERING CONTEXT

Software engineering suffers from many afflictions:

Client
'Our business operation needs a new information system. We've got a reasonable feeling for what we want it to do for us, so we've outlined some ideas and possible solutions in this document ...'

Software Engineer
'We've sketched out a specification of the software component of your required system that we think will give you what you seem to be asking for in your initial document. We're confident we can have it implemented and delivered to you by the agreed deadline ...'

Quality Controller
'We're almost at the end of some extensive system testing. We have, of course, uncovered a number of bugs en route; but we've rectified them—no problem. The system is now working fine with all the representative test data we can manage to throw at it, so we're confident you are going to get a really good product ...'

User Representative
'On-site trials have quickly revealed that the software system as delivered is totally unacceptable. Quite apart from the unusable interface, it frequently crashes; and when it is operational, it sometimes behaves in ways which are simply wrong or which we never asked for. Even some of the facilities that we wanted don't seem to be present ...'

Software Manager
'Our valued client who commissioned system XXXX is hopping mad, and it's going to cost us a lot of extra time, money and staff to put right. I'd like a word with the guys responsible for its development ...'

This scenario, contrived and exaggerated though it is, reflects an ongoing concern that the delivery of poor quality software is an ever-present problem in software engineering. Since an underlying theme of this book is software quality—loosely, the software works as intended and is found to be satisfactory in all other respects considered important by the client—we will now investigate why such quality is all too often an endangered species and how traditional methods of attempting to control and assure software quality might be improved upon.

It is assumed that the reader is familiar with the rudiments of software engineering, but if not, a diagram like that in Figure 1.1 will help.

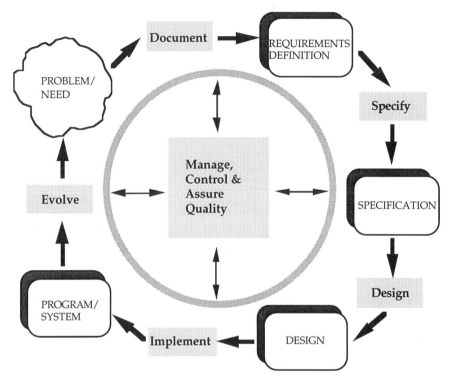

Figure 1.1 A simplified software engineering life cycle model.

This diagram models the engineering process, albeit in a very simplified fashion; rectangles are activities, 'soft' boxes are deliverables. The model is broadly applicable regardless of the kind of artifact being built. In software engineering, it is often referred to as the *life cycle*, though this is not everybody's favourite term, and the life cycle is not everybody's favourite model. Many variations of the life cycle have been devised, and many alternative process models have been constructed in an attempt to devise improved frameworks for software engineering; but Figure 1.1 will suffice for our purposes (see also Figure 1.2 on page 11).

The main quality issues of concern in software engineering, and the deliverables to which they relate, are as follows:

REQUIREMENTS DEFINITIONS
Relevant issues here are:

• Do the stated requirements express what the client and potential users of the software really want? For example,
  – are there any omissions?
  – has anything been included which is unnecessary?
  – are there any conflicts?

- Is the requirements document
  - free of obscurity?
  - unambiguous?
  - consistent and complete?

Note that the two sets of questions relate to different aspects of capturing/eliciting requirements and then documenting them. The first deals with what a client and users actually want; the second deals with whether the requirements have been expressed with a sufficient degree of accuracy and clarity.

It is universally accepted that deciding the requirements for a new system is the hardest part of the life cycle. In stating this, we are assuming client-procured software, or software aimed at a market need. There can, of course, be situations where the application is so new and innovative that it requires a certain amount of experimental software development just to understand the problem.

Since a requirements definition is largely an informally expressed document using natural language and client-friendly diagrams, the above questions are—indeed, can only be—answered by *review*. In the introductory scenario, we can imagine that the draft requirements document produced by the client would have to be significantly firmed up before it could be presented for approval as a basis for subsequent development of the system. Basing specification, design, etc. on a set of inadequately articulated requirements is not a recipe for success.

SPECIFICATIONS

Important questions to be asked about specifications are:

- Can the specification of the proposed software be given an unambiguous watertight interpretation?

- If so, does this interpretation conform to what is expressed in the client requirements definition?

We will avoid using terms like 'requirements specification'. The distinction we will make between a 'requirements definition' and a 'specification' is quite simple. The former is written on behalf of clients, for clients, and describes what the client wants. The latter is a document written by software engineers for software engineers and represents the first technical description of the system to be built. As such, therefore, there is no mandate for a specification to be intelligible to the client. Rather, there is a need for it to be as precise as possible in terms of the notations used, given that we wish to be able to answer the above two questions with a high degree of confidence.

EXERCISE 1.1

Constructing some safety-critical software, you come across the following exception condition in the specification:

Caution!
To avoid risk of explosion, if valves A and B or C are closed, the system must shut off supply of ethylene from pipe D or pipe E if the vessel pressure is above 50 atmospheres.

Sketch an algorithm that would implement the functionality expressed in this description.

Exercise 1.1 provides a simple example of poor specification. Here is another, further emphasizing that even in small natural language descriptions a host of problems can lurk:

The system manipulates three counters. The value of one counter must always lie between the other two. As regards these latter two counters, the one must never exceed a certain specified value; a similar stipulation applies to the other.

Although the system being described here is ostensibly simple, the paragraph is anything but clear and unambiguous. The questions that need answering to obtain a single clear interpretation include:

- What is a 'counter'? Does 'counter' mean its value is a whole number? If so, is it the case that each counter can never be negative?

- Does the second sentence mean 'one counter always lies between the other two, though which counter this is can vary', or is this 'middle' counter fixed? Even if the latter, are the other two counters allowed to 'swap roles' in terms of which is the 'bottom' counter and which is the 'top' counter, or are these roles fixed too?

- Does 'lie between' mean 'strictly lie between'? That is, does it mean that the 'lying between' counter must not equal either of the other two, or is this allowed in either or both cases?

- In the third sentence, presumably 'must never exceed' implies 'can be equal to'? Also, does the sentence mean that both counters referred to (presumably the 'bottom' and 'top' ones) must not exceed the *same* specified value, or can this limit value be different for the two counters?

- Is/are the limit value(s) fixed or can it/they vary dynamically?

The reader will come across the 'counters' specification again in an exercise of Chapter 3. There are, of course, any number of examples one could give of this kind of thing; for a less trivial example discussed in the literature, try Meyer (1985). It is also worth pointing out that use of tables and diagrams to augment natural language text has considerable value, but can add its own batch of problems. A diagram, for example, is not intrinsically free of defects just because it is 'a diagram'.

It is not enough to defend use of natural language for specification by claiming that one simply needs to be careful with one's phrasing. Another main problem with natural language is that its syntax and semantics is complex and clumsy, making it wholly inappropriate as a medium for expressing technical concepts precisely and concisely, and to an appropriate level of abstraction (see Section 2.2). Also, use of natural language would hardly facilitate the automatic processing of specifications—a desirable capability, not least because of the valuable CASE tool support which it is then possible to provide (CASE: Computer Aided Software Engineering; CASE is the usual acronym applied to any software designed to support the software engineering process in some way).

The fact is that use of natural language frequently and unintentionally suffers from a variety of defects that we must avoid in any kind of technical description, such as

- noise   (extraneous text)
- inelegance   (verbosity/clumsiness)
- omission   (e.g., failing to define terminology used)

- ambiguity   (more than one interpretation)
- contradiction (two or more aspects impossible to satisfy simultaneously)
- obscurity   (lack of clarity in what is being conveyed)
- inconsistency (e.g., different ways of representing the same thing).

Reducing these internal defects, which means reducing reliance on natural language as the specification medium, will help to answer the quality control question on page 3 that asks: *can the specification be interpreted unambiguously?* This in turn will facilitate answering the question which follows it: *does the specification describe a software product which conforms to what the client wants?* Traditionally, quality control in specification manifests itself in terms of reviews. The problem is that if, as we might suppose in our scenario, there is little or no attempt to address the external issue of validating the specification against requirements, and/or the requirements are inadequately documented anyway, then it is virtually guaranteed that a system will be built which turns out to be unacceptable to its users.

DESIGNS

The main problems here are:

- Is the design correct? That is, does it in some sense 'correctly conform to' the specification?

- Is the design put together well? In particular, is it appropriately 'modular', i.e., composed of internally cohesive software components that interface with each other in well-defined ways?

Clearly, the first question is meaningless if the specification is internally defective. In addition, the question is pointless if the specification, no matter how good it is in other respects, fails the external test, i.e., it describes a system which will not satisfy the requirements when implemented. Note that the answer to the second question can be *no*, even though the answer to the first is *yes*. Modularity in its various guises is a key element of internal quality, and internal quality is just as important in the long term as regards maintenance and evolution of the system, as external, user-perceived quality (though one could plausibly argue that there is some coupling between the two). Again, the traditional approach to establishing design correctness and appropriateness is that of review, such as a *walkthrough* or *inspection* (see any textbook on software engineering, such as Pressman (1992)). Our introductory scenario did not mention design—it was already doomed by a defective specification anyway.

Design is generally portrayed as a pivotal activity in engineering, often with an implied emphasis on flair and creativity on the part of designers. Yet software may differ here. There is possibly a stronger technical coupling between specification, design and implementation in software engineering than in other engineering disciplines (see Chapter 9). It is true that the terms 'specification', 'design' and 'implementation' tend to conjure up different levels of abstraction—even different artifacts—in the software development process. Whilst this distinction is applicable to some development methods, there is a sense in which the terminology is slightly over-rich, possibly leading to some confusion. For example, a design can be regarded as a specification that contains a degree of computer-oriented detail not present in the (abstract) specification. Similarly, an implementation in a high-level language is a completely executable specification of a design. Moreover, in some methods such as Jackson System Development (Cameron 1989), the first specification product of the development process already contains extensive operational detail, i.e., detail that would be traditionally regarded as design. There is no subsequent, separately identifiable design step as such, but rather a transformation of the specification to the required implementation.

IMPLEMENTATIONS

Quality problems at this stage include:

- Is the code a correct translation of the specification/design?

- Will the behaviour of the implementation be consistent with the original requirements and hence satisfy the client?

Coding can be a hand-crafted activity, or—with some development methods—carried out automatically from a computerized form of the design or even specification. Once code begins to appear, another traditional quality control technique becomes applicable: that of *testing*, by which we mean computerized execution of the software. Testing is fine for answering the second question above. In fact, testing is the obvious and only means available, for how else would we expect a client to decide whether to accept a system except by using it live on site, putting it through a series of rigorous acceptance trials? Even with market-oriented (non-bespoke) software, the product can be loaned out to potential off-the-shelf buyers who use it 'in anger' and then convey their experiences back to the developer.

The problem with testing lies in answering the first question, which it cannot, in general, do so adequately. The example at the beginning of Gries (1981) acts as an incisive illustration of this fact (as well as an indicator of a more effective alternative to achieving software correctness). The next exercise serves to highlight the main cause of testing's inadequacy.

EXERCISE 1.2

You have invented a super-fast algorithm for sorting an array of 10 integers or less. On how many test cases should you try out your algorithm so as to be able to conclude that it is completely correct?

The limitations of testing arise for the following reasons:

- Correctness of software must at least mean 'entirely free of logical errors' when its functionality is judged against its specification. Yet testing can verify this with 100% certainty only if the software has been *exhaustively* tested, i.e., tested with all possible inputs consistent with its specification. Note that 'all possible inputs' will include error inputs as well as valid inputs if the specification covers error cases.

- In general, exhaustive testing is completely impracticable since the 'input space' of the software is far too large, although there can obviously be specific situations where exhaustive testing is possible. Thus, testing is usually *inductive* in the sense that, if the observed software behaviour conforms to its specification with a certain set of chosen tests, we induce—rather than *prove*—the conclusion that the software is correct.

- However, the induced conclusion can easily be wrong because there might well be errors lurking in the software that the tests simply have not detected. We cannot be sure of the absence of errors, since an error is known to be present only when a test discovers it—which is what testing is meant to do, i.e., *discover* errors.

- The problem is this: how do we design sets of test cases so that they 'adequately' test the software—that is, if no errors are detected, we feel sufficient confidence in our conclusion about the software's correctness? The difficulty of designing adequate test sets obviously increases with size-related software complexity.

Testing can sometimes shoulder a huge responsibility. This is especially so if a system is of the critical kind, i.e., something bad is likely to happen if the software malfunctions; e.g., a medical support system, or an aircraft navigation system. If a business information system 'falls over', the result might well be a lot of frustrated people and some degree of financial loss; but if an aircraft navigation system goes wrong, several hundred people might end up dead. In our introductory scenario, the project was coming off the rails right from the start. Even if it was on some kind of rails when testing began, no amount of system testing and bug elimination could guarantee an error-free system.

Summary

What conclusions can we arrive at from the above analysis and critique? Here are some possibilities:

- Documents using natural language should be avoided.

- Reviews are an ineffective quality control mechanism that need to be replaced by other techniques.

- Testing needs to be eradicated as much as possible from the development process.

However, *each one of these conclusions is invalid*. Non-technical, human-understandable documents are an essential means of communication between client and developer; and natural language is an important adjunct to explicating technical descriptions. Properly organized reviews are an effective means of quality control. Testing will always have a valuable corroborative role to play for the developer, as well as being the main vehicle by which clients judge the acceptability of delivered systems. Yet it is just as important to appreciate the limitations of all these facets of the software engineering process, as well as recognizing their value. This is where 'formal methods' enter the picture.

1.2 'FORMAL METHODS'

Objectives

It is mythology to think that so-called 'formal methods' are intended to replace reviews, testing, etc., or eradicate the use of natural language from technical documentation. On the contrary, formal methods are intended to *augment* these traditional features of software development with an additional level of sound engineering practice. The term 'formal method' is actually a misnomer since it is not the method which is formal, but rather the notations which are used. However, the term is now entrenched in the software engineering dictionary.

There are some who consider formal methods not to be software engineering. This is a strange position to take. Consider one of the central objectives of formal methods:

O1. (Greater descriptive accuracy) To construct technical descriptions of software systems and their components which are as precise and defect-free as possible.

Technical description is an engineering discipline, no matter what the form of engineering involved. For example, we do not expect bridges and roads to be built from imprecise specifications; we do not expect any form of hardware, mechanical or electrical, to be built from imprecise specifications. So we should not expect software to suffer this fate either.

The other main objective of formal methods is

O2. (Improved quality control) To produce software systems and components thereof that are verifiably correct with respect to their technical descriptions.

This is clearly a laudable objective, notwithstanding that we need to be clear about exactly what we mean by 'correct with respect to'. Verifying correctness requires the construction of *proofs*, which in turn involves the application of reasoning via some system of logic. In fact, working backwards, we cannot construct effective proofs unless the specifications and designs we wish to reason about are accurately described in terms of notations underpinned by relevant mathematics. We come back full circle to O1, an objective that can be viewed in two complementary ways. Either we can view precision in description as a necessity that (with the appropriate notations) has a useful additional benefit, namely that it facilitates reasoning about the properties of the software we are trying to build. Or, given that such reasoning is an objective, then descriptive accuracy is necessary anyway: we cannot have O2 without O1.

Let us accept the desirability of objectives O1 and O2, and the larger aim that embraces them, which is to improve the quality of the software artifacts we build above and beyond what traditional software engineering technology is capable of producing. The consequences are then clear. We need to infuse the software development process, both notationally and from the standpoint of verification, with an appropriate degree of relevant formal/mathematical rigour. Again, there should be no reason why software engineering should be treated differently to any other engineering discipline in this respect. We expect an electronics engineer to construct accurate descriptions of electronic circuits using notations suited to the task. Equally, we expect the engineer to be knowledgeable of the laws and associated mathematics underlying the behaviour of electronic circuits. Further, we expect the engineer to apply that knowledge when verifying that a given circuit design meets its specification. It is perhaps unfortunate, then, that the difficulties involved in realizing similar expectations in software engineering have been compounded by an unwarranted amount of resistance and scepticism, even hostility, on the part of some in the computing community (see Section 9.3 for a brief discussion of some of the issues).

Remark
We are of course assuming that software artifacts are amenable to mathematically-based description and analysis. This is perhaps not an entirely obvious fact, but one which the reader will have to take for granted for the moment.

Potential Benefits of Formal Methods

REQUIREMENTS

It is perhaps not fully appreciated that formal methods have a valuable role to play here. A requirement can be accommodated within a formal description only if the requirement can be understood. In fact, the very act of trying to formalize something tends to generate the kind of questions that users need to be asked in order to obtain clarification, resolve inconsistencies, discover omissions, etc. That this is the case will be evident to anyone who has ever tried to construct a formal specification, having been given a requirements definition.

SPECIFICATIONS

By the application of appropriate formal notations, the main benefit here is precise, unambiguous specifications free from the defects mentioned earlier that plague natural language narrative. Also, specifications can be reasoned about formally to check that they possess certain desirable properties. The obvious point is sometimes made that formal specifications are not going to be client- or user-intelligible. As was indicated earlier (toward the bottom of page 3), it should be equally obvious that they are not meant to be; this is true of all technical specifications, regardless of the development approach. What is important is to be able to validate a specification to the satisfaction of all concerned. How formal methods contribute here is discussed in Section 9.1.

DESIGNS

Designs can be derived from, and proved to be correct with respect to, specifications. Moreover, it is inherent in most formal methods that a specification, and hence the design derived from it, carries a strong *data abstraction* characteristic. Data abstraction is widely accepted as representing an excellent basis for modularity, and is also strongly related to the object-oriented view of software architecture, which is currently much in vogue (with some justification, most would consider).

IMPLEMENTATIONS

Implementations can likewise be derived that are provably correct with respect to designs, and hence with respect to specifications. We can show how this results with a modicum of formality, the first instance of such in the book! Our basic model of the software development process after requirements definition will be as follows:

> *All deliverables are technical descriptions, or 'specifications', of some kind. Each technical description subsequent to the first is derived from its immediate predecessor by the process of 'refinement' until code is reached.*

This model blurs conventional distinctions between 'specifications', 'designs' and 'implementations'. That this is a reasonable stance to take in a formal methods context has been hinted at earlier. Thus, suppose D_1 is the top-level or 'most abstract' description of what is to be built, i.e., a specification in conventional terms. By various refinement processes, this gets transformed into a description D_2, which in turn gets transformed into a description D_3, etc. Eventually, we arrive at a description D_n fully expressed in the target language. Let us represent the result of each step by

$$D_i \sqsubseteq D_{i+1}$$

where $\sqsubseteq$ is the symbol conventionally used to mean 'is refined by', or 'is correctly realized by'. $\sqsubseteq$ is an example of what is called a 'relation'. Let us claim (i.e., without proof) that $\sqsubseteq$ is 'transitive'; that is, it has the following property, where X, Y and Z are to be taken as arbitrary descriptions:

if $X \sqsubseteq Y$ and $Y \sqsubseteq Z$ **then** $X \sqsubseteq Z$

Then, no matter how many intermediate descriptions lie between D_1 and D_n, by appeal to the transitivity of $\sqsubseteq$, it must follow that

$D_1 \sqsubseteq D_n$

Thus, the final description—the software coded in the target language—correctly implements the original, most abstract description. Of course, we need ways of showing that our development decisions are correct, but that is another story. Refinement is not a topic covered in detail in this book, though it is overviewed in Section 9.2.

EXERCISE 1.3

1. Assuming normal family relationships, state which of the following relations are transitive:

   isTheFatherOf, isTheSisterOf, isARelationOf
   isMarriedTo, isAMemberOfTheSameFamilyAs.

2. Name some transitive relations between numbers.

The ability to verify the correctness of design and implementation decisions also alleviates testing from alone carrying the burden of verification. Unit and integration testing now play a subsidiary role. Unit testing addresses modules individually, whereas integration testing exercises software entities built from unit-tested modules as the entire system is gradually fabricated. In fact, both forms of testing can now concentrate more on checking problematic, exceptional or extreme input cases.

GENERAL ASPECTS
The development effort curve is likely to peak earlier in formal methods than in a conventional approach. This is because greater time is spent getting the abstract specification and its design transformation correct. The expected pay-off is a significantly reduced level of testing and subsequent corrective maintenance, resulting in a net saving in costs compared to those that would otherwise be incurred in a conventional approach.

As well as the obvious benefits that accrue from precise description and verification in technical development activities, there are other advantages. As suggested earlier, if descriptions are fully formalized, it is then possible to build CASE tools that can manipulate descriptions in a variety of useful ways. Further discussion of 'practice' issues like CASE tools is also left until the last chapter of the book.

A 'Formal Method'

Figure 1.2 on the next page shows how formal methods can be viewed as augmenting software development within a conventional framework of phases, control points and defect-fixing iterations. A central aim of formal methods is to reduce these costly, time-consuming iterations in both frequency and scope.

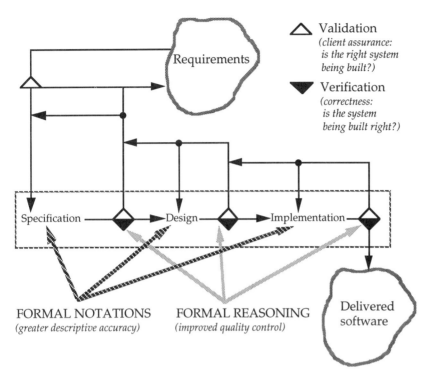

Figure 1.2 Augmentative contribution of formal methods to software development.

Even at this early stage, we have enough backcloth to sketch out the main features of a formal method:

- From analysis of the problem domain, derive a formal specification of the system to be built in some notation specifically devised for the purpose. Validate the specification, i.e., verify that the specification is internally consistent and possesses other desirable properties, and confirm that it meets the requirements to the satisfaction of the client/users.

- Next, refine the specification into another in which computer-oriented detail begins to emerge. As part of the refinement, verify that the new, more concrete description correctly implements the previous specification.

- Repeat the second step, essentially a design step, through further appropriate levels of decreasing abstraction, which is essentially a process of gradual implementation, until the description is expressed fully in the target language.

- Perform whatever corroborative unit testing is deemed necessary on the software and its individual components.

Thereafter, the remainder of development depends on the software artifact being built. For example, if the intention is to build a complete system, then a phase now ensues in which the implemented components must be integrated and fitted into a separately built scheduling framework such as a main program. Here, testing concentrates on interfacing and communication between components. At some later stage, system testing and client acceptance trials, as appropriate, will take place.

Of course, the previous summary glosses over many aspects, but it is sufficient to give a general flavour of what is involved. This book covers in depth only the first main phase of formal methods: specification. For reasons of economy of size, relatively little is said about proof or refinement, though much of Chapter 9 is devoted to providing a rounded picture of the whole discipline. However, specification is arguably the most important, as well as being the most maturely developed and understood, component of formal methods. Formal specifications not only feed back into requirements validation and feed forward into the design and implementation processes, but can also act as clear, unambiguous baselines for:

- contractual purposes
- software experimentation, e.g., trying out different designs
- communication and discussion amongst software personnel
- constructing other documentation, e.g., user manuals
- acting as yardsticks for software testing strategies
- supporting future modification and update.

By the end of the book, the aim is to have moved readers from a starting position that assumes no prior exposure to the discipline to a point where they will have sufficient knowledge, practical skills and confidence to tackle the specification of a wide range of software artifacts, from simple data types to non-trivial systems.

SUMMARY OF CHAPTER 1

- The main weak points in the quality control/assurance processes that are typically applied in conventional software engineering are highlighted.

- The main benefits that can accrue from applying formal methods in the technical development phases of the software life cycle are outlined.

2

ASPECTS OF SPECIFICATION: FORMALIZATION AND ABSTRACTION

Key Topics   Formal systems: rules, proofs; syntax, semantics; applications. Abstraction: omission, suppression, generalization. Specification notations: programming languages, discrete mathematics; discrete systems. Models of computation; specification paradigms.

2.1   WHAT IS 'FORMAL'?

Formal Systems

People often take the 'formal' in 'formal methods', etc. to mean 'expressed in symbols' and/or 'mathematical'. Looking up a dictionary definition is useful:

FORMAL
... having the outward form only; ... essential

FORMALIZE
... to make precise or give a clear statement of ...

(these fragments are extracted from *The Chambers Dictionary, 1993*).

Thus, a formal notation enables us to describe the 'outward form' or *essence* of something in a *precise* and *clear* way. This implies at the very least that a formal notation has a precise syntax—that is, the syntax can be described in such a way that it is possible to decide mechanically (e.g., via a computer program) whether or not an arbitrary construct expressed in the symbols of the notation is syntactically correct. Such decision-making is, of course, something that a compiler does. So programming languages, high level or otherwise, form a particular class of formal notation. However, most programming languages are suitable for description only at a fairly detailed operational level, e.g., specifying how an algorithm is to be executed by some, usually abstract, machine.

A more technical characterization of 'formal' can be obtained via the mathematical concept of a *formal system*. A formal system provides us with:

- An *alphabet* of symbols from which *well-formed formulas* (wffs), i.e., syntactically correct strings of symbols, are constructed;

- A collection of *rules* which tell us how to derive the wffs of the system.

Here is a simple example:

Alphabet: <, >

Rules: (r1) $\dfrac{}{<>}$ (r2) $\dfrac{F}{<F>}$ (r3) $\dfrac{F \quad G}{FG}$

The alphabet is comprised of two symbols '<' and '>'. There are three rules, which are ascribed the names r1, r2 and r3 for easy reference. Each rule has the form

$$
\text{(rule\_id)} \quad \frac{\text{A1 A2 ... An}}{\text{C}}
$$

In general, the *premise* part of a rule (its top line) is a list of zero or more wffs and/or wff patterns Ai. By 'pattern' is meant a syntactic structure that is generalized by the use of wff *variables*, like F and G in the example. Wff variables stand for arbitrary wffs of the system, and they can also occur in the rule's *conclusion* C (its bottom line), which is itself either a specific wff or wff pattern of some kind.

The rules of a formal system represent a sort of 'symbol pushing' apparatus. Each rule is interpreted as follows: for any actual wff(s) syntactically matching the rule's premise pattern(s), another actual wff can be constructed according to its conclusion pattern. Thus, rule r2 on page 13 states that a new wff can be constructed by taking a wff and enclosing it in a pair of angle brackets; rule r3 states that a new wff can be constructed by concatenating two wffs. Rule r1 has an empty premise part, which means that its conclusion is well-formed 'by definition'. The conclusions of such rules are called *axioms*. Clearly, since the axiom of a rule like r1 contains no variables, it therefore represents a single wff.

It should not be too hard to see that our example formal system defines—or generates, depending on one's viewpoint—a set of formulas which, loosely, are 'all strings made up of left and right angle brackets that are properly matched and balanced'. So the following constructs are wffs of the formal system:

<>   <><>   <<<>>>   <><<>><>   <><<><><<>>>

but these are not:

<   ><   <><>>   <<<<>>   (( ))   <><<><><<>>

Note, though, that any member of this latter list could be well-formed according to some other formal system we have not described.

Inherent in the concept of a formal system is the idea of *closure*. This means that the only wffs that belong to a formal system are precisely those that can be derived from its rules. Thus, to verify whether a claimed wff actually is well formed according to some formal system, we can attempt to build the claimed wff 'from scratch' using the system's rules. With our simple formal system, this is easy. For example, consider the string <><<><><<>>> (the end wff in the first list above). Then:

1.	<>	— r1
2.	<><>	— r3 on 1 and 1
3.	<<>>	— r2 on 1
4.	<><><<>>	— r3 on 2 and 3
5.	<<><><<>>>	— r2 on 4
6.	<><<><><<>>>	— r3 on 1 and 5

Each step in what we refer to as a *proof* of <><<><><<>>> is numbered for easy reference, and is justified by appeal to application of one of the rules. When we apply a non-axiomatic rule, one or more wffs that have already appeared in the proof must match the wff pattern(s) on the rule's top line. The wff described in the step is then derived from the justifying rule's conclusion pattern. This matching process is trivial with our example system, but with more complex rules, care must be taken that their premise patterns are correctly matched to previous wffs in the proof. Obviously, a good software tool could relieve us of any error-proneness here.

Syntax and Semantics

Although formal systems are not a direct concern of this book, the preceding overview serves to highlight the distinguishing features of 'formalness'. Firstly, it should be observed that a formal system operates *at a purely syntactic level*. This attribute lies at the heart of what formalness really is: without regard to 'meaning' or 'interpretation', or what we generally refer to as *semantics*. Secondly, the rules of a formal system represent precise, mechanical manipulations of syntactic patterns. When a rule is applied, there is absolutely no doubt about whether its application is correct or not. For example, in the previous proof, each step can be checked (by a human or computer program) for errors, again without regard to what the wffs in the proof might actually mean.

Formal systems, however, are not just neat ways of playing games with symbols. Their practical significance includes the following:

a. Using a formal system, the syntax of a language can be defined in a precise, rule-driven way. A formal system which does this is called a *grammar*. In practice, the grammar rules of a formal language are presented in a somewhat different style to the rules of our example formal system.

b. Using a formal system, deductive-style manipulations on the constructs of a language can be defined in a precise, rule-driven way ('if we have this, then we can derive this', etc.). A formal system which does this represents a system of proof or *inference*. The rules of such a system are usually presented in the style shown in the previous example.

It is important to appreciate that (a) and (b) are two quite separate applications of formal systems. With (a), we have a means of defining and mechanically checking the usage of a language's syntax; with (b), we have a means of constructing and mechanically checking proofs.

Sometimes, (a) and (b) reside together under the same roof. For example, in constructing formal specifications, an obvious concern is to adhere correctly to the syntax of the notation used. This book uses a specification notation called Z, whose syntax is described informally in subsequent chapters; a proper grammar for Z can be found in Spivey (1992). A main ingredient of Z is something called *predicate logic*. An important consequence of this is that we are able *to reason about the specifications we write in Z*, since predicate logic possesses properties that allow us to construct logical arguments in systematic ways. These properties can also be expressed as a formal system (which is quite separate from any grammar), providing us with a rule-driven capability for handling descriptions based on predicate logic in a reasoning capacity.

Note the important duality operating here. Predicate logic is acting as a medium for description, as well as an apparatus for reasoning. The latter capability is perhaps more obvious than the former; after all, that is what logic is intended for—to allow us to 'prove things'. The duality, as manifested in notations like Z, turns out to be a powerful combination, and it is this which makes such notations potent description weapons in the armoury of the software engineer.

Nevertheless, the reader may feel perturbed by the emphasis on syntax and 'mechanical' rules, apparently at the expense of semantics. We seem to be giving the impression that when we construct a formal description or reason about it, we do not care what it means! *On the contrary, its interpretation is just as important as its syntax.* Clearly, in any practical application of a language, we are concerned with what its constructs mean and not just their syntactic structure. The language defined by our previous example formal system has little application because, given its trivial structure, there is little that its constructs could usefully mean. Notations applied in formal methods are immensely richer in alphabet and syntactic structure, enabling them to be used to describe a whole variety of scenarios from aspects of the real world to complex computer systems.

The following simple example may help to dispel any fears that semantics is being ignored. Suppose we wish to describe formally the following fact: water flows in pipe p1 or pipe p2 if, and only if, valve v7 is open. We might write

$f(x)$ to mean 'water flows in pipe x'
$o(x)$ to mean 'valve x is open'

Given the interpretation usually reserved for the symbols $\vee$ and $\Leftrightarrow$ (see Section 4.2), the following would act as a suitable formal description:

$$f(p1) \vee f(p2) \Leftrightarrow o(v7) \tag{2.1}$$

The reader should assume this sentence to be a wff according to some grammar that we will not bother to specify. The grammar permits constructs called 'predicates' (say), some having the shape Name(Argument), others the shape Predicate $\vee$ Predicate, and so on.

Now imagine we have at our disposal a formal inference system for reasoning about the descriptive notation, one rule of which is

$$(\rho) \quad \frac{P \vee Q \Leftrightarrow R}{R \vee \neg Q}$$

Treating the P, Q and R as wff variables, we can match the premise pattern of this rule to our previous sentence (2.1). If we do this, we obtain the conclusion sentence

$o(v7) \vee \neg f(p2)$

According to the meaning ascribed to the symbols involved, we interpret the result as saying that 'either valve v7 is open or no water flows in pipe p2'. In other words, we have reasoned that this is a consequence, by rule ρ, of 'water flows in pipe p1 or pipe p2 if, and only if, valve v7 is open'.

In fact, because everything is formal, it actually does not matter what $f(x)$ and $o(x)$ are intended to mean. For example, if instead

$f(x)$ means 'person x is overweight'
$o(x)$ means 'account x is overdrawn'

then the above, albeit trivial, reasoning step has shown that

'either account v7 is overdrawn or person p2 is not overweight'

is a consequence of

'person p1 is overweight or p2 is overweight if, and only if, account v7 is overdrawn'

Of course, this is basically meaningless, but that is our problem and not the fault of the notation or rule ρ. Given this second interpretation, perhaps we should not have written f(p1) ∨ f(p2) ⇔ o(v7) in the first place. Having given meaning to symbols, it is our responsibility to ensure that what we construct with them is meaningful.

Actually, there is an even greater level of generality at work here. The point is that rule ρ, and any other rule like it, operates in a completely generalized way through its wff variables. Not only is it unimportant what meanings are involved when rule ρ is used, its wff variables P, Q and R can stand for *any* actual wffs we like, and not just the ones used in the example. There is thus no limit to the syntactic, hence semantic, complexity of inferences we can make even using just a single rule.

Clearly, there are advantages in being able to suppress meaning and operate at a purely syntactic level. Providing we are careful with our formalization, we can achieve useful things syntactically without compromising the intended meaning of the constructs we handle. Obviously, though, we are required to have considerable faith in rules like ρ opposite: we do not want them ever to produce invalid results, i.e., results that do not interpret correctly back into the modelled scenario. The fact that we are able to invent rules which do not misbehave in this way is certainly non-obvious.

Examples of reasoning about Z specifications do occasionally occur in later chapters, especially Chapter 9, but they are expressed in a mainly informal style, which suffices for our purposes. Hence, we will not be describing any formal apparatus for reasoning about Z specifications. Nevertheless, it is useful for the reader to be aware that we could place our examples on a formal, rule-driven basis if we wished. If we did so, we would be demonstrating that our informal reasoning was not flawed in any way. That, after all, is the central thrust of formalization: to maximize precision and minimize errors.

EXERCISE 2.1

1. Specify the following language as a formal system (use single upper-case letters for wff variables):

    - The language is called PropLog and its basic wffs are just individual lower-case letters.

    - If any one of the symbols

      $$\land \qquad \lor \qquad \Rightarrow \qquad \Leftrightarrow$$

      is placed between two wffs of PropLog and the whole construct is parenthesized, e.g., (p ⇔ q), then the result is also a wff of PropLog.

    - Placing parentheses around a wff is also well-formed, as is placing the symbol ¬ in front of any wff.

2. State which of the following are wffs of PropLog:

    $$\Rightarrow \qquad a \qquad (ab) \qquad (a \Rightarrow \neg b) \qquad (A \Rightarrow B) \qquad (a (\Rightarrow) b)$$
    $$(a \Rightarrow b) \Rightarrow c \qquad (a \neg b) \qquad \Rightarrow (a \Rightarrow b) \qquad (a \Rightarrow b) (c \Rightarrow d)$$
    $$((a \Rightarrow \neg b) \Rightarrow (a \Rightarrow ((\neg \neg c))))$$

3. If a formal system existed for reasoning about descriptions written in PropLog which included the rule

$$\frac{(\, \text{P} \Rightarrow \text{Q}\,) \quad \text{P}}{\text{Q}}$$

what conclusions, if any, can be derived from the wffs in (2) using the rule?

2.2   ABSTRACTION IN DESCRIPTION

Abstraction Techniques

Abstraction is the tool *par excellence* for describing complex entities to a level of detail appropriate to the task at hand. Abstraction allows us to concentrate on the essence of something relative to a particular context. The main methods of abstraction are

- *omission*: discarding detail considered to be irrelevant
- *suppression*: suppressing detail at a certain level of description
- *generalization*: capturing commonality between related descriptions.

Each of these methods is relevant to software development in general, and formal specification in particular.

Consider first *omission*, which is basically a domain modelling tool. Typically, what we do is observe some part of reality, or *domain*, in which our interest lies and construct an abstract description of it using suitable, often diagrammatic, notation(s). The description then contributes, in some way that is development-method dependent, to the specification of a computer system that is going to provide a service to that reality. As part of the modelling process, we have to make (often very hard) decisions about a domain model's *scope*, i.e., which facets of the domain to include in, and which to omit from, the model.

A variety of domain analysis/modelling techniques are used in software engineering. Some development methods concentrate on 'entities' and their 'attributes' and relationships, while others concentrate on flows of data and what happens to the data in those flows; yet others concentrate on events and their time orderings that occur in the domain. There is no single approach to domain modelling that has established itself above all others as being the best choice for interfacing with formal specification. One possible choice that seems suited to a certain class of problem is outlined in the case study beginning in Chapter 5.

Whereas omission is a scoping technique, *suppression* is used to control the complexity of descriptions. Various techniques come under the category of suppression. One such technique is *subsumption*, which allows us to invent constructs that 'stand for', and may eventually 'expand out into', greater detail (yet to be worked out) at some lower level of description. *Decomposition* allied to subsumption is the main technique for constructing hierarchical descriptions in a top-down fashion. Suppression can also be achieved by the opposite of subsumption, namely *synthesis*, whereby we take some detail and abstract it away from consideration in an act of 'bottom-up' construction. We will see that suppression can be usefully exploited in simple ways in specification work.

A mechanism related to suppression is *encapsulation*. Encapsulation can be likened to the 'enforcement of suppression' of information and is used to establish an unimpeachable opaque barrier around detail whose public visibility would be an irrelevance to anything external to the abstraction in question. In programming languages, encapsulation is effected by 'modules' (or similar), and is typically used to hide implementation of a routine, representation of a data type, or a collection of the former coupled with the latter, which is called 'data abstraction'. Structures with encapsulating properties also occur in formal notations.

Generalization can play a part in both domain modelling and specification. For example, suppose we are building a computer system that deals with people. We decide to model a person purely on the basis of name, age and gender. Thus, we are saying in an act of omission that a person's address, social class, ethnic origin, degree of obesity, etc., is 'out of scope' and irrelevant. Here, implicit generalization is at work, for we are also implying that the model of a person is sufficiently general to act as a descriptor of *every* person in which we are interested.

Explicit generalization in descriptions is achieved, or increased, by *parametrization*. Parametrization is a notational device that enables us to factor out the detailed differences amongst a group of related models and so represent each of them by a single description. The parametrized description acts as a template from which a 'concrete instance' can be derived by providing the template parameters with actual values that characterize the instance required. Parametrization is provided in a variety of forms in formal notations. An aspect of parametrization arises out of the following exercise.

EXERCISE 2.2

§ The answer is given overleaf.
Study the following two separate fragments of 'Esperanto' code on this and the next page. What is there of a non-trivial nature that is common between them?

```
{fragment A}
constant MAX = ...;
type
  ALPHA = record
    S:array[1..MAX] of CHAR;
    L:0..MAX
  end rec;

procedure A1(inout X:ALPHA;
                in E:CHAR);
begin
  with X do
    if L = MAX then ERROR
    else
      L := L + 1;
      S[L] := E
    end if
  end with
end A1;


function A2(in X:ALPHA) return 0..MAX;
begin
  return X.L
end A2;
```

```
{fragment B}
type
  BETA = pointerto ND;
  ND = record
    I:INTEGER;
    N:BETA
  end rec;

function B1(in Y:BETA)
  return 0..MAX;
begin
  if Y = nil then return 0
  else
    return 1 + B1(Y.N)
  end if
end B1;


procedure B2(inout Y:BETA);
begin
  if Y = nil then ERROR
  else
    Y := Y.N
  end if
end B2;
```

```
procedure A3 (inout X:ALPHA);
begin
  if X.L = 0 then ERROR
  else
      X.L := X.L - 1
  end if
end A3;
```

```
procedure B3 (inout Y:BETA;
                    in X:INTEGER);
  NN:BETA
begin
  NN := new ND;
  with NN do
    I := X; N := Y
  end with;
  Y := NN
end B3;
```

Specification Notations

It seems entirely incorrect to state that the two code fragments in Exercise 2.2 are identical, but at a certain level of abstraction this is true. They are behaviourally identical, or nearly so, in the sense that both are different ways of implementing the same thing: a stack data structure (fixed-size array with index, or linked list) with operations such as finding the length of a stack (A2, or B1), adding a new item to the top of a stack (A1, or B3) and deleting the top of the stack (A3, or B2). There is also a more subtle point: stack behaviour is independent of stack element type, which is CHAR and INTEGER in the two fragments. At an abstract descriptive level, what we would like is a notation that enables us to specify the behaviour of a stack, parametrized with respect to element type, without suggesting in any way how this behaviour might be implemented.

Clearly, abstraction is of little use unless we can represent our desired abstract constructions in a suitable notation. High-level programming languages are abstract notations designed to specify operational constructs such as algorithms so that machine-level detail is subsumed. We prefer to work with a high-level language rather than machine code for describing implementations because of the messy detail that the high-level language suppresses. In turn, the constructs we build using the language are closer to the intellectual abstractions we construct when designing computer-executable solutions to problems.

Yet, by the same token, high-level programming languages are unsuitable for specifying systems, since their use would result in specifications being cluttered with unwanted detail at an inappropriately low level of abstraction. We would be guilty of 'overspecification': constraining *how* a computerized solution might be built, instead of simply describing *what* essential properties and features the solution should possess. We can hardly think of either code fragment in Exercise 2.2 as 'specifying *what* a stack is'. To do this, we require a notation with far greater powers of abstraction than a programming language.

Enter discrete mathematics and logic. The fact that mathematical notation of any kind is formal and possesses considerable powers of conciseness and abstraction comes as no surprise. What is less obvious perhaps is that discrete mathematics is capable of specifying computer systems and their components to any degree of abstraction that is judged appropriate. The operative word here is 'judged'. As we will see, specification is a skill that requires considerable judgement to be exercised on the part of the specifier in determining the exact level(s) of abstraction to express in a description. This is task dependent. Some specifications, because of their intended function, will need to suppress much more detail than others. All the specifications in this book are intended as problem/domain-level descriptions of software artifacts to be built, prior to design and implementation. They are therefore expressed to a high level of abstraction.

Note that we are concerned with *discrete* mathematics. This is because we are interested in the specification, design and implementation of only discrete systems or their components, i.e., systems whose 'information content' can exist in separate, uniquely identifiable 'states', as opposed to a continuum of possibilities. To illustrate, consider a wrist-watch which

- shows the time with traditional minute and hour hands
- displays the date, in DD/MM/YY format, say.

Using a notation based on discrete mathematics, there would be no difficulty in modelling the way in which the watch handles dates. Dates are discrete in a self-evident way. However, time and its passage is continuous, and this is mirrored by the apparent (albeit very slow) continuous movement of the watch hands. We could not use our notation to model this aspect of the watch's behaviour unless we discretized it in some way, i.e., by modelling time as a progression of 'ticks', in one-hundredth second intervals, say. The model would be approximate, but the approximation may be entirely suitable for our purpose. Indeed, the example illustrates how we would attempt to model any continuous value space with a discrete-based notation. We would need to project that space onto a discrete model whose granularity was sufficiently fine to enable us to capture adequately whatever we were trying to describe.

EXERCISE 2.3

State whether each of the following scenarios is discrete or continuous. For each of the latter cases, briefly describe one way in which the scenario could be modelled discretely.

a. traffic light signals
b. a sphere's position on a two-dimensional plane over which it can move
c. the positions of aircraft within a country's airspace
d. staff and the offices they occupy
e. music produced by a pianist
f. floating point arithmetic of a computer.

Returning briefly to our model of post-requirements software development in a formal methods environment as overviewed in Section 1.2, we can now better understand what occurs in this process. Our first description is an abstract, mathematically-oriented specification of something to be built; our last description is that of the built solution expressed in a programming language. As we progress down the development route, each new description we generate is distinguished from its predecessor by the replacement of abstractions with more concrete, computer-oriented detail. It is precisely because formal notations are used that, as part of this so-called refinement process, each new, less abstract description can be formally verified to conform correctly to its predecessor.

Models of Computation

Although we concentrate on specification in this book, our wider interest lies in developing computer systems that provide required services to various domains. The concept of a 'system' is rather hard to define, although we generally regard a system as exhibiting a 'behaviour over time' which is detectable externally at the interface between itself and the environment in which it is embedded. The behaviour manifests itself as input/output activity, i.e., flows of data into and out of the system. In fact, systems can be described purely in terms of this observable property. In effect, we are viewing a system as something which 'maps' inputs to outputs. This purely *functional* view of systems has a certain elegance and simplicity that lends itself to formalization.

An alternative model is illustrated in Figure 2.1. This model imparts to the internal architecture of a system a component (Σ in the diagram) known as its *state*. The state of a system can be thought of as 'the information content of a system that persists throughout its lifespan'. The existence of a state component fundamentally affects our view of the nature of system behaviour. There is now a further basic ingredient to system activity: *state transition*. Thus, from time to time, the system carries out some activity that updates its state. Since the state persists, this change manifests itself to the next strand of activity that the system carries out.

Two consequences of 'state' are thus:

- All *operations* (OP1, OP2, etc. in the diagram) that a system carries out have a state-transition component. Depending on its required behaviour, a given operation might or might not cause a change to the system state and/or exhibit input/output activity.

- A system can remember previous states by maintaining these as part of its current state. Thus, if desired, a system can be organized to record the history of (part of) its previous behaviour or revert back to some previous state.

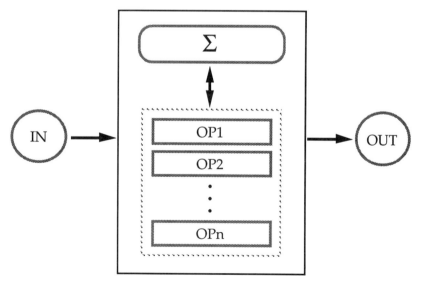

Figure 2.1 A state-based view of system behaviour.

There are certain strong arguments favouring the functional approach to software description:

- it is less complex: there is no notion of 'state'
- it is mathematically cleaner: system behaviour is purely functional
- it simplifies certain processes central to formal methods such as proof: it is easier to reason about functional behaviour.

Despite this, software engineering continues to be dominated by the development of state-based software, partly because most computers are still state-based and, hence, so are the majority of programming languages used to program them. The general approach adopted in this book will also be state-based, but this is not due to a desire merely to conform to the status quo. Rather, our stance results from adopting the following 'axiom': that any useful computer system must necessarily embody an appropriate model of the external domain that it services. Without this internalized model, a system will be unable to interact reliably in the intended manner with its outside environment. Moreover, our perception of a wide variety of external-world subsystems is very much state-based. Consider as a simple example the everyday domain of banking. A bank maintains a set of current accounts. The natural view of these accounts is as information content of the banking system that changes state over time (i.e., when money is put into, or withdrawn from, an account); the accounts can, of course, also be inspected (e.g., when a customer makes an account balance enquiry). If we wish to build a computerized version of this banking system that reflects our view of the domain, it should therefore be state-based. In effect, we are trading off certain acknowledged advantages of the functional model against a better fit with our day-to-day interpretation of the way the world works.

There are two main languages currently used for state-based specification: the language associated with the Vienna Definition Method (VDM) (see for example Andrews and Ince 1991; Jones 1990; Jones and Shaw 1990) and the Z notation (see for example Diller 1990; Hayes 1993; Ince 1988; Lightfoot 1991; McMorran and Powell 1993; Potter *et al*. 1991; Spivey 1992; Woodcock and Loomes 1988; Wordsworth 1992). Both languages are rich, formal notations for specifying discrete systems in general, and hence digital computer systems in particular. Though we use Z in this book, the reader is strongly encouraged to discover the flavour of VDM from the references given. Comparison will reveal that the pragmatic and technical, as opposed to syntactic, differences between the two are relatively few, if not necessarily completely trivial; see Hayes (1992) for one comparitive study.

Specification Scope and Paradigms

As previously explained, when specifying at the most abstract level we are primarily concerned with describing external behaviour that is to be exhibited, and not any particular means, methods, or materials by which the behaviour might be realized. The aim of the specifier must be accurately to document required features without unnecessarily constraining the skills and flair of those whose task will be to build the software to specification. Of course, it could be the case that a client requirements document states that the software shall be written in Cobol. However, such *non-functional* requirements do not lie within a formal specifier's remit. It is not that such requirements are less important, but that they serve a different purpose. As far as designers and implementors are concerned, all requirements are germane to their task: to realize software that conforms to its abstract specification, whilst keeping within any restrictions on the possible solution space that are imposed by non-functional requirements.

Bearing the foregoing in mind, we might expect a state-based formal specification to cover the following:

- description of state
- state-transition behaviour
- input/output behaviour.

Further, if we are attempting to specify systems completely, we also need to include

- behaviour over time
- user-system interface
- performance.

We shall concentrate on the first set of categories, since their formalization is now a well-developed technology. Formal description associated with any category in the latter set lies outside the scope of this introductory text.

We now have in place the basic characterization of our main specification paradigm. Briefly, from an analysis of the problem domain, we construct an abstract description of the state component of the software to be built. This is followed by abstract descriptions of required software behaviour based on the state model. This approach to specification is generally referred to as *model-oriented*, or the 'abstract model' approach. The name reflects the fact that we construct *models* of state, these models being expressed in terms of available mathematical structures.

Two other major specification paradigms are *property-oriented* and *process-oriented*. For a comparison of the three approaches, the interested reader can try Cohen *et al.* (1986). Z is rich enough to be used in a property-oriented style, and so this form of specification is covered briefly in a later chapter. Process-oriented specification is suited to the description of concurrent systems, which lie outside Z's scope. Such systems are the realm of notations like CSP (Communicating Sequential Processes), and the interested reader can try something like Hoare (1985), though this work is not for the faint-hearted.

SUMMARY OF CHAPTER 2

- The reader is introduced to the essence of formalness via the notion of *formal system* and two main applications of the latter: *language syntax description* and *inference systems*.

- The role played by *abstraction* in formal methods is emphasized, with particular reference to techniques and notations.

- The main paradigms addressed by this book are characterized, namely *discrete state-based* computation and *model-oriented* specification.

THE DIGITAL WATCH:
FUNDAMENTALS OF SPECIFICATION USING Z

Key Topics   Schemas, declarations, predicates. Variables, types; normalization, signatures, properties. State models: static properties; bindings. Operations: dynamic properties; decoration, schema inclusion. Global names, axiomatic definitions. The Δ and Ξ conventions. Partial and total operations, preconstraints. Initial states, proof obligations.

3.1   STATE MODELLING: SOME BASIC Z CONSTRUCTS

A First Case Study

Our first main case study does not deal with a computerized system. Although it is readily implementable as such, the system is more likely to be realized as a piece of hardware that you wear round your wrist. Consider the problem of specifying the following:

The Digital Watch System
A digital watch keeps track of the time in hours and minutes using the 24 hour clock. The watch automatically increments the time by 1 minute when appropriate, although the time can be reset by the user to any desired value (the hours and minutes components are separately adjustable incrementally by the use of buttons on the side of the watch).

In addition, the watch keeps track of the date, which it shows in day/month/year format. The day is shown as two digits, the month as a three-letter code Jan, Feb, Mar, etc., and the year is shown fully as four digits. A factory-fitted constraint is that the watch handles years only from YYYY onwards, where the factory varies YYYY as its watch production proceeds from year to year (typically, YYYY is CCD0, where CC is the current century and D0 the current decade). The date is also user-adjustable, forwards or backwards. The watch increments the date by one day when appropriate, automatically adjusting month and year as necessary. Using a liquid-crystal display, the watch continuously shows the time. The date is shown by request (the wearer presses yet another button on the side of the watch) and the display lasts for about 8 seconds.

When confronted with an informal description of a simple system that is to be formally specified, one way to start is to make a preliminary inventory of the components of the system that the specification will have to cover in terms of state and operations. A first attack on the Digital Watch system might yield the analysis on the following page. This analysis is only a first shot, and we may need to alter it as we construct the specification. This is not atypical; the process of formalization often uncovers omissions and defects of various kinds in our initial understanding of the domain. One of the great strengths of formalization is that it tends to highlight issues about the system or requirements that need to be addressed or clarified—issues that might otherwise be overlooked, possibly with costly consequences.

STATE:

Component	Description
Time	The time of day, externally displayed as two components: • an hours value: an integer in the range 00 to 23 inclusive • a minutes value: an integer in the range 00 to 59 inclusive.
Date	The date, externally displayed as three components: • the day: an integer in the range 01 to 31 inclusive • the month: a three-letter code such as Jan, Feb, etc. • the year: an integer from YYYY onwards (YYYY is factory-set).

OPERATIONS:

Name	Description
Add1Min	The watch adds one minute to the time, adjusting the hours component if appropriate
Add1Day	The watch increments the date by one day, adjusting year and/or month component(s) if appropriate
ResetMin	The user incrementally resets the minutes component only
ResetHr	The user incrementally resets the hours component only
ResetDateUp	The user resets the date forwards
ResetDateDown	The user resets the date backwards
ShowTime	The watch displays the time (which it does continuously)
ShowDate	The watch displays the date (on request, only for 8 seconds).

In this analysis, we can already presume to have clarified one aspect omitted in the informal description of the digital watch: how midnight is displayed. We suppose this to be 00.00, not 24.00, which is why the hours values have been given the range 00 to 23.

Returning briefly to certain ideas expressed in Section 2.2, it is clear that our Digital Watch specification is going to be based on models of real-world time and dates, the former discretized to the granularity of minutes, which is fairly coarse but sufficient. The operations Add1Min and Add1Day model the passage of time and days in the real world. The six other operations identified are there to make the system useful; without them, the system would faithfully model real-world time and the passing of days, but it would hardly be useful! Alternatively, if the system provided various user functions, but its model of time or dates was wrong, it would still not be very useful. Either kind of defect—functional inadequacy or invalid state model—can easily afflict software, as can another problem: a poorly designed user interface. Formal description can help avoid functional inadequacy and trap defective state models, though its application to human–computer interaction is still a research area; the interested reader can try Harrison and Thimbleby (1990).

Schemas

Formal Z text comprises a sequence of *paragraphs* of various kinds, which impart an ordely top-level structure to a specification. One of the most important kinds of paragraph is the *schema*. Loosely, a schema is akin to a 'module' that embodies a mathematical description of some feature of the system we want to specify, such as (a component of) the system state or an operation. Usually, the following box-like framework with an open right-hand side is used to present schemas (but see also page 31); many authors omit the two small vertical lines on the extreme right:

```
┌─ SchemaName ─────────────────────────────────────────────┐
│ DeclarationPart                                           │
│ ────────────────                                          │
│ AxiomPart                                                 │
└───────────────────────────────────────────────────────────┘
```

More specifically:

*   The name of the schema is inserted into the top line of the box. A schema name becomes global to the specification from the point of its introduction, and *cannot be used for any other purpose in the specification text*.

*   In the schema's declaration part one or more *variables* are introduced. Each variable has a name and type; its scope extends through the axiom part *but does not include the declaration part itself*. Although the schema variables are local, there are ways in which they can be made visible to other Z paragraphs.

*   The axiom part is optional. If present, it comprises a *predicate* which references one or more of the schema variables declared, and possibly other variables as well that are in scope. The predicate is axiomatic in the sense that it describes a 'given' property of the schema variables, i.e., the variables by definition (are required to) satisfy the predicate.

In a schema modelling a state, the axiom part is used to impose constraints on the variables in order that the state model is valid, i.e., does not permit 'meaningless' states. In a schema modelling an operation on a state, the axiom part describes the operation's behaviour, i.e., what state transition it accomplishes and what input/output activity it exhibits.

Remark

In the text, the syntax of Z constructs will be described in an informal manner. The syntax adheres to the *de facto* standard (Spivey 1992), though see page 44 concerning commentary. We use a sans-serif font to describe syntactic elements or generalized constructs. It is customary to use an *italic font* in Z text, but we use `Courier font` (mainly for names, e.g., see below), retaining italicization for its normal usages.

Formal description of a system necessarily begins with the system state, since specification of the operations depends directly on the state model we construct. For simplicity, we will begin by considering just the time component of the state of the digital watch, which we might specify with the following schema:

```
┌─ TimeHM ──────────────────────────────────────────────┐
│ hrs : 0..23                                            │
│ mins : 0..59                                           │
└────────────────────────────────────────────────────────┘
```

Here, the time model is captured wholly by the declared variables themselves and so the schema has no axiom part, hence no inner horizontal line separator. Note that declarations have the syntax NameList : Expression.

Special symbols apart, an 'undecorated' name in Z (see page 35 for 'decorations') can be any sequence of upper/lower-case letters, digits and underscores, starting with a letter, though not ending with an underscore; note that letter case is significant. We will adopt our own style of naming within this permitted syntax as follows:

- *Schemas:* A schema name will normally consist of letters and digits only, starting with an upper-case letter; in certain special circumstances, the initial letter will be Greek. Example: `TimeOfDay`.

- *Variables:* Variable names may contain any permitted characters but will always start with a lower-case letter. Example: `timeAfterDusk`.

- *Types:* A name occurring to the right of ' : ' in declarations will normally consist of letters only, starting with an upper-case letter. Sometimes, all the letters will be upper-case. Example: `TIME`.

Generally, upper-case letters will be used in preference to underscores to highlight a name's structure. So, we prefer `timeAfterDusk` to `time_after_dusk`, for example.

Variables and Types

It is important to understand that a variable in Z is a *mathematical* variable and must not be confused with the common notion of 'variable' in the procedural programming world. In the latter case, a variable is the name of a *location* in some store; but in the formal world, a variable is just a symbol that denotes a unique 'element', i.e., a *value* which has a *type*. A Z variable is 'variable', not because it is 'updatable', but because the value it denotes is often non-specific, as in a schema, and covers a range of possibilities. In the declaration

    x : X

the role of expression `X` is to fix the type of the value denoted by `x`, and assert that the value is 'drawn from' the collection of values described by `X`. For example, schema `TimeHM` on the previous page specifies that the variable `hrs` denotes a value drawn from the range `0..23` inclusive and its type is 'integer' (see later). Thus, wherever `hrs` subsequently appears in the specification text in the scope of its declaration in `TimeHM`, it denotes *the same integer value in each instance*, whatever value that might be. A variable in Z text is therefore little more than a 'syntactic place marker' for some value. We must be a little careful, however. It is possible in Z, as in most formal notations, to declare: (i) 'constants' (see later); (ii) variables with the same name in different scope regions.

The concept of *type* permeates the programming world, though not always with quite the clarity and precision that such a fundamental concept deserves. Fortunately, Z adopts a simple approach to typing. A type denotes a *non-empty set* of values which is treated as 'maximal'. Although we leave proper discussion of sets until subsequent chapters, it suffices here to regard a set as a collection of *distinct* objects which are *of the same type*. Suppose, therefore, that S is the set of values denoted by a type τ. The fact that S is a 'maximal set' means that *all* values of type τ are contained in S. Moreover, S contains *nothing but* τ values. This simple notion of type has two important aspects:

- a type denotes a set that is not contained in any 'wider' set
- the type of any Z expression can be determined by an algorithm, irrespective of the value that the expression denotes.

The first point means that there is no notion of 'subtype' in Z. The significant practical consequence of both points is that it is possible to construct a program which performs type checking on Z specifications. This would not be possible if Z's type structure permitted subtypes, because decision-making about subtypes would then require the construction of proofs, and proof construction is a process that cannot be automated as a general algorithm.

Every Z specification needs one or more *basic types* with which to describe objects whose internal make-up is of no relevance to the specification. Values of a basic type are regarded as 'atomic'. Throughout this book we will treat 'integer' as a basic type. This type is written as the symbol $\mathbb{Z}$, which denotes the set of all integer numbers, and which is assumed to be 'given' to every specification, i.e., it is always available for use whenever we need it. In fact, $\mathbb{Z}$ is the *only* basic type automatically provided by standard Z. This may seem rather alarming. The reader, mindful of programming languages, might ask: what about booleans, characters, real numbers, enumerated types, etc.? Despite the seeming lack of basic type provision, the Z specifier is not disadvantaged in any way, as will become apparent in later chapters.

For convenience, there are also symbols for two major subsets of the integers: $\mathbb{N}$ for the *natural numbers* (zero and the positive integers) and $\mathbb{N}_1$ for the *positive integers* only. Like $\mathbb{Z}$, these two sets are infinite. If we wish to denote a *finite* unbroken *increasing* subrange of the integers, then we can use the notation used in schema `TimeHM`, namely

```
i..j
```

where `i` and `j` are expressions denoting integers and $i \le j$. If we wished to denote a finite set of integers that do not form a continuous subrange, then we would need to use notation that is not discussed until Chapter 5.

EXERCISE 3.1

1. § The answer is discussed on the next page.
   State the type of each variable in the following declaration list:

   ```
   w : N
   x : Z
   y : 1..100
   z : N₁
   ```

2. Suppose a variable `v` is declared

   ```
   v : ξ1..ξ2
   ```

   such that $\xi 1 > \xi 2$. What is `v`'s type, and what value(s) do you think it can denote?

3. Comment on the following schema:

   ```
   ┌─ ThreeIntVars ────────────────────────────────┐
   │ i,j : Z                                        │
   │ k : i..j                                       │
   └────────────────────────────────────────────────┘
   ```

It should now be evident that when a variable is declared, the right-hand side of the declaration not only fixes the variable's type but may also provide an additional *constraint* that narrows down the possibilities for the variable's value. For example, in Exercise 3.1(1), although w is of type $\mathbb{Z}$, its declaration imposes the additional constraint that w denotes only 0 or a positive integer. It is possible to *normalize* a declaration so that the type and any additional constraint the declaration conveys are explicitly revealed. For example, the normalized forms of the declarations in Exercise 3.1(1) could be individually described as follows, revealing that all four variables are of type $\mathbb{Z}$:

$$w : \mathbb{Z} \mid w \geq 0$$
$$x : \mathbb{Z}$$
$$y : \mathbb{Z} \mid 1 \leq y \leq 100$$
$$z : \mathbb{Z} \mid z \geq 1$$

Here, the symbol '|' has been used to separate the normalized declaration from the additional constraint. In fact, | is equivalent to the horizontal line dividing a schema box into its two main parts. So the syntax Declarations | Constraint is nothing more than a different way of describing *schema text*. As we will see, schema text can occur in many places in Z descriptions.

Remark
Z symbols which are introduced but otherwise not commented upon ($\geq$, $\leq$, etc.) have their expected meaning.

The following two schemas can now be seen to 'say the same thing as' TimeHM at the bottom of page 27:

```
┌─TimeHMNorm─────────────────────────────────────────────┐
│ hrs : ℤ                                                 │
│ mins : ℤ                                                │
│ ─────────────                                           │
│ 0 ≤ hrs ≤ 23                                            │
│ 0 ≤ mins ≤ 59                                           │
└─────────────────────────────────────────────────────────┘
```

```
┌─ TimeHMNat ────────────────────────────────────────────┐
│ hrs : ℕ                                                 │
│ mins : ℕ                                                │
│ ─────────────                                           │
│ hrs ≤ 23                                                │
│ mins ≤ 59                                               │
└─────────────────────────────────────────────────────────┘
```

Note that the ordering of declarations and predicate components is immaterial. When all the declarations in a schema are normalized as in TimeHMNorm, the schema's *signature*—the names and types of its variables, and the schema's *property*—the overall predicate on its normalized variables, become fully revealed.

The flexibility available in schema construction prompts the question: which style is preferred—normalized form or not? There are no rigid guidelines to follow, but generally, the most constraining ('strongest') form of variable declaration is chosen since this minimizes the amount of detail that has to be written in schema axiom parts.

A further choice in defining schemas is also available. Instead of the box format, an equivalent 'horizontal' schema definition syntax can be used:

SchName ≙ SchemaExpr

One possibility for SchemaExpr is square-bracketed schema text, as illustrated in the following definition, which is equivalent to the box-definition of TimeHMNat on the opposite page:

TimeHMNat ≙ [hrs : ℕ; mins : ℕ | hrs ≤ 23 ∧ mins ≤ 59]

Semicolons are used to separate declarations in schema text; this is also permitted in box presentation. The symbol ∧ can be verbalized as 'and'; we say more about it in the next chapter. An advantage of vertical box presentation is that line breaks can be used for 'anding' top-level (but *not* nested) predicate components; this facilitates reader-friendliness in the layout of schema predicates.

Here are some further examples of horizontal definition:

TimeHMNatDecs ≙ [hrs : ℕ; mins : ℕ]
TimeHMNatNorm ≙ [hrs : ℤ; mins : ℤ | 0 ≤ hrs ≤ 23 ∧ 0 ≤ mins ≤ 59]
TimeHMNatDecsNorm ≙ [hrs : ℤ; mins : ℤ | 0 ≤ hrs ∧ 0 ≤ mins]
TimeHMNatSig ≙ [hrs : ℤ; mins : ℤ]

Our terminating name elements Decs, Norm and Sig are intended to have their obvious interpretations with respect to the 'root' of the schema name, whether used singly or combined. (Read from left to right, the reader might care to note that NormDecs conveys the same as Sig, i.e., normalized and declarations only!)

Given this choice in presenting schema definitions in specifications, which do we use? In general, the box form is chosen because of its greater visual impact when embedded in natural language text. However, there are situations where horizontal schema definition is more appropriate. This is generally when the right-hand side of the definition can be constructed as a schema expression involving operators, rather than just being schema text. A simple example occurs on page 50 of this chapter.

EXERCISE 3.2

1. Construct two equivalent horizontal schema definitions for the date component of the state of the digital watch along the following lines:

   a. a schema called DateVars that introduces as compactly as possible three variables suitable for modelling a date in day/month/year form
   b. the normalized variant of DateVars (call it DateVarsNorm).

   Consider only DateVars's declarations; do not attempt to construct its predicate.

2. § One possible solution is given in Exercise 3.3 on page 33.
   Consider the vague 'counters' specification given at the top of page 4. Construct a state model ThreeCntrs which formalizes this scenario. Record all assumptions you make in arriving at your model.

Bindings

We can think of any schema Sch as defining a 'space' populated by *bindings* (an idea we develop more formally in Section 7.2). If Sch is a state model, we can call this space a *state space*, since it defines all possible individual states which are permitted. A binding associates variables with values. To indicate that a variable Var in some binding is bound to the value of the expression Expr, we will write

Var ⇒ Expr

Complete bindings are described between large angle brackets. Below are listed some of the bindings defined by the *signature* of TimeHM on page 27.

⟨ hrs ⇒ -5, mins ⇒ -3 ⟩   (*)
⟨ hrs ⇒ 0, mins ⇒ -5 ⟩   (*)
⟨ hrs ⇒ 0, mins ⇒ 0 ⟩
⟨ hrs ⇒ 5, mins ⇒ 3 ⟩
⟨ hrs ⇒ 5, mins ⇒ 63 ⟩   (*)
⟨ hrs ⇒ 24, mins ⇒ 3 ⟩   (*)
⟨ hrs ⇒ 3, mins ⇒ 24 ⟩

However, the state space which TimeHM defines is 'smaller' than the collection of bindings defined by its signature alone. This is due to TimeHM's property, which has a narrowing effect: the actual state space defined by TimeHM comprises only those bindings defined by its signature which satisfy its property, i.e., make its property true.

It can be seen that, of the bindings enumerated above, those marked (*) are *not* part of TimeHM's state space. They lie in area B of Figure 3.1 below, but not in area A since, whilst they are consistent with TimeHM's signature, they do not satisfy its property.

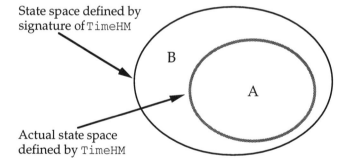

State space defined by signature of TimeHM

Actual state space defined by TimeHM

Figure 3.1   State-space relationship between a state model and its signature.

Although the above binding notation is not directly used in Z constructs, the concept of a binding helps us to understand what Z descriptions mean.

The behaviour of a system must never violate its state model in any way, otherwise the system would become inconsistent with the domain it is supposed to provide a meaningful service to. A state schema's property is a fixed part of the state model just as much as its signature is, and the model in its entirety must never be compromised. For this reason, a state model's property is sometimes referred to as the (state) *invariant*. Thus, whatever our digital watch does, the time component of its state always belongs to the state space described by the signature *and* invariant of TimeHM—or TimeHMNat, or `TimeHMNorm` since, as stated earlier, all these models are equivalent. We now have a sensible interpretation of 'equivalent schemas': they define precisely the same collection of bindings. We will call such schemas 'variants' of each other.

A state model documents a required *static* property of a system: the model characterizes a fixed property that is time-independent. In contrast, an operation schema documents some required *dynamic* property of a system, and we now need to see how schemas are used to specify operations.

EXERCISE 3.3

Consider the following state model as one possible answer to Exercise 3.2(2):

$$\texttt{ThreeCntrs} \; \hat{=} \; [\; \texttt{c1,c2,c3} \; : \mathbb{N} \; | \; \texttt{c1} \leq \texttt{n} \wedge \texttt{c3} \leq \texttt{m} \wedge \texttt{c1} \leq \texttt{c2} \leq \texttt{c3} \;]$$

Although the names n and m are not declared in the schema, the reader should assume they are correctly declared elsewhere.

1. Using the name-suffix conventions of page 31, draw a diagram incorporating a sufficient number of labelled 'bubbles' to depict the state-space relationship between the schemas: `ThreeCntrs`, `ThreeCntrsDecs`, `ThreeCntrsNorm`, `ThreeCntrsSig`, and `ThreeCntrsDecsNorm`.

2. Assuming that $n = 10$ and $m = 8$, determine which of the following bindings belong to the state space of `ThreeCntrs`:

    $\beta 1$: $\langle\, c1 \Rrightarrow 0, c2 \Rrightarrow 5, c3 \Rrightarrow 8 \,\rangle$
    $\beta 2$: $\langle\, c1 \Rrightarrow 1, c2 \Rrightarrow 1, c3 \Rrightarrow 1 \,\rangle$
    $\beta 3$: $\langle\, c1 \Rrightarrow 3, c2 \Rrightarrow 2, c3 \Rrightarrow 1 \,\rangle$
    $\beta 4$: $\langle\, c1 \Rrightarrow 3, c2 \Rrightarrow 6, c3 \Rrightarrow 9 \,\rangle$
    $\beta 5$: $\langle\, c1 \Rrightarrow 8, c2 \Rrightarrow 8, c3 \Rrightarrow 8 \,\rangle$
    $\beta 6$: $\langle\, c1 \Rrightarrow 1, c2 \Rrightarrow 7, c3 \Rrightarrow 7 \,\rangle$

3.2 TOWARDS SPECIFYING OPERATIONS

A General Model for Operations

To understand how a Z description of an operation in a state-based system is constructed, we must consider what such an operation in general accomplishes. This has already been indicated in Section 2.2 and is suggested by Figure 2.1 on page 22. Summarizing again, an operation's behaviour on a state

a. exhibits a state transition (though this does not necessarily mean the state changes)
b. may, though not necessarily,
   – require inputs and/or
   – produce outputs.

Clearly, there are different possible combinations of these features, although component (a) is a compulsory part of the description of *any* state-based operation.

In order to model mathematically the concept of a state transition, we need two equivalent but distinguishable state 'instances'. Let us call these State and State '. We can think of State as representing the 'before state', i.e., the state of the system just before the operation is imagined to take place. Similarly, we can use State ' to represent the 'after state', i.e., the state of the system just after the operation is imagined to have taken place. It is by expressing a relationship between State and State ' that we describe the nature of the transition. As a simple example, if an operation does not change the state—it *observes* the state, but does not *update* it—then we would specify in an appropriate manner that State and State ' are equal.

State and State ' can loosely be thought of respectively as a kind of extra 'input' and 'output' to an operation. This is sometimes a source of confusion for people. The difference between state and actual input/output is that, whereas the state is regarded as a *persistent* feature of a system, inputs and outputs are *transient* data manifested at the operation's interface—'transient' in the sense of being consumed/produced, but not persisting. Moreover, at the user-interface level, it is only via the mapping of inputs to outputs that we are able to observe operation behaviour; state transition is purely an internal matter.

The main ingredients in the specification of an operation AnOp are thus the following, where we have used the name suffixes Decs and Pred to stand for respectively the declarations and predicate of a schema:

- the before-state State, as described by the schema text StateDecs | StatePred
- the after-state State ', as described by the schema text StateDecs' | StatePred'
- declarations of any input(s) In? required
- declarations of any output(s) Out! produced
- *what* the operation does, which covers
  - constraints on the operation's applicability, if any   (*)
  - consumption of inputs, as appropriate
  - production of outputs, as appropriate
  - state transition effected,
  all of which will be encompassed by a predicate we will refer to as OpBhvr.

For present purposes, the component of operation behaviour marked (*) can be ignored. We will return to this feature towards the end of Section 3.4.

An operation with all these ingredients might be described in a schema box thus:

```
┌─ AnOp ──────────────────────────────────────────────────────────────────┐
│ StateDecs                      — the before-state variables               │
│ StateDecs'                     — the after-state variables                │
│ In?                            — any inputs required (could be none)      │
│ Out!                           — any outputs produced (could be none)     │
│ ─────────────────────                                                     │
│ StatePred                      — the before-state predicate               │
│ OpBhvr                         — the predicate describing what the operation does │
│ StatePred'                     — the after-state predicate                │
└──────────────────────────────────────────────────────────────────────────┘
```

It should be remembered that there is no obligation to adopt a particular ordering when writing down the components of either main part of a schema; the orderings used here are simply those that most would probably find reasonably natural.

Although the OpBhvr component models the operation's behaviour as regards input–output mapping and state transition, we necessarily also have two state predicates, each coupled to the appropriate collection of state variables: one for the before-state model and one for the after-state model (these two models are of course equivalent). Thus, an operation specification emphasizes the fundamental role played by state models in the description of system behaviour: the fact that a state model describes an invariant property of a system, and no matter what a system does dynamically, its behaviour cannot violate that invariant.

The declaration and axiom parts of an operation schema look quite complex, lengthy descriptions. As we will see, Z provides us with a number of syntactic devices that enable us to abbreviate our descriptions quite significantly.

Decorations

It is not purely arbitrary that special terminating characters have been tagged onto some of the names used in AnOp opposite. These characters are examples of what are called *decorations*. A decoration is a sequence of one or more special characters terminating the name of an object. The most commonly used decorations in Z are the single characters `' '`, `'?'` and `'!'`, though combinations of these are also permitted. Here are some examples of names incorporating decorations:

> `hrs'`   `day?`   `hr24!`   `TimeOfDay'`   `d!?`   `year''`

A decoration is an integral part of a name. Thus, v, $v?$, v', etc. are *different* names of (therefore) *different* variables. Certain decorations tend to have fixed usages:

- the name of any input variable has a ? decoration
- the name of any output variable has a ! decoration
- a ' decoration identifies an 'after' state (component).

It must be emphasized that these are syntactic *conventions* only, although they have become part of standard Z usage and so can be assumed always to apply, unless otherwise stated. Thus, in an appropriate context, the names `var` and `var'` would denote respectively a state component *before* an operation is considered to have its effect, and the corresponding component of the state *after* that operation has occurred. It is tempting to regard `var` and `var'` as 'the same variable with a different value', as though the programming operation of 'assignment', say, is somehow being described. *The temptation must be resisted*. `var` and `var'` are two separate variables belonging to two separate (but equivalent) state models. It is the relationship formally expressed by a predicate between the two variables/state models that describes mathematically the familiar programming idea of 'update'.

We can now see from the generalized schema AnOp that, if this were some operation on the `TimeHM` state model of the digital watch (page 27), then

> StateDecs   is `hrs : 0..23; mins : 0..59`
> StateDecs' is `hrs' : 0..23; mins' : 0..59`

Since these two texts represent the complete before- and after-state models, no explicit pair of state predicates StatePred and StatePred' would appear in the axiom part of the operation schema. Alternatively, if we chose the `TimeHMNat` variant of the state model (page 30), then

> StateDecs   is `hrs : ℕ; mins : ℕ`
> StateDecs' is `hrs' : ℕ; mins' : ℕ`

and

StatePred   is hrs ≤ 23
                 mins ≤ 59
StatePred′   is hrs′ ≤ 23
                 mins′ ≤ 59

These two predicates *would* appear in the axiom part of the operation schema.

A further important aspect of decoration is that it is also permissible to decorate a schema name, though only once the schema has been specified—*schema names must be undecorated when first defined*. Schema decoration is better viewed as an operation, the effect of which is to decorate all names that are introduced in the schema's declaration part consistently wherever they occur in the schema's text. For example,

TimeHMNat′ = [hrs′ : ℕ; mins′ : ℕ | hrs′ ≤ 23 ∧ mins′ ≤ 59]

Note that global names referenced in a schema, including special names like ℕ and ≤, are *not* affected by schema decoration.

EXERCISE 3.4

Write out the texts of

a. TimeHMNorm′′ (see page 30)
b. ThreeCntrs?   (see Exercise 3.3 on page 33 for ThreeCntrs).

We will now partially sketch out the specification of one of the watch operations, namely Add1Min. For reasons explained earlier, we choose the most compact form of the time state model, i.e., TimeHM. The operation will look something like this:

```
┌─Add1Min────────────────────────────────────────────┐
│ hrs : 0..23                                          │
│ mins : 0..59                                         │
│ hrs′ : 0..23                                         │
│ mins′ : 0..59                                        │
│ ─────────────────────                                │
│ OpBhvr                                               │
└──────────────────────────────────────────────────────┘
```

Since the effect of Add1Min is purely a state transition, it consumes no input and produces no output; its sole objective is to keep the system time model in track with real-world time. OpBhvr thus merely describes a relationship between 'time-before' (hrs and mins) and 'time-after' (hrs′ and mins′). The overall relationship is fairly obvious: the time-after is one minute further on from the time-before. However, in order to express this with a predicate over the two sets of state variables, we need to break it down into more detail. Although there is no particular recipe for doing this, the following tactics will often help:

a. where possible, determine individual state transition relationships between corre-sponding variable pairs in the two state models
b. identify any obvious 'special cases' that the relationship needs to encompass.

These two tactics are in evidence in the following breakdown of what Add1Min's predicate must convey:

- If mins < 59, then it will be the case that mins′ = mins + 1.
  On the other hand, if mins = 59 (a special case), then mins′ = 0.

- If mins < 59, the hours component stays the same, that is hrs′ = hrs.
  However, if mins = 59 (the special case again), the hours component changes thus:
  - if hrs < 23, then it will be the case that hrs′ = hrs + 1
  - alternatively, if hrs = 23 (another special case), then hrs′ = 0.

Arriving at such analyses is a matter of practice and experience. However, we will defer formalizing descriptions like these until later. In any case, a description of Add1Min will now be obtained by a different route.

State Modelling Revisited

In general, there will be many different ways in which a model of a system state can be constructed. This should not be unduly surprising. For example, in programming there are many different data structures that can be constructed to hold items for look-up (arrays, binary trees, hash tables, etc.). The question is: what criteria might be used in deciding which state model is to be preferred out of a number of alternatives? We must be careful not to stretch the programming analogy too much. For example, we might well prefer one program data structure to another on the grounds of search efficiency. Yet in the world of abstract specification, the same notion of efficiency is a meaningless criterion to apply. This is *not* to say, however, that we are ultimately unconcerned in formal methods with the efficiency of implementations produced.

Deciding upon the model of a state is often a non-trivial issue, and is a topic we will discuss at some length in later case studies. For now, the question might be asked: is there any sensible alternative to the TimeHM time model for the digital watch? Consider this schema:

```
┌─ Time ──────────────────────────────────────────────┐
│                                                      │
│  t : 0..1439                                         │
│                                                      │
└──────────────────────────────────────────────────────┘
```

What we have done is simply model the time of day in minutes alone, absorbing the hours value (there are 1440 minutes in a day). The fact that the watch *displays* the time in 24-hour clock format is a separate issue. It is important to separate physical presentation of data at the user interface from internal representations. A state model is not obliged to mirror the former; the only obvious requirement is that there must be ways of mapping state data to output.

EXERCISE 3.5

§ The answer is given near the start of Section 3.3 on pages 42–43.
Return to Exercise 3.2(1.a) on page 31. Can you devise an alternative set of variables on which a state model of the watch's date component could be based?

Choosing schema Time as our time model has an immediate consequence: the specification of Add1Min is easier to write. Its OpBhvr component now has only to express

- if t < 1439, then t′ = t + 1
- if t = 1439, then t′ = 0.

This relationship between t' and t is actually 'adding 1 modulo 1440' which, by using the Z mod operator for integers (briefly, i mod j evaluates to the remainder of dividing i by j), can be expressed succinctly as

$$t' = (t + 1) \bmod 1440$$

or, of course,

$$(t + 1) \bmod 1440 = t'$$

It must be remembered that state transition descriptions are *predicates* and *not* commands. In many instances, these predicates happen to be equality relations. The reader will be aware that if $\alpha = \beta$, then also $\beta = \alpha$. The danger to be avoided is in thinking of an equality relation with a single '-decorated variable written on the left-hand side (a style commonly used) as denoting an imperative 'update instruction', like an assignment statement in a program. This relates to the warning given on page 35 concerning the interpretation of '-decorated variables.

Using Time, which we will now make our primary time model, Add1Min is thus:

```
┌─ Add1Min ──────────────────────────────────────┐
│ t,t' : 0..1439                                   │
│─────────────────────────────────                │
│ t' = ( t + 1 ) mod 1440                          │
└──────────────────────────────────────────────────┘
```

However, other operations (e.g., see below) are less pleasing. The point is that state modelling often involves choices that can be made only after some experimentation.

Remark
Whereas we use the term 'variant' to describe schema texts that are equivalent as defined earlier, the term 'version' will be used to describe schema texts that are non-equivalent alternatives. So, Time and TimeHM are two *versions* of a time state model.

To construct specifications of ResetMin and ResetHr, we need to understand exactly what these two operations mean. In reality, a user resets the minutes value by pressing a button on the watch which causes the watch to step up through the minutes range, leaving the hours value unchanged; similarly for the hours value. It is not possible to model continuous pressing of a button and the rapid step-through which this causes; but we can view this as the user repeatedly applying one simple operation: changing the hours/minutes value by one unit. So:

```
┌─ ResetMin ─────────────────────────────────────┐
│ t,t' : 0..1439                                   │
│─────────────────────────────────                │
│ t' = ( t div 60 ) * 60 + ( t + 1 ) mod 60        │
└──────────────────────────────────────────────────┘
```

```
┌─ ResetHr ──────────────────────────────────────┐
│ t,t' : 0..1439                                   │
│─────────────────────────────────                │
│ t' = ( t + 60 ) mod 1440                         │
└──────────────────────────────────────────────────┘
```

EXERCISE 3.6

1. Explain the equality for `t'` in `ResetMin`. Why is it not simply

    $$t' = (\,t + 1\,) \bmod 1440 \ ?$$

2. Respecify `ResetMin` and `ResetHr` assuming the watch stepped through time values *decrementally*.

3. § The answer is discussed immediately below.
    Respecify operation `ResetMin` (incremental version) using the `TimeHMNat` version of the time model (page 30); call it `ResetMinNat`.

Question (3) in the previous exercise focuses on a vital point. If your answer was something like

```
┌─ ResetMinNat ────────────────────────────────────────────────┐
│ hrs,mins : ℕ                                                  │
│ hrs',mins' : ℕ                                                │
├───────────────────────────────────────────────────────────── │
│ hrs ≤ 23                                                      │
│ mins ≤ 59                                                     │
│ mins' = ( mins + 1 ) mod 60                                   │
│ hrs' ≤ 23                                                     │
│ mins' ≤ 59                                                    │
└───────────────────────────────────────────────────────────── ┘
```

then you could not complain if, when you used the built watch to change the minutes value, the hours value changed as well! You could protest about the design being wrong, but you would not get your money back since the design, though eccentric, conforms to the specification! The problem lies in the omission from `ResetMinNat` of

`hrs' = hrs`

As it stands, `ResetMinNat` permits `hrs'` to be any value, subject only to the obligation to respect its declaration and the after-state predicate. A similar error can be perpetrated with `ResetHrNat` where we must remember to include `mins' = mins`. You might think that a watchmaker with any vestige of common sense would not implement a watch in such a perverse way, even if, technically, the maker was 'keeping to the specification'. Yet the reader can no doubt appreciate the dangers of any methodology which entertains reliance on the 'common sense' of implementors to disentangle dubious features of specifications!

Important conclusion: using Z, we take the position that if something is omitted from a specification, the implementor is free to choose how to tackle the omitted feature (provided, of course, the choice does not compromise conformity with the specification). When specifying an operation, we are expressing a relationship between the *complete* before and after states. Hence, it is just as important to specify explicitly which state components *do not* change as it is the updates that do occur.

Schema Inclusion

Imagine that we were constructing a specification requiring a complex state model State, i.e., one with many components with lengthy type descriptors and a highly non-

trivial predicate. It would clearly be tiresome writing out the texts corresponding to
StateDecs, StateDecs', StatePred and StatePred' in every operation specification.
Fortunately, this can be avoided. This is because it is possible for one schema to
'import' the text of another by referencing the name of the latter in its declaration part,
a device called *schema inclusion*. In fact,

```
┌─ NewSchema ──────────────┐        ┌─ NewSchema ──────────────┐
│ ...                      │        │ ...                      │
│ ExistingSchema           │        │ ExistingSchemaDecs       │
│ ──────────────           │        │ ──────────────────       │
│                          │        │                          │
│ ...                      │        │ ...                      │
│                          │        │ ExistingSchemaPred       │
└──────────────────────────┘        └──────────────────────────┘
```

is equivalent to

Thus, an equivalent text for NewSchema can be imagined by expanding the *schema
reference* ExistingSchema into its schema text. The declarations of ExistingSchema become
implicitly incorporated into the declaration part of NewSchema, and likewise the
predicate of the former is implicitly added to the axiom part of the latter. There are
some potential complications, e.g., if the two schemas contain variables with common
names, but we will deal with this issue much later in Section 8.2.

Using schema inclusion for the watch operations, for Add1Min we get

```
┌─ Add1Min ────────────────────────────────────────────────────┐
│ Time; Time'                                                   │
│ ───────────                                                   │
│ t' = ( t + 1 ) mod 1440                                       │
└───────────────────────────────────────────────────────────────┘
```

There is little gain here because Time is a compact description in the first place. There
would be a bigger gain with operations on, say, the TimeHMNat state model. For
example, compare the following with its variant (when corrected) on page 39:

```
┌─ ResetMinNat ────────────────────────────────────────────────┐
│ TimeHMNat; TimeHMNat'                                         │
│ ─────────────────────                                         │
│ mins' = ( mins + 1 ) mod 60                                   │
│ hrs' = hrs                                                     │
└───────────────────────────────────────────────────────────────┘
```

It is important to grasp thoroughly the effect of schema inclusion and its 'macro-like'
qualities. For example, we have not omitted the before-state and after-state predicates
from ResetMinNat—they are merely subsumed by the two included state model
schema references.

Schema inclusion is a major technique for facilitating specification construction and
is just one of many operations on schemas that we will meet in due course, collectively
put under an umbrella called the 'schema calculus'. The schema calculus, dealt with at
length in Chapter 8, is an important contributor to Z's expressive power and can be
seen as a natural consequence of the schema construct itself—there would be far less
use in composing descriptions into named units if the latter could not then be referenced by name in other parts of the specification.

EXERCISE 3.7

1. Write a schema text equivalent to `AvCntrVal` below *without* using schema inclusion (for `ThreeCntrs`, see Exercise 3.3 on page 33):

    $AvCntrVal \mathrel{\hat{=}} [\, ThreeCntrs;\ ThreeCntrs';\ acv! : \mathbb{N}\ |$
    $acv! = (\,c1 + c2 + c3\,)\ div\ 3\ \wedge$
    $c1' = c1 \wedge c2' = c2 \wedge c3' = c3\,]$

2. Suppose we had constructed a normalized variant of the `Time` model on page 37. Use schema inclusion to rewrite the specifications of `Add1Min` on page 40, and `ResetMin` and `ResetHr` on page 38.

Observation and Output

The informal description of the watch on page 25 refers to the display of the time as 'continuous', though this is not a property that we can formalize in Z. However, we can regard the persistence of the display as being a function of the liquid crystal read-out mechanism itself. Thus, consider the operation `TimeOut` described below. Unlike the other operations so far considered, which are *updates*, `TimeOut` is purely an *observer* operation. Such operations are characterized by the fact that the before and after states are identical. So an observer operation will include in its specification an equality of the form $var' = var$ for each before and after variable pair in the two state models (eventually, we will meet other ways of saying the same thing).

```
┌─TimeOut──────────────────────────────────────────────┐
│ Time; Time'                                           │
│ hrs! : 0..23                                          │
│ mins! : 0..59                                         │
├───────────────────────────────────────────────────────┤
│ hrs! = t div 60                                       │
│ mins! = t mod 60                                      │
│ t' = t                                                │
└───────────────────────────────────────────────────────┘
```

Note that the equalities for `hrs!` and `mins!` in `TimeOut` could correctly refer to t' instead of t. Where choice exists, consistent style throughout a specification is preferred. If corresponding before- and after-state variables are equal, we will generally use the former in expressions.

The time display now appears to have been dealt with satisfactorily, *but this is not so*; there is an aspect of the watch we have not captured. Although the display itself is continuous, the time which is displayed changes because we expect the watch to update the display in line with the passage of time! This means that every instance of the watch updating the time by another minute should be accompanied by a time display operation so that the new time is shown by the watch. In other words, the `Add1Min` and `TimeOut` behaviours really need to be combined.

One possible solution is to revise the specification by deleting `TimeOut` and inserting an output behaviour into `Add1Min`. This means we will no longer have a separate time display operation, but then the watch's behaviour does not require this. So `Add1Min` is modified to

```
┌─ Add1Min ──────────────────────────────────────────────┐
│ Time; Time'                                             │
│ hrs! : 0..23                                            │
│ mins! : 0..59                                           │
├─────────────────────────────────────────────────────────┤
│ t' = ( t + 1 ) mod 1440                                 │
│ hrs! = t' div 60                                        │
│ mins! = t' mod 60                                       │
└─────────────────────────────────────────────────────────┘
```

Further aspects of this modification are dealt with in the following exercise. Another, perhaps superior, way of handling the coupling between the time's update and its display occurs in a later exercise.

EXERCISE 3.8

1. Why do the equalities for hrs! and mins! in the revised Add1Min now refer to t', rather than t as in the discarded TimeOut operation?

2. Explain what is wrong with defining the new version of Add1Min by combining its old version with TimeOut, i.e., something like

    NewAdd1Min ≙ [Add1Min; TimeOut]

3. Identify any other operation(s) covered so far in the text that need to be subjected to a change similar to Add1Min, and give the modified specification(s).

3.3   FURTHER STATE AND OPERATION DESCRIPTION

A Date Model

To make further progress with the case study, we need to construct a model for the date component of the digital watch's state. A variables-only attempt might yield

```
┌─ DateVars ──────────────────────────────────────────────┐
│ dy : 1..31                                              │
│ mn : 1..12                                              │
│ yr : ℕ                                                  │
└─────────────────────────────────────────────────────────┘
```

There are two points worth reiterating that were first made in Section 3.2. Firstly, the fact that the physical display of a month is a three-letter code does not invalidate the DateVars model—there is an obvious mapping between the state variable mn and its displayed form. Secondly, there are alternative ways of modelling dates. Two possibilities are

```
┌─ DateVarsDY ────────────────────────────────────────────┐
│ doty : 1..366                                           │
│ yr : ℕ                                                  │
└─────────────────────────────────────────────────────────┘
```

and

```
┌─DateVarsDD──────────────────────────────────────────────┐
│ days : ℕ
│
└──────────────────────────────────────────────────────────┘
```

In `DateVarsDY`, the months have been absorbed into a days-of-the-year counter `doty`. In `DateVarsDD`, absorption has been taken to its ultimate degree: `days` merely counts the passing of days from some 'date zero'. This latter model is possible because the informal problem description indicates that the watch handles years only from some year YYYY. Thus, January 1st of year YYYY can act as 'the beginning of days'.

Even these simple examples highlight the trade-offs we often have to make when constructing formal specifications. In assessing the three versions of the date model, the following should be apparent:

- Specifying `Add1Day` will be easiest with `DateVarsDD` since a trivial state transition is involved. It will be the most complex with `DateVars` since a state transition involving possible changes to day, month and year components must be described.

- Mapping state data onto the user interface will be the most complex with `DateVarsDD` since month and year boundaries will have to be calculated. The mapping will be easiest with `DateVars` since a trivial one-to-one correspondence exists.

We will choose `DateVars`, not only because it is the most natural model of the three, but also for ulterior motives related to the following question: what extra constraints need to be added to `DateVars` to ensure that it constitutes a valid date model?

Consideration of `DateVars` should lead one rapidly to the conclusion that it is wholly inadequate as a model of the date component of the digital watch's state. This is because the state space defined by `DateVars`, whilst it includes all valid dates, also contains a range of bindings, none of which could be interpreted as valid dates. For example, assuming year YYYY is 1900, consider these bindings allowed by `DateVars`:

$$\beta1: \ \langle \, dy \Rrightarrow 31, \ mn \Rrightarrow 9, \ yr \Rrightarrow 1956 \, \rangle$$
$$\beta2: \ \langle \, dy \Rrightarrow 29, \ mn \Rrightarrow 2, \ yr \Rrightarrow 1923 \, \rangle$$
$$\beta3: \ \langle \, dy \Rrightarrow 29, \ mn \Rrightarrow 7, \ yr \Rrightarrow 1872 \, \rangle$$

Binding $\beta1$ interprets to the 31st September, which is non-existent; $\beta2$ interprets to the 29th February, which was non-existent in 1923; and $\beta3$ is invalid because its year component precedes the assumed value for YYYY. What is needed in the date model is a predicate imposing additional constraints on `DateVars` which excludes precisely such bindings as these.

The required predicate turns out to be quite complex. To help us with the task of expressing it, we will assume that we have the special predicate symbols `ajsn` and `leapYr` available with the following interpretations:

- `ajsn( m )` means: 'm is the month of either April, June, September, or November'; e.g., `ajsn( 6 )` is true, but `ajsn( 12 )` is false.

- `leapYr( y )` means: 'y represents a leap year'; e.g., `leapYr( 1992 )` is true but `leapYr( 1990 )` is false.

Armed with this notation, we can express an adequate date model `Date` as described overleaf, where `bottomYr` is assumed to denote the lowest year the watch handles. To express different cases, a new symbol ⇒ has been used. For each case, a case-characterizing predicate comes first, followed after the ⇒ by the necessary consequence for that case. In Chapter 4, we will give a proper explanation of the ⇒ symbol. For now, P ⇒ Q can be verbalized as 'if P is the case, then Q must hold as a consequence'. Note that in the second case, the reader may feel that leapYr(yr) should be 'and-ed' with mn = 2, but this is actually redundant given the third case. The new symbol ¬ in the third case in effect inverts the logic of its operand and can be read as 'not'.

```
┌─ Date ─────────────────────────────────────────────────────────────┐
│ DateVars                                                            │
│ ──────────────────                                                 │
│                                                                    │
│ yr ≥ bottomYr              — built-in watch constraint             │
│ ajsn(mn)                   — case: month is April, May, June, or September │
│   ⇒ dy ≤ 30                                                        │
│ mn = 2                     — case: month is February               │
│   ⇒ dy ≤ 29                                                        │
│ mn = 2 ∧ ¬ leapYr(yr)      — case: month is February and it is not a leap year │
│   ⇒ dy ≤ 28                                                        │
└────────────────────────────────────────────────────────────────────┘
```

Note that the author-chosen commentary syntax

— TextNotContainingNL **NL**

(**NL** is 'new line') is *not* covered in Spivey (1992), though it is useful to be able to mix informal annotations unambiguously with Z text. This is permitted by Brien and Nicholls (1992).

EXERCISE 3.9

Specify the predicates that need to be added to the following schemas (pages 42 and 43) in order to create a valid date model for the Digital Watch specification:

a. DateVarsDY   b. DateVarsDD

Global Variables

A new feature occurs in schema Date: it makes reference to a name bottomYr that is not declared in the schema and is not provided by the included DateVars. Variable bottomYr is the earliest year the watch will handle. Recall that this factory-fitted constraint is not user-adjustable. There are two problems:

• where is bottomYr declared?
• what value is bottomYr?

Declaration rules are very simple in Z: all names must be declared, and the declaration of a name must textually precede any of its applied occurrences. Now bottomYr is not part of the Date model itself; it is not a state component that (potentially) undergoes transitions, but is more akin to a 'constant' that helps define the state space described by Date. This is why its declaration is not placed within Date. In fact, bottomYr is declared as a *global* variable. Its scope thus becomes the whole of the specification text from its declaration onwards.

Instead of using schemas, which localize names, global variables are declared in definition paragraphs called *axiomatic descriptions*. These look somewhat like schema boxes with the top and bottom borders removed, as the following shows:

$$
\begin{array}{|l}
\text{DeclarationPart} \\
\hline
\text{AxiomPart}
\end{array}
$$

Clearly, `bottomYr` is a natural number, but what more should we say about it? There is no single value it denotes since the factory keeps changing it. The best we can do is give it some sensible lower bound. Since the meaning of `leapYr` used in schema `Date` will depend on the modern calendar, which began in 1753, the following Z paragraph *preceding* that of `Date` suffices:

$$
\begin{array}{|l}
\text{bottomYr} : \mathbb{N} \\
\hline
\text{bottomYr} \geq 1753
\end{array}
$$

Some Additional Schema Structuring

Unlike the deleted operation `TimeOut`, which got absorbed into operations like `Add1Min`, an analogous observer operation `ShowDate` is certainly required and easily specified. For reasons that may not be clear at this point, we will split up its specification across two schemas:

$$
\begin{array}{|l}
\text{---}\ \text{DateOut} \text{---} \\
\text{Date; Date}' \\
\text{d! : 1..31; m! : 1..12; y! : } \mathbb{N} \\
\hline
\text{d! = dy}' \\
\text{m! = mn}' \\
\text{y! = yr}' \\
\end{array}
$$

$$
\begin{array}{|l}
\text{---ShowDate---} \\
\text{DateOut} \\
\hline
\text{dy}' = \text{dy} \\
\text{mn}' = \text{mn} \\
\text{yr}' = \text{yr} \\
\end{array}
$$

We are not concerned with how output data gets mapped into its surface presentation; conversion of a month value to a three-letter code will be treated as a matter for the watch's interface.

`DateOut` looks strange because it describes an operation that allows *any* state transition to occur to the date component (why? see page 39). However, its purpose is not to model a complete system operation. Just as we are capturing the full state model of the digital watch via more than one schema, so we can do the same with its operations. In general, modularization into several contributing schemas is performed for a variety of reasons. For the state model in Digital Watch, it effects a 'separation of concerns'. For the ShowDate operation, it is a piece of 'bottom-up' pragmatism, as Exercise 3.10(2) below should make clear.

Like Add1Min, we need an operation Add1Day that is an internal state transition which keeps the watch's state consistent with the real world date. To specify Add1Day, we will assume declaration of the following additional predicate symbol eom ('is end of month'):

eom(d,m,y)   means: 'd, m and y form a date where d is the last day of month m in year y'; e.g., eom(29,2,1992) is true (1992 was a leap year), but eom(30,10,1990) is false.

```
┌─ Add1Day ─────────────────────────────────────────────┐
│ Date                                                   │
│ Date'                                                  │
│────────────────────────────────────────────────────── │
│ eom( dy,mn,yr ) ∧ mn = 12        — case: end of December (hence of year) │
│   ⇒ dy' = 1 ∧ mn' = 1 ∧ yr' = yr + 1                   │
│ eom( dy,mn,yr ) ∧ mn < 12        — case: end of month but not December │
│   ⇒ dy' = 1 ∧ mn' = mn + 1 ∧ yr' = yr                  │
│ ¬ eom( dy,mn,yr )                — case: not end of a month │
│   ⇒ dy' = dy + 1 ∧ mn' = mn ∧ yr' = yr                 │
└────────────────────────────────────────────────────────┘
```

As with schema Date on page 44, we see more vividly the point first made on page 36 concerning the tactic of decomposing a complex description by 'case analysis'. One approach is to try to identify the most specialized cases first, and then work out the more general ones. In Add1Day, the cases are listed in decreasing order of specialization, though of course any order would do. Once again, it should be noted how schema inclusion simplifies schema construction. The reader might ponder what the full expanded form of Add1Day would be.

Unlike Add1Min, operation Add1Day does not have a display component. However, we have yet to address ResetDateUp and ResetDateDown, which *are* required to have a display effect like (the modified) ResetMin and ResetHr. These two remaining date operations are tackled in the next exercise, which also features the time reset operations.

EXERCISE 3.10

1. Specify an operation Sub1Day ('reduce date by one day'). Tackle it in the style of Add1Day using a 'by cases' approach and expressing the predicate as illustrated in Date and Add1Day. However, Sub1Day is more involved than Add1Day, partly because you have to decide how to deal with the following complication: what happens if the date is January 1st of bottomYr?

2. Specify ResetDateUp and ResetDateDown (easy using schema inclusion). Could ResetMin and ResetHr have been dealt with in a similar way? Explain.

The Δ and Ξ Conventions

As well as schema inclusion, there are other devices to reduce the formal text we have to write. For example, the following pattern occurs in any operation on a state:

```
┌─ AnOp ───────────────────────────────────────────────────────┐
│ State                                                          │
│ State′                                                         │
│ ...                                                            │
├────────────────────────────────                               │
│                                                                │
│ ...                                                            │
└────────────────────────────────────────────────────────────────┘
```

It has been established by convention in Z that the prefixes Δ and Ξ can be attached to a schema name, and the effect is as though the following definitions had occurred:

$$\Delta\text{State} \; \hat{=} \; [\text{State}; \text{State}']$$
$$\Xi\text{State} \; \hat{=} \; [\Delta\text{State} \mid v1' = v1 \wedge v2' = v2 \wedge \ldots \; vk' = vk]$$

where $v1$–vk inclusive are the variables of State. Unless a specification says otherwise, its use of Δ and Ξ is by default as described here and there is no need to provide explicit definitions. Note that these two conventions are applicable only to schemas modelling states.

The Δ and Ξ conventions can save a considerable amount of writing with operations. As regards Add1Day, there would be little saving since Date; Date′ would simply be replaced by ΔDate; a similar comment applies to the other update operations. However, with ShowDate (page 45), there is a bigger gain:

```
┌─ ShowDate ────────────────────────────────────────────────────┐
│ ΞDate                                                          │
│ DateOut                                                        │
└────────────────────────────────────────────────────────────────┘
```

Note that both inclusions supply Date and Date′ models. This is fine: in the expanded text, only one instance of each state variable declaration (and likewise state predicate) is considered to be present. The matching variables are said to be *merged*, a process discussed later in Section 8.2.

Use of the Δ and Ξ conventions is strongly recommended, not least because of their visual impact when reading specifications. It is much easier to distinguish updates from observations if the conventions are used.

EXERCISE 3.11

1. Specify the variables n and m appearing in the ThreeCntrs model (see Exercise 3.3), given that they must both be odd natural numbers with n no bigger than m.

2. Using the Δ and Ξ conventions, construct specifications for the following operations on the ThreeCntrs state:

    *   ResetC1, which resets counter c1 to c3 mod (c1 + 1)

    *   CntrDiffs, which outputs the differences between the c1 and c2 counters and between the c2 and c3 counters.

3.4 COMPLETING THE SPECIFICATION

A System View

Thus far, we have treated the time and date components of the watch in isolation, as two separate components. Were this really the case, our specification would end up as precisely that: a description of two independent subsystems. However, the time and date components of the watch *are* dependent (how? see below). So we must treat the digital watch as a coherent single system, and adjust the specification to reflect this fact.

Firstly, the complete system state of the digital watch can be documented by

```
┌─ DigitalWatch ─────────────────────────────────────┐
│ Time                                                │
│ Date                                                │
│                                                     │
└─────────────────────────────────────────────────────┘
```

Secondly, all main operations, namely

```
Add1Min, ResetMin, ResetHr,
Add1Day, ResetDateUp, ResetDateDown, ShowDate
```

must now be regarded as operations over a state described by `DigitalWatch`. The first three operations update the state, though only the `Time` component, whereas the next three operations also update the state, though only the `Date` component; `ShowDate` leaves the complete state unchanged. However, before we effect any modifications, we need to understand the coupling that exists between `Time` and `Date`. The fact is that whilst the static properties of the two subsystems are independent, their dynamic properties are not. The reason for this is simple: the date must change on each occasion that the time moves on from the end of one day to the beginning of the next. That is, `Add1Day` *must occur precisely and only when* `Add1Min` *occurs at the end of a day.* At the moment, our specification fails to capture this essential dynamic property.

What we need to do is express in our specification the conditions under which either or both of `Add1Min` and `Add1Day` occur. Noting that the end of the day is represented by a system state where $t = 1439$, we therefore have

- if $t < 1439$, then the next state change is `Add1Min` only (leaving `Date` unchanged)
- if $t = 1439$, then the next state change is `Add1Min` *and* `Add1Day`.

These requirements can be expressed in two new schemas:

```
┌─ TimeOnlyChange ───────────────────────────────────┐
│ ΔDigitalWatch                                       │
│ Add1Min; ΞDate                                      │
├─────────────────────────────────────────────────────│
│ t < 1439                                            │
│                                                     │
└─────────────────────────────────────────────────────┘
```

```
┌─ TimeAndDateChange ────────────────────────────────┐
│ ΔDigitalWatch                                       │
│ Add1Min; Add1Day                                    │
├─────────────────────────────────────────────────────│
│ t = 1439                                            │
│                                                     │
└─────────────────────────────────────────────────────┘
```

Since `Add1Min` and `Add1Day` provide ΔTime and ΔDate respectively, the reference to ΔDigitalWatch in each of the new schemas is redundant; however, its inclusion helps to emphasize that we now have two `DigitalWatch`-level update operations. The inclusion of ΞDate in `TimeOnlyChange` is necessary since we need to specify that the operation leaves the date component of the state unchanged. `TimeAndDateChange` combines the effects of `Add1Min` and `Add1Day`. These latter two operations stay as specified—their status is now that of two subsystem operations contributing to a higher level of description.

Partial and Total Operations

The conditions under which the two new system-level operations opposite can occur have been added to the axiom parts of their schemas. These conditions, `t` < 1439 and `t` = 1439, are examples of the general feature indicated by (*) on page 34 but not elaborated upon. That is, predicates can be included in an operation schema to define the 'start conditions' under which the operation is applicable. We will call such predicates 'preconstraints'. A preconstraint is always a predicate on the before state and/or input(s) of the operation concerned.

If an operation is not applicable under all circumstances, as with `TimeOnlyChange` and `TimeAndDateChange`, it is *partial*; otherwise it is *total*. The inclusion of a preconstraint in an operation's description is thus an explicit indication that the operation is partial. However, *absence of any explicit preconstraint does not necessarily mean the operation is therefore total.* Consider this simple example:

```
┌─ Decrement ─────────────────────────────────────────────────┐
│  x,x' : ℕ                                                     │
│ ─────────────────────────────────────────────────────────── │
│  x' = x - 1                                                   │
└──────────────────────────────────────────────────────────────┘
```

Clearly, `Decrement` is partial because the transition would violate the constraint of the declaration of x' ($x' \geq 0$) if $x = 0$. Nevertheless, the fact that we have not included an explicit precontraint requiring $x > 0$ does *not* make `Decrement`'s description invalid. It is a separate issue whether we should, for reasons of good style, make operations like `Decrement` 'honest' by revealing their partialness with explicit preconstraints.

It can be seen that the area of operation partialness and preconstraints is rather more subtle than may first appear. With `Decrement`, it does not matter whether we include or omit $x > 0$; we are still basically describing the same operation. But we could not omit `t` < 1439 from `TimeOnlyChange`, or `t` = 1439 from `TimeAndDateChange`, because then we certainly would be describing operations different to the ones we wanted! The difference in the two situations is really this. Some preconstraints if omitted, e.g., $x > 0$ in `Decrement`, can be deduced from the operation text alone, and so their omission is 'harmless'. Others if omitted, e.g., `t` < 1439 in `TimeOnlyChange`, can be deduced *only by understanding the reality we are trying faithfully to describe*. Their omission is harmful in the sense that our formal description would then not adequately interpret to the reality (domain) being addressed. If we omitted, say, `t` < 1439 from `TimeOnlyChange`, it would still be a legal operation specification, but it would not be valid in the domain of the digital watch—it would require the time only to change and not the date, even when the time was just one tick away from midnight.

Lest these issues seem rather confusing at this early juncture, we will adopt the following stance: when specifying what we understand to be a partial operation, we will make its perceived partialness as explicit as possible with preconstraints. Later, in Section 8.4, we will encounter an important feature of Z—a way of accurately calculating an operation's partialness in terms of what is called its *precondition*.

EXERCISE 3.12

Refer back to the `ThreeCntrs` state model described in Exercise 3.3, page 33. Determine which of the operations listed below are possible on this state. For each possible operation, state whether it is partial or total, and if partial, give the full preconstraint that defines the extent of the operation's applicability.

a. incrementing the counter `c1` by `1`
b. decrementing the counter `c3` by `c2`
c. resetting `c3` to its maximum allowed value `m`
d. swapping the values `c1` and `c2`
e. resetting `c1` and `c3` respectively to two input values $x?, y? : \mathbb{N}$
f. displaying how many times `c2` has equalled `c3`'s value
g. displaying whether or not `c1` divides `c2` exactly.

Examining the watch's behaviour further, we see that, as each minute passes by, the watch changes state either by `TimeOnlyChange` or by `TimeAndDateChange`. We can think of this 'either/or change of state per minute' as the top-level state change operation automatically carried out by the watch system. We can even define it:

$$\text{WatchChange} \;\hat{=}\; \text{TimeOnlyChange} \vee \text{TimeAndDateChange}$$

The $\vee$ symbol is an operator meaning 'either one or the other (or, if both are applicable, choose either one)'. Note that the preconstraints of the two operations ensure that only one is ever applicable and never both, since $t < 1439$ and $t = 1439$ cannot both apply at the same time. We say that the choice between the two operations, and hence `WatchChange` itself, is *deterministic*.

The watch's automatic behaviour over its lifespan is thus effectively

for each minute of real-world time that ticks by **do** `WatchChange` **end do**

(*NB*: This '**for** statement' is *not* part of Z!) The four `Reset` operations and observation `ShowDate` provide the watch user with a useful degree of operational control. There are still aspects of the watch's behaviour the specification does not cover. For example, the watch must have a scheduling policy for dealing with a user-initiated operation if it occurs at the same time as a `WatchChange`. One possibility is that all `Reset` operations override `WatchChange`, whereas `Showdate` and `WatchChange` can happily occur concurrently. However, these considerations are really implementation issues, and so we will not discuss them any further.

EXERCISE 3.13

Describe how the specifications of the four `Reset` operations and `ShowDate` must be altered to raise them to the status of operations on `DigitalWatch` (the changes are simpler than those in which `Add1Min` and `Add1Day` are involved).

Initial States

The state in which a system starts its life must be consistent with the general state model. If this were not so, it would hardly be a recipe for implementing a system exhibiting meaningful behaviour. This aspect is dealt with by giving a suitable initial state description using a schema. For the initial state of the digital watch, we will imagine that it is factory-set to the time 00.00 on the 1st of January of the current year of manufacture (say `cym?`). The following schema describes this choice of initial state:

```
┌─ InitDigitalWatch ─────────────────────────────────────────┐
│ DigitalWatch'; cym? : ℕ                                     │
├─────────────────────────────                               │
│ t' = 0                                                      │
│ dy' = mn' = 1                                               │
│ yr' = cym?                                                  │
└─────────────────────────────────────────────────────────────┘
```

This schema describes a *family* of acceptable initial states rather than just one state, since the initial value permitted for the state component `yr'` covers a range of possibilities represented by `cym?`. It is conventional to give the initial state schema of a state model State the name `InitState`. Note that `DigitalWatch'`, not ΔDigitalWatch, appears in `InitDigitalWatch` because an initial state schema defines a static system property, not a state transition. However, because there is a sense in which the state we are specifying is 'an outcome of an initialization', we prefer the prime-decorated form of a state model in the specification of an initial state. This is well-established Z style.

Proof Obligations

The requirement of general/initial state model consistency is not something we can take for granted. In fact, it is a *proof obligation*—a property of our system development (in this case, of the specification) that we ought to prove. Discharging appropriate proof obligations is an integral part of the development process throughout all phases of a formal methods approach. The argument below represents a very informal proof. As Section 2.1 indicated, it could be formalized given a suitable set of 'reasoning rules'.

Consider `InitDigitalWatch`. We can see immediately that the value chosen for `t'` respects the declaration/constraint of `t'`, so there are no problems here. But what of the date components? Clearly, the values 1, 1 and `cym?` must represent a valid date. Now, we know that the 1st of January of any year will never cause a problem. So the acceptability of the initial state rests on the value `cym?`. The one requirement here is that it must not be less than the value chosen for `bottomYr`. Thus, we appear to have omitted the following crucial requirement from `InitDigitalWatch`:

$$cym? \geq bottomYr$$

However, let us represent the predicate of `Date'` as `DatePred( dy',mn',yr' )`. From the following equalities in `InitDigitalWatch`:

$$dy' = mn' = 1 \quad \text{and} \quad yr' = cym?$$

it follows that `DatePred( 1,1,cym? )` holds by the simple process of 'substituting equals for equals'. If we expand this predicate out by replacing 1 for each instance of `dy'`, 1 for each instance of `mn'` and `cym?` for each instance of `yr'`, we get

$$\begin{aligned}
&\texttt{cym?} \geq \texttt{bottomYr} && (3.1)\\
&\texttt{ajsn(1)} \Rightarrow \texttt{1} \leq 30\\
&\texttt{1} = \texttt{2} \Rightarrow \texttt{1} \leq 29\\
&\texttt{1} = \texttt{2} \wedge \neg \texttt{leapYr(cym?)} \Rightarrow \texttt{1} \leq 28
\end{aligned}$$

Logic allows us to 'ignore' any case expressed using $\Rightarrow$ which has a false case-defining predicate. This applies to all three cases, which leaves just the first line (3.1). Thus, the requirement concerning `cym?` is actually a direct consequence of the predicate of `InitDigitalWatch` anyway, which means that it would be redundant, though not incorrect, to include the requirement in the schema.

Does this mean `InitDigitalWatch` is acceptable? Almost. Strictly, we should show that it is possible to choose a value for `cym?` which satisfies (3.1). This is obviously so—in fact, any natural number equal to, or exceeding, `bottomYr` will do. Hence we conclude that `InitDigitalWatch` is acceptable and consistent with `DigitalWatch`.

Documentation

The Digital Watch specification, like the other case studies in this book, is presented in a deliberate discovery/expository mode which is designed to lead the reader step by step through a sequence of concepts. The text is not intended to be indicative of the way specifications are presented in practice as software engineering documents. Later in Section 8.4 (page 216), we comment on the structure of specification documents.

EXERCISE 3.14

1. Give 'honest' specifications for operations (a,b,g) in Exercise 3.12.

2. Remark upon the behaviour of the following operation `OpAorB`:

    `OpAorB` $\triangleq$ `OpA` $\vee$ `OpB`

    where `OpA` and `OpB` are operations (a) and (b) referred to in Question (1).

3. Identify, then specify, some additional operations that a real-world digital watch might possess which have not been mentioned in the case study. If necessary, invent extra watch features, e.g., an optional hourly 'beep'.

SUMMARY OF CHAPTER 3

- An overall 'look and feel' for formal specification in Z is provided via a single, fairly simple case study, but without getting too immersed in predicate logic or sets.

- The fundamental concepts and constructs on which Z specifications are based are introduced, particularly as regards the *schema* and its associated repertoire of notational devices and conventions.

- The reader is lead step by step through the development of a specification, illustrating how its structure evolves as construction proceeds, highlighting the main issues to be addressed and indicating where important areas of decision-making lie.

PREDICATE LOGIC:
A LANGUAGE FOR DESCRIPTION

Key Topics   Basic predicates: relations; environments, interpretation, truth values; free variables. Propositional operators and structures, truth-functional and intuitive interpretation; truth calculation; contingencies, contradictions, tautologies; propositional laws, equivalences. Universal and existential quantifiers, bound variables; multiple instances of quantifiers; bound variable renaming; schema-text syntax; predicate laws. Axiomatic description of relations; tuples; cartesian product, powerset.

4.1   BASIC PREDICATES

Relations

Chapter 3 shows how Z specifications can be constructed that comprise mathematical models of states and descriptions of operations over states. States, operations, and global features of a specification are modelled by asserting axiomatic properties (i.e., properties 'given by definition') over collections of carefully chosen mathematical variables. These axiomatic assertions, or *axioms*, are expressed in (to give its full title) *first-order predicate logic*; we will usually drop the 'first-order'. The axioms in a Z specification are examples of *logical expressions* called *predicates*.

A predicate in its simplest form is expressed using an *n-ary* or *n-place* name called a *relation*. For now, *n-ary* can be taken to mean that when the relation name is applied, it 'requires n arguments'; we can also say that a relation's *arity* is n. Later in Section 4.4 we revise this view slightly, more accurately treating an n-ary relation as a name requiring a *single* argument with n components. The difference is less superficial than it seems.

The two most fundamental relations in Z are equality (=), a familiar binary (i.e., 2-ary) relation that is used extensively in specifications; and set membership ($\in$), another binary relation which is introduced in the next chapter. Here again are the three additional relations, with their interpretations, that we found useful in the Digital Watch specification:

- `ajsn( m )`:   m is the month of either April, June, September, or November
- `leapYr( y )`:   y represents a leap year
- `eom( d, m, y )`:   d, m and y form a date where d is the last day of month m in year y.

Thus, `ajsn` and `leapYr` are *unary* (1-ary) relations, and `eom` is a *tertiary* (3-ary) relation. All four relation names are *prefix*, i.e., they are written *before* their arguments (= and $\in$ are *infix*, i.e., written *between* their arguments). In the Digital Watch specification, we merely assumed the availability of these three relations. However, while Z provides us with a host of useful predefined relations in its 'mathematical toolkit', there are none for dates, etc. In Section 4.4, we see how to define our own relations.

Remark
Z's mathematical toolkit is an extensive suite of predefined names/symbols of various kinds, organized into different categories, which provides a wide range of mathematical structures that can be utilized in formal descriptions. The toolkit will be gradually revealed over ensuing chapters. An authoritative source like Spivey (1992) acts partly as a reference manual for the toolkit.

Syntactically, predicates are often referred to as *formulas*. A *basic formula* of predicate logic consists of a relation name applied to the correct number of arguments with the correct type(s) and placed in the correct order. For example, the following predicates are all basic formulas:

a. `ajsn( 4 )`
b. `leapYr( 1900 )`
c. `eom( 31,7,1856 )`.

However, relation arguments are not restricted to just constants. In general, they are *terms* (or *expressions*), meaning that they can be built from an arbitrarily nested mix of constants, variables and applications of function names to sub-terms. For example, given

$$i, j : \mathbb{N}$$

then the following is a well-formed predicate:

d. `eom( i mod 31 + 1, j, bottomYr * j - i )`

It is true that, with the declarations as given, the second argument `j` might not be a number in the range `1..12` inclusive and the third argument might be less than 1753 (even negative), but they are both of the correct *type*, i.e., integer.

Generally, we think of a function application

$$f(a_1, a_2, \ldots a_n)$$

as 'evaluating to' a value which depends on the function `f` and its arguments a_i, $i = 1..n$. Functions are applied with prefix syntax in Z, except where an alternative is allowed—for example, infix operators such as `+`, etc. These operators are simply 2-ary functions in a different syntactic guise. In fact, all terms could be written in Z using purely prefix form. For example, the third argument of (d) above can be expressed alternatively as

$$(\_-\_)((\_*\_)(bottomYr, j), i)$$

where (`_-_`) and (`_*_`) are the full prefix functional names of the two operators. Underscores are used in a function name to indicate the positions of arguments when the name is applicable in non-prefix form. For obvious reasons of readability, a non-prefix syntax for a function is preferred if it provides a more natural form. This is also true of relations, especially binary relations. We prefer to read and write `i < j` rather than any other formulation (which would actually be (`i,j`) ∈ (`_<_`), but that is jumping ahead).

Environments and Interpretations

The informal definitions given for the relations used in the Digital Watch specification are 'semantic' in the sense that they state what we want the relation to mean when translated into the reality we are dealing with. Semantically, a predicate is a *truth-valued* expression, i.e., it is either true or false, with no other possibilities like 'unsure'. Given the intended meaning of the Digital Watch relations, we are able to conclude that, of the example predicates (a)–(d) on the opposite page,

- (a) and (c) are true
- (b) is false
- (d) is either true or false, but we need further information to decide which.

More generally, to determine the truth-value of a predicate, we need an *interpretation* for all the different names/symbols appearing in it; put simply, we need to know what they mean.

In Z, interpretations are derived from what are called *environments*. An environment can be thought of as an association between names and elements (recall that an element is a value with a type). Thus, the Z mathematical toolkit mentioned in the *Remark* on page 54 provides an environment common to all specifications. Each specification *enriches* this environment with its own declared names, such as schemas and global variables introduced in axiomatic definitions. Provided we know the types and values of elements associated with the various names appearing in a predicate, we can determine the predicate's truth value.

Consider the problem of evaluating a simple predicate like $\text{isP}(\alpha, \beta)$ in some environment ENV, where α and β are two terms. If the name isP is not known in ENV, we cannot proceed any further: the predicate is ill-formed because we would be guilty of applying a name not in scope (e.g., it may be undeclared). We still cannot get anywhere if ENV contains isP but the element associated with isP is not a binary relation: the predicate is still ill-formed. Even if isP is associated with a binary relation, there may still be problems. The types of the arguments α and β must agree with the type of binary relation associated with isP; if not, the predicate is ill-typed and its evaluation is meaningless. Recall that type checking in no way requires actual *values* of names to be known—it is something a Z syntax checker can do in exactly the same way that a compiler does for a strongly typed programming language.

Similar checks must be carried out on the terms α and β. Assuming the predicate passes all its syntax and type checks, we can attempt the task of its evaluation. Let us make the example more specific. Suppose isP is associated with a binary relation such that $\text{isP}(\text{x1}, \text{x2})$ interprets to 'the integer x1 is greater than the integer x2'. Then

$\quad$ $\text{isP}(0, -3)$ $\qquad\qquad$ is true

but

$\quad$ $\text{isP}((2 * 8) + 1, 17)$ $\quad$ is false

If, however, the same predicates occur in a different environment where the interpretation of $\text{isP}(\text{x1}, \text{x2})$ is 'the integer x1 is less than, or equal to, the integer x2', then the first predicate is false and the second true. In either environment, we are able to determine the truth values of both predicates because, as well as knowing the relation associated with isP, we are able to evaluate the four terms $0, -3, (2 * 8) + 1$ and 17. This is because the constant names $0, 1, 2, 3, 8$ and 17, the prefix name $-$, and infix names $*$ and $+$, are provided by Z and have their standard meaning.

Remark

Given either of the previous meanings for isP, we might regard isP as a poorly chosen name. When we introduce names, we usually have particular interpretations for them already in mind. In that case, we often choose a name that is suggestive of the interpretation we wish the name to have. However, we must be careful never to provide an interpretation based purely on names alone. A relation isLessThan might be defined such that isLessThan(x1, x2) means 'integer x1 is greater than integer x2'. We could justly complain that either the name or its meaning is utterly perverse; but that is all we could do.

EXERCISE 4.1

1. Write down in Z-like syntax the prefix form of

   $$(-b + \surd (b^2 - 4ac)) / 2a$$

   assuming sqrt and / were available real-number functions.

2. Consider predicate (d) on page 54. List all the names that would need to be recorded in an environment to make it possible in principle to determine (d)'s truth value.

Free Variables

Part of the expressive power of predicate logic stems from the fact that we can construct predicates involving terms that contain variables as well as constants. To be strict, we mean *free* variables, but the full significance of 'freeness' will not be apparent until Section 4.3. For now, the terms 'variable' and 'free variable' will be used synonymously. In a Z specification, free variables are those declared globally and those introduced in the declaration part of a schema.

Recall that a variable denotes some unique element, but usually we do not know which one; the type is fixed by the variable's declaration but the value is drawn from a range of possibilities given by the declaration's right hand side after the ' : '. Thus, consider the predicate

    bottomYr < 1990   (4.1)

where bottomYr is the Digital Watch global variable. We cannot determine this predicate's truth value because bottomYr is not a constant; we know from its declaration that it names an element of integer type whose value is 1753 or greater, but that is all we know. A more involved example is predicate (d) on page 54. Here, the predicate contains instances of three different variables.

The term 'n-ary' can be applied to predicates as well as relations. A predicate is n-ary if it contains instances of n distinct (free) variables. In fact, relations and predicates are really the same in the sense that predicates are used to define the meaning of relations, as Section 4.4 shows. In general, if the terms of a predicate contain one or more free variables, it is not possible to determine the predicate's truth value. Thus, we were able to determine the truth values of the previous two predicates

    isP(0, -3)   and   isP((2 * 8) + 1, 17)

since they are *0-ary* predicates or *propositions*, i.e., contain no free variables; but predicate (d) on page 54 is a tertiary predicate and predicate (4.1) above a unary predicate.

To determine the truth value of an n-ary predicate (n ≥ 1), we also need to be provided with a constant for each distinct free variable occurring in the predicate's terms. If we then *substitute* the instances of the variable(s) consistently with the constant(s) given, the predicate becomes 0-ary and truth evaluation is possible. For example, consider predicate (d) on page 54 and the binding

$$\langle\, \text{i} \Rightarrow 28, \text{j} \Rightarrow 2, \text{bottomYr} \Rightarrow 1940 \,\rangle$$

Then, since all terms in the binding are constants, we can calculate thus:

    eom(i mod 31 + 1, j, bottomYr * j - i)
    — by substitution from given binding:
    ≡ eom(28 mod 31 + 1, 2, 1940 * 2 - 28)
    — by evaluating terms (applications of mod and *):
    ≡ eom(28 + 1, 2, 3880 - 28)
    — by evaluating terms (applications of + and -):
    ≡ eom(29, 2, 3852)
    — by evaluating predicate (application of eom):
    ≡ true.

The *equivalence* symbol ≡ means 'logically identical to' (see page 64 and onwards).

A 0-ary predicate has a constant truth value in some given environment, though in another environment, its truth value might be different; an example of this was given earlier involving the hypothetical relation isP. In Z, there are two special 0-ary predicates true and false, which are the *constant* predicates. They are constant because true is true *in any environment*, and false is false *in any environment*. It should be understood that true and false are *predicates*, not truth values; the distinction is subtle but important.

EXERCISE 4.2

Give the truth value of, or otherwise comment upon, each of the following predicates in an environment where

- the variables i, j : ℕ are in scope and c denotes the integer 100
- isP(x, y) has a 'less than' interpretation between integers x and y.

a. isP(i, j)   b. isP(j * 2, 64)   c. isP(16, d)
d. isP(5, c)   e. isP(-3, i).

4.2   THE PROPOSITIONAL OPERATORS

Propositional Structures

Certain *propositional operators*, or *connectives*, have already been introduced in Exercise 2.1, page 17, where the syntax of a simple propositional logic language was defined by a formal system. Four of these operators were used in Chapter 3. To summarize, the names of the standard propositional operators are

      ∧   ∨   ⇒   ⇔   (all are infix binary)
      ¬   (unary).

Z restricts itself to these five operators, though there are actually fifteen more (see Exercise 4.6 on page 62). The operators are used in predicate logic just as they are in propositional logic: to build more complex logical expressions from simpler ones. Propositional logic is a much weaker language than predicate logic as it deals only with propositions. It has no formal syntax for relations, terms, etc., no variables, and no 'quantifiers' (see Section 4.3).

EXERCISE 4.3

In the formal world of predicate logic, propositions are 0-ary predicates. In the informal world of natural language, identification of propositions is not necessarily so simple. Study the following sentences:

a. 1992 is a leap year
b. 1992 might be a leap year
c. Is it true that 1992 is a leap year?
d. 1992, 1993, and 1994 are all leap years
e. Either 1992 or 1992 is a leap year
f. 1992 isn't a leap year if 1993 is
g. To say that 1992 is a leap year is exactly the same as saying 1993 is a leap year
h. There are no leap years between 1900 and 1903 inclusive
i. 1968 was the most revolutionary leap year for the UK prior to 1992.

State which of these sentences are proper propositions, i.e., factual assertions that are either true or false.

The reason that propositional logic is completely inadequate for specifying software (but not necessarily other artifacts, e.g., low-level computer hardware) is because it is essential to be able to formalize descriptions which: (i) assert properties over a range of possible values via variables; (ii) assert the ideas of 'universality' and 'existence'. Consider these statements:

- the years 1992 and 1993 are exactly divisible by 4
- if yr is a leap year, then yr is exactly divisible by 4
- all leap years are exactly divisible by 4
- there are years exactly divisible by 4 that are not leap years.

Propositional logic can cope with the first statement, being a combination of two simple propositions (what are they?), but it needs predicate logic to express the second (it involves a variable). The third statement asserts a universal property of leap years (they are all divisible by 4), and the fourth asserts the existence of years exactly divisible by 4 which do not have the leap year property. Clearly, the last two statements are either true or false, and we can determine which, so they are propositions. Yet, in predicate logic, their formalization must involve a relation like $leapYr$, so we cannot regard them as 'atomic' assertions of fact with no internal logical structure, as we would in propositional logic.

From now on, to avoid explicit description of irrelevant predicate detail, upper case letters will be used as formula variables in logical expressions; for example,

$$((\neg (\neg P)) \Rightarrow (Q \Rightarrow (R \wedge P)))$$

Use of such variables indicates that the (well-formed!) formulas they stand for are arbitrary and have no bearing on the issues being discussed. Note, though, that separate instances of the same formula variable in a sentence (e.g., P) stand for the same formula, whatever that might be. When a formula is expressed purely in terms of formula variables and the propositional operators, we refer to its structure as *propositional*; we use this terminology even if the formula is a predicate logic formula.

Propositional Operators

To avoid excessive use of parentheses in compound logical expressions, Z has the following *priority* and *associativity* rules for its five propositional operators:

PRIORITY
The list below is in *decreasing* order of priority from top to bottom; it also provides an informal interpretation of each operator:

$\neg$	'not'	$\neg$ P asserts that P is false
$\wedge$	'and'	P $\wedge$ Q asserts that both P and Q are true
$\vee$	'or'	P $\vee$ Q asserts that either P, or Q, or both, are true
$\Rightarrow$	'implies'	P $\Rightarrow$ Q asserts that either P is false, or Q is true, or both
$\Leftrightarrow$	'if and only if'	P $\Leftrightarrow$ Q asserts that P and Q are either both true or both false.

ASSOCIATIVITY
All the infix propositional operators 'associate to the left' except $\Rightarrow$, which, like $\neg$, 'associates to the right'. Thus, when prOp is $\wedge$, $\vee$ or $\Leftrightarrow$, we have

$$P \text{ prOp } Q \text{ prOp } R \equiv (P \text{ prOp } Q) \text{ prOp } R$$

but $P \Rightarrow Q \Rightarrow R$ is equivalent to $P \Rightarrow (Q \Rightarrow R)$.

From these rules, it should be clear that, for example,

$$\neg \neg P \Rightarrow Q \Rightarrow R \wedge S \equiv ((\neg (\neg P)) \Rightarrow (Q \Rightarrow (R \wedge S)))$$

As one would expect, parentheses can be used, even when they are redundant.

EXERCISE 4.4

1. Reduce parentheses to a minimum in the following:

   a. $\neg (P \wedge ((Q \Rightarrow P) \Rightarrow Q))$ b. $(((\neg P \wedge Q) \Rightarrow P) \Rightarrow Q)$
   c. $((\neg P) \wedge Q) \Rightarrow (P \Rightarrow Q)$

2. Fully parenthesize the following constructs without overriding priorities:

   a. $\neg P \wedge Q \Rightarrow P \vee Q \Leftrightarrow \neg P$ b. $P \Rightarrow Q \wedge \neg P \Leftrightarrow \neg Q \vee P$

If the propositional structure of a logical expression is

$$P1 \vee P2 \vee \ldots Pn$$

then it is called a *disjunction* and each P_i is a *disjunct*. So 'or-ing' and 'disjoining' mean the same thing. Logical expressions of the forms

$$\neg P \qquad P \Rightarrow Q \qquad P \Leftrightarrow Q$$

are referred to as *negations*, *implications*, and *equivalences*, respectively. In an implication, the left and right arguments are referred to as the *antecedent* and *consequent*.

If the propositional structure of a logical expression is

$$P1 \wedge P2 \wedge \ldots Pn \qquad (4.2)$$

then it is called a *conjunction* and each P_i is a *conjunct*. So 'and-ing' and 'conjoining' mean the same thing. Semicolon separators in box predicates are just *top-level* $\wedge$'s in disguise. Thus

$$\mid P1;\ P2;\ \ldots Pn$$

is the same as (4.2) though possibly with fewer parentheses than (4.2) needs since semicolons used this way act like special 'ands' with the lowest priority of all.

Similarly, the box predicate:

```
P1
P2
...
Pn
```

is the same as (4.2) because two consecutive predicates separated by a sequence of one or more line breaks in a schema or axiomatic description are also treated conjunctively. Note that use of semicolons or elision of $\wedge$ by line breaks works only at the outtermost level of predicate syntax. Also, if we wish to connect predicates with an operator other than $\wedge$, the operator must be written explicitly. Consider the predicate

```
P1 ∨                                                        (4.3)
   P2
   P3
```

This predicate is *not* equivalent to

$$P1 \vee (\ P2 \wedge P3\ ) \qquad (4.4)$$

but instead is equivalent to

$$(\ P1 \vee P2\ ) \wedge P3$$

This is because indentation has no effect and the line break after the $\vee$ is not significant, whereas the line break after P2 is (line breaks are insignificant in expected places such as before and after infix symbols). If (4.4) is required, an explicit $\wedge$ must be placed between P2 and P3 in (4.3).

EXERCISE 4.5

Formalize all the proper propositions of Exercise 4.3 using `leapYr`, and state whether each is true or false.

Interpretation

TRUTH-FUNCTIONAL INTERPRETATION
Propositional operators are given meaning by a truth-functional approach. That is, a unique truth-value result is assigned to each different possible truth interpretation of the argument(s) of the operator. Because of the small number of different argument cases for each operator, the definitions are easily presented in tabular form.

¬P	P	Q	P ∧ Q	P ∨ Q	P ⇒ Q	P ⇔ Q
true	false	false	false	false	true	true
false	true	false	false	true	false	false
	false	true	false	true	true	false
	true	true	true	true	true	true

Table 4.1   Truth-functional definition of Z's five propositional operators.

By default, the propositional operators have this truth-functional meaning in every environment. The reader might find different symbols used in notations other than Z, such as ~ instead of ¬, or → instead of ⇒, but this is mere name-changing.

We can see that there are 12 other binary propositional operators that can be defined. This follows because there is a total of 16 different result columns that can be constructed from 4 different argument-pair cases, given that the result for each of these cases is one of 2 possibilities ($16 = 2^4$). Similarly, there are 3 other unary propositional operators apart from ¬. Most of these 15 extra operators have no practical use in predicate descriptions, and all can be defined in terms of those that Z provides (see next exercise). Even Z's complement of the 5 standard operators is over-rich, but the gain is one of expressive power. Reducing the operators to a minimum needed to express any propositional structure would often result in clumsy and unreadable descriptions.

INTUITIVE INTERPRETATION

The readability of descriptions using the standard operators stems from their reasonable accord with intuition. This is at least so with ¬, ∧ and ∨. The one point to make is that ∨ is *inclusive*, not *exclusive*, i.e., P ∨ Q is true when either or *both* of its arguments are true. As regards ⇔, there is some danger in viewing P ⇔ Q as merely another way of writing P = Q. This must be avoided because ⇔ and = are different kinds of symbol: ⇔ is a binary *operator* symbol with a particular truth-functional interpretation, whereas = is a binary *relation* symbol used to assert that two *terms* denote the same value. Also, ⇔ is often read as 'equivalent to' as well as 'if and only if' (often abbreviated to *iff*), so there is potential for confusing it with the equivalence symbol ≡, which we have also used. The difference between the two symbols is clarified shortly.

Intuitive interpretations of ⇒ work the least well, especially when judged against its formal definition. Earlier, we described P ⇒ Q as 'either P is false, Q is true, or both', which does not sound very intuitive at all. 'If P then Q' sounds much better and conveys the idea of *consequence*. The main pitfall is that 'if… then…' is overloaded, with uses varying from expressing conditional selection in algorithms to the idea of causality in natural language, as in

if Lola fails her Formal Methods exam in June, then she retakes it in September.

Causality is the main danger because there is *no* causality expressed with ⇒. Letting p be 'Lola fails her Formal Methods exam in June' and q be 'Lola retakes her Formal Methods exam in September', then

p ⇒ q

is a perfectly respectable logical expression, one of whose interpretations is that p is false and q is true. This particular interpretation does not make causal sense in the real world, but logically the implication is true. To emphasize further the non-intuitiveness of $\Rightarrow$, consider

> 39 is a prime number $\Rightarrow$ 1993 is a leap year

The antecedent and consequent are entirely unrelated semantically, and we are unlikely ever to need to construct an implication like this; but it is still well-formed (what is its truth value?).

It is best for the reader simply to accept the truth-functional interpretation of $\Rightarrow$ given in the previous table and apply the symbol correctly. Use of the antecedents of implications as case-defining expressions is quite a common style of writing certain predicates, as we have already seen in Chapter 3 (e.g., operation Add1Day on page 46). However, partly because $\Rightarrow$ is the least intuitive of the standard propositional operators, some prefer to avoid its usage (though this is not a stance we adopt). We will see ways of doing this shortly.

> EXERCISE 4.6
>
> 1. Of the twelve other binary propositional operators, two are
>
>   a. 'exclusive or': P xor Q is true if either operand is true, but not both
>   b. 'nand': P nand Q is true if either or both operands are false.
>
>   Show how both can be equivalently re-expressed using the standard operators.
>
> 2. What are the three other unary propositional operators, and why, therefore, would their provision in no way enhance expressive power?

Some Propositional Laws

TRUTH CALCULATION
An obvious consequence of functionality of the propositional operators is that the truth value of any compound predicate built from basic predicates and the operators can be calculated on the same simple systematic basis as one would evaluate any kind of term or expression. As an example, consider

> $\neg\,\neg\,P \Rightarrow Q \Rightarrow R \wedge P$

under the truth interpretation

> P is true, Q is false, R is false.

Then

> $\neg\,P$ is false; $\neg\,\neg\,P$ is true; $R \wedge P$ is false; $Q \Rightarrow R \wedge P$ is true;
> hence $\neg\,\neg\,P \Rightarrow Q \Rightarrow R \wedge P$ is true.

As usual, one simply has to take care with priorities and associativities.

Truth calculation of a propositional structure is more interesting if carried out for all possible truth value interpretations of its formula variables. If the latter are small in number, it is practicable to display the calculation in tabular form. On the next page is the 'truth table' for the propositional structure $\neg\,P \vee Q \Leftrightarrow P \Rightarrow Q$:

P	Q	$\neg P$	$\neg P \lor Q$	$P \Rightarrow Q$	$\neg P \lor Q \Leftrightarrow P \Rightarrow Q$
false	false	true	true	true	true
true	false	false	false	false	true
false	true	true	true	true	true
true	true	false	true	true	true

Table 4.2   A truth-table calculation.

The general procedure for building such a table is to start with n columns for each of the n distinct formula variables, and then systematically enumerate in 2^n rows all the different combinations of truth values for those variables. Columns are then added progressively that build up interpretations of the separate subformulas comprising the overall propositional structure, working outwards through the latter. The final column constructed is the result column, giving the structure's interpretation in all possible circumstances.

Depending on the interpretations of its formula variables, a propositional structure like $\neg P \land Q \Rightarrow P$ can be true or false; we say it is *contingent*. In contrast, a structure such as $\neg (Q \Rightarrow P \Rightarrow Q)$ is said to be *contradictory* because it is always false, regardless of the truth values of its constituents. The opposite is the case for the propositional structure $(P \Rightarrow Q) \land P \Rightarrow Q$, which is always true regardless; such logical expressions are *tautological*. We can see from Table 4.2 that $\neg P \lor Q \Leftrightarrow P \Rightarrow Q$ is a tautology. The important point to appreciate is that it is *structure* alone which governs whether a formula is a contingency, contradiction or tautology, and has nothing to do with the inner make-up of the components of its structure—remember that the variables P, Q, etc. stand for *arbitrary* formulas. So, for example, $\neg P \lor Q \Leftrightarrow P \Rightarrow Q$ is a tautology irrespective of what P and Q stand for.

Truth table construction provides a cast-iron method for determining whether—or checking a claim to the effect that—a given propositional structure is contingent, contradictory or tautological; but even truth tables may not be necessary. Consider

$$\neg (a \lor b) \lor c \land a \land d \Leftrightarrow (a \lor b) \Rightarrow c \land a \land d$$

Without the need for any complicated calculation, a brief analysis of this structure will tell us that it is tautological. This is because the structure can be mapped onto $\neg P \lor Q \Leftrightarrow P \Rightarrow Q$, which we already know to be tautological, by making the following 'match':

P is matched with $(a \lor b)$,   Q is matched with $c \land a \land d$

Recall that this simple idea of syntactic pattern matching was briefly introduced in Section 2.1 in the context of applying rules of a formal system.

EXERCISE 4.7

Prove the claims the text has made to the effect that

- $\neg P \land Q \Rightarrow P$ is a contingency
- $\neg (Q \Rightarrow P \Rightarrow Q)$ is a contradiction
- $(P \Rightarrow Q) \land P \Rightarrow Q$ is a tautology.

LAWS

Tautological structures are particularly important because they represent the propositional forms *which are true under any interpretation,* provided, of course, that the standard meanings of the operators are applied. We call them propositional *laws* (of predicate logic). Here are some simple examples:

$$\text{true,} \qquad \neg\,\text{false,} \qquad P \vee \text{true,} \qquad P \vee \neg P, \qquad \text{false} \Rightarrow P$$
$$P \Rightarrow \text{true,} \qquad P \Rightarrow P, \qquad P \Leftrightarrow P, \qquad \neg\,(\,P \wedge \text{false}\,)$$

Some laws are given names; for example, the fourth law in the list is known as the 'Law of the Excluded Middle' because it requires that a logical expression must be either true or false—there is no 'in between'.

Many propositional laws have the structure

$$\text{Form1} \Leftrightarrow \text{Form2}$$

This structure is tautological precisely if it is the case that whenever Form1 is true so is Form2 and whenever Form1 is false so is Form2. This special relationship between Form1 and Form2—*that under any interpretation they always have the same truth value*—can be described by writing

$$\text{Form1} \equiv \text{Form2} \qquad\qquad (4.5)$$

We say that 'Form1 and Form2 are equivalent (formulas)'. Here lies the terminological danger referred to earlier. When we write Form1 $\Leftrightarrow$ Form2, this is an *assertion* of equivalence which is either true or false under some given interpretation. The notion of equivalence embodied in $\equiv$, which is a relation and *not* another propositional operator, is of a higher order (if you like, it is 'meta'). (4.5) is a statement to the effect that Form1 and Form2 are equivalent in the sense that they are interchangeable formulas, i.e., they are logically identical under all circumstances. Here is the tautology tabulated on the previous page now rewritten as a (meta)equivalence:

$$\neg P \vee Q \equiv P \Rightarrow Q$$

This law could be called 'Definition of Implication'. Other useful laws include

$$P \Leftrightarrow Q \equiv P \Rightarrow Q \wedge Q \Rightarrow P$$
$$\neg(\,P \vee Q\,) \equiv \neg P \wedge \neg Q$$
$$\neg(\,P \wedge Q\,) \equiv \neg P \vee \neg Q$$

The latter two laws are called DeMorgan's laws.

There is an arbitrary number of propositional laws since there is no limit to the complexity of the propositional structures we are allowed to write down. In practice, we handle this situation by constructing a number of basic laws from which all others can be derived. We can use equivalence laws to explore different ways of writing a particular predicate. For example, an equivalent way of writing the predicate of the Date schema on page 44 (see also Question (3) in the next exercise) which side-steps use of implications is as follows:

$$yr \geq bottomYr$$
$$\neg\,ajsn(\,mn\,) \vee dy \leq 30$$
$$mn \neq 2 \vee dy \leq 29$$
$$mn \neq 2 \vee leapYr(\,yr\,) \vee dy \leq 28$$

Here, avoidance of $\Rightarrow$ is at the expense of some understandability. Better results can be achieved with the following 'implication-avoiding' case-style equivalence:

$$(P \Rightarrow Q) \wedge (\neg P \Rightarrow R) \equiv P \wedge Q \vee \neg P \wedge R$$

Clearly, this equivalence is applicable when there are two mutually exclusive cases which are defined by a predicate and its negation.

EXERCISE 4.8

1. How could an equivalence law be obtained from each of the simple tautologies listed at the top of page 64? How could such a law be obtained from a contradiction?

2. Consider the integers $\mathbb{Z}$ and operators +, - and *. Let a, b and c be *arbitrary* integers. Then some basic laws of this 'algebraic system' are as follows:

    *   + and * are *commutative* (though binary minus is not); that is,

        $$a + b = b + a \qquad \text{— similarly for } *$$

    *   + and * are *associative* (though, again, binary minus is not); that is,

        $$(a * b) * c = a * (b * c) \qquad \text{— similarly for } +$$

    *   * *distributes over* both + and - (though neither of the latter two distribute over *); for example:

        $$a * (b + c) = (a * b) + (a * c) \qquad \text{— similarly for } * \text{ over } -$$

    *   Unary minus has the property that:

        $$- - a = a$$

    By analogy with these properties, construct some more propositional equivalence laws. If unsure, remember you can check conjectured laws via truth tables.

3. The re-expression of the `Date` predicate given on the opposite page can be obtained mainly by applying the following laws to its original form (page 44), possibly more than once and not necessarily in the order given:

    *   Definition of Implication (see text)   — L1
    *   DeMorgan (second version in text)   — L2
    *   associativity of $\vee$ (see Question (2))   — L3
    *   a property of $\neg$ (see Question (2)).   — L4

    Explain this justification in detail, i.e., work out the symbol re-arrangements involved, referring to the laws by the identifiers given on the right-hand side. Why does the introductory sentence to this question say 'mainly'?

4. The symbol $\equiv$ has several important properties, including *transitivity* (see page 10):

    if $P \equiv Q$ and $Q \equiv R$ **then** $P \equiv R$

    What is wrong with formalizing this law as

    $$(P \equiv Q) \wedge (Q \equiv R) \Rightarrow (P \equiv R)?$$

4.3 THE QUANTIFIERS

Universal and Existential Quantification

The statements

a. all leap years are exactly divisible by 4
b. for any leap year y, y is exactly divisible by 4

are two different ways of asserting informally that all leap years have a common property: exact divisibility by 4. Statements like these are said to be *universal* because the property is asserted to hold for all objects in the 'universe' in which we are interested (here, leap years). Despite the occurrence of a variable name in (b), note how both statements are 0-ary, i.e., we can interpret each statement as either true or false according to our model of leap years and their properties. The zero arity of the second statement is because the name y occurring in it is *not* a free variable, but merely acts as a device to facilitate assertion of the universality of the property concerned. This property can be formalized as

$$y \bmod 4 = 0$$

given that we regard y as some *arbitrary* leap year. The assertion in (a) or (b) is then:

for any leap year y, $y \bmod 4 = 0$

Assuming the availability of a set `LeapYrs` which represents all objects in the universe that are leap years, the statements (a) and (b) can be formalized as the predicate

$$\forall y : \text{LeapYrs} \bullet y \bmod 4 = 0$$

The symbol $\forall$ is called the *universal quantifier*, for which read 'for all/each/any ...' or similar. Variables like y are called *bound variables* and, unlike free variables, cannot be replaced by terms (compare the truth calculation on page 57 involving substitution of free variables). The 'spot' symbol $\bullet$ merely acts as a separator between the quantifier part and the predicate quantified.

Remark
From now on, we will use parametrized formula variables as in $P(x)$, $Q(x, y)$, etc., to represent generalized predicates in which at least the parameter names (but possibly others too) occur as free variables.

In general, if we wish to assert that *all* elements of set X have property P, we write

$$\forall x : X \bullet P(x)$$

Here are two further examples; note how universality can be implicit in natural language :

- a positive integer exactly divides itself
  $$\forall k : \mathbb{N}_1 \bullet k \bmod k = 0$$
- the product of an odd positive integer with itself is also odd
  $$\forall k : \mathbb{N}_1 \bullet k \bmod 2 = 1 \Rightarrow (k * k) \bmod 2 = 1$$

The form of the second predicate is

$$\forall x : X \bullet P(x) \Rightarrow Q(x) \tag{4.6}$$

In effect, the antecedent $P(x)$ of the implication reduces the universe of interest to something 'narrower' than X. The form provides a way of saying 'all those x from X which are P are also Q', or similar. We can use this form for formalizing the statements (a) and (b) opposite. Instead of making appeal to a set LeapYrs, we can quantify over ℕ, say, and narrow ℕ down further to just leap years with the Digital Watch relation leapYr. Thus:

$$\forall y : ℕ \bullet \text{leapYr}(y) \Rightarrow y \bmod 4 = 0 \qquad (4.7)$$

Remark

In (4.6), the antecedent of the implication is true only if x is P (has property P). Yet if some x is not P, we would not want this fact alone to cause our assertion about those X objects which *are* P to collapse into falsehood. This collapse does not occur because a false antecedent yields a true implication overall, which perhaps provides the reader with some feel for why $\Rightarrow$ is given the particular truth-functional definition that it has.

Now consider these statements:

c. there are years exactly divisible by 4 that are not leap years
d. there exists a year y, where y is exactly divisible by 4, but y is not a leap year.

Like the earlier examples (a) and (b), these two statements express the same idea, but this time the assertion is one of *existence*. Again, variable y is bound and not free in (d) as it is merely a device for constructing the existential assertion. Such assertions—that there is *at least one* element x with property P in the universe of interest X—have the form

$$\exists x : X \bullet P(x)$$

where the symbol $\exists$ is the *existential quantifier*. So we can formalize (c) and (d) as

$$\exists y : \text{YrsDivBy4} \bullet \neg \text{leapYr}(y)$$

assuming YrsDivBy4 defines those years exactly divisible by 4. Here are two more simple examples:

- some positive integers are not exactly divisible by 2
  $$\exists k : ℕ_1 \bullet k \bmod 2 \neq 0$$
- there is a positive integer which is prime and exactly divisible by 2
  $$\exists k : ℕ_1 \bullet \text{prime}(k) \wedge k \bmod 2 = 0 \qquad (4.8)$$

where we have used the unary relation prime, assumed given, in the obvious way. The form of the second predicate, which is

$$\exists x : X \bullet P(x) \wedge Q(x) \qquad (4.9)$$

is also quite important like form (4.6) earlier. Here, we can view the conjunct $P(x)$ as narrowing down further the universe of interest. The form provides a way of saying 'some of those in X which are P, are also Q', or similar. We can use this form to formalize the previous statements (c) and (d). Instead of making appeal to a set YrsDivBy4, we can quantify over ℕ, say, and write

$$\exists y : ℕ \bullet y \bmod 4 = 0 \wedge \neg \text{leapYr}(y) \qquad (4.10)$$

We will return to forms (4.6) and (4.9) later in this section.

Sometimes it is required to assert unique existence: 'there is *exactly one member* of the set X with property P'. The symbol $\exists_1$ enables such an assertion to be written succinctly. For example, as there is only one prime number exactly divisible by 2, instead of (4.8) previously we could have written the much stronger but still valid assertion

$$\exists_1 k : \mathbb{N}_1 \bullet \text{prime}(k) \wedge k \bmod 2 = 0$$

Shortly, we will see that we can express unique existence anyway just using the standard quantifier symbols. So the symbol $\exists_1$ is just for convenience.

Remark

Imagine a single universe W in which all possible values reside. If W was 'typeless', quantification syntax would simply be

$$\forall x \bullet P(x) \qquad \text{or} \qquad \exists x \bullet P(x)$$

since there is only one universe over which to assert universality or existence. Any further narrowing down of W would be achieved by sub-predicates of P, typically using forms (4.6) and (4.9) described earlier. However, the semantics of Z rests on a universe partitioned by type into disjoint sets. So quantification in Z is always with respect to some *type* and not an all-encompassing W. Hence, we use the syntax

$$\forall x : X \bullet P(x) \qquad \text{or} \qquad \exists x : X \bullet P(x)$$

since we must say over which type the quantification operates, though note that, as with declarations in schemas etc., the set X can be 'narrower' than just a type.

> EXERCISE 4.9
>
> Imagine a binary relation loves, whose two arguments are each of type PERSON, such that loves(x,y) means 'x loves y', or equivalently 'x is a lover of y', i.e., 'lover' is used to describe any person who loves some other person. loves does *not* include people who love themselves. Using loves, formalize the following:
>
> a. nobody loves nesta
> b. carrie loves bill but doesn't love anybody else
> c. some people love both bill and carrie
> d. bill has only one lover but it isn't nesta
> e. carrie's lovers are also nesta's lovers
> f. carrie loves nesta's lovers.

Multiple Instances of Quantifiers

Using relation loves of the previous exercise, consider the problem of formalizing:

> there are two people who do not love each other.

We need two quantifiers with different bound variables to 'introduce' each of the two people:

$$\exists p : \text{PERSON} \bullet \exists q : \text{PERSON} \bullet p \neq q \wedge \neg \text{loves}(p,q) \wedge \neg \text{loves}(q,p)$$

Note the importance of including $p \neq q$ since we need to make p and q refer to *different* people. We could also write

$$\exists q : \text{PERSON} \bullet \exists p : \text{PERSON} \bullet p \neq q \wedge \neg \text{loves}(p,q) \wedge \neg \text{loves}(q,p)$$

because $\exists$ is *commutative* (see Exercise 4.8(2)); so too is $\forall$. In fact, one $\exists$ is sufficient since several variables, possibly of different types, can be introduced by a single quantifier:

$$\exists p,q : \text{PERSON} \bullet p \neq q \wedge \neg \texttt{loves}(p,q) \wedge \neg \texttt{loves}(q,p)$$

Combinations of the two quantifiers need some care, however. For example,

$$\forall p : \text{PERSON} \bullet \exists q : \text{PERSON} \bullet \texttt{loves}(p,q)$$

i.e., 'everybody loves somebody', is clearly not equivalent to

$$\exists q : \text{PERSON} \bullet \forall p : \text{PERSON} \bullet \texttt{loves}(p,q)$$

i.e., 'some people are loved by everybody' (see also Exercise 4.10 on the next page).
We could assert unique existence as in

$$\exists_1 p : \text{PERSON} \bullet \texttt{loves}(p,\texttt{carrie})$$

i.e., 'carrie has just one lover', by equivalently asserting that:

carrie has a lover p, and everyone other than p isn't a lover of carrie's.

We can formalize this assertion as follows; note the requirement to bracket a quantification when used as an operand of a propositional operator:

$$\exists p : \text{PERSON} \bullet \texttt{loves}(p,\texttt{carrie}) \wedge$$
$$(\forall q : \text{PERSON} \bullet p \neq q \Rightarrow \neg \texttt{loves}(q,\texttt{carrie}))$$

This example prompts the more general question: what is the scope of a quantifier?
The structure of this last predicate is

$$(\ \exists p : \text{PERSON} \bullet \ \dots\dots\dots\dots\dots \ \text{scope of } p \ \dots\dots\dots\dots\dots$$
$$(\ \forall q : \text{PERSON} \bullet \ \dots\dots \ \text{scope of } q \ \dots\dots \ ) \ )$$

The scope of the $\exists p : \text{PERSON}$ extends over the whole predicate. In effect, the scope of a quantifier is to the right as far as possible. One can think of $\forall$ or $\exists$ as a kind of prefix operator which binds less tightly than any infix propositional operator. So, letting Qntfr stand for any quantifier symbol, and prOp any propositional operator, we have that

$$\text{Qntfr} \ x : X \bullet P \ \text{prOp} \ Q \qquad \text{and} \qquad (\text{Qntfr} \ x : X \bullet P) \ \text{prOp} \ Q$$

are quite different.

A little care is needed in box presentations. 'As far to the right as possible' then means to the next predicate separator, i.e., semicolon or *significant* line break. So the following two box fragments are *not* the same:

|
| $\forall x : X \bullet$
| $\quad P(x) \wedge$
| $\quad Q(x)$

|
| $\forall x : X \bullet$
| $\quad P(x)$
| $\quad Q(x)$

In the left-hand fragment, occurrence of the $\wedge$ ensures that the scope of the $\forall$ includes $Q(x)$. In the right-hand fragment, its scope stops just after $P(x)$ because of the significant line break (recall that indentation is not significant). So this latter fragment is actually the same as

$$(\forall x : X \bullet P(x)) \wedge Q(x)$$

which would probably be a syntax error (e.g., second x instance undefined). In any case, it would be wrong if it is not what the specifier intended. Even if it is what the specifier intended, it is poor style: we have two different variables in the same predicate with the same name.

Statements can be difficult to formalize because natural language often elides universality, etc., as we have already seen. Here is a particularly awkward example:

$$\text{everybody loves a lover.} \tag{4.11}$$

We note first that if p is a lover, there has to be someone—q, say—whom p loves. So

$$\exists\, q : \text{PERSON} \bullet \text{loves}(p,q)$$

makes p a lover. Moreover, if p is a lover, (4.11) asserts that everybody (excluding p) loves p:

$$(\exists\, q : \text{PERSON} \bullet \text{loves}(p,q)) \Rightarrow (\forall\, r : \text{PERSON} \bullet r \neq p \Rightarrow \text{loves}(r,p))$$

This leaves the problem of introducing p. The point is that statement (4.11) is really making a claim about *any* lover: everybody loves a lover, *whoever that lover is*. So we arrive at

$$\begin{aligned}\forall\, p : \text{PERSON} \bullet \\ (\exists\, q : \text{PERSON} \bullet \text{loves}(p,q)) \Rightarrow \\ (\forall\, r : \text{PERSON} \bullet r \neq p \Rightarrow \text{loves}(r,p))\end{aligned} \tag{4.12}$$

Fortunately, statements we wish to formalize in Z are not usually this contorted.

EXERCISE 4.10

1. Give the truth value of

   a. $\forall\, x : \mathbb{Z} \bullet \exists\, y : \mathbb{Z} \bullet x + y = 7$
   b. $\exists\, y : \mathbb{Z} \bullet \forall\, x : \mathbb{Z} \bullet x + y = 7$
   c. $\exists\, y : \mathbb{Z} \bullet \exists\, x : \mathbb{Z} \bullet x + y = 7$
   d. $\forall\, x : \mathbb{Z} \bullet \forall\, y : \mathbb{Z} \bullet x + y = 7$.

2. Using relation loves again, formalize the following assertions:

   a. some people love nobody
   b. some people are loved by one person only
   c. there are people who have exactly the same lovers
   d. bill has at least three lovers.

3. Express as succinctly and naturally as possible in your own words the following:

   a. $\forall\, x : \text{PERSON} \bullet$
      $\text{loves}(\text{nesta}, x) \Rightarrow (\exists\, y : \text{PERSON} \bullet y \neq \text{nesta} \wedge \text{loves}(y, x))$
   b. $\exists\, x : \text{PERSON} \bullet$
      $\text{loves}(x, \text{bill}) \wedge (\forall\, y : \text{PERSON} \bullet y \neq \text{bill} \Rightarrow \neg\, \text{loves}(x, y))$.

On Free and Bound Variables

In a quantification

$$\text{Qntfr } x : X \bullet P(x)$$

the name of the bound variable is immaterial. For example,

$\forall \, x : \mathbb{N} \bullet \, \texttt{leapYr}(\, x \,) \Rightarrow x \bmod 4 = 0$
$\forall \, \texttt{annum} : \mathbb{N} \bullet \, \texttt{leapYr}(\, \texttt{annum} \,) \Rightarrow \texttt{annum} \bmod 4 = 0$
$\forall \, \texttt{yr} : \mathbb{N} \bullet \, \texttt{leapYr}(\, \texttt{yr} \,) \Rightarrow \texttt{yr} \bmod 4 = 0$

and any of an arbitrary number of other formulas of this form differing only in the name of the bound variable, are equivalent. In principle, therefore, we can change the name of a bound variable without affecting the meaning of the predicate involved. However, consider

$\texttt{Qntfr} \; x : X \bullet \texttt{P}(\, x , y \,)$

We cannot rename the bound variable to y, for then y, which was free in P, becomes captured by Qntfr and the resulting predicate

$\texttt{Qntfr} \; y : X \bullet \texttt{P}(\, y , y \,)$

is not equivalent to what it was previously.

The problem of free variable capture, which can also happen with other manipulations such as term substitution, does not have much impact on specification. Renaming, substitution, etc., are operations we perform in formal reasoning. Here, it is simply worth bearing in mind that 'boundness' and 'freeness' are relative to syntactic context. Consider again predicate (4.12) opposite. Observe that p is

- free in $r \neq p$
- free in $\texttt{loves}(\, r , p \,)$
- free in $r \neq p \Rightarrow \texttt{loves}(\, r , p \,)$
- free in $\forall \, r : \text{PERSON} \bullet r \neq p \Rightarrow \texttt{loves}(\, r , p \,)$
- free in $\texttt{loves}(\, p , q \,)$
- free in $\exists \, q : \text{PERSON} \bullet \texttt{loves}(\, p , q \,)$
- free in $(\exists \, q : \text{PERSON} \bullet \texttt{loves}(\, p , q \,)) \Rightarrow (\forall \, r : \text{PERSON} \bullet r \neq p \Rightarrow \texttt{loves}(\, r , p \,))$
- bound in $\forall \, p : \text{PERSON} \bullet (\exists \, q : \text{PERSON} \bullet \texttt{loves}(\, p , q \,)) \Rightarrow$
  $\qquad\qquad\qquad (\forall \, r : \text{PERSON} \bullet r \neq p \Rightarrow \texttt{loves}(\, r , p \,)).$

Similarly, q is

- free in $\texttt{loves}(\, p , q \,)$
- bound in $\exists \, q : \text{PERSON} \bullet \texttt{loves}(\, p , q \,)$

but is elsewhere not in scope in (4.12).

EXERCISE 4.11

1. In predicate (4.12), which of its bound variables could be renamed

   a. as p ?   b. as q ?   c. as r ?   d. as x ?

   Consider each case in isolation.

2. Consider a predicate whose structure is

   $\texttt{Qntfr1} \; x : X \bullet$
   $\qquad \texttt{P}(\, x \,) \; \texttt{prOp1} \; (\texttt{Qntfr2} \; y : Y \bullet \texttt{Q}(\, x , y \,) \; \texttt{prOp2} \; \texttt{R}(\, x , y , z \,))$

   a. Give all the subpredicates in which x is free
   b. What predicate results if x is renamed as y and *simultaneously* y is renamed as x? Is it equivalent to the original form?
   c. What problems, if any, might occur in substituting z with some term?

Further Aspects of the Quantifiers

SCHEMA-TEXT SYNTAX
Instead of narrowing down the universe of interest defined by Decs in

> Qntfr Decs • Predicate

by suitable subpredication in Predicate, we can include constraints with declarations in schema-text style by writing

> Qntfr Decs | Constraint • Predicate

where Constraint is a predicate with the required narrowing effect. For verbalization purposes, it often works to say 'such that' for '|'. Here are two examples that are equivalent to the two predicates (4.7) and (4.10) given earlier on page 67:

> $\forall y : \mathbb{N}$ | leapYr(y) • y mod 4 = 0
> $\exists k : \mathbb{N}$ | y mod 4 = 0 • ¬ leapYr(y)

In fact, the schema-text syntax is related to forms (4.6) and (4.9) on pages 66–67 thus:

> $\forall$ Decs | Constraint • Predicate ≡ $\forall$ Decs • Constraint ⇒ Predicate
> $\exists$ Decs | Constraint • Predicate ≡ $\exists$ Decs • Constraint ∧ Predicate

The schema-text form is thus avoidable, though its usage simplifies the main predicate after the •, and this can improve readability. As always, where there exists choice, one has to make judgements. The reader will find that the syntax

> SchemaText • ...

where we have written SchemaText for Decs | Constraint, occurs in many other situations too.

SOME PREDICATE LAWS
Consider the predicate

> ¬ ($\forall$ p : PERSON • loves(p, carrie))

i.e., 'not everyone loves carrie'. One might equally well say: 'there are some people who do not love carrie', which is

> $\exists$ p : PERSON • ¬ loves(p, carrie)

More generally, the negation of universality 'not every x from X is P' is identical to asserting that 'there is at least one x from X which is not P'. We have the equivalence

> ¬ ($\forall$ x : X • P(x)) ≡ $\exists$ x : X • ¬ P(x)

and also

> ¬ ($\exists$ x : X • P(x)) ≡ $\forall$ x : X • ¬ P(x)

i.e., 'there is no x from X which is P' is identical to 'every x from X is not P'.

The reader may detect a similarity between these last two equivalences and DeMorgan's laws:

> ¬ (P ∧ Q) ≡ ¬ P ∨ ¬ Q
> ¬ (P ∨ Q) ≡ ¬ P ∧ ¬ Q

Indeed, they can be seen as generalizations of DeMorgan's laws if one views universal and existential quantification in the following way:

$$\forall x : X \bullet P(x) \equiv P(x1) \wedge P(x2) \wedge \ldots \tag{4.13}$$
$$\exists x : X \bullet P(x) \equiv P(x1) \vee P(x2) \vee \ldots \tag{4.14}$$

where $x1$, $x2$, etc. are the individual elements of X. So $\forall$ ($\exists$) is like distributing assertion of P conjunctively (disjunctively) over the entire universe of interest X. However, it must be stressed that whilst this interpretation of the two quantifiers is helpful, (4.13) and (4.14) are proper equivalences only if X is *finite*.

Below is a summary of equivalence laws involving quantifiers that we have covered thus far. They can be added to the laws discussed towards the end of Section 4.2. There are many more laws involving the quantifiers which we will not mention.

- all the quantifiers are commutative
- bound variables can be renamed (providing no capture occurs)
- DeMorgan's laws for $\wedge/\vee$ can be extended to $\forall/\exists$
- $\forall/\exists$ predicates are reducible to conjunctions/disjunctions for *finite* universes
- schema-text forms for $\forall/\exists$ convert to basic $\forall/\exists$ forms involving $\Rightarrow/\wedge$.

For specification purposes, equivalences can be regarded simply as providing alternatives, since two equivalent predicates 'express the same thing logically'. Their main usefulness lies in transforming predicates in reasoning tasks.

A NOTE ON TRUTH CALCULATION
Determining the truth of a quantification poses some difficulties. Faced with

$$\neg(\forall x : X \bullet P(x)) \quad \text{or} \quad \exists x : X \bullet P(x)$$

we simply have to find one element of X which is not P, or is P, respectively. That will be sufficient to establish the predicate as true. However, what do we do if we suspect either predicate is *false*? In that case, we would be in effect trying to establish

$$\forall x : X \bullet P(x) \quad \text{or} \quad \neg(\exists x : X \bullet P(x))$$

as true. We could inspect each member of X if X is finite to determine whether the member is P or not, laborious though this would be for large sets; but this method is obviously of no use if X is infinite. In that case, we might be able to make some appeal to the intended semantics of the relation P with respect to X.

You were in effect doing this kind of semantic reasoning in Exercise 4.10(1) (we all know what arithmetic 'means'). Clearly, though, it would be preferable if there were some other, *systematic* process, not requiring appeal to what things mean, for determining the truth of a predicate, however simple or complex the predicate is and whether or not it contains quantifiers. That process is formal proof, as briefly aired in Section 2.1 (though discussion of the precise relationship between *proof* and *truth* is outside the scope of this book).

EXERCISE 4.12

1. Use schema-text syntax to formalize the following over the integers $\mathbb{Z}$:

   a. For any number you can think of, there is always a prime number that exceeds it

b. For any number k greater than 2, there are no positive integers x, y and z for which the following holds:

$$x^k + y^k = z^k$$

Assume a function $power(a, n) = a^n$.

2. State what you think each of the following is equivalent to, if anything. Is the same true for $\forall$?

a. $\exists x : X \bullet P(y)$ — x is not free in P
b. $\exists x : X \bullet \exists x : X \bullet P(x)$
c. $(\exists x : X \bullet P(y)) \wedge Q(x)$ — x is not free in P.

3. Where possible, give an equivalent formula for each of the following such that the quantification '$Qntfr\ x : X \bullet$' involved occurs exactly twice (*Hint*: be careful):

a. $\forall x : X \bullet P(x) \wedge Q(x)$
b. $\exists x : X \bullet P(x) \wedge Q(x)$
c. $\forall x : X \bullet P(x) \vee Q(x)$
d. $\exists x : X \bullet P(x) \vee Q(x)$.

4.4 DEFINING RELATIONS AXIOMATICALLY

The Digital Watch Relations

We have now covered sufficient predicate logic to deal with the loose ends remaining from the Digital Watch specification, i.e., providing definitions of the relations `ajsn`, `leapYr`, and `eom`. Their descriptions must obviously be axiomatic, since the relations augment the specification globally, making it easier to express predicates in various schemas. Taking `ajsn` as an example, we therefore expect to see (in outline)

> `ajsn _ : SomeUnaryRelationType`
> ———————————————
> `PredicateDescribing ajsn`

Note the underscore, since we wish to apply `ajsn` as a *prefix* symbol, as in

`ajsn(m)`

Without the underscore, we would have to write the less friendly-looking

`m ∈ ajsn`

The reason for this will emerge in Chapter 5.

Fairly obviously, the predicate for `ajsn` should express our desired interpretation for `ajsn`, namely

`ajsn(m)` means: 'm is the month of either April, June, September, or November'

The right-hand side, the 'body' of the definition, is easily formalized:

$m = 4 \vee m = 6 \vee m = 9 \vee m = 11$

The clue to completing the defining predicate is firstly to realize that 'means' in the informal definition works out as 'equivalent to', i.e., we wish to assert axiomatically that the left and right-hand sides are the same logically. That is:

$$\text{ajsn}(m) \Leftrightarrow m = 4 \lor m = 6 \lor m = 9 \lor m = 11$$

This leaves us with one problem: declaring m. This is easily dealt with when we further realize that the m in the definition stands for an *arbitrary* month: for *any* month m, m having the ajsn property is the same as m being either 4, 6, 9 or 11. In other words, *arbitrariness of variables is essentially just universal quantification*. The full axiom for ajsn is therefore as given in the following almost complete axiomatic description:

> ajsn _ : SomeUnaryRelationType
> ---
> $\forall$ m : 1..12 •
>   ajsn(m) $\Leftrightarrow$ m = 4 $\lor$ m = 6 $\lor$ m = 9 $\lor$ m = 11

Note how the quantification serves as the mechanism for declaring m as well as making it arbitrary. Also, the axiom part uniquely fixes what the variable ajsn 'stands for', and so ajsn is a 'constant' in the usual sense. Shortly, we find out what values relations such as ajsn actually denote.

From this example, we can generalize to an 'axiomatic description template' for an arbitrary n-ary prefix relation nAryRel:

> nAryRel _ : SomeNaryRelationType
> ---
> $\forall$ DeclarationsOf x1, ... xn •
>   nAryRel(x1, ... xn) $\Leftrightarrow$ SomeDefiningPredicateOver x1, ... xn

This axiom template does not represent the only way to define a relation, but it is a frequently used way of doing so. The x1, ... xn are the 'arbitrary argument variables' needed to express the defining predicate. Since $\Leftrightarrow$ is commutative, its two operands could be switched, though putting the defining predicate on the right-hand side is more natural to read.

In the Digital Watch specification, we might expect to see an axiomatic description like that below. The extra tertiary relation isDate has its uses (see next exercise).

> bottomYr : $\mathbb{N}$
> ajsn _ : SomeUnaryRelationType1
> leapYr _ : SomeUnaryRelationType2
> isDate _ : SomeTertiaryRelationType1
> eom _ : SomeTertiaryRelationType2
> ---
> bottomYr $\geq$ 1753
> $\forall$ m : 1..12 • ajsn(m) $\Leftrightarrow$ m = 4 $\lor$ m = 6 $\lor$ m = 9 $\lor$ m = 11
> $\forall$ y : $\mathbb{N}$ • leapYr(y) $\Leftrightarrow$ SomeDefiningPredicateOver y
> $\forall$ d : 1..31; m : 1..12; y : $\mathbb{N}$ •
>   isDate(d,m,y) $\Leftrightarrow$ y $\geq$ 1753 $\land$ (ajsn(m) $\Rightarrow$ d $\leq$ 30) $\land$
>   (m = 2 $\Rightarrow$ d $\leq$ 29) $\land$ (m = 2 $\land$ $\neg$ leapYr(y) $\Rightarrow$ d $\leq$ 28)
> $\forall$ d : 1..31; m : 1..12; y : $\mathbb{N}$ •
>   eom(d,m,y) $\Leftrightarrow$ SomeDefiningPredicateOver d,m,y

One is not obliged to introduce all global names in a single axiomatic description. Nor must all axiomatic descriptions precede schema paragraphs, though this is the usual style. Adherence to the rule of 'definition before use' is what is obligatory. Bearing that in mind, careful ordering and grouping of definitions can pay dividends. In defining new global names, some accompanying or earlier definitions may be of use. The application of `leapYr` in the definition of `isDate` illustrates this.

EXERCISE 4.13

1. Explain how tertiary relation `isDate` defined in the text could be of use in the Digital Watch specification.

2. Give a suitable complete axiomatizing predicate, but not the declaration, for each of the following relations:

    a. `prime _`
    `prime( k )` means 'k is a prime number'; i.e., it is a positive integer exceeding 1 that is exactly divisible by 1 and itself only

    b. `_ < _`

    c. `raTri _`
    `raTri( a , b , c )` means that summing the squares of two of the arguments equals the square of the other, where a, b, and c are positive integers.

3. Complete the defining predicates for `leapYr` and `eom` in the axiomatic description in the text. *Hint*: with `eom`, make other relations work for you.

    Note: a year `WXYZ` is a leap year if either `WXYZ` is divisible by 400, or `YZ` ≠ '00' and `YZ` is divisible by 4. This definition holds for all years after 1753, which is also the minimum value allowed for `bottomYr` in Digital Watch.

Relation Declarations

To complete our picture of defining relations axiomatically, we need to know how to write their declarations. This problem relates to an important topic left outstanding from Section 4.1: given some relation, how do we describe its type and value in Z?

Remark
A similar problem arises with functions. For example, what is the type and value of the function denoted by (`_+_`), say? In this chapter, we consider relations only, though the reader may care to note that the description of a function's type and value is very similar. You may be able to work this out, in advance of Chapter 6.

Consider again our arbitrary n-ary prefix relation `nAryRel`. Whenever `nAryRel` is applied, we write a predicate with this syntax:

$$nAryRel(a_1, a_2, \ldots a_n)$$

Instead of thinking of `nAryRel` as having n arguments, as we did at the start of Section 4.1, we can regard `nAryRel` as being applied to a *single* object, namely the *n-tuple*

$$(a_1, a_2, \ldots a_n) \tag{4.15}$$

This view is convenient because all relations of whatever arity can then be viewed uniformly. Even $i < j$, say, can be thought of as 'less than' acting on the 2-tuple (i, j).

A tuple of *dimension* k, or k-tuple, is an *ordered* structure of k elements (k ≥ 2) of possibly varying types. Note that there is no such object as a 'uni-tuple'. In fact, disregarding the need to use parentheses to override priorities as in a * (b + c), say, (Expression) in Z is just the same as Expression on its own. As an example, the definition of `leapYr` could be written thus:

$$\forall\, y : \mathbb{N} \bullet \text{leapYr } y \Leftrightarrow \ldots$$

Similarly `ajsn`, etc. Most of us are heavily conditioned into putting parentheses round singleton arguments of prefix symbols, but it is not necessary in Z, either when defining or applying such a symbol. Naturally, redundant parentheses can still be used for 'psychological security'. For the moment, the text will continue to use them in the majority of cases, switching to a leaner style only in Chapter 7 and beyond.

An explicit tuple is written by enclosing a list of its component elements in parentheses (these parentheses are *not* redundant of course!). The type of a tuple is easily described. For the previous n-tuple (4.15), its type would be

$$\tau_1 \times \tau_2 \times \ldots\ \tau_n$$

where the types of a_1, a_2, etc., are respectively τ_1, τ_2, etc. The symbol × is the *cartesian product* operator, and we will say much more about it in the next chapter. As examples, we could describe the arguments of each relation in Exercise 4.13(2) as follows:

(prime_) has arguments taken from: $\mathbb{N}_1$
(_ < _) has arguments taken from: $\mathbb{Z} \times \mathbb{Z}$
(raTri_) has arguments taken from: $\mathbb{N}_1 \times \mathbb{N}_1 \times \mathbb{N}_1$

Of course, the actual *types* of the arguments of `prime` and `raTri` are $\mathbb{Z}$ and $\mathbb{Z} \times \mathbb{Z} \times \mathbb{Z}$ respectively, but × is an operator on sets, so we are allowed to incorporate extra constraints directly in the usual way into constructs involving ×.

Describing the argument type of a relation is one thing, but it does not describe the type of the relation itself, since a relation is not a single element or tuple. Here lies the clue to what we are seeking. *An n-ary relation is characterized by precisely ALL those elements (n-tuples, if n ≥ 2) which satisfy its defining predicate.* In other words, the value of a relation is exactly that 'space' of individual elements *for which the relation is true*. To illustrate, here are some members of the spaces defining (the values of) the above three relations (all three spaces happen to be infinite):

(prime_):   2,3,5,7,11,13,17,19,23,29,31,37,41,43, ...
(_ < _):   (0,1),(0,2), ... (-1,0),(-1,1), ... (1,2),(1,3), ...
(raTri_):   (3,4,5),(3,5,4),(4,3,5),(4,5,3),(5,3,4),(5,4,3), ...

If a space is populated by elements of type τ, the type of the space itself is written as $\mathbb{P}\,\tau$. The symbol $\mathbb{P}$ is the *powerset* operator, and like the cartesian product operator ×, we will say much more about it in the next chapter. Suffice it to say here that a full grasp of × and $\mathbb{P}$, and the roles these two operators play in the general scheme of things, is vital to a proper understanding of the Z notation and its mathematical toolkit.

We are now able to describe the type of an arbitrary n-ary relation. For `nAryRel` on the opposite page, it is $\mathbb{P}\,(\,\tau 1 \times \tau 2 \times \ldots \tau n\,)$. For the three example relations above, we will have the declarations

$$prime \_ : \mathbb{P}\,\mathbb{N}_1 \qquad \text{— a space of positive integers}$$
$$\_ < \_ : \mathbb{P}\,(\,\mathbb{Z} \times \mathbb{Z}\,) \qquad \text{— a space of ordered pairs (i.e., 2-tuples) of integers}$$
$$raTri \_ : \mathbb{P}\,(\,\mathbb{N}_1 \times \mathbb{N}_1 \times \mathbb{N}_1\,) \qquad \text{— a space of positive integer triples}$$

The subsequent defining axiom for each relation then fixes precisely which space the relation actually is. Note the need for parentheses to take into account that $\mathbb{P}$ has greater priority than $\times$. As we will see, $\mathbb{P}\,(\,\mathbb{Z} \times \mathbb{Z}\,)$ is not the same as $\mathbb{P}\,\mathbb{Z} \times \mathbb{Z}$, for example.

EXERCISE 4.14

1. Give the declarations of all the Digital Watch relations on page 75.

2. a. Give the complete space which is the value of the relation `ajsn`
   b. Give those five members of `leapYr`'s value space which come first after 1790
   c. Give the members of `eom`'s value space relating to the first half of 1992
   d. Give the complete space which is the value of the unary relation `isn` whose defining axiom is

$$\forall\, i : \mathbb{Z} \bullet isn(\,i\,) \Leftrightarrow i > i$$

SUMMARY OF CHAPTER 4

- The fundamentals of the language of (first-order) predicate logic, as it is manifested in the Z notation, are elaborated.

- The concept of a relation is introduced, showing how relations are modelled in Z and how they are axiomatically defined in Z specifications.

THE VAN HIRE SYSTEM (PART I):
FROM REAL WORLD TO STATE MODEL

Key Topics   Domain analysis, data models; entities, attributes, binary relations; state models. Basic types: given sets; free types. Types and sets. Sets by extension. Constructed types: powerset; cartesian product, projection. Sets by comprehension. Set relations and operators; some laws of set theory. Data types. Abbreviation definitions.

5.1   A SYSTEM DEVELOPMENT PROBLEM

Problem Scenario

The main activities in the early life-cycle phases of system development are:

- Understanding and documenting the problem domain, i.e., the external context which the eventual computer system will be embedded in and provide a service to.

- Deriving a set of client/user requirements for the new system and from these constructing a technical specification of the software to be built.

These activities are general to all system development. The one distinguishing feature for us is that the technical specification will be expressed using Z.

The second case study is a system development problem, and so is more representative than Digital Watch of the practical use of formal specification. The problem domain relates to a business operation briefly described in the following overview:

The Van Hire Business

A garage runs a van hire business. The business is ticking over satisfactorily but it is likely that the just-tolerable efficiency of the current manual system, already under strain, will soon decrease to unacceptable levels. The garage has put into motion plans to expand the business by enlarging its premises and increasing its fleet size. The results of a feasibility and cost-benefit study have produced the strong recommendation that the garage should, as part of the expansion, computerize its hire business to increase efficiency, profitability and quality of service to the customer. A brief preliminary analysis of the current business operation has revealed the following set-up:

- *From time to time, new vans of different kinds are acquired in batches from various manufacturers to augment or replace the existing fleet.*

- *Not all vans in the fleet are available for hire at any given moment. For example, a van might be off the road for service or repair. Also, a new van is given a thorough pre-check before being released for hiring.*

- *Basically, a van is hired by a customer making a booking. Advance bookings require payment of a minimum deposit. There is no facility for provisional booking, so a booking firmly enters a customer into a contract with the garage. Vans are collected by customers from the garage's hire centre and subsequently returned there at the end of hire periods.*

- *The garage adopts a regular replenishment policy, and eventually vans are withdrawn, either to be disposed of as scrap if suffering excessive accident damage, or sold off on the second-hand market.*

As the result of a market survey and consultant advice, the garage has come down in favour of bespoke software rather than an off-the-shelf data-management product, mainly because of the dedicated features that can be built into the former. The software house which has won the contract to develop the system happens to be a forward-looking company. It tends to adopt a formal methods approach to development work for outside clients where it judges that the technology is appropriate and will not be over-stretched on the project. Past experience has shown that formal methods are particularly cost-effective with computerization of small-to-medium sized information systems whose scope and functionality are relatively stable and well understood.

In any system development problem like this, the two requirements definition objectives which will have the greatest impact on the technical Z-based specification are identification and documentation of:

- the 'relevant domain subject matter' that the system needs 'to keep track of' so that it is able to provide the services desired by the client
- the system functionality that will provide the client with those desired services.

The first of these two sets of requirements will form the basis of a Z state model; out of the second set of requirements will come the operation specifications.

> EXERCISE 5.1
>
> § Answer to part (a) is in this chapter, part (b) in the next chapter.
> Sketch some preliminary ideas concerning what you expect to be the client's
>
> a. data requirements   b. functional requirements.

Some Analysis

The business outline is obviously insufficient on its own to act as the basis for developing an acceptable computer system. Thus, we will imagine a period of extensive consultation with the client during which the developer has sought to clarify a number of important issues, including the following:

Q. *Over what length of period can a customer hire a van?*
A. Up to a maximum of 28 days, though we reserve the right to refuse a booking from a potential customer—especially a customer previously unknown to us—who requires a hire period length at or near the maximum. Hire periods are defined in terms of their start and end dates; these, of course, cannot be days like Sundays, bank holidays, etc.

Q. *Presumably, though, times are just as important as dates?*
A. Yes, but times merely dictate what we charge the customer. For the first day of hire, we charge a full day's rate for hirings starting up till 13.00 and thereafter half the full day rate. There are, however, no such variations relating to the return time of a van. A return time that keeps to contract is by definition any time during the last day of hire before close of business (18.00 each working day), up to and including 08.45 of the following day *but no later*. Obviously, vans

can be returned only on working days; intervening Sundays, holidays, etc. must be paid for as part of the hire period booked.

Q. *Suppose a pre-booked customer is late in collecting, or even fails to collect, a van; or suppose a customer is late in returning a van?*

A. This situation is taken care of by the standard hire contract, a copy of which we have given to you. The relevant small print says that if a customer has not arrived to collect a van by close of business on the agreed start day, the contract is made void; also, the customer receives no refund. For late returns, we levy a minimum of twice one full day's rate for the first day, plus quadruple this rate for each subsequent day. These heavy surcharges act as a strong disincentive to potential late returners. In practice, the disincentive works—there have been only two late returns in the last six months. We can of course reduce or waive these penalties at our discretion.

Q. *We are under the impression that you permit customers to hire only one van at a time. If so, isn't that a bit restrictive and not good business strategy?*

A. Our customers are mainly individual members of the general public; we don't operate hire agreements with firms—that is not the slice of the business we target. So nearly all our customers require just one van to fit a certain job they have in mind. In fact, although one van per customer used to be our policy, we haven't operated it for at least a year. Now we just use our discretion. Requests for more than one van at a time are actually quite rare. Where this happens, we treat each individual van request as a separate booking. Note that we offer five different types of van for hire—more than some of our rivals—which, in our view, cater for all needs. The van types are: mini, transit, light, medium, and heavy-duty, the latter mainly being used for home contents removal work.

Q. *Is it the case that when customers make bookings, they are allocated specific vans at the time of booking?*

A. Only when a booking is immediate, i.e., hiring is to start straight away. For advanced bookings, what we do is merely earmark particular van classes as being reserved, as per the customer's requirements. In doing this, we check in principle that we are not overbooking. We know of some hire firms that adopt this dubious practice, but not us. When the customer turns up on the hire start date, we allocate available vans in the requested class(es).

Q. *How can you be sure of van availability, and what do you mean by 'in principle' in your answer to the previous question?*

A. We mean that we make a quick check against the size of our fleet to see if a van of the required class is available over the desired period, but we do not take into account vans that are currently unavailable, e.g., late in being returned or off the road for repair. This approach works well enough in practice. Late returns are extremely rare, and the number of vans we have off the road simultaneously for any length of time is always arranged to be as small as possible (unpredictable accident repair notwithstanding).

Q. *But this procedure does not GUARANTEE availability.*

A. No, of course not, but almost. Naturally, customers making immediate bookings have to take what is available and risk being disappointed. But for advance bookings, a minimum 24 hours notice enables us virtually to guarantee customer satisfaction. If we think there is the slightest risk of an availability problem, we contact certain local external suppliers who normally can produce vans of the right kind for us within the hour; the vans then temporarily become part of our fleet. However, we try to avoid this since it increases our costs substantially, and is the main reason why we are absolutely rigorous about not over-booking. In the very unlikely event that a customer, having made an advance booking and despite our checks etc., arrives on the start date to find we have insufficient vans available, we offer either a re-arrangement of the hire period free of charge or a complete refund. This has happened only once since we started up the business about three years ago.

Q. *Ok, but how do you manage the interleaving of bookings with vans off the road for servicing. Could you clarify please?*

A. When a van is approaching its next service point, we simply fit the van's service into any spare time slot that we can find for it. This is typically an afternoon or evening since most vans get returned either early in the morning or late afternoon, and a service does not usually take more than two hours. If necessary, we get one of our mechanics to do some overtime.

Q. *Can you please confirm that there are no such things as 'provisional bookings'?*

A. Confirmed. Enquiries are welcomed, e.g., by phone, but a booking is made only by the customer making a personal call to our hire centre and either paying up in full or, for an advance booking, making a minimum deposit of 30% of the total charge. However, subject only to using our discretion again, booking can be done any time in advance of the desired hire start date to avoid disappointment.

Q. *Presumably a customer can cancel a booking. What then?*

A. There is a sliding scale of cancellation fees depending on how close to the hire start date the cancellation is made, working up to the full deposit paid if the cancellation is made within two days of the start date.

Q. *Can a customer make multiple bookings?*

A. If you mean bookings with different, possibly overlapping, hire periods, then yes, but again it is entirely at our discretion; we tend to permit it only for regular customers. Remember that we also treat a request for more than one van over the same hire period as a multiple booking. Actually, multiple bookings are relatively infrequent. They are just about worth it, even though they complicate the paperwork. Presumably that is at least one problem which computerization will help alleviate!

Conducting interviews is a standard part of the requirements elicitation repertoire. Much of the above is simply trying to understand the domain of van hiring as operated by the garage. In a real sense, therefore, we are also understanding the computer system to be built, since that system will in effect partly be a computerized version or model—even 'emulation'—of the domain it is servicing.

Of course, the developer needs other information as well as that contained in the answers to the previous questions. For example, answers are needed to questions like:

- What query/report functionality would you like? For example, do you want to be able to see the extent of booking day by day over a specified period?

- What kind of interface do you want, e.g., when entering booking data?

Nevertheless, although the above imagined interview mainly addresses clarification of the domain, it suffices for present purposes—making progress with developing a Z specification.

Data Model for the Van Hire System

First, some terminological clarification. By (conceptual) *data model*, we mean a model as constructed by analysis techniques such as entity–relationship modelling. The closest, though not entirely equivalent, construct in a Z specification would be a a *state model*. Thus, we reserve 'data model' for domain descriptions and 'state model' for system state descriptions. The former lies in the realm of requirements engineering, the latter in the realm of technical software specification. It is important to appreciate that a Z specification is *not* a 'requirements specification' in the sense of being a client/domain-oriented description of some kind. Of course, certain manifestations of client functional requirements and domain features will be directly visible in, or recoverable from, Z specifications. Even so, a Z specification is an abstract description of *the software to be built*, written by and for software engineers; it is not intended as a statement of *what the client requires*, written by/for the client. Clearly, though, it is essential for a Z specification to conform to the latter, and this is addressed by specification validation, a topic covered in Section 9.1.

Remark
Z specifications are sometimes discussed in the literature from the viewpoint of being descriptions of external domains. At least in a software development context, the distinction made in this text is, in the author's view, the accurate position to take.

Back to the development problem. The reason why we are focusing on domain data modelling is that it is capable of providing a sound basis for Z state modelling, particularly for the kind of system under consideration here. The Van Hire business is an entity-rich domain, and such domains yield information that is vital to a meaningful state model. The data model we will construct for the van hire business uses standard parlance such as 'entities', 'relationships' and 'attributes'. Data modelling is a skill and a craft in its own right with many associated techniques, discussion of which lies outside the scope of this book. There are many textbooks on the subject for the uninitiated reader, such as Howe (1983).

A common feature of data modelling is an *entity–relationship* description, which scopes the domain in terms of relevant entity types and how they are related. Typically, certain real-world entities stand out as obvious candidates for incorporation into the data model, and in the Van Hire system we would surely include VANs and CUSTOMERs in this category. However, it would soon be apparent that a richer basket of entity types is needed to support the client's functional requirements, and that inclusion of VANCLASS entities in the model is also necessary. We might try to sketch out the relationships perceived to exist between these entity types in an entity–relationship (E–R) diagram as in Figure 5.1. Diamonds are relationships, each of which is given a name that is meaningful when read in one direction. Boxes are entity types.

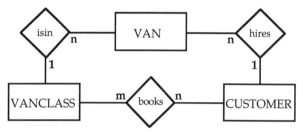

Figure 5.1 Entity–relationship diagram for the van hire domain (first version).

We can see that each relationship happens to be binary. With a binary relationship, *cardinalities* between participating entity instances can be specified. Thus, the 'n' in the n-to-1 assignation of isin means that *many* vans can exist in a van class, with the '1' of n-to-1 further ensuring that any particular van can exist in *one van class only*. If we view the isin relationship in the 'inverse' direction (we might then call it 'has', say), then the cardinality is 1-to-n, meaning that one van class can have many vans.

Binary relationships bestow certain advantages (later, we see that this has implications for descriptions written in Z). One benefit is that the smaller the arity of a relationship, the less complex its structure and hence in principle the more it is to be preferred. Generalizing and simplifying somewhat, a model with several relationships of small arities is preferable to one with the same 'information content' which has less components but as a result relies on more complex relationships of a higher order.

There are some problems with Figure 5.1 as it stands. For example, there is no way of relating the vans that customers hire to the van classes customers book; also, there is no sensible entity to allocate attributes like hire periods. The inadequacy of the model can be removed by introducing a booking entity to bind the other entities together into a meaningful structure. Figure 5.2 is a reworked model in which the entity BOOKING has replaced relationship books, and the hires relationship has been discarded in favour of a relationship between BOOKINGs and VANs. Now, for a given booking, we can identify the customer involved, the van class reserved and the van (eventually) allocated; and attributes like hire periods clearly belong to bookings.

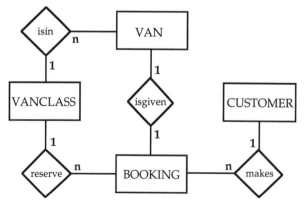

Figure 5.2 Entity–relationship diagram for the van hire domain (second version).

Note the effect of changing relationship books into entity BOOKING: two new binary relationships of reduced cardinality (many-to-1) are generated. This is quite a common procedure in data modelling, i.e., replacing a many-to-many relationship, or a relationship of arity greater than 2, by a new entity type. This always increases the number of relationships in the model, but the gain is that they are of reduced complexity.

In practice, the E–R diagram of Figure 5.2 might well have been constructed in the first place. Whilst such diagrams help fix upon entity relationships, we need to supplement them with additional explanation. An important issue concerns the time dimension. For example, is Figure 5.2 intended to cover the life history of the garage's van hiring or some time span of lesser scope? If the former, it would certainly be wrong. This is because, over a period of time, a given van can be allocated to several bookings; in which case, the isgiven relationship should be many(bookings)-to-1(van).

The main determinant for whether the semantics of relationships in a data model should include historical information is the client's functional requirements. For the van hire system, suppose we have elicited that the client has no interest in historical data of any kind. Hence isgiven is a 1-to-1 relationship—at any isolated moment, a van can be allocated to one booking only. The cardinalities of the other three relationships are unaffected by history. For example, as well as over a period of time, one customer can have several bookings associated with him/her at some given moment in time. As we will see, time is a factor to consider in state modelling too (see pages 89-90).

The description below attempts to clarify our data model by expressing in words the E–R diagram of Figure 5.2, attaching important additional real-world constraints (these are the letters on the right-hand side, which reference constraints defined in *Constraints* sections), and providing further definitional information.

A. *Van Hire entity types, relationships and constraints*

- VAN
  Definition: A VAN is a vehicle which is part of the garage's hire fleet.
  Relationships:
  Each van can be associated with at most one booking at a time   (a)
  Each van has only one van class.
  Constraints:
  a. The booking's hire period must be 'active', i.e., vans are allocated no earlier than the start of hire periods.

- VANCLASS
  Definition: A VANCLASS characterizes a van as one of five different kinds.
  Relationships:
  Each van class has many different vans
  Each van class can be associated with many bookings.   (b)
  Constraints:
  b. Nominal overbooking for a van class is not permitted. 'Nominal overbooking' means: on a given day, more vans in a class are booked than exist in the fleet.

- CUSTOMER
  Definition: A CUSTOMER is an individual person who has contracted to hire vans from the garage.
  Relationships:
  Each customer makes one or more bookings.

- BOOKING
  Definition: A BOOKING is a contract between one person and the garage to hire one van of a particular class over an agreed period of time.
  Relationships:
  Each booking is associated with one customer
  Each booking requests one van class
  Each booking is allocated one van.   (c)
  Constraints:
  c. As constraint (a) for VAN.

Global constraints:
No historical data, such as previous customers, cancelled/completed bookings etc., is to be handled.

The origin of most of Section A can be located in the business outline and interview given previously. Section B below supplements (A) with attribute lists for entities, though without any data typing. Those 'attributes' which are really references to other entities are enclosed in parentheses.

B. *Van Hire entity attributes*

- VAN
  registration number
  manufacturer
  model
  date purchased
  date last serviced
  whether or not available for hire
  (class)

- VANCLASS
  class name
  max. usable height, width and depth
  maximum payload
  average mpg: city and long journey
  approximate top speed
  fuel type

- CUSTOMER
  customer identifier
  name
  address
  date of birth
  date passed driving test
  traffic conviction record
  day-time telephone number

- BOOKING
  booking reference code
  hire period
  whether or not active
  total charge
  deposit
  method of payment (cash, cheque, etc.)
  credit card number (where applicable)
  accounting period
  (customer who has made booking)
  (requested van class)
  (van allocated when booking is active)

As well as justifying the above data model to the client, the developer will also make it clear that if the model is used as the basis for developing the computer system, then the system will be able to support actions such as:

- Responding to an event like: 'Customer X has booked a van in class C for period P' (the system will perform the required update to remain valid with respect to the domain).

- Servicing a request like: 'How many vans are due to be hired out on day D?'.

However, the system will not be able to support actions such as:

- Dealing with an event for historical purposes, e.g: 'Customer X has just booked a van for the third time in the current quarterly period'.

- Answering queries like: 'What is the total number of times van V has been hired?'.

We will imagine that the client is happy with the suggested data model, formally approved at a subsequent review, and wants the system to support actions like those in the first group, but has no interest in actions such as those in the second group. It is this kind of information concerning a system's functional dependency on its data model that the developer will have used in constructing the latter. However, as actual services to be provided by the system are otherwise rarely at issue in this chapter, detailed consideration of client functional requirements will be left until Chapter 6.

Remark
Determining salient aspects of a real-world domain, expressing these in data and other kinds of model, and then deriving a state model description in Z may take many weeks of analysis and experimental modelling to finalize. The system case study here is not in absolute terms particularly complex, and a skilled Z specifier could 'knock up' a draft Z state model quite quickly with little explicit reliance on the data modelling detail we have gone into here. We are proceeding in a deliberate manner to emphasize the fact that bridging the gap between real-world domains and formal specifications in general requires a systematic approach that is appropriate to the particular class of problem being addressed.

> EXERCISE 5.2
>
> The *relationships* of a data model are no different *mathematically* to *relations* such as those we were defining in Section 4.4 to support the Digital Watch specification. Treating entity class names (VAN, CUSTOMER, etc.) as though they are sets like $\mathbb{Z}$, etc., describe in Z the types of:
>
> a. each relationship in Figure 5.1
> b. § The answer to this part is developed in the next section.
>   each relationship in Figure 5.2.
>
> You may need to go over the material of Section 4.4 again.

5.2 FROM DATA MODEL TO STATE MODEL

The Beginnings of a Specification

It seems a reasonable proposition that the main information structures of a Z state model can be derived from a domain data model of the kind described in Section 5.1. Yet the Van Hire data model is awash with detail, which is not something we expect to see in an abstract specification. However, recall the discussion in Section 2.2 concerning abstraction. In building the data model of Section 5.1, we have scoped the domain; that is, we have abstracted the real world by omitting certain of its features judged to be of no relevance to the task at hand. In deriving a Z state model from the data model, a different 'golden rule' of abstraction dominates: we suppress all information that is not needed for the description to fulfil its intended role effectively. This principle means that we need to make manifest in the abstract description of a system's state

- the main entities and their types
- the relationships between those entities
- entity–attribute detail, but *only* where the attribute information is essential
- the constraints that must operate on and between entities.

In other words, it is Figure 5.2 and section (A) of the Van Hire data model which is the primary focus for deriving a Z state model. Most, though not all, of section (B)—the attribute analysis—is of subsidiary importance at this stage. Including a full-blown attribute analysis in an abstract state model would clutter it with unnecessary and distracting detail.

Bearing the foregoing in mind, the basis of the data-to-state model manoeuvre we require is as follows: every relationship expressed in the E–R diagram becomes a mathematical relation of exactly the same kind in the state model. Suppose for the moment we assume the following types:

- CUSTOMER: the complete class of customer entities
- VAN: the complete class of van entities
- VanClass: all the different possible van classes
- BOOKING: the complete class of booking entities.

Using the operators $\mathbb{P}$ and $\times$ introduced in Section 4.4 to describe the types of relations, the beginnings of a Z state model can be described by the following first-shot, incomplete schema (references to relationships in comments refer to Figure 5.2):

```
┌─VanHire─────────────────────────────────────────────────────────────┐
│ custom : ℙ( CUSTOMER × BOOKING )          — the makes relationship   │
│ commit : ℙ( BOOKING × VanClass )          — the reserve relationship │
│ activeHires : ℙ( BOOKING × VAN )          — the isgiven relationship │
│ fleet : ℙ( VAN × VanClass )               — the isin relationship    │
│ OtherVars                                                            │
├──────────────────────────────────────                               │
│ custom is a 1-to-many relation                                       │
│ commit is a many-to-1 relation                                       │
│ activeHires is a 1-to-1 relation                                     │
│ fleet is a many-to-1 relation                                        │
│ RestOfPredicate                                                      │
└──────────────────────────────────────────────────────────────────────┘
```

We have informally documented each relation's cardinality in the predicate part, but for the moment subsumed any other variables or constraints that might be needed, including those pertaining to attribute-level description.

Relation cardinalities represent important model detail that must not be overlooked. Consider the custom component of VanHire. Its state is a 'space' (the $\mathbb{P}$ symbol) of pairings (the $\times$ symbol) between customers and bookings. So if customer c has a current booking b, the pair (c , b) will contribute to the value of custom. The same customer c could be associated with bookings other than b since one customer is allowed to make many bookings. However, no booking can be associated with more than one customer in custom; otherwise 'multiple customer' bookings would be allowed, which does not occur in the domain—one booking is associated with one customer only. The declaration of `custom` on its own is not sufficient because it allows `custom` to be an arbitrary—that is, *many-to-many*—relation, and hence allows values for `custom` that are invalid with respect to the domain. That is why the invariant '`custom` is a 1-to-many relation' is necessary. Similarly for the other three relations.

More generally, if a binary relation between X objects and Y objects is many-to-many with no other special properties, then nothing is needed beyond declaring it as a $\mathbb{P}(X \times Y)$ relation. However, for more restricted relations, i.e., many-to-1, 1-to-many, or 1-to-1, the declaration must be supplemented by the appropriate constraint. We will deal with formalizing constraints like these in Section 5.5, and again in Section 6.1.

Initially, it may strike the reader as strange to treat a *state* component as a relation. We think of the axiomatically defined global relations of the Digital Watch specification—`ajsn`, `leapYr`, etc.—as 'constants' of a special kind which are applicable to arguments to construct predicates that are either true or false. Their role seems to have little in common with that of the state variables `custom`, `commit`, etc., in the `VanHire` schema. Nevertheless, whilst *roles* are different, the *underlying mathematical model* is exactly the same. For example, the global `ajsn` relation of Digital Watch and `custom` component in the `VanHire` schema are each just a 'space' of a particular type.

The mode of thinking which desires to treat state components as somehow different from 'operational objects' in Z descriptions is perhaps engendered by procedural programming—a paradigm in which one is trained to think of 'state' as 'data', and 'relations' (less than, equals, etc.) as 'conditional operations' to be applied to data in algorithms. However, in the abstract world, relations are just mathematical structures of a certain kind that are as applicable to modelling states as they are to contributing to the axiomatic basis of a specification; the same observation applies to functions, dealt with in Section 6.1. Consider `custom` again in `VanHire`. At any imagined moment, `custom` is some relation of the $\mathbb{P}(\text{CUSTOMER} \times \text{BOOKING})$ variety. When the real-world changes—e.g., a customer returns a van and completes a booking, or a new customer makes a booking—this update in the real world is modelled partly as a change to the value of `custom`. The new `custom` value is still a $\mathbb{P}(\text{CUSTOMER} \times \text{BOOKING})$ relation; it is simply a different relation—i.e., a slightly different space of (customer, booking) pairs—to what it was just before the change took place.

DIFFERENCES

Despite the impression we may have created, it is important to appreciate that a Z state model is not a mechanical translation of (mainly) some E–R diagram. Many differences can exist between data and state models. One of these concerns time. A history-wide data model might be constructed as a matter of methodology, even though this full model is not necessary to support actual functional requirements. Contrast this with a state model, which should be thought of as representing an arbitrary state of the system *at some 'frozen' moment in time*. The distinction is important. Take the Van Hire data model of Section 5.1. As pointed out earlier, the difference between the model as-is and a model with history semantics would be this: in the latter, the isgiven relationship in the E–R diagram would be many-to-1 from bookings to vans, not 1-to-1. Suppose we now simply translated this wider data model into a state model as described. Given that the functionality of the Van Hire system requires no historical information, then the `VanHire` state schema *would contain a completely unnecessary slice of history in it,* which is obviously not sensible. Thus, even if isgiven was many-to-1 in the data model, it should be reduced to 1-to-1 in the state model.

Possible reduction in cardinalities due to time considerations is just one cause of differences between data and state models. A state model can also contain components additional to, or derived from, the basic domain relationships. The inclusion of such components might be related solely to judgement concerning a specification's clarity, understandability, ease of construction, mathematical elegance, and/or separation of concerns. For example, if we *did* need to include the full history of the isgiven relationship in the state model, we might split the relation in VanHire into two:

| pastHires : $\mathbb{P}$ (BOOKING $\times$ VAN) | — historical many-to-1 component |
| activeHires : $\mathbb{P}$ (BOOKING $\times$ VAN) | — current 1-to-1 component |

The 'sum' of these two relations in the state model would now correspond to the isgiven relationship in the data model. The reason for this splitting, which is not mathematically necessary, could be that it improves understandability of the specification, making operations clearer and simpler to describe, for example.

Actually, we will see that binary relations are good for many of the 'specification desiderata' mentioned in the previous paragraph. It was hinted earlier that binary relation(ship)s are simple, elegant constructs which make them particularly useful in data/state modelling. So it is unlikely that we will need to re-structure the initial four components of VanHire to any significant extent to improve the quality of the model.

Generally, the Z equivalent of an E–R description will not be sufficient on its own to support the specification of required system operations, and additional state components will be needed. These will typically involve attributes of particular entity types. For example, consider the following problem concerning the VanHire schema:

How can we tell which bookings are late in completing; or which are to start on a given date in the future; or which are supposed to start today but the customers involved have not turned up yet to collect their vans?

The relation activeHires gives us some relevant information. We know that the bookings of this relation are those which are under way and so must have hire periods starting no later than the current date; but that is all we can say. We cannot answer questions like the above unless we make explicit in the state model at least the hire period attribute of bookings. To do that requires adding to the model without disturbing the four basic relation components already there.

Exactly what further work needs to be done to VanHire will be described in Section 5.5. Before then, we need a thorough grounding in some further Z basics. In particular, we need to know how to introduce types like CUSTOMER and VanClass into specifications. We also need to understand properly the two fundamental constructor mechanisms $\mathbb{P}$ and $\times$ we have used in the type description of relations, but with little explanation of the underlying mathematics. More generally, we need to gain a proper understanding of *sets*.

EXERCISE 5.3

§ Answers are developed in subsequent sections.
Describe *informally* some additional constraints needed in VanHire's predicate.

Basic Types: Given Sets

Whatever types underpin a particular Z specification, some will inevitably be *basic*, being used to describe objects regarded as primitive. Basic types other than $\mathbb{Z}$ needed in a specification are introduced with paragraphs of the form

[Name_1 , Name_2 , ...]

The names are those of *given sets* and act as basic types; each is global to the rest of the specification and can be used in any subsequent declaration. Here is an example:

[VIDEO, PERSON]   (5.1)

This paragraph might introduce a type VIDEO to denote videos hired out by a video club, and a type PERSON to identify club members. The paragraph serves to assert that the two sets exist, that they are non-empty (since an 'empty type' is not meaningful), and that they have no members in common. The last property holds because, since VIDEO and PERSON are *types*, it is therefore impossible for an object to belong to both.

Note that we have no way of describing the values of a given set. We cannot write down a particular VIDEO or PERSON value because we have no representation for it. This is not as bad as it first sounds. By introducing a given set into a specification, we are saying not only that it is a basic type but also, as a corollary, that its internal structure serves no useful purpose in the specification. In other words, it can be inferred from (5.1) that the specification has no need to refer to *actual specific* VIDEO or PERSON values. Thus, in a simple yet powerful way, we can use given sets to suppress unwanted detail. Of course, suppose we declare, say

vid1, vid2 : VIDEO

and subsequently assert that

vid1 ≠ vid2

Then vid1 and vid2 are certainly different members of VIDEO (which, by inference, must therefore contain at least two members!), but that is all we are saying; we have no way of describing what the actual values of vid1 and vid2 are.

Remark
It is best to think of the symbol $\mathbb{Z}$ as a special case of a basic type. Firstly, $\mathbb{Z}$ is in effect 'given' to all specifications. Secondly, we are able to construct constants denoting specific values of type $\mathbb{Z}$ by a special facility: decimal notation.

What given sets are needed in the Van Hire specification? A general starting point is to assume that a given set will be needed for each main entity type appearing in the state model. This follows from our earlier statement that detail which is an unnecessary distraction in an abstract specification should be suppressed. Given sets do this simply and effectively. However, for reasons explained shortly, van classes will be dealt with slightly differently. So for Van Hire we will have the given sets

[VAN,	— uniquely identifies all possible vans
CUSTOMER,	— uniquely identifies all possible customers
BOOKING]	— uniquely identifies all possible bookings

Note the comment 'uniquely identifies all possible ...'. Although VAN, for example, is an opaque box of elements, each element is regarded as pertaining to a unique van. Moreover, VAN is deemed to cater for all possible vans. Obviously, in the actual Van Hire system, only a subset of VAN will be in use at any given moment. When the system is implemented, a representation for type VAN will be chosen such that the implicit requirements for VAN— 'uniqueness of van identification', 'being large enough', etc.— are realized. Typically, the representation will be based on some 'identifier' attribute. In the case of VAN, the choice might well be van registrations, which are then used to key into the 'attribute tuples' for the van entity instances stored in the system. A similar set of comments applies to CUSTOMER and BOOKING.

Since we also wish to treat the entity type VANCLASS as basic, we might choose to use a given set. Yet there are differences between VANCLASS and the other three entity types. Firstly, we know that VANCLASS comprises exactly five instances distinguished by the following classification: mini, transit, light, medium, heavy-duty. Secondly, we might need to refer explicitly to a particular van class in the specification. This would be necessary if, for example, we had to specify an operation like: 'in each van class, give those vans currently out on hire'. Under these circumstances, it is appropriate to define the type not as a bare given set, but in a way that allows us easily to distinguish between its members.

One simple way to achieve this would be to model the type using an existing type or types. For VANCLASS, we could choose a five-element integer subrange such as $0..4$, where 0 denotes the van class 'mini', and so on. However, analogously to program design, it is better style in such cases to define a type comprising 'meaningful symbolic names'. We can do this in Z with a paragraph called a *free type* definition:

```
VanClass ::= mini | transit | light | medium | heavyDuty
```

More generally, the syntax of a free type definition is

$$\text{Name} ::= \text{Alt}_1 \mid \text{Alt}_2 \mid \dots$$

where Name is the name of the new type and the alternatives Alt_1, Alt_2, etc. exhaustively define all the different values of the type. In the simplest case, as with VanClass, the alternatives are just names which are constants, rather like an 'enumeration type' in certain programming languages. Much later in Section 7.5, more general forms of free type definition are discussed.

We can view a free type definition like that for VanClass as another mechanism for introducing basic types into specifications, which—unlike a given set—enables us via the definition's 'literal constants' to write down members of the new type. This seems to contradict our earlier statement that the basic types in a specification are its given sets (plus $\mathbb{Z}$). There is actually no contradiction because a free type is just a given set in disguise. For example, the definition of VanClass above is just a more compact, 'sugary' way of saying the following:

[VanClass]

```
mini,transit,light,medium,heavyDuty : VanClass
```

A predicate stating that:
    VanClass has precisely five distinct values which are denoted by the names
    mini, transit, light, medium **and** heavyDuty

We know enough logic to formalize the predicate, though it would be rather clumsy (see also Exercise 5.4(3) below); by the end of this chapter, we will be able to express the predicate elegantly. Obviously, we would normally choose a free type definition in preference to its much more verbose axiomatic, given-set equivalent.

EXERCISE 5.4

1. Using some imagination, invent given sets that are likely to be needed in the abstract specification of

   a. a library system
   b. a system for controlling user access to a set of computers
   c. an airline reservation system.

2. Write down the definition of a type suitable for modelling different classes of degree that can be awarded by a higher education institution.

3. Give an axiomatic description based on a given set which is equivalent to the following free type definition:

   ```
   Gender ::= male | female
   ```

   The required predicate is fairly simple to express.

5.3   SETS AND THEIR CONSTRUCTION

Preamble: Types and Sets

In an untyped world, there would be just be a 'universe of objects' W. A set could be any collection of objects selected from W that we wished to clump together. In a typed world, however, only objects *of the same type* can be constructed into a set. Thus, we can have a particular set of VAN values, but we cannot construct a set some of whose members are VAN values and others of which are VanClass or CUSTOMER values, say. The inability to mix objects in this way is a straightforward consequence of having types, and avoids certain mathematical difficulties that would otherwise arise.

Let us pursue the relationship between types and sets further. An object ω in Z has just one type only. Importantly, this type can be determined (by a human, or computer program) from the expression we have written for ω. Suppose the type of ω is τ. Then we know (page 28) that τ itself determines a special 'maximal' set. This set contains *all* and *only* objects of type τ (so it will contain ω in particular). However, given any set Ψ constructed from τ objects, then ω might or might not be a member of Ψ—it just depends which set Ψ happens to be. For example, suppose ω is the number 4. Then its type is $\mathbb{Z}$, which denotes the 'set of integers', of which 4 is one particular member. Suppose that Ψ happens to be the negative integers; then clearly 4 is not a member of this set. However, if Ψ were the even integers, then 4 would be a member of this set. In fact, because the set denoted by $\mathbb{Z}$ is infinite, we can construct an arbitrary number of different sets of integers to which 4 belongs, and to which 4 does not belong. Nevertheless, 4 has only one type, namely $\mathbb{Z}$.

Remark

We often speak of a set 'containing' a member. This intuitive terminology is rarely misleading, but you should understand that, strictly, a set *is* its constituent members and is not some kind of 'container' with a certain contents.

It often helps to visualize set relationships, using simple shapes—rectangles, bubbles, etc.—to depict sets (or 'spaces' as we have sometimes called them) as illustrated in Figure 5.3.

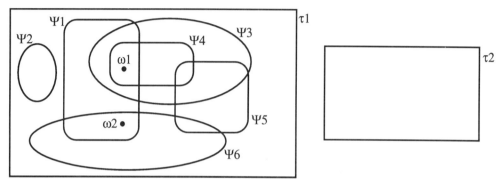

Figure 5.3 Two types and some sets.

Here, $\tau1$ and $\tau2$ are two types, say two given sets such as VAN and CUSTOMER. The two rectangles represent the (maximal) sets denoted by these types. Thus, for example, all and only objects of type $\tau1$ lie within the rectangle labelled $\tau1$. Commonality of membership across two or more sets is represented by an appropriate overlapping of shapes. So the two rectangles cannot possibly overlap since this would contradict the fact that $\tau1$ and $\tau2$ are types. On the other hand, consider particular subsets of $\tau1$. We can see that $\omega1$ is a member of sets $\Psi1$, $\Psi3$ and $\Psi4$, but not sets $\Psi2$, $\Psi5$, or $\Psi6$. Similarly, $\omega2$ is a member of $\Psi1$ and $\Psi6$, but not $\Psi2$, $\Psi3$, $\Psi4$ and $\Psi5$.

The linkage between types and sets applies whether the type in question defines objects we think of as primitive or as structured. As we have already seen, it is the given sets of a specification which are its basic types and which define the objects which the specification regards as primitive. There are three different kinds of structured object in Z: *sets*, *tuples* and *bindings*. Bindings will not be discussed from a type viewpoint until Section 7.2.

Constructing Sets by Extension

The simplest way to construct a particular set is to enumerate all the elements that belong to it. This mode of set construction is called definition *by extension*. It is applicable if: (a) we are able to write down terms for the elements of the set; (b) the set we wish to construct is finite and reasonably small. In an extensional set definition, curly brackets are used to delimit the enumeration; for example:

$$\{\,8,9,7,6\,\}$$

which is a particular (sub)set of (the) integers. Apart from the essential characteristic that all members of a set must be of the same type, there are two other basic properties sets possess: a set is an *unordered* structure, and its members are *distinct*. Thus:

- The following sets are identical to each other and to the preceding one:

  { 6,8,7,9 }   { 8,7,6,9 }   { 7,9,8,6 }

  Of course, an ordering can be imposed on the four elements of this set, but this would be via a binary relation like ≤, for example, and would not arise through any inherent property of the set structure itself.

- Writing something like

  { 7,9,8,8,6,9,9 }

  is well-formed, but the element duplication is redundant. Although the enumeration contains seven terms, the set which the expression denotes comprises four elements only; in fact, of course, it is exactly the same set as that denoted by the previous examples.

Terms in extensional definitions are not limited to just constants. So given the variables i,j : ℕ, the following is a legal example of a set construction, since all terms denote elements of type ℤ:

{ i * i,i + j,6,j * 2,j * j - i * i,i * 2 + 1 }

Moreover, if we have the binding

⟨ i ⇒ 3,j ⇒ 4 ⟩

then the set is the same as that denoted by all the previous examples in this section.

The subrange notation lwb . . upb is a shorter way of defining a set by enumerating all integers from lwb up to upb inclusive. Here are some set equalities that are all true:

6..9 = { 6,7,8,9 }   — which is the same set as in previous examples
8..8 = { 8 }
j..i = { }   — assuming the above binding

If lwb = upb, as in the second example, the subrange is equal to a *singleton* set, i.e., a set comprising one element only. If lwb > upb, as in the third example, the subrange is empty, or strictly, the *empty set of integers*. An empty set can be written as { } or denoted by the special symbol ∅; we will generally use the latter. Note that the previous sentence begins '*An* empty set …'. This is because there is not just one empty set, as there would be in an untyped world, but arbitrarily many—one for each type, in fact.

EXERCISE 5.5

1. Suppose that, in order to model the natural numbers 0 . . 7 in *binary* form, we choose the following eight set representations:

   { 0,0,0 }   { 0,0,1 }   { 0,1,0 }   { 0,1,1 }
   { 1,0,0 }   { 1,0,1 }   { 1,1,0 }   { 1,1,1 }

   Explain why this model is inadequate.

2. Consider type Gender in Exercise 5.4(3):

   a. Write down all the different sets that can be defined by extension from this type.
   b. What is wrong with the expression: { male,medium,female,light } ?

c. In the answer to Exercise 5.4(3), explain why the following equality on its own would be insufficient as the predicate in the axiomatic definition:

$$Gender = \{ male, female \}$$

3. Work out how many different sets can be constructed from the elements of type VanClass on page 92 (just count the sets, do not bother to define them). There is actually a simple formula involving the number 2 that can be used to calculate the answer. Can you work out what this formula is?

Powerset Construction

Since a set is itself a (structured) value, it must have a type *and hence belong to a set itself*. Consider the set { 8,6,9,7 }. Informally, it is natural to describe the type of this set as a 'set of integers'. Thus, if we declare a variable setOfInt to be a 'set-of-integers variable', this should mean—in the absence of further constraints—that setOfInt can be *any* set whose elements are integers, such as { 8,6,9,7 }. To declare setOfInt, we would use the powerset operator $\mathbb{P}$:

$$setOfInt : \mathbb{P}\,\mathbb{Z}$$

For this to make sense, the expression $\mathbb{P}\,\mathbb{Z}$ must denote a set whose elements *are sets themselves*, these being different sets of integers. In fact, $\mathbb{P}\,\mathbb{Z}$ must therefore denote *the set of all possible sets which can be constructed from the elements of* $\mathbb{Z}$—that is, all different possible *subsets* of $\mathbb{Z}$. Note carefully that the subsets of $\mathbb{Z}$ include $\varnothing$ and $\mathbb{Z}$ itself.

As a simple example of what $\mathbb{P}$ does, suppose we have the free type

$$Colour ::= red \mid green \mid blue$$

one consequence of which is that the following equality holds:

$$Colour = \{ red, green, blue \}$$

In the declaration

$$hue : Colour$$

hue can be any element of Colour, namely red, green or blue. But in the declaration

$$palette : \mathbb{P}\,Colour$$

palette can be any *(sub)set* of Colour elements. As an expression denoting a set itself, the members of $\mathbb{P}\,Colour$ are all possible sets constructible from Colour elements. $\mathbb{P}\,Colour$ must therefore satisfy the following equality:

$\mathbb{P}\,Colour = \{$
— the empty set of Colour elements
  $\varnothing$,
— all singleton sets of Colour elements
  { red }, { green }, { blue },
— all doubleton sets of Colour elements
  { red, green }, { red, blue }, { green, blue },
— the maximal set of Colour elements
  { red, green, blue } }

palette is thus one of the eight different possible sets of type $\mathbb{P}\,Colour$.

In constructing the powerset $\mathbb{P}\, S$ of some set S, there is no restriction on the set that S is allowed to be. So the construction $\mathbb{P}\,(\,\mathbb{P}\, X\,)$, for example, is perfectly acceptable. It is the set of all sets that can be constructed from the elements of $\mathbb{P}\, X$, i.e., it defines the set of all different subsets of $\mathbb{P}\, X$. Since the members of $\mathbb{P}\, X$ are sets themselves, the members of $\mathbb{P}\,(\,\mathbb{P}\, X\,)$ must be sets whose elements are also sets. To provide an example within reasonable bounds, consider type Gender in Exercise 5.4(3). Then

$$\mathbb{P}\, \texttt{Gender} = \{\, \varnothing, \{\, \texttt{male}\, \}, \{\, \texttt{female}\, \}, \{\, \texttt{male}, \texttt{female}\, \}\, \}$$

but $\mathbb{P}\,(\,\mathbb{P}\, \texttt{Gender}\,)$ will be as follows:

$\mathbb{P}\,(\,\mathbb{P}\, \texttt{Gender}) = \{$
— the empty set of $\mathbb{P}\, \texttt{Gender}$ elements
   $\varnothing,$
— all singleton sets of $\mathbb{P}\, \texttt{Gender}$ elements
   $\{\varnothing\}, \{\{\texttt{male}\}\}, \{\{\texttt{female}\}\}, \{\{\texttt{male}, \texttt{female}\}\},$
— some of the doubleton sets of $\mathbb{P}\, \texttt{Gender}$ elements
   $\{\varnothing, \{\texttt{male}\}\}, \{\varnothing, \{\texttt{female}\}\}, \{\varnothing, \{\texttt{male}, \texttt{female}\}\},$
— see next exercise for remaining elements
   $\dots\,\}$

Considerable care is needed with $\varnothing$. Note how $\varnothing$ and $\{\,\varnothing\,\}$ are not at all the same. $\varnothing$ is the empty set (of something), but $\{\,\varnothing\,\}$ is a *singleton* set having the empty set (of something) as its sole element.

Another reason why $\varnothing$ needs to be treated with care is because it is *generic*, i.e., stands for 'similar objects of different types'. In full form, we should write

- $\varnothing\,[\,\mathbb{Z}\,]$ for the empty set of integers
- $\varnothing\,[\,\text{VAN}\,]$ for the empty set of vans
- $\varnothing\,[\,\mathbb{P}\, \texttt{Gender}\,]$ for the empty set of $\mathbb{P}\, \texttt{Gender}$ sets

and so on. Whenever a generic construct is applied, we must be able to work out which actual object is intended in that particular instance. Usually, the syntactic context in which the generic construct is applied is enough to determine this information, but where this is not the case, we must provide the necessary type information in square brackets as illustrated. Nearly all our usages of $\varnothing$ will be 'context sensitive' as regards type, and so writing $\varnothing$ on its own will be sufficient.

From the examples so far, we can generalize as follows. For any set S, the empty set $\varnothing$ and S are members of $\mathbb{P}\, S$. If S's elements are members of type τ, then $\varnothing$, S and every other member of $\mathbb{P}\, S$ are sets of type $\mathbb{P}\, \tau$. For example, the following sets are all members of $\mathbb{P}\, \mathbb{N}$; so each is of type $\mathbb{P}\, \mathbb{Z}$ since the members of $\mathbb{N}$ are of type $\mathbb{Z}$:

$\{\, \texttt{bottomYr} * \texttt{bottomYr} - 1\, \}$
$0\,..\,9999$
$\{1, 2, 4, 8, 16, 32, 64, 128, 256, 512, 1024\,\}$

Moreover, since every set constructed from values of type τ is of type $\mathbb{P}\, \tau$, this must apply to the specific set denoted by τ itself. Hence,

- $\mathbb{Z}$ as a *value* is a set of *type* $\mathbb{P}\, \mathbb{Z}$
- CUSTOMER as a *value* is a set of *type* $\mathbb{P}\, \text{CUSTOMER}$
- Colour as a *value* is a set of *type* $\mathbb{P}\, \texttt{Colour}$

etc.

Furthermore,

- VAN as a *value* is a set of *type* $\mathbb{P}$ VAN
- $\mathbb{P}$ VAN as a *value* is a set of *type* $\mathbb{P}$ ($\mathbb{P}$ VAN)
- $\mathbb{P}$ ($\mathbb{P}$ VAN) as a *value* is a set of *type* $\mathbb{P}$ ($\mathbb{P}$ ($\mathbb{P}$ VAN))

etc.

All this sounds less curious only when you have fully assimilated sets, types, and the powerset operator. Note that if we drew a diagram depicting, say, the sets S, $\mathbb{P}$ S and $\mathbb{P}$ ($\mathbb{P}$ S), none of the three spaces would overlap or contain each other. If they did, we would be asserting that there exist certain elements common to the sets involved, but this is impossible since the members of S, $\mathbb{P}$ S and $\mathbb{P}$ ($\mathbb{P}$ S) are quite different in type.

INFINITE AND FINITE SETS

Informally, a set S is *finite* if its members can be counted to give its size as a natural number. If S has (in)finitely many members, then so correspondingly does $\mathbb{P}$ S. Where S is infinite, some members of $\mathbb{P}$ S will themselves be infinite. The fact that a subset of an infinite set can itself be infinite should come as no surprise; after all, $\mathbb{N}$ is a subset of $\mathbb{Z}$, for example.

In specification work, we occasionally need to be explicit about the fact that certain sets are finite. One way to do this is to use $\mathbb{F}$ instead of $\mathbb{P}$ in declarations. $\mathbb{F}$ S means 'the set of all *finite* subsets of S'. For example:

```
finSetOfInt : F ℤ
```

Note that if S is infinite, then so is $\mathbb{F}$ S, even though each member of $\mathbb{F}$ S is itself finite (*remark:* infinity is a strange concept!). On the other hand, if S is finite, then $\mathbb{P}$ S and $\mathbb{F}$ S are terms denoting identical sets and it does not matter which we use. However, it must be remembered that, in general, $\mathbb{P}$ S and $\mathbb{F}$ S are *not* the same. Only $\mathbb{P}$ constructs *types*; $\mathbb{F}$ is just a useful extra operator embodying an additional constraint.

There is no 'golden rule' about when to use $\mathbb{P}$ and when to use $\mathbb{F}$ in declarations. For constructing abstract descriptions, $\mathbb{P}$ generally suffices. Sometimes, however, imposing a finiteness constraint of some kind is necessary. The necessity could be mathematically based, for example when dealing with objects like sequences (see Section 7.3); or it could be imposed by development considerations, such as designing program data structures to implement an abstract state model. Even then, explicit use of the constructor $\mathbb{F}$ might not be necessary. Sometimes, finiteness can be inferred from the various predicates in which a set variable is involved. As a trivial but quite common example of this, suppose we declare

```
setOfInt : P ℤ
```

and attach the predicate

```
#setOfInt ≤ maxSize
```
(5.2)

The prefix operator # calculates the size of a *finite* set. So (5.2) fixes `setOfInt` to be no more than `maxSize` elements big. Axiomatically, (5.2) can hold only if `setOfInt` is finite, even though we have used $\mathbb{P}$ in its declaration.

The four components so far included in the `VanHire` schema all happen to be sets, each modelling a binary relation, and all are declared using $\mathbb{P}$. In practice, of course, no actual van hiring business could be 'infinitely large'. But worrying about real-world finiteness and imposing upper limits on the sizes of various sets in the Van Hire specification would be an unnecessary distraction in this case study; so these considerations will not figure in our state model.

EXERCISE 5.6

1. Where possible, give the type of, or otherwise comment on, the following:

   a. $\{\}$ b. $\{0,0\}$ c. $\{\{0,0\},0\}$ d. $\{\{0,0\},\{0,0\}\}$

2. a. Give a more succinct term for: $\{\{1\},\varnothing,\{1,0\},\{0\}\}$
   b. What is the type of:
      i. $\varnothing$ in (a)?   ii. the overall set in (a)?
   c. Complete the following declaration: $\mathbb{N},\mathbb{N}_1 : \ldots$

3. Consider the following types:

   $$\text{VanClass,} \quad \mathbb{P}\,\text{VanClass,} \quad \mathbb{P}(\mathbb{P}\,\text{VanClass})$$

   Pair each term below with one of these types where possible, otherwise give an appropriate comment:

   a. $\varnothing\,[\,\text{VanClass}\,]$ b. $\{\,\text{light}\,\}$ c. $\{\varnothing,\{\,\text{light}\,\}\}$ d. $\{\{\,\text{light}\,\}\}$
   e. light f. $\{\varnothing,\{\{\,\text{light}\,\}\}\}$ g. $\{\varnothing\}$ h. $\{\,\text{light},\varnothing\,\}$

4. Complete the definition by extension of $\mathbb{P}(\mathbb{P}\,\text{Gender})$ started on page 97.

5. Suppose U is the set $\{1\}$. In each of the following declarations, give all possible values the variable could denote:

   $$s : \{1\}; \ u : U; \ su : \mathbb{P}U$$
   $$ssu : \mathbb{P}(\mathbb{P}U); \ sssu : \mathbb{P}(\mathbb{P}(\mathbb{P}\{1\}))$$

Cartesian Product Construction

The operator $\mathbb{P}$ enables us to construct and describe unordered collections of objects of the same type. Another fundamental requirement is to be able to construct and describe combinations of possibly different types of object. As we first saw in Section 4.4 and subsequently have seen in the outline VanHire schema, mixed-type combinations are handled via the *cartesian product* operator $\times$. Like $\mathbb{P}$, the symbol $\times$ is another type constructor.

In general, the expression $X \times Y$ defines the set of all *ordered pairs* (x,y) such that x is a member of set X and y is a member of set Y. As a simple illustration:

$$(0..1) \times \text{Gender} = \{(0,\text{male}),(0,\text{female}),(1,\text{male}),(1,\text{female})\}$$
$$\text{Gender} \times (0..1) = \{(\text{male},0),(\text{female},0),(\text{male},1),(\text{female},1)\}$$

Clearly, $X \times Y \neq Y \times X$ unless X and Y are the same set. As a reminder from Section 4.4, cartesian product construction can be defined over n *co-ordinates* thus:

$$X_1 \times X_2 \times \ldots X_n \tag{5.3}$$

which is the set of *n-tuples* $(x_1, \ldots x_n)$, where (for all i) the co-ordinate x_i in each n-tuple is a member of X_i. Further, if the members of X_i are of type τ_i, then each member of (5.3) is an n-tuple of type

$$\tau_1 \times \tau_2 \times \ldots \tau_n$$

and (5.3) itself must therefore construct a set of type

$$\mathbb{P}\,(\,\tau_1 \times \tau_2 \times \ ... \ \tau_n\,) \tag{5.4}$$

As we have seen, n-ary relations where n ≥ 2 have types with the structure of (5.4). This is because such a relation is modelled as a set (the $\mathbb{P}$ part), where each member is a tuple of dimension n (the $\tau_1 \times \tau_2 \times \ ... \ \tau_n$ part).

We must be careful with parentheses and tuples. Recapping from Section 4.4, empty tuples ( ) are illegal, and 'uni-tuples' do not exist. If we write (x), say, this is just the same as writing x on its own (ignoring the possible need for parentheses to override operator priorities, etc.). In addition, consider the following expressions:

$$A \times B \times C \qquad (A \times B) \times C \qquad A \times (B \times C)$$

The first denotes the set of triples (a , b , c); the second denotes the set of ordered pairs ((a , b) , c) where the first co-ordinate is also an ordered pair; the third also denotes a set of ordered pairs but with the structure (a , (b , c)), i.e., the second co-ordinate is an ordered pair. This non-associative behaviour of × is necessary to permit arbitrarily nested tuple structures, though it is not what we would expect by simple analogy to, say, numerical multiplication.

The importance of the operators × and $\mathbb{P}$ cannot be over-emphasized. × and $\mathbb{P}$ can be arbitrarily combined to yield objects with internal structures of any required complexity. As we have seen, when we apply × and $\mathbb{P}$, their arguments do not have to be types but can be any sets. However, we must be careful to remember what the underlying types actually are, especially if normalization (see page 30) is an issue. As subsequent chapters will show, by using these two operators and adding appropriate restrictions, a variety of mathematical objects more specialized than relations can be constructed that are extremely useful in specifying discrete systems.

EXERCISE 5.7

1. (See also Exercise 5.5(1) on page 95.)
   Describe an adequate way of modelling the integers $0\,..\,7$ in binary.

2. Give the type of, or otherwise comment on, each of the following:

   (0); { (1)}; ({ 1 }); (0 , { 1 }); { 0 , (1)}; ({ 0 }, { 1 })
   { 0 , (0 , 1)}; { (0 , 0) , (1 , 1)}; { { 0 } , (1 , 1)}; ({ 0 } , (1 , 1))
   ((0 , 0) , (1 , 1)); { (0 , { 1 }, (0 , 0) , { 0 , 1 })}

3. § The answer is discussed in Section 5.5.
   Find further potential uses for × and $\mathbb{P}$ in the Van Hire case study.

PROJECTION
The following two schemas illustrate what seems to be a potential dilemma:

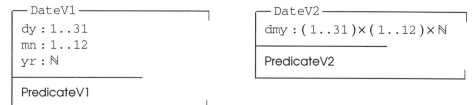

Which is the preferable state model of a date? Do we have separate state variables or utilize more complex cartesian product types? The answer is that we should always construct a specification in a way that is judged to provide the clearest exposition of what the specification is supposed to be describing. As a general guideline, if the state of component x potentially varies over the lifespan of a system, we should see x declared as a variable in some schema. This argues for `DateV1` if the three date components can separately vary, as they do in Digital Watch. The cartesian product model would be more suitable where a date, once entered into a system, does not suffer changes to its individual components, i.e., state changes occur only to *whole* dates.

If we choose the `DateV2` model, there is the problem of how to construct its predicate. In a loose sense, a predicate 'equivalent' to `PredicateV1` is needed, but to express it, we need to access the individual components of dmy. How? The answer is by using what are called *projection functions*. A projection function takes an n-tuple of some particular type and 'projects out' a specific component of it. For ordered pairs, Z provides two generic projection functions called `first` and `second`. Thus, if p is the ordered pair (x, y), `first(p)` gives x, and `second(p)` gives y. The names of these two functions are indicative of the more general fact that tuple component selection is essentially an accessing operation *by position*.

For cartesian product types with more than two co-ordinates, specific projection functions must be defined—there is no built-in `third`, `fourth`, etc. This is required even if we wish to access only the first and/or second components of an n-tuple where n > 2; the functions `first` and `second` are *for ordered pairs only*. In Chapter 7, we see how to define our own projection functions. For date triples in schema `DateV2` above, we can imagine that we have defined the following (d is assumed to be constrained to the set (1..31) × (1..12) × $\mathbb{N}$):

- `dayOf( d )` gives a positive integer in the range 1..31
- `monthOf( d )` gives a positive integer in the range 1..12
- `yearOf( d )` gives a natural number.

Using terms like these, the predicate of `DateV2` can be constructed. In the `VanHire` schema, all tuple structures are binary, so `first` and `second` would be sufficient unless we wanted projection functions with more 'meaningful names' for particular types of binary relation.

Remark
Something strongly resembling projection comes 'for free' with the third type-structuring mechanism discussed in Section 7.2, which involves the use of schemas. That reason alone, though possibly others too, might easily tip the balance in favour `DateV1`.

Constructing Sets by Comprehension

Specification *by comprehension* is a general method of constructing sets whether finite or infinite. The method involves giving an exact characterization, via terms and/or predicates, of the elements we wish a set to consist of. There are three related ways of doing this in Z. In the following, P(x) stands for some predicate and E(x) for some term in which the variable x is freely involved.

SET COMPREHENSION USING PREDICATES

The first variation of the technique uses schema-text syntax. Consider

$$x : X \mid P(x)$$

This means that x is an element drawn from set X which satisfies the constraint P. If we simply enclose this syntax in curly brackets:

$$\{x : X \mid P(x)\}$$

then this means 'the set of *all* elements x drawn from the set X which satisfy P' (note that x is now a local variable to the set comprehension). Here are some examples. The latter two involve using `VanHire` schema variables in declarations. There is nothing special about this. If a variable is a set, then it can be used in a declaration. Remember that what can follow the ' : ' in declarations is any legal set expression.

a. $\{n : \mathbb{N} \mid n \bmod 2 = 0\}$
b. $\{k : \mathbb{N} \mid \mathrm{lwb} \leq k \leq \mathrm{upb} \wedge \mathrm{prime}(k)\}$
c. $\{c : \mathrm{CUSTOMER} \mid (\exists \, \mathrm{cbPr} : \mathrm{custom} \bullet c = \mathrm{first}(\mathrm{cbPr}))\}$
d. $\{v : \mathrm{VAN} \mid (\exists \, \mathrm{vcPr} : \mathrm{fleet} \bullet \mathrm{vcPr} = (v, \mathrm{mini}))\}$

Informally:

- the natural numbers which are even
- the natural numbers between lwb and upb inclusive which are prime
- the customers who currently have a booking with the garage
- the mini vans in the fleet.

The role of $\exists$ in examples (c) and (d) is worth noting. In effect, $\exists$ is being used to introduce a further 'local variable' so that the required constraint in the set comprehension can be constructed. For example, with the third set, we have to say in effect

$$\{c : \mathrm{CUSTOMER} \mid \text{there is a customer-booking pair with } c \text{ as the customer}\}$$

Remember that the given set $\mathrm{CUSTOMER}$ identifies *all possible* customer entities, and in set comprehension (c) we are interested in only a particular subset of these (those with bookings).

Set comprehensions are not limited to single variables. For example:

e. $\{n, m : \mathbb{Z} \mid (\exists k : \mathbb{N} \bullet n = m + k)\}$
f. $\{a, b, c : \mathbb{N}_1 \mid a + b > c \wedge b + c > a \wedge c + a > b\}$

Each set constructed comprises those tuples, derived from the *characteristic tuple* of the declarations, which obey the constraint. For (e) and (f), these sets are respectively:

- the integer pairs (n, m) such that n is at least as big as m
- the positive integer triples (a, b, c) such that the sum of any two exceeds the third.

Determining the characteristic tuple in examples like these is quite straightforward—if the declaration part is $x_1 : X_1; \ldots x_n : X_n$, then the characteristic tuple will be $(x_1, \ldots x_n)$. However, schema references are allowed to occur in the declaration part of *any* construct; i.e., schema referencing is not just a feature limited to schemas themselves. So schema references can appear in set comprehensions. When they do, the situation is potentially more involved. Consider this example which involves schema `Date` from the Digital Watch specification:

$$\{\mathrm{Date} \mid \mathrm{leapYr}(\mathrm{yr}) \wedge 1900 \leq \mathrm{yr} \leq 1999 \wedge \mathrm{mn} = 2\}$$

Contrary to what might first be expected, this does *not* in fact construct a set of date triples (dy , mn , yr) representing February dates in twentieth century leap years. This is because of the way in which schema references contribute to characteristic tuples, which is not discussed until Section 7.2. Till then, we will avoid examples like this.

SET COMPREHENSION USING TERMS

A second variation of set comprehension has the syntax

$$\{ x : X \bullet E(x) \}$$

where E is a term rather than a predicate. This form means 'the set of all elements calculated by E(x) where x is drawn from the set X'. Note thus that the set's type is derived from the type of E(x), not x. Whereas the predicate P in the schema-text form acts like a 'filter', the term E(x) in this form acts like a 'generator', calculating all the members of the set to be constructed. Here are some examples, of which (g) and (h) merely respecify respectively the two sets defined earlier in (a) and (c):

g. $\{ n : \mathbb{N} \bullet 2 * n \}$ — alternative to (a)
h. $\{ cbPr : custom \bullet first(cbPr) \}$ — alternative to (c)
i. $\{ a, b, c : \mathbb{N}_1 \bullet ((a, b, c), a + b + c) \}$

As can be seen, use of terms can result in more elegant set comprehension expressions. Example (i) constructs all pairs of positive integer triples and their sums.

SET COMPREHENSION USING PREDICATES AND TERMS

The most general form of set comprehension is a combination of the previous two:

$$\{ x : X \mid P(x) \bullet E(x) \}$$

This means 'the set of values calculated by E(x), where x is drawn from the set X and satisfies P(x)'. Here are some of the previous sets respecified using this form:

j. $\{ k : \mathbb{N} \mid lwb \leq k \leq upb \wedge prime(k) \bullet k \}$ — alternative to (b)
k. $\{ vcPr : fleet \mid second(vcPr) = mini \bullet first(vcPr) \}$ — alternative to (d)
l. $\{ n, m : \mathbb{Z} \mid (\exists k : \mathbb{N} \bullet m + k = n) \bullet (n, m) \}$ — alternative to (e)

In examples (j) and (l), the term which constructs the set is just the characteristic tuple made explicit (the characteristic tuple of a singleton variable declaration is just the variable itself). None of these examples really benefits from using the full form; but consider this:

m. $\{ a, b, c : \mathbb{N}_1 \mid a * a + b * b = c * c \bullet a * b \, div \, 2 \}$

This set constructs the areas of all right-angled triangles with integer sides. The reader should try writing this using just the schema-text form of set comprehension (see next exercise).

We can now see that the following 'template equalities' hold:

$$\{ \, Decs \mid Pred \, \} = \{ \, Decs \mid Pred \bullet CharacteristicTupleOfDecs \, \}$$
$$\{ \, Decs \bullet Term \, \} = \{ \, Decs \mid true \bullet Term \, \}$$

In practice, having just the schema-text form of set comprehension would be sufficient, since it is always possible to construct a predicate, no matter how inelegant, to characterize a set's members. Given this rich syntax for set comprehension, in any given instance we generally choose the form that is judged to win on elegance and simplicity.

EXERCISE 5.8

1. Specify the 'set of the squares (0, 1, 4, 9, 16, etc.) of the natural numbers' by each of the three comprehension methods.

2. Specify each of the following sets by comprehension using the most appropriate method:

   a. { mini, transit, light }   — see page 92
   b. the empty set of integers
   c. the pairs (x, y) for which x is a natural number and y is its square
   d. the VanHire customers who have made bookings reserving heavy-duty vans
   e. the triples representing the lengths of the sides of all right-angled triangles (*Note*: for positive integers n and m, the terms $n^2 - m^2$, 2mn and $n^2 + m^2$ give the sides of a right-angled triangle).

3. a. Consider example (l) in the set comprehensions in the text. Give an alternative name for this set (*Hint*: see Section 4.4)
   b. Give a simpler expression for the set { i, j : $\mathbb{Z}$ | i ≤ j • i * j }
   c. Give a simpler expression for the set
      { v : VAN; vc : VanClass |
         (∃ vcPr : fleet • v = first(vcPr) ∧ vc = second(vcPr)) }
   d. Specify by extension the set { a : $\mathbb{Z}$ | 1 ≤ a * a ≤ 20 • a - 1 }
   e. Express example (m) in the text using the purely schema-text form of set comprehension.

5.4   MORE ON SETS

Any particular set will be of type $\mathbb{P}\ \tau$, for some type τ. If we regard the τ as arbitrary, rather like a parameter, then we can treat $\mathbb{P}\ \tau$ as a generic type and derive a single 'theory' of sets based on the constants, relations and functions associated with $\mathbb{P}\ \tau$. This theory, a collection of generalized laws, will provide us with useful and interesting properties that sets exhibit. Since there is only one constant of type $\mathbb{P}\ \tau$, namely the empty set $\varnothing\ [\ \tau\ ]$, which we have already covered, we will concentrate on the main set relations and functions, and then overview their properties.

Throughout this section we will use the Greek letter τ to emphasize that τ stands for an arbitrary type. Of course, we cannot use Greek letters in this way when constructing actual descriptions in Z.

Set Relations

To assert that some element is (not) a member of some set, we have the binary relations

   _ ∈ _   'is a member of'
   _ ∉ _   'is not a member of'

where x ∉ s is equivalent to ¬ (x ∈ s). Thus, the following three propositions are true:

   3 ∈ { x : $\mathbb{N}$ | x mod 2 ≠ 0 }
   0 ∉ $\mathbb{N}_1$
   ¬ (0 ∈ $\mathbb{N}_1$)

On the other hand

$3 \notin \text{VanClass}$

is ill-typed, even though intuitively it must be true (3 certainly is not a member of
VanClass). Care must always be taken with generic relations and functions to make
sure that their arguments are type-consistent. In the case of $\in$ or $\notin$, if the left argument
is of type τ, the right argument must be of type $\mathbb{P}\,\tau$. Thus, $\in$ and $\notin$ are binary relations
of type $\mathbb{P}\,(\,\tau \times \mathbb{P}\,\tau\,)$.

Obviously, we have the universal relations $=$ and $\neq$. Two sets are one and the same
set if and only if they contain precisely the same members. This is not difficult to
express formally. Let a and b be sets of type $\mathbb{P}\,\tau$; then

$$a = b \;\Leftrightarrow\; (\,\forall\, e : \tau \bullet e \in a \Leftrightarrow e \in b\,)$$

So, for example,

$\{\,x : \mathbb{N} \mid x < x\,\} = \varnothing$ is true
$\{\,a, b\,\} \neq \{\,a, b, b, a\,\}$ is false

Two important relations are

$\_\subseteq\_$ 'is a subset of'
$\_\subset\_$ 'is a *strict* subset of'

Informally, for any sets a and b be of type $\mathbb{P}\,\tau$, $a \subseteq b$ if and only if every member of a is
also a member of b. $a \subset b$ holds if and only if every member of a is also a member of b
but b also contains elements that are not in a. Thus, $\subseteq$ is a *weaker* relation than $\subset$. One
relation $\rho 1$ is weaker (stronger) than another $\rho 2$ of the same type if the space defining
when $\rho 1$ ($\rho 2$) is true wholly contains the space defining when $\rho 2$ ($\rho 1$) is true.

Two or more sets are *disjoint* if no two of them have any elements in common. If we
wish to assert that sets $s_1, \ldots s_n$ ($n \geq 2$) are disjoint, we can use the unary relation
disjoint thus:

$$\text{disjoint}\,\langle\, s_1, \ldots s_n\,\rangle \tag{5.5}$$

The angle-bracketed construct is actually a sequence, for which see Section 7.3. Again,
we must take care with types. For example, it is true that at a 'meta' level sets such as
VAN and CUSTOMER are disjoint; but we *cannot* express this fact by writing

$$\text{disjoint}\,\langle\, \text{VAN}, \text{CUSTOMER}\,\rangle$$

since the s_i in (5.5) must all be sets of the same type.

As a more substantial illustration of the set relations discussed, consider the following axiomatic definition of a tertiary relation isTri, where isTri holds for the triple
of positive integers (x_1, x_2, x_3) if and only if the triple is capable of forming the sides
of a triangle:

> isTri : $\mathbb{P}\,(\,\mathbb{N}_1 \times \mathbb{N}_1 \times \mathbb{N}_1\,)$
> ───────────────────
> $\forall\, a, b, c : \mathbb{N}_1 \bullet$
> $(\,a, b, c\,) \in \text{isTri} \;\Leftrightarrow\; a + b > c \land b + c > a \land c + a > b$

The following are true propositions involving isTri:

$isTri \in \mathbb{P}(\mathbb{Z} \times \mathbb{Z} \times \mathbb{Z})$
$isTri \subseteq \mathbb{Z} \times \mathbb{Z} \times \mathbb{Z}$
$(5, 12, 13) \in isTri$
$disjoint \langle \{(-2, -1, 4), (0, 0, 0), (2, 4, 6)\}, isTri \rangle$
$\forall i : \mathbb{N}_1 \bullet (i, i, i) \notin isTri$
$\{i : \mathbb{Z} \mid i > 1 \bullet (i, i + 1, i + 2)\} \subset isTri$
$isTri = \{a, b, c : \mathbb{N}_1 \mid a + b > c \wedge b + c > a \wedge c + a > b\}$

In fact, we could have written this last equality as the defining axiom for $isTri$. By defining a relation directly in terms of the space of elements for which it is true, we sidestep the $\forall / \Leftrightarrow$ technique typified by the definition of $isTri$ actually given.

There is a trade-off between declaring the relation as $isTri$ as opposed to $isTri\_$. Choosing the latter, we could keep $isTri$'s definition and the examples as they stand, provided we replaced each instance of $isTri$ by $(isTri\_)$. For example:

$(isTri\_) \in \mathbb{P}(\mathbb{Z} \times \mathbb{Z} \times \mathbb{Z})$

Note the need to parenthesize names of prefix or infix symbols when used as (set) objects in their own right. This is a slight disadvantage as it leads to somewhat inelegant expressions. On the other hand, the gain with making $isTri$ prefix is that we could, if we wished, exploit this feature by rewriting $isTri$'s definition and the third and fifth examples above as follows:

$$\mid \quad \text{... ... ...}$$
$$isTri(a, b, c) \Leftrightarrow a + b > c \wedge b + c > a \wedge c + a > b$$

$isTri(5, 12, 13)$
$\forall i : \mathbb{N}_1 \bullet \neg isTri(i, i, i)$

The syntax is now more pleasing. So, the answer to the question 'what syntax should we give a relation like $isTri$?' simply depends on how we intend to use it. If most of our usage is going to treat $isTri$ overtly as a set, writing predicates like the above examples, then our choice would tend to be as on the previous page. If, however, $isTri$ is to be used mainly as a predicate symbol asserting a certain property (triangle-ness) over positive integer triples, then the choice of prefix syntax is clearly superior.

Related to this discussion is a convention concerning the declaration and use of binary relations. If a binary relation abr is declared as

$abr : \mathbb{P}(X \times Y)$

then, despite the omission of surrounding underscore markers, we can still use abr as an infix name providing we underline it, as in

$x \ \underline{abr} \ y$

This is a useful convention, enabling us to enjoy the best of both syntaxes—infix and set membership assertion—without having any underscore markers in names. It works particularly well in schemas where we want to use a binary relation variable both in its capacity as a set and as an infix predicate symbol. We could use the underline convention for all the current variables of $VanHire$, though some name changing (back to something like those in Figure 5.2, page 84) would be warranted to improve readability; obviously (for $v \in VAN$, $vc \in VanClass$)

$v \ \underline{isin} \ vc$ \qquad reads better than \qquad $v \ \underline{fleet} \ vc$

So the choice of names for the binary relation variables in the `VanHire` schema has been somewhat pre-emptive.

EXERCISE 5.9

1. Express the relationship between $\mathbb{Z}$, $\mathbb{N}$ and $\mathbb{N}_1$ as a single predicate.

2. Give the truth value of, or else comment upon, the following predicates:

   a. $\neg\,(\emptyset \subset \{\,1,4,9,16\,\})$ b. $\emptyset \notin \mathbb{P}\,\{\,1,4,9,16\,\}$
   c. $s \in \mathbb{P}\,T \;\Leftrightarrow\; s \subseteq T$ d. $100 \in \mathbb{P}\,\{\,1,4,9,16\,\}$
   e. $\forall s : \mathbb{P}\,T \bullet \texttt{disjoint}\,\langle\,s,\emptyset\,\rangle$ f. $\mathbb{F}\,T \subset \mathbb{P}\,T$

3. Complete the axiomatic description of type `VanClass` sketched on page 92.

4. A set of sets `ptn` is said to be a *partition* of another set `s` of type $\mathbb{P}\,T$ if and only if
   - every member of `ptn` is non-empty
   - each pair of members of `ptn` is disjoint
   - every element of `s` is located in some member of `ptn`
   - no member of `ptn` contains elements not in `s`.

   e.g. $\{\,\{\,1\,\},\{\,2,3,5,7\,\},\{\,4,6,8,9,10\,\}\,\}$ is one possible partition of $1\,.\,.\,10$.

   Write down `ptn`'s declaration and a predicate that constrains `ptn` to be a partition of `s`.

5. With reference to the variables of the `VanHire` schema, formalize the following predicates. Assume that `vansHireable` is a set of type $\mathbb{P}$ VAN.

   a. The vans `vansHireable` are part of the fleet
   b. The bookings referenced in `custom` are all different
   c. The bookings recorded in `custom` and `commit` are the same bookings
   d. None of the `vansHireable` vans is on hire to anyone.

6. Consider the true statements about relation `isTri` given in the text. Write down a structurally analogous set of true statements about the relation `_<_`. In doing so, make use of the tuples $(\,0,-1\,)$, $(\,-1,0\,)$, $(\,0,0\,)$ and $(\,1,0\,)$.

Set Operators

Figure 5.4 shows three basic set operators; the result of each is given by the shading.

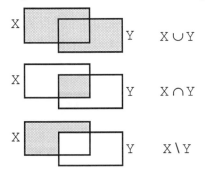

X $\cup$ Y

X $\cap$ Y

X $\setminus$ Y

Figure 5.4   Diagrammatic representation of basic set operators.

Briefly, *union* $x \cup y$ gives the 'join' of two sets; this is a set comprising precisely the elements of both, though remember that there can be no duplicated elements. *Intersection* $x \cap y$ gives a set comprising precisely the elements common to its two set arguments. *Difference* $x \setminus y$ gives a set comprising precisely those elements of the first set that are not in the second set. More formally, given x and y of type $\mathbb{P}\,\tau$, then

$$x \cup y = \{\, e : \tau \mid e \in x \vee e \in y \,\}$$
$$x \cap y = \{\, e : \tau \mid e \in x \wedge e \in y \,\}$$
$$x \setminus y = \{\, e : \tau \mid e \in x \wedge e \notin y \,\}$$

Once again, remember the necessity for type consistency of arguments.

There are generalizations of union and intersection over families of sets. Given $\mathtt{setOfSets} : \mathbb{P}\,(\mathbb{P}\,\tau)$, then

$$\bigcup \mathtt{setOfSets} = \{\, e : \tau \mid (\exists\, s : \mathtt{setOfSets} \bullet e \in s) \,\}$$
$$\bigcap \mathtt{setOfSets} = \{\, e : \tau \mid (\forall\, s : \mathtt{setOfSets} \bullet e \in s) \,\}$$

Thus, $\bigcup$ gives all elements which belong to the set members of its argument, and $\bigcap$ gives all elements which are common to every set member of its argument.

Usage of the above operators is illustrated by the following. Given the two equalities:

$$\mathtt{squares} = \{\, n : \mathbb{N} \bullet n * n \,\}$$
$$\mathtt{notSquares} = \{\, i : \mathbb{N} \mid \neg\,(\exists\, j : \mathbb{N} \bullet i = j * j) \,\}$$

then the following equalities are all true as a consequence:

$$\#\{\, n : \mathtt{squares} \mid n \leq 100 \,\} = 11$$
$$\mathtt{squares} \cup \mathbb{N} = \mathbb{N}$$
$$\mathtt{notSquares} \cup \mathtt{squares} = \mathbb{N}$$
$$\mathbb{N} \cap \mathtt{notSquares} = \mathtt{notSquares}$$
$$\mathtt{squares} \cap \mathtt{notSquares} = \varnothing$$
$$\mathbb{N} \setminus \mathtt{squares} = \mathtt{notSquares}$$
$$\bigcup \{\{0\}, \mathbb{N}_1, \{\, i : \mathbb{N}_1 \bullet -i \,\}\} = \mathbb{Z}$$
$$\bigcap \{\, \mathtt{squares}, 10..24, (1..25) \setminus \mathtt{notSquares} \,\} = \{16\}$$

Clearly, if two sets are disjoint their intersection will be $\varnothing$. This is illustrated by the fifth equality above, providing an alternative to $\mathtt{disjoint}\,\langle\, \mathtt{squares}, \mathtt{notSquares} \,\rangle$.

EXERCISE 5.10

1. Which enclosed segment in Figure 5.4 represents the set $(X \cup Y) \setminus (X \cap Y)$?

2. Suppose the sets $\mathtt{vansHireable}$, $\mathtt{vansOnHire}$ and $\mathtt{vansOffTheRoad}$, all of type $\mathbb{P}$ VAN, have the following properties: (a) they are disjoint; (b) together they comprise exactly the vans recorded in the $\mathtt{VanHire}$ component $\mathtt{fleet}$. Formalize properties (a) and (b), avoiding the $\mathtt{disjoint}$ relation for expressing (a).

3. For each of the following terms, give a single set to which it is equal:

    a. $\mathbb{N} \cup \mathbb{Z}$ b. $\mathbb{Z} \cap \mathbb{N}_1$ c. $\mathbb{N} \setminus \mathbb{N}_1$ d. $\mathbb{N}_1 \setminus \mathbb{N}$
    e. $\bigcup \{\mathbb{N}, \mathbb{Z}, \mathbb{N}_1\}$ f. $\bigcap \{\mathbb{N}, \mathbb{N}_1, \mathbb{Z}\}$

4. Give the value of each of the following terms, where

$$\text{Units} = 0..9$$

a. $\#(\text{Units} \cup (\text{Units} \setminus \mathbb{Z}))$ b. $\text{Units} \cap \{n : \mathbb{N} \bullet n * n\}$
c. $(\text{Units} \setminus \mathbb{N}) \cap \mathbb{N}_1$ d. $(\text{Units} \cap \mathbb{N}_1) \cup (\text{Units} \setminus \mathbb{N}_1)$
e. $(\text{Units} \cup \mathbb{N}_1) \setminus (\text{Units} \cap \mathbb{N}_1)$

5. § Answers are in the main text following.
Using Exercise 4.8(2) on page 65 as a guide, write down some properties which you think the operators $\cup, \cap$ and $/$ possess.

Some Laws of Set Theory

The laws of a data type theory express interesting properties that are possessed by the constants, relations and functions of the data type. As an example, some laws of the integer data type—type $\mathbb{Z}$ and its operators—were informally described in Exercise 4.8(2). Certain laws of a data type theory will be axiomatic, whilst all others can be derived by proof. (Discussion of data types occurs in Section 5.5. The distinction between 'type' and 'data type' is clarified further in Section 7.1.)

Data type laws are expressed as statements in predicate logic. They are assumed to be universally quantified over the variables that appear in them, if this is not explicitly stated; this is because the laws are describing *universal* properties of the objects to which they refer. Thus, for the laws that are listed below, you should assume that w, x and y are type-consistent set variables, i.e., all are of type $\mathbb{P}\,\tau$ for some *arbitrary* type τ, and that each law is implicitly prefixed by an appropriate universal quantification, such as '$\forall\, w,x,y : \mathbb{P}\,\tau \bullet$' for the third law below. It is usual to drop such quantification when expressing data type laws since in effect it serves only to introduce the arbitrary variables needed to express each particular law—the quantification is little more than 'formal clutter'.

Some laws of set theory involving relations:

$$x \subseteq x$$
$$\neg(x \subset x)$$
$$w \subseteq x \wedge x \subseteq y \;\Rightarrow\; w \subseteq y \qquad\qquad \text{— also for } \subset$$
$$x \subseteq y \wedge y \subseteq x \;\Leftrightarrow\; x = y$$

Properties of $\subseteq$ and $\subset$ expressed in these laws are examples of basic properties that binary relations in general can possess; further discussion of these properties occurs in Section 6.3. Note that the fourth law could be regarded as a definition of set equality.

Some laws of set theory involving operators:

$$x \cup x = x \qquad\qquad\qquad\qquad\qquad\quad \text{— also for } \cap$$
$$x \cup y = y \cup x \qquad\qquad\qquad\qquad\quad \text{— also for } \cap$$
$$w \cup (x \cup y) = (w \cup x) \cup y \qquad\quad \text{— also for } \cap$$
$$w \cup (x \cap y) = (w \cup x) \cap (w \cup y) \quad \text{— also if } \cap \text{ and } \cup \text{ are interchanged}$$
$$\#(a \cup b) = \#a + \#b - \#(a \cap b) \quad \text{— for } \textit{finite} \text{ sets only, i.e., } a, b : \mathbb{F}\,T$$
$$x \setminus x = \emptyset \setminus x = \emptyset$$
$$x \setminus \emptyset = x$$
$$(w \setminus x) \setminus y = w \setminus (x \cup y)$$
$$(x \setminus y) \cap y = \emptyset$$

In order, the first four laws state that: $\cup$ is idempotent, commutative, and associative (all of which also apply to $\cap$), and that $\cup$ distributes over $\cap$ ($\cap$ also distributes over $\cup$). The fifth law gives us a way of counting the members in the join of two finite sets. Unlike $\cup$ and $\cap$, the $\setminus$ operator is neither idempotent, nor commutative, nor associative. There are many laws like the last showing how $\setminus$ interacts with $\cup$ and $\cap$. In the next exercise, you are asked to prove this law.

On a simplistic level, the practical value of data type theories is that the two sides of an equality law provide different ways of calculating the same thing (cf. the equivalence laws of logic). Thus, if we have a law

$$\alpha = \beta$$

then whenever the syntactic pattern of α occurs anywhere in a term, it can be written instead in β's form, or vice versa. For example, if we wanted to write

$$(\, s1 \cup (\, s2 \cap s3 \,)\,) \cap (\, s1 \cup s2 \,) \tag{5.6}$$

we can actually simplify this to

$$s1 \cup (\,(\, s2 \cap s3 \,) \cap s2 \,) \tag{5.7}$$

by applying the distributive law for sets given above thus: substitute w, x and y in the law by $s1$, $(\, s2 \cap s3 \,)$, and $s2$ respectively. Doing this, the law's right-hand side becomes (5.6). So we can rewrite (5.6) in the form given by the law's left-hand side, which is (5.7). In fact, we can do even better than this—see the next exercise.

There is a much more fundamental role for data type laws than effecting minor adjustments to the elegance of expressions written in specifications. Coupled with laws of logic, they are indispensable ingredients in *reasoning* about specifications, a topic we overview in Chapter 9. A simple example of specification reasoning occurred at the end of Section 3.4. Further examples occur in Sections 8.4, 9.1 and 9.2.

> EXERCISE 5.11
> 1. Simplify (5.7) in the text, justifying each step in your simplification.
> 2. Try to prove this law for sets: $(\, x \setminus y \,) \cap y = \varnothing$
>   by making use of the definitions of $\notin$, $\cap$ and $\setminus$ given in the text, some simple laws of logic, and the following additional equivalence:
>
> $$e \in \{\, x : X \mid P(\, x \,)\} \;\Leftrightarrow\; e \in X \wedge P(\, e \,)$$
>
>   *Hint*: via a sequence of simple steps, try to rearrange the left-hand side of the equality using the suggested definitions/laws so that it becomes equal to $\varnothing$.

5.5   THE STATE MODEL ELABORATED

Some Additions and Restructuring

The state model of the Van Hire specification will be developed in two ways:

a. additional variables will be incorporated
b. the model will be split over more than one schema.

An impetus for (a) has already been aired in Section 5.2—the model needs explicit hire period information if the system is going to deal with the timing of bookings properly.

Here is another reason for (a). We cannot tell from the model as it stands which vans are *available* for hire. We need to know this to be able to describe updates on the state component `activeHires` when bookings become active, i.e., customers arrive to collect vans at the start of hire periods. We can tell which vans are definitely *not* hireable, namely those which contribute to `activeHires`. But of the rest of the fleet, only a proper subset might be hireable because some vans could be off the road for maintenance or repair. At present, there is no information content in the model that conveys which of the 'not-currently-on-hire' vans are actually hireable (or, alternatively, which are not hireable).

To some extent, (b) is a consequence of (a). Schema `VanHire` already involves four binary relations requiring a fairly complex predicate to constrain them into modelling only states consistent with the domain. By adding further variables, we are in danger of creating a schema that is 'over-busy', containing too many components to feel comfortable with 'in one go' (a pragmatic limit that has some basis in psychological studies is not to exceed more than 5–7 components). By using smaller schemas and schema inclusion, we can inject a useful degree of decomposition into the model. Especially with models more complex than that in the Van Hire specification, there may be more than one way of achieving this, and which is the best choice (if there is a 'best') may not be clear. In Digital Watch, there was an obvious, natural division of the state. In Van Hire, a sensible division is not so immediately apparent.

The decomposition we will actually apply is to base the Van Hire model on two main components:

A. a component that deals with the bookings
B. a component that deals with the garage's vans.

This division has a reasonable basis because, to a large extent, vans and bookings are separate facets of the business. If a booking is made or cancelled, say, it has no effect on the vans; similarly, if a van comes off the road for repair or is disposed of for scrap, it will have no effect on the bookings. Of course, there is some overlap between (A) and (B) as represented by the component `activeHires`, which records the vans that have been allocated to active bookings. This interaction can be dealt with when components (A) and (B) are combined.

Schema `Bookings` below deals with component (A).

```
┌─ Bookings ─────────────────────────────────────────────┐
│ custom : ℙ( CUSTOMER × BOOKING )                        │
│ commit : ℙ( BOOKING × VanClass )                        │
│ hirePeriods : ℙ( BOOKING × Period )   — hire period of each booking │
│ activeBkngs : ℙ BOOKING               — those bookings currently active │
│─────────────────────────────────────────────────────────│
│  a.  custom is a 1-to-many relation                      │
│  b.  commit is a many-to-1 relation                      │
│  c.  hirePeriods is a many-to-1 relation                 │
│  d.  Each of the first three variables handles precisely the same set of bookings │
│  e.  activeBkngs members come from those handled by any of the other variables │
│  f.  A hire period cannot exceed maxHireLen days in length │
└─────────────────────────────────────────────────────────┘
```

The individual constraints contributing to the schema predicate have been itemized for convenience. Several new names appear in `Bookings`. One of these is `maxHireLen`, referred to in constraint (f). `maxHireLen` is a global constant representing the integer 28, the maximum hire length in days the garage allows. Other new names are `Period` and the variable `hirePeriods` to whose declaration `Period` contributes. `Period` denotes the set of all possible hire periods; we deal with its definition later. `hirePeriods` typifies one simple technique for getting attribute information into a state model—we pair each instance of the entity type involved with the value of the attribute in question, using a suitable set (here `Period`) to describe the 'value space' of the attribute.

The other new name in `Bookings` is `activeBkngs`. What we are trying to do is capture everything relevant about bookings in the `Bookings` schema without reference to van entities. The first three variables cannot tell us which bookings are active, so we define another variable which has this role. The declaration of `activeBkngs` in effect says 'let this set be those bookings that are active'. The role of `activeBkngs`, like `hirePeriods`, is to make attribute information manifest in the model, though in a different way to `hirePeriods`. Suppose `ENTITY` is a class of entity with an attribute `attr`. Suppose also that a state model needs to identify those instances of `ENTITY` that possess the same particular value for `attr`. Then we include in the model

   `entSet : ℙ ENTITY`

which 'by definition' stands for those `ENTITY` instances with the particular value of `attr` in question. The incorporation of `activeBkngs` adopts this approach.

The following predicate insists that if two pairs in `custom` have the same booking, they must also have the same customer:

   ∀ cbPr1 , cbPr2 : custom •
       second(cbPr1) = second(cbPr2) ⇒
                       first(cbPr1) = first(cbPr2)

In fact, this is sufficient to formalize constraint (a)—it rules out `custom` being many-to-many. Constraints (b) and (c) are similar. The necessity for (a), (b) and (c) was explained in Section 5.2. Constraint (d) is also essential to ensure integrity of the model. Without it, the declarations of `custom`, `commit` and `hirePeriods` could satisfy constraints (a), (b) and (c) respectively, but otherwise the bookings that contribute to each variable need not necessarily exhibit any particular relationship. In the domain, a booking establishes a hire period and reserves one van of the requested class, as well as identifying a customer. Hence the need for (d). Remember that there is only so much constraint-wise that can be captured in declarations alone.

With the presence of `activeBkngs`, constraint (e) is clearly essential for model integrity, for otherwise `activeBkngs` could comprise *any* members of the given set `BOOKING`. Constraints like (e) are quite different to constraint (f). The latter arises because it corresponds to a requirement imposed by the domain. In contrast, (e) results from the internal structure of the mathematical model itself. If (f) was removed, `Bookings` would still meaningfully model a van booking/hiring domain, but one where there was no hire length limit in operation. Remove (e), however, and the model loses its integrity *given the intended meaning of* `activeBkngs`.

The second contributory schema to the full state model displays some features in common with `Bookings`. The need for the constraints included should now be reasonably clear.

```
┌─ Vans ──────────────────────────────────────────────────────────────────┐
│ fleet : ℙ ( VAN × VanClass )                                             │
│ vansOnHire : ℙ VAN            — those vans currently hired out to customers │
│ vansHireable : ℙ VAN          — those vans which can be allocated to customers │
├──────────────────────────                                                │
│ g.  fleet is a many-to-1 relation                                        │
│ h.  vansOnHire and vansHireable are vans in the fleet                    │
│ i.  vansOnHire and vansHireable share no vans in common                  │
└──────────────────────────────────────────────────────────────────────────┘
```

The two new variables are of the same general nature as `activeBkngs` in `Bookings`, i.e., each is an 'entities with the same particular value for a certain attribute' variable. The attribute involved happens to be the same for both variables, namely a van's availability-for-hire status.

Instead of `vansOnHire` and `vansHireable`, we could adopt the approach used for `hirePeriods` in `Bookings`. To do this, we would need a set for the value space of the attribute, which in this case would probably be a free type, say:

```
VanStatus ::= offTheRoad | onHire | free
```

A binary relation could now be introduced into the model to record which entities have which value for the attribute in question. The `Vans` schema would become:

```
┌─Vans1──────────────────────────────────────────────────────────────────┐
│ fleet : ℙ ( VAN × VanClass )                                            │
│ vanAvlblty : ℙ ( VAN × VanStatus )         — availability of each van   │
├──────────────────────────                                               │
│ Predicate                                                               │
└─────────────────────────────────────────────────────────────────────────┘
```

The predicate that would be needed is left as an exercise. The 'information content' of `Vans` is now captured in a different way in `Vans1`; this is also dealt with in the next exercise. As to which approach is superior, there is no definitive answer. For a given specification task, the answer might become apparent—in terms of, say, improved clarity, elegance, etc.—only after some experimentation. Formal specifications are subject to just as much trial and error, backup, and reworking as any other artifact of the software development process.

Finally, we construct the full model as shown on the next page. In bringing together the submodels for bookings and vans, the fourth main binary relation `activeHires` derived from the conceptual data model at last plays its role. The extra variable `today` adds some necessary icing to the cake; as with `Period`, the set `Date` will be dealt with shortly. The necessity for the inclusion of `today` is connected with component `hirePeriods` in `Bookings`. Without reference to the current date, we could not tell which hire periods are current, which are to start in the future, etc. (this presupposes some connection between `Date` and `Period`, to be revealed shortly). The need for constraint (m) should be obvious. Constraint (n) is now a natural consequence of `today`'s inclusion and appropriately strengthens in the model the idea of what is 'active'. The 'nominal' mentioned in constraint (o) refers to the assumption that there are no late vans to be returned or vans off the road. In other words, these two possibilities in the real world are ignored for the purposes of expressing (o).

```
┌─VanHire──────────────────────────────────────────────────────┐
│ Bookings                                                      │
│ Vans                                                          │
│ activeHires : ℙ ( BOOKING × VAN )                            │
│ today : Date                                   — today's date │
├──────────────────────────────────────────────────────────────┤
│ j.   activeHires is a 1-to-1 relation                        │
│ k.   activeBkngs from Bookings is precisely the bookings in activeHires │
│ l.   vansOnHire from Vans is precisely the vans in activeHires │
│ m.   Every van on hire must match the class requested in the corresponding booking │
│ n.   Every active booking cannot have a hire period starting later than today │
│ o.   There is no nominal overbooking                          │
└──────────────────────────────────────────────────────────────┘
```

A final observation on the state model is that variables `activeBkngs` and `vansOnHire` are not strictly necessary, for reasons you are asked to determine in the next exercise. That is, they are redundant, or *derived*, and could be removed (the exercise below also asks you to examine this). Via variable `activeHires`, they also slightly increase the coupling between schemas `Bookings` and `Vans`. Whether variables such as `activeBkngs` and `vansOnHire` should be included in a state model is, however, a matter of judgement concerning clarity, purpose, etc., and has nothing to do with 'correctness'. Part of the philosophy attached to using Z is that abstract specifications should be constructed to be readable and understandable, even if this is at the expense of, say, optimality, i.e., using the minimum of components to construct an adequate description. Often, one model is no 'better' than another; they just reflect different sets of compromises the specifier has made. Redundancy is acceptable and even encouraged if a specifier judges it to achieve a desirable balance of features in a specification. This does not mean that any such redundancy should be mirrored in the implementation. An abstract specification is a *what* document constructed for its mathematical elegance, etc.; it is not a software engineer's '*how* to build the implementation' blueprint.

EXERCISE 5.12

1. Work out and informally express the predicate for schema `Vans1` in the text.

2. Explain how schemas `Vans` and `Vans1` convey the same information content.

3. Explain why variables `activeBkngs` in schema `Bookings` and `vansOnHire` in schema `Vans` are redundant (derived).

4. Describe all the changes that would have to be made throughout the `VanHire` state model if variables `activeBkngs` and `vansOnHire` were removed.

Data Types

We are left with `Period` and `Date` to consider. Clearly, they have to be global sets; but should they be declared as given sets or what? Introducing `Period` as a given set would be a poor choice for the reason that it is natural to model a hire period as a pair of dates. If `Date` is available, this is easy—we can simply define `Period` as a set of `Date` pairs, with one restriction: it is intuitive and reasonable to insist that the first date of a pair is the start date of the hire period and the second is the end date. Whilst this constraint will make life easier, to express it requires an appropriate ordering relation for `Date` values. Suppose we have:

$$
\begin{array}{|l}
\_ \, \texttt{isOnOrBefore} \, \_ : \mathbb{P} \, (\, \texttt{Date} \times \texttt{Date} \,) \\
\hline
\forall \, \texttt{d1,d2} : \texttt{Date} \bullet \\
\quad \texttt{d1 isOnOrBefore d2} \iff \text{`date d1 occurs no later than date d2'}
\end{array}
$$

(we need not worry here about how the defining predicate of `isOnOrBefore` might be formalized). A suitable axiomatic description of `Period` can now be constructed :

$$
\begin{array}{|l}
\texttt{Period} : \mathbb{P} \, (\, \texttt{Date} \times \texttt{Date} \,) \qquad\qquad \text{— Period is some set of Date pairs ...} \\
\hline
\text{— ... and we want it to be precisely this one:} \\
\texttt{Period} = \{ \, \texttt{d1,d2} : \texttt{Date} \mid \texttt{d1 isOnOrBefore d2} \, \}
\end{array}
$$

Recall that the implicit term over which the set comprehension operates will be the characteristic tuple (`d1`, `d2`).

Having declared the global set `Period`, we can now use it after the ':' in declarations. This is quite a common specification technique: we declare a global set, and then use that set in the declaration of subsequent names. Since, in a declaration `x : X`, the expression `X` can be any set expression (subject to scope rules of names, etc.), a name such as `Period` is perfectly acceptable. Note carefully, though, that `Period` is *not* a type, unlike `VAN` and `CUSTOMER`, say; it is just a 'value space' that has been modelled in terms of other available (`Date`) objects.

Having `Period` available to declare variables is one thing, but making it really useful is another. The projection functions `first` and `second` provide access to the start and end dates of members of `Period`, but how could we

a. calculate the length of a hire period?
b. determine whether two hire periods overlap?
c. determine whether a given date falls in a particular hire period?
etc.

We at least know that (a) is going to be necessary (why?).

What is required is to make `Period` into a 'data type', by which we mean a set over which a collection of operations—relations and functions—has been defined. We can imagine a `length` function for (a), a binary `overlaps` relation for (b), a binary `fallsIn` relation for (c), and so on. To declare operations like these, we need in turn to exploit operations defined over `Date`, since dates are the main ingredient used to model hire periods. Thus, we also need `Date` to be a suitably rich data type. In fact, we have already supposed a relation `isOnOrBefore` over the set `Date` in defining `Period` itself. We can easily imagine this relation to be accompanied by at least three others: `isBefore`, `isOnOrAfter`, and `isAfter`. It is now apparent that defining `Date` merely as a given set thus:

[`Date`]

would be insufficient. `Date` would be just an opaque box of elements, unable to support the construction of `Period` or be of any use in expressing the predicates of the Van Hire specification where dates are involved.

Constructing data types is an important specification activity, and much more will be said about this topic in Chapter 7. We merely touch upon the process in the next chapter via set `Period` and the few hire period operations needed to support the Van Hire specification. To avoid getting bogged down in too much peripheral axiomatic description activity in the case study, we will suppose that a previous specification document called `Date_Adt` has been written which provides all the material needed; i.e., a set `Date` that can be used in declarations, accompanied by a basket of useful relations and functions for handling `Date` values. We can imagine that `Date_Adt` exports this data type so that it can be imported by any other specification that needs it. To achieve this, a paragraph is included in the importing specification along the following lines:

import `Date_Adt`

In Section 7.1, an example specification is given which shows what the internals of `Date_Adt` might be.

It must be emphasized that the **import** construct is *not part of* Z but purely an invention on our part. Nevertheless, this kind of facility is something we might reasonably expect a CASE support environment for Z to provide. It promotes a vital software engineering activity: *reuse*—here, specification reuse. If someone develops a data type that other specifications might find useful, we would want a controlled means of making the data type available. Note that the Van Hire specification cannot 'see inside' the `Date_Adt` document; neither by extension can the specifier. The imported data type `Date` is treated as *abstract*. As viewed by Van Hire, `Date` acts rather like a given set enriched by a collection of relations and functions whose defining predicates are encapsulated in `Date_Adt`. If a specifier tried to exploit any illicit knowledge gained about the internals of `Date_Adt`, we expect the sophisticated syntax checker of our Z support environment to trap such misdeeds.

Remark
Readers familiar with, say, Modula-2 or Ada® will recognize a strong analogy between the above scenario and constructing abstract data types in these languages.

EXERCISE 5.13

§ The answer is given in Section 7.1 and its exercises.
In the same manner as for `Period`, define a set that provides a suitable value-space model for `Date`. Using your model, complete the formalization of relation `isOnOrBefore` given on page 115. Now define the other relations `isBefore`, `isOnOrAfter`, and `isAfter` (*Hint*: this is easy, given `isOnOrBefore`).

® Ada is a registered trademark of the US Government Ada Joint Program Office.

Summary: the Van Hire Specification So Far

GLOBALS

This and the next subsection summarize everything we have so far constructed as part of the Van Hire specification. Firstly, we bring together the non-schema paragaphs. As can be seen, the declaration of `Period` is expressed differently to that on page 115; `maxHireLen` has also been declared in this new style.

> — There are four basic types, one of which—`VanClass`—is a free type
> `[ VAN , CUSTOMER , BOOKING ]`
> `VanClass ::= mini | transit | light | medium | heavyDuty`

> — The following imports a data type `Date` which is 'abstract' to the Van Hire specification
> — Remember that the import construct is our own invention
> **import** `Date_Adt`

> — The next paragraphs define a data type `Period` to support the Van Hire specification
> `Period == { d1,d2 : Date | d1 isOnOrBefore d2 }`
> Axiomatic descriptions of useful relations and functions for `Period`

> — An integer constant
> `maxHireLen == 28`

A '`==`' paragraph is a useful 'equals by definition' construct called an *abbreviation definition*. It is typically used to define a syntactically briefer and/or neater way of expressing the right-hand side. Remember, though, that neither this, nor the previous, definition of `Period` creates a new type—`Period` is simply another way of denoting the set it is defined to be equal to. An abbreviation definition perhaps better conveys this, since the left- and right-hand sides of such a definition are interchangeable.

Simple forms of abbreviation definition have the syntax

> Name == Expression

which can be read as 'let Name be the value of Expression'; a more general form allows generic definitions (see later). No restriction is placed on the complexity of Expression, whose inferred type becomes the type of Name. An abbreviation definition is just a shorter way of writing

$$\frac{\text{Name : TypeInferredFromExpression}}{\text{Name = Expression}}$$

So usage of abbreviation definitions comes down to convenience and clarity of style.

STATE SCHEMAS

For convenience, we repeat here the detail of earlier pages. It is perhaps worth summarizing the origins of the various state variables:

- Four variables (`custom`, `commit`, `fleet`, `activeHires`) are binary relations corresponding to the relationships expressed in an E–R model of the domain.

- Four variables (`hirePeriods`, `activeBkngs`, `vansOnHire`, `vansHireable`) incorporate vital attribute semantics of certain entities (using two modelling techniques as described in the text). Of these 'attribute variables', two are redundant (`activeBkngs`, `vansOnHire`), but have been included to improve model clarity.

- Another variable (today) is needed to tighten up the state model with respect to what is in the past, what is current and what lies in the future.

The reader is asked to accept that the main binary relations, four attribute variables and today together create a state model capable of supporting the client's required functionality. This functionality has mainly been left implicit rather than explicitly stated (see Section 6.2).

```
┌─Bookings─────────────────────────────────────────────────┐
│ custom : ℙ ( CUSTOMER × BOOKING )                         │
│ commit : ℙ ( BOOKING × VanClass )                         │
│ hirePeriods : ℙ ( BOOKING × Period )                      │
│ activeBkngs : ℙ BOOKING                                   │
├───────────────────────────────────────────────────       │
│ a.  custom is a 1-to-many relation                        │
│ b.  commit is a many-to-1 relation                        │
│ c.  hirePeriods is a many-to-1 relation                   │
│ d.  Each of the first three variables handles precisely the same set of bookings │
│ e.  activeBkngs members come from those handled by any of the other variables │
│ f.  A hire period cannot exceed maxHireLen days in length │
└───────────────────────────────────────────────────────────┘
```

```
┌─ Vans ────────────────────────────────────────────────────┐
│ fleet : ℙ ( VAN × VanClass )                              │
│ vansOnHire, vansHireable : ℙ VAN                          │
├───────────────────────────────────────                    │
│ g.  fleet is a many-to-1 relation                         │
│ h.  vansOnHire and vansHireable are vans in the fleet      │
│ i.  vansOnHire and vansHireable share no vans in common    │
└───────────────────────────────────────────────────────────┘
```

```
┌─VanHire────────────────────────────────────────────────────┐
│ Bookings; Vans                                             │
│ activeHires : ℙ ( BOOKING × VAN )                         │
│ today : Date                                               │
├───────────────────────────────────────                    │
│ j.  activeHires is a 1-to-1 relation                       │
│ k.  activeBkngs from Bookings is precisely the bookings in activeHires │
│ l.  vansOnHire from Vans is precisely the vans in activeHires │
│ m.  Every van on hire must match the class requested in the corresponding booking │
│ n.  Every active booking cannot have a hire period starting later than today │
│ o.  There is no nominal overbooking                        │
└───────────────────────────────────────────────────────────┘
```

The main lesson the reader should derive from our efforts so far with Van Hire is that, beginning with even a relatively simple real-world domain, deriving a state model of a system that is to be implemented to serve that domain is a non-trivial process. Entity–relationship modelling is one technique that provides a sound basis for deriving some of the main information structures contributing to a state model. That is but a beginning, however. Further attribute-significant components usually have to be added to obtain a model sufficiently rich to support specification of the required functionality.

Even then, considerable experimentation may take place in casting the model into a form that is judged to achieve an acceptable balance of quality indicators, such as clarity, mathematical elegance, and separation of concerns.

The main danger with a state model lies in it not being 'strong enough', i.e., we forget to include some invariant that excludes certain states which are inconsistent with the domain. State modelling requires care, much time and attention to detail. So it should. A major plank on which any specification rests is the consistency and validity of its state model. This is so, whether or not the development method is 'formal'. The beauty of mathematical models, quite apart from their abstraction and conciseness, is that we can check for their consistency and other desirable properties by various processes of logical analysis and reasoning, as Chapter 9 later describes.

We could continue and complete the Van Hire specification based on the state model as-now-is. However, in the light of material in the next chapter, parts of the model will be expressed more compactly before system operations are addressed. The eventual final form of the state model is something we would probably have constructed in the first place. Taking an extended route to get there has afforded us extra space in which to introduce important concepts across a range of topics, from mathematical structures like sets, tuples and relations, to domain and state modelling techniques.

EXERCISE 5.14

1. Consider this constraint:

    For any van class c, if there are no vans of class c in the fleet, then there can be no bookings requesting class c.

    The constraint is clearly necessary. Explain, then, why we have not included it anywhere in the Van Hire state model schemas.

2. Formalize constraints (b)–(o) inclusive of the predicates of the Van Hire state model schemas. You will need to exercise some imagination as regards Date and Period operations for expressing constraints (f), (n) and (o). Constraints (m) and (n) are quite tricky. Constraint (o), the 'no overbooking' invariant, is difficult; try to express it in words first.

SUMMARY OF CHAPTER 5

- A system development problem is introduced as a second case study that is reasonably representative of a software engineering task to which formal specification using Z can be effectively applied.

- Problem domain analysis and state modelling are discussed, showing how entity–relationship models and attribute analysis provide one method of deriving the bulk of a Z state model and the types needed to underpin it.

- The basics of types, sets, set construction, and set operations, plus some simple set theory, are imparted, using the case study to illustrate application of these concepts in the mathematical modelling of a non-trivial system state.

6

THE VAN HIRE SYSTEM (PART II):
FROM STATE MODEL TO OPERATIONS

Key Topics Domain, range, image, inverse. Functions: partial, total; injections, surjections, bijections. Term undefinedness. Restriction operators, override. Properties of relations: reflexivity, symmetry, etc.; equivalence relations, orders. Closure, composition, iteration.

6.1 POLISHING THE STATE MODEL

Further Aspects of Binary Relations

Of all possible classes of relation, binary relations are the most important because

a. The idea of pairing of things together is intuitively very natural, arises frequently in the real world, and can be exploited to considerable advantage when constructing state models.

b. An important subclass of binary relations are the *functions*. Functions offer further properties that can be put to beneficial use in specifications.

c. A rich theory of binary relations and functions exists, provided by Z's mathematical toolkit. The theory involves a collection of useful operators obeying laws that describe interesting properties exhibited by the (generic) mathematical types 'binary relation' and 'function'.

We have seen (a) much in evidence in the previous chapter. In this current section, we look at (b) in particular. Throughout the chapter, and particularly in Section 6.3, various aspects of (c) will be introduced.

A useful abbreviation definition provided by Z is the following:

$$X \leftrightarrow Y \; == \; \mathbb{P}(X \times Y)$$

This definition is generic because X and Y are effectively parameters—they can be any types (hence sets) we wish. For the purposes of discussion, we will sometimes refer to X (Y) as the *left (right)* set of the relation. We could use the abbreviation for each binary relation variable incorporated into the Van Hire state model, as in:

```
custom : CUSTOMER ↔ BOOKING
```

It must be remembered, though, that the two sides of an abbreviation definition are interchangeable. The $\leftrightarrow$ symbol (which associates to the *right*) provides a more pleasing way of declaring binary relations, but it does *not* represent some new kind of type constructor, for example. The only constructed types in the proper Z sense are sets and tuples (plus 'schema types'; see Section 7.2). Other mathematical types such as relations and functions are modelled in terms of sets and tuples.

Whilst it is not obligatory to use the $\leftrightarrow$ notation, its usage better conveys the idea of pairing and the fact that binary relations in Z are modelled in terms of their *graphs*, i.e., as sets of ordered pairs. This graphical view can be emphasized by usage of another optional notation. Instead of writing an ordered pair as a two-tuple thus:

$$(x, y)$$

we can write it as a *maplet* using the infix ordered pair constructor $\mapsto$ thus:

$$x \mapsto y$$

The two notations are effectively equivalent, though it is inferior style to mix them up in the same expression. To illustrate, consider the `custom` component of `Vanhire`. If customer `c` has made bookings `bx` and `by`, then we could express this fact as

$$\{ c \mapsto bx, c \mapsto by \} \subseteq custom$$

Note that $\mapsto$ has the lowest priority of any infix operator. Hence, except in stock situations such as extensional set construction, it is safest to place maplets in parentheses. An example state of `custom` is shown in Figure 6.1:

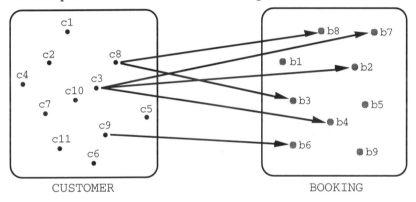

Figure 6.1   A graphical view of a binary relation.

Thus, `custom` in this state is

$$\{ c3 \mapsto b2, c3 \mapsto b4, c3 \mapsto b7, c8 \mapsto b3, c8 \mapsto b8, c9 \mapsto b6 \}$$

Visualizing binary relations in this graphical way can aid understanding. Obviously, the convention is that the direction of the arrows indicates the direction of the relation.

For the customers and bookings making up `custom`, we could write respectively

```
{ cbPr:custom • first( cbPr )}
{ cbPr:custom • second( cbPr )}
```

but there is actually an easier way. The *domain/range* of a binary relation is the set of left/right co-ordinates that contribute to the relation. Z provides us with two generic prefix operators, `dom` and `ran`, which calculate these sets. Thus, given

```
abr : X ↔ Y
```

then

```
dom abr = {x:X; y:Y | ( x ↦ y ) ∈ abr • x}
ran abr = {x:X; y:Y | ( x ↦ y ) ∈ abr • y}
```

Assuming the state of `custom` to be as in Figure 6.1, then

```
dom custom = { c3,c8,c9 }
ran custom = { b2,b3,b4,b6,b7,b8 }
```

These two operators can be used to good effect in the predicates of the Van Hire state model, which is something you are asked to investigate as part of the next exercise.

The operators dom and ran are but two of a large number associated with binary relations. Two more are illustrated in Figure 6.2: *image*, which has a special syntax, and *inversion*, one of the few Z *postfix* operators.

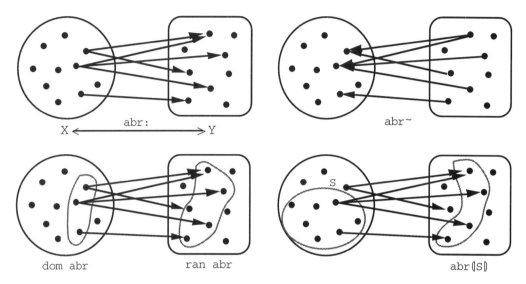

Figure 6.2 (Anticlockwise, from top left) A binary relation abr and: abr's domain and range; the image of a set through abr; abr's inverse.

Relational image is a binary operator with the syntax $\_(\!|\_|\!)$, as in

abr$(\!| \; S \; |\!)$

S must be a set of type $\mathbb{P}X$, given that abr is of type $X \leftrightarrow Y$. The expression calculates those right co-ordinates of abr (as a $\mathbb{P}Y$ value) to which abr relates members of S (if any). Thus:

abr$(\!| \; S \; |\!)$ = { x : X; y : Y | x ∈ S ∧ (x ↦ y) ∈ abr • y }

Here are some true equalities, based on Figure 6.1 on page 121:

custom$(\!|$ { c3 } $|\!)$ = { b2 , b4 , b7 }
custom$(\!|$ { c5 , c8 , c10 } $|\!)$ = { b3 , b8 }
custom$(\!|$ { c1 , c2 , c5 , c6 } $|\!)$ = ∅

Relational *inversion* can be defined as

abr$^\sim$ = { x : X; y : Y | (x ↦ y) ∈ abr • y ↦ x }

Inversion calculates that $Y \leftrightarrow X$ relation which comprises the inverted maplets of its argument. Combining this with relational image, we have for example:

custom$^\sim$ $(\!|$ { b2 , b4 , b5 , b7 } $|\!)$ = { c3 }
custom$^\sim$ $(\!|$ { b8 } $|\!)$ = { c8 }
custom$^\sim$ $(\!|$ { b1 , b5 , b9 } $|\!)$ = ∅

Again, these equalities relate to Figure 6.1.

EXERCISE 6.1

1. Explain the structure of an object declared as:

    obj : W ↔ X ↔ Y

2. a. Is it possible for the domain or range of a relation to be empty? Explain
    b. Is dom(abr1 ∪ abr2) = (dom abr1) ∪ (dom abr2) true? Explain
    c. Is dom(abr1 ∩ abr2) = (dom abr1) ∩ (dom abr2) true? Explain
    d. Are the answers to (b) and (c) the same for ran?

3. For each term below, give another term to which it is equal (where
    abr : X ↔ Y). Although first is a function, treat it as a binary relation that
    relates any ordered pair (x, y) to x; similarly, second relates (x, y) to y.

    a. first ⦇ abr ⦈   b. second ⦇ abr ⦈   c. second ⦇ abr~ ⦈
    d. abr ⦇ dom abr ⦈   e. abr~ ⦇ ran abr ⦈

4. Consider the relation divEx : $\mathbb{N}_1$ ↔ $\mathbb{N}_1$, where divEx relates i to j *iff* i is
    exactly divisible by j and i > j > 1. Give the values of the following
    (informally express answers where this is more convenient):

    a. dom divEx   b. ran divEx   c. divEx ⦇ 1..9 ⦈
    d. divEx ⦇ { 5, 13, 19 } ⦈   e. divEx~ ⦇ { 2 } ⦈

5. § The answer is given below.
    Re-express the predicates of the Van Hire state model wherever use of the
    domain and range operators is beneficial.

A Return to the Van Hire State Model

Comparison of the following modified Van Hire state schema predicates with those
given in the answer to Exercise 5.14 shows what improvements can be gained by
exploiting even the simplest of operators. Only those predicates which present an
obvious beneficial use of dom and ran have been re-formalized; the remainder have
been kept informally expressed (see the answer to Exercise 5.14 for example formal-
izations of these). The opportunity has also been taken to use the ↔ abbreviation.
Letters cross-reference the constraint identification scheme as used in Section 5.5. Recall
that length is a Period function assumed to have been declared.

```
┌─Bookings────────────────────────────────────────────────┐
│ custom : CUSTOMER ↔ BOOKING                              │
│ commit : BOOKING ↔ VanClass                             │
│ hirePeriods : BOOKING ↔ Period                          │
│ activeBkngs : ℙ BOOKING                                  │
├─────────────────────────────────────────────────────────┤
│ a.   custom is a 1-to-many relation                      │
│ b.   hirePeriods is a many-to-1 relation                 │
│ c.   commit is a many-to-1 relation                      │
│ ran custom = dom commit = dom hirePeriods    — constraint (d) │
│ activeBkngs ⊆ ran custom                     — constraint (e) │
│ ∀p : ran hirePeriods • length( p ) ≤ maxHireLen  — constraint (f) │
└─────────────────────────────────────────────────────────┘
```

```
┌─ Vans ─────────────────────────────────────────────────┐
│ fleet : VAN ↔ VanClass                                  │
│ vansOnHire : ℙ VAN                                      │
│ vansHireable : ℙ VAN                                    │
├─────────────────────────────────────                    │
│ g.  fleet is a many-to-1 relation                       │
│ vansOnHire ∪ vansHireable ⊆ dom fleet      — constraint (h) │
│ vansOnHire ∩ vansHireable = ∅              — constraint (i) │
└─────────────────────────────────────────────────────────┘
```

```
┌─ VanHire ───────────────────────────────────────────────┐
│ Bookings                                                 │
│ Vans                                                     │
│ activeHires : BOOKING ↔ VAN                              │
│ today : Date                                             │
├─────────────────────                                     │
│ j.  activeHires is a 1-to-1 relation                     │
│ activeBkngs = dom activeHires              — constraint (k) │
│ vansOnHire = ran activeHires               — constraint (l) │
│ m.  Every van on hire must match the class requested in the corresponding booking │
│ n.  Every active booking cannot have a hire period starting later than today │
│ o.  There is no nominal overbooking                      │
└──────────────────────────────────────────────────────────┘
```

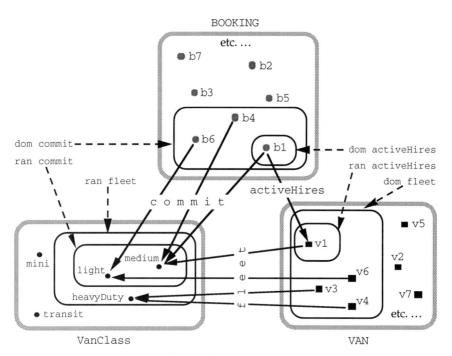

Figure 6.3 Visualization of part of an example Van Hire state.

Figure 6.3 is a visualization of part of the Van Hire state model, which for reasons of practicality, is depicted in a highly contrived simple state. The relations commit, fleet and activeHires are shown together with the domain and range of each. The visualization supposes a state in which there are currently just three bookings (b1, b4, b6) and a fleet that comprises just four vans (v1, v3, v4, v6) with classes as indicated. Note that the fleet has no transit or mini vans, and that only booking b1 is active. The 'etc. ...' in the BOOKING and VAN bubbles is intended to indicate that both sets are imagined to contain other members which have not been shown. Of course, the identifiers b1, b2, etc. and v1, v2, etc. used to pinpoint individual members of (given) sets are purely for convenience, as in all such diagrams.

Although using dom and ran in the Van Hire state predicates has reduced clutter considerably, we can do even better than this by exploiting the next concept.

Functions

The most general form of binary relation is one with a many-to-many cardinality. This means that an element in the left set can be related to 0 or more elements in the right set, and vice versa; essentially, there are no restrictions in the relationship expressed. More constrained forms of binary relation are many-to-1, 1-to-many and, more constrained still, 1-to-1. For example, with a many-to-1 relation, a left set element can be related to at most one element in the right set. Properties like this are now explored further.

Consider the different situations enumerated below, with small stretches of the imagination where necessary, pertaining to this real-world domain:

Some of the administrative staff of an organization occupy a block of desirable, newly refurbished offices. Staff are uniquely identified by elements of the set STAFF, and offices by elements of the set OFFICE. To model which staff currently occupy which offices, the following binary relation will be used:

_ hasDeskIn _ : STAFF ↔ OFFICE

In the following scenarios, we will assume that the total populations of STAFF and OFFICE are respectively eight (s1,s2, ...s9) and five (o1,o2, ...o5).

OFFICE SCENARIO I (the fully flexible office allocation system)
An example state of hasDeskIn might be

{ s1 ↦ o2, s1 ↦ o3, s1 ↦ o5, s2 ↦ o3, s5 ↦ o3, s6 ↦ o1, s6 ↦ o2 }

The offices are of different sizes and so can accommodate different maximum numbers of staff. Some offices (e.g., o4) are not occupied by any staff, whilst some less lucky staff (e.g., s4) remain ensconced in an open-plan area and are not associated with the desirable office block at all. Also, there are some offices (e.g., o3) occupied by several members of staff; and there are some staff (e.g., s1) with desks in more than one office.

OFFICE SCENARIO II (the rationalized office allocation system)
Management decides that, though in principle a member of staff could be given a desk in more than one office, in practice past experience suggests that this does not work well, often making people hard to find and creating a 'who-does-what-and-where?' confusion. So each staff member in the office block is allocated to just one office. An example state of hasDeskIn might be

{ s1 ↦ o4, s3 ↦ o3, s4 ↦ o2, s6 ↦ o3, s7 ↦ o2, s8 ↦ o4 }

OFFICE SCENARIO III (the isolationist rationalized office allocation system)
This is as Scenario II, but the office block has been refurbished as a collection of single-person offices (on the insistence of management who consider that when several people occupy an office, much productive work is lost through idle chatter). So every occupied office has only one member of staff in it. An example state of `hasDeskIn` might be

$$\{\, s2 \mapsto o3, s3 \mapsto o2, s4 \mapsto o1, s9 \mapsto o5 \,\}$$

OFFICE SCENARIO IV (the efficient rationalized office allocation system)
Again, this is related to Scenario II, but management considers it a waste of space resources not to have all offices occupied. So every office has at least one staff member allocated to it, and preferably more where possible. Thus, an example state of `hasDeskIn` might be

$$\{\, s1 \mapsto o3, s2 \mapsto o2, s3 \mapsto o1, s4 \mapsto o5, s6 \mapsto o2, s7 \mapsto o4, s9 \mapsto o1 \,\}$$

OFFICE SCENARIO V (the efficient isolationist rationalized office allocation system)
This is basically a combination of III and IV. Nobody has a desk in more than one office, each office is single-person, and all offices are occupied. For example:

$$\{\, s1 \mapsto o5, s3 \mapsto o1, s4 \mapsto o4, s7 \mapsto o3, s8 \mapsto o2 \,\}$$

OFFICE SCENARIOS I', II', III', IV', V' (egalitarian variations)
These are variations of Scenarios I–V inclusive. *All* administrative staff are allocated offices in the office block to avoid acrimony, accusations of favouritism, etc. To ensure this is achievable in each scenario, an upper bound is placed on staff numbers (imagine this to be the size of STAFF in each case) so that it is equal to the total number of staff the offices can accommodate.

EXERCISE 6.2

1. What is the cardinality of each relation I–V inclusive?
   Do relations I'–V' have the same cardinalities as their counterparts in I–V?
   Is there a class of binary relation not covered by the examples? If so, give an example state of `hasDeskIn` consistent with the class you have identified.

2. § The answer is involved in the discussion below.
   Consider in turn each of the following predicates, and state for which of the relations (I–V and I'–V') the predicate is true:

   a. $\forall s : \text{STAFF}; o1, o2 : \text{OFFICE} \bullet$
      $s \text{ hasDeskIn } o1 \wedge s \text{ hasDeskIn } o2 \Rightarrow o1 = o2$

   b. $\forall s1, s2 : \text{STAFF}; o : \text{OFFICE} \bullet$
      $s1 \text{ hasDeskIn } o \wedge s2 \text{ hasDeskIn } o \Rightarrow s1 = s2$

   c. $\forall o : \text{OFFICE} \bullet \exists s : \text{STAFF} \bullet s \text{ hasDeskIn } o$

   d. $\forall s : \text{STAFF} \bullet \exists o : \text{OFFICE} \bullet s \text{ hasDeskIn } o$

If we generalize property (a) expressed in Exercise 6.2(2) to some arbitrary binary relation, then it means that every member of the relation's left set is related to *at most one* member of its right set. In other words, the relation is X-to-1 (X could be 'many' or '1'). Recall that this kind of constraint is required several times in the Van Hire model.

Only relations I and I', which are many-to-many, do *not* satisfy constraint (a). Nor would a relation that is 1-to-many (like `custom` in schema `VanHire`), though an example of such does not occur in the office illustration.

If a binary relation obeys constraint (a) of Exercise 6.2(2), then the binary relation possesses a special extra property: that of being *functional*. So all relations modelling the previous scenarios, except relations I and I', are functions. We have made use of several Z functions already, e.g., `first`, `second`, `dom` and `ran`. Remember, too, that all operators whatever their syntax are also functional, e.g., $\# \_$, $\_ \cup \_$, $\_ ^{\sim}$ and $\_ \lparen \_ \rparen$.

Suppose `phi` is a function 'from X to Y', i.e., its left set is X and its right set is Y. Then an additional syntax becomes available: that of *function application*, as in the term

> phi x

or

> phi(x)

if the redundant parentheses are preferred. This term calculates that member y of phi's right set to which x is related, given that x is in phi's domain; if it is not, *the term is undefined*. Note that y is unique because of the functional constraint operating on phi. In normal parlance, we would say something like 'the function phi applied to argument x evaluates to y', which can be expressed as the equality

> phi(x) = y

although this is no different from writing

> (x ↦ y) ∈ phi

or

> (x ↦ phi(x)) ∈ phi

The advantage of function application is that it allows us to *calculate* the right set member to which the function's argument is related.

There is, however, much more to functions than just being binary relations with an X-to-1 property. Functions can be split into different subcategories depending on certain additional properties they might possess (phi is as above in what follows):

- PARTIAL FUNCTIONS: A function phi is *partial* if dom phi ⊆ X, i.e., its domain is a subset of its left set, hence possibly a strict subset. Since this property is true for *all* functions, partial functions represent the complete class of functions. The term 'partial' clearly stems from the fact that phi(x) will not be defined if dom phi ⊂ X and x ∉ dom phi. Scenarios II–V would each be modelled by a partial function, since it is not necessarily the case that each staff member occupies an office.

- TOTAL FUNCTIONS: When dom phi = X, the function is said to be *total*. In that case we know phi(x) is always defined. Totalness is property (d) in Exercise 6.2(2) and applies to scenarios II'–V'. The non-functional scenario I' is also 'total' in the same sense, though totalness is a property normally confined to discourse about functions.

- INJECTIONS: A function is said to be *injective*, or *one-one*, if every element in its range is paired with only *one* element in its domain. Injectivity is properties (a) and (b) combined in Exercise 6.2(2). Scenarios III, V, III' and V' would each be modelled by a function which is injective since each office can be occupied by only one staff member. Note that a function modelling scenario II, II', IV or IV' could not be injective.

- SURJECTIONS: A function is said to be *surjective* , or *onto*, if its range is the whole of its right set, i.e., `ran phi` = Y. This is property (c) in Exercise 6.2(2). Scenarios IV, IV',V and V' would be modelled by a function which is surjective since every office is occupied. However, note that scenarios II, II', III and III' are not surjective.

- BIJECTIONS: We can see that the functions modelling scenarios V and V' would be injective and surjective. Functions with both these properties are called *bijections*.

It is worth re-emphasizing that 'partial' applies to *all* functions, including those that are total. Often the term 'partial' is used in the more specific sense of 'non-total', i.e., a function whose domain is a strict subset of its left set. One can always use the term 'non-total' where confusion might otherwise arise.

The reader might find the above list of function properties a little bewildering on first encounter, but they are of considerable importance with respect to simplifying specifications. In fact, there are special symbols to convey these properties. When declaring a function `phi`, we write

> `phi` : LeftSet RightPointingArrow RightSet

There are different forms for the symbol RightPointingArrow depending on the properties that we want `phi` to have. The basis of the symbol is $\rightarrow$, but with the following embellishments:

- small vertical bar in middle, i.e., $\nrightarrow$: the function is *partial*
- absence of vertical bar in middle, i.e., $\rightarrow$: function is *total*
- tail to arrow, i.e., $\rightarrowtail$, $\rightarrowtail$: function is *injective*
- double head, i.e., $\twoheadrightarrow$, $\twoheadrightarrow$: function is *surjective*
- tail and double head, i.e., $\rightarrowtail\!\!\!\rightarrow$: function is *bijective*.

Note that Z does not accommodate 'partial bijections', so the symbol $\rightarrowtail\!\!\twoheadrightarrow$ is illegal.

Until one gets used to these 'herring bone' symbols, they can be confusing and even irksome. By using them, however, we can express desired constraints on variables directly in declarations and thereby dramatically reduce the complexity of the predicates we have to write. To illustrate this point, suppose `toBi` is a (total) bijection, sometimes called a *one-one correspondence*, between sets X and Y. We would declare `toBi` thus:

> `toBi` : X $\rightarrowtail\!\!\!\rightarrow$ Y   (6.1)

If there was no special constraint notation for functions, we would have to declare `toBi` as

> `toBi` : X $\leftrightarrow$ Y   — or of course $\mathbb{P}$ (X $\times$ Y)

and add to the axiom part of the appropriate paragraph the following four predicates:

> $\forall$ x : X; y1,y2 : Y $\bullet$
>   (x,y1) $\in$ `toBi` $\wedge$ (x,y2) $\in$ `toBi` $\Rightarrow$ y1 = y2   — `toBi` is functional
> dom `toBi` = X   — ... and total
> $\forall$ x1,x2 : X; y : Y $\bullet$
>   (x1,y) $\in$ `toBi` $\wedge$ (x2,y) $\in$ `toBi` $\Rightarrow$ x1 = x2   — ... and not many-to-1
> ran `toBi` = Y   — ... and surjective

The declaration (6.1) captures all this, so it clearly pays to use Z's herring bones!

A point of syntax to note is that no trailing underscore is needed after `toBi` in (6.1) or indeed in *any* function declaration. This is because when a name is applied prefix-edly to an argument, the default interpretation is that this is function application syntax. Some care is needed, though. Function application constructs *terms*. When a name is applied prefixedly in its capacity *as a relation* to construct *a predicate*, this is *not* 'function application'. If we wish to apply a relation of our own in prefix style, the trailing underscore in the relation's name *is* necessary when it is declared (see also page 106).

EXERCISE 6.3

1. For each of the following, all of which are to be regarded as $\mathbb{P}(\mathbb{N} \times \mathbb{N})$ relations defined in terms of their graphs (sets of maplets),

   - state whether the relation is functional, and if so, which kind *relative to* $\mathbb{N}$
   - give the relation's domain and range.

   a. $\{i : \mathbb{N} \bullet i \mapsto 0\}$ b. $\{i : \mathbb{N}_1 \bullet i \mapsto i - 1\}$ c. $\{i : \mathbb{N} \bullet i \mapsto i + 1\}$
   d. $\{i : \mathbb{N} \bullet i \mapsto i * i\}$ e. $\{i : \mathbb{N} \bullet i \mapsto i\}$ f. $\{i : \mathbb{N} \bullet i \mapsto i \text{ div } 2\}$

2. Given that f and g are both $\mathbb{P}(X \times Y)$ functions, state the circumstances (if any) under which each of the following is functional:

   a. $f \cap g$ b. $f \cup g$ c. h, where $h \subseteq f$ d. $\varnothing[X \times Y]$ e. $f^\sim$

3. Calculate $obj(\!| 1..5 |\!)$ for each of the six relations obj in Question (1).

4. § The answer is given below.
   a. Which relations in the Van Hire state model can be expressed as functions? Alter schema declarations and predicates accordingly.
   b. For those predicates remaining which were left unformalized on pages 123–124, try to formalize them by exploiting the changes in (a) so as to improve upon the answers given to Exercise 5.14.

A Final Return to the Van Hire State Model

All binary relations in Van Hire's model can be expressed as functions. This is so even of `custom` *if we invert the relation type into a many-to-1* BOOKING $\leftrightarrow$ CUSTOMER *relation*. The inversion necessitates a change to the first two conjuncts in schema `Bookings`. A major benefit of exploiting functions is evident—five messy constraints have disappeared from predicate parts, absorbed into declarations. Of the five functions, only `activeHires` in the `VanHire` schema has any special properties—it is injective. `length`, `start` and `fallsIn` are part of data type `Period`; we declare them shortly.

```
┌─ Bookings ─────────────────────────────────────────────────┐
│ custom : BOOKING ↠ CUSTOMER                                 │
│ commit : BOOKING ↠ VanClass                                 │
│ hirePeriods : BOOKING ↠ Period                              │
│ activeBkngs : ℙ BOOKING                                     │
├─────────────────────────────────────────────────────────────┤
│ dom custom = dom commit = dom hirePeriods                   │
│ activeBkngs ⊆ dom custom                                    │
│ ∀ p : ran hirePeriods • length( p ) ≤ maxHireLen           │
└─────────────────────────────────────────────────────────────┘
```

```
┌─ Vans ────────────────────────────────────────────────┐
│ fleet : VAN ⇸ VanClass                                 │
│ vansOnHire, vansHireable : ℙ VAN                       │
├────────────────────────────                           │
│ vansOnHire ∪ vansHireable ⊆ dom fleet                  │
│ vansOnHire ∩ vansHireable = ∅                          │
└────────────────────────────────────────────────────────┘
```

```
┌─ VanHire ──────────────────────────────────────────────┐
│ Bookings                                                │
│ Vans                                                    │
│ activeHires : BOOKING ⤔ VAN                             │
│ today : Date                                            │
├─────────────────────────────                           │
│ activeBkngs = dom activeHires                           │
│ vansOnHire = ran activeHires                            │
│ ∀ b : activeBkngs •                                     │
│    fleet( activeHires( b )) = commit( b ) ∧             │
│    start( hirePeriods( b )) isOnOrBefore today          │
│ ∀ vc : VanClass • ∀ d : Date •                          │
│    #{ b : dom commit | commit( b ) = vc ∧ d fallsIn hirePeriods( b )} │
│       ≤ #{ v : dom fleet | fleet( v ) = vc }            │
└─────────────────────────────────────────────────────────┘
```

Further benefits of the changes can be seen in the predicate of VanHire where formalization of the more difficult constraints is now more simple. It is possible even to improve slightly on the last conjunct, the 'no nominal overbooking' invariant, though we would need to use an operator that has yet to be discussed.

FUNCTION APPLICATION AND UNDEFINEDNESS

The use of function application in the Van Hire model is worth further discussion. Consider for example the 'correct class of van has been allocated' invariant in the VanHire schema:

$$\forall \, b : \text{activeBkngs} \bullet \textbf{fleet(activeHires(b))} = \text{commit(b)} \qquad (6.2)$$

The term emboldened takes an active booking b and applies the activeHires function to it to calculate the van allocated, i.e., activeHires(b). This term is then used as the argument of the fleet function to calculate the van's class. The latter is also calculated by applying the commit function to the active booking b. The two results are asserted to be equal for any active booking.

Firstly, if we were being more minimalist with parentheses, the emboldened term could be written

        fleet(activeHires b)

but *not*

        fleet activeHires b

because *function application is left-associative* and expects a single argument. It follows that

        fleet activeHires b = (fleet activeHires) b

which is obviously *not* what we want. It is also a syntax error (`fleet` expects a `VAN` argument), though later in Chapter 7 we see that 'applying a function to a function' can be perfectly sensible in certain situations.

When handling partial functions, term undefinedness caused by applying a function to an argument outside its domain becomes an important issue. Term undefinedness may cause undefinedness of the predicate in which the term appears, and this must be avoided. In (6.2), the 'booking universe' in the quantification is that of `activeBkngs`. Thus, definedness of `activeHires` applied to b, `fleet` applied to `activeHires( b )`, and `commit` applied to b is guaranteed by the various predicates of the `VanHire` model (why?). So the equality 'makes sense' in all situations catered for. Had the quantification been simply

$$\forall b : \text{BOOKING} \bullet \text{fleet}(\text{activeHires}(b)) = \text{commit}(b)$$

then this is not good enough since each function application is now potentially undefined for certain values of b. In fact, in the scope of the $\forall$, we would have an equality

$$\xi 1 = \xi 2$$

where either $\xi 1$ or both $\xi 1$ and $\xi 2$ could be undefined. The truth value of the equality then becomes problematic. This is precisely the kind of situation we must avoid. Of course, it might just be that `activeBkngs = BOOKING`. But then that is just one extreme possible state of `activeBkngs` (which is highly unlikely in reality!), and state predicates characterize static system properties that hold *in the arbitrary case*.

There might still seem to be a difficulty, however, since (6.2) can be unwound into

$$\forall b : \text{BOOKING} \mid b \in \text{activeBkngs} \bullet$$
$$\text{fleet}(\text{activeHires}(b)) = \text{commit}(b)$$

or

$$\forall b : \text{BOOKING} \bullet$$
$$b \in \text{activeBkngs} \Rightarrow \text{fleet}(\text{activeHires}(b)) = \text{commit}(b)$$

Consider the latter form. Suppose b drawn from BOOKING is such that we have $b \notin \text{activeBkngs}$. Then the function applications in the consequent are potentially undefined. Surely this is a problem? The answer is *no*, as the consequent is 'guarded' by $b \in \text{activeBkngs}$. If this is false, the truth value of the consequent is irrelevant—the implication overall is true. Where $b \notin \text{activeBkngs}$, we think of each function application in the consequent as calculating something in the function's right set, but we simply do not care what it is. A similar, common situation that arises particularly in operation specifications is something typified by

> x ∈ dom f   — f is partial, say a state variable
> ...
> PredicateInvolving f(x)

One might ask: suppose $x \notin \text{dom } f$; what then the value of f(x)? The answer is essentially the same: it does not matter because, if $x \in \text{dom } f$ were false, then the whole schema predicate would be too, which makes the value of f(x) immaterial.

Term undefinedness, which can occur by other means too (see pages 175–176, for example), is rarely a problem in practical specification work. The issue impinges more on logic and proof, though that lies outside the scope of this text. Providing we exercise caution in the way objects like partial functions are applied, all will be well.

DEVELOPMENT OF DATA TYPE `Period`

The following axiomatic description, which we would include near the beginning of the Van Hire specification, provides us with the `Period` operations we have used in the Van Hire state model, plus a few extras. It makes use of various operations assumed to be imported as part of the abstract data type `Date`.

$$
\begin{aligned}
&\texttt{start,end : Period} \rightarrow \texttt{Date} \\
&\texttt{length : Period} \rightarrow \mathbb{N} \\
&\texttt{datesIn : Period} \rightarrow \mathbb{P}\,\texttt{Date} \\
&\texttt{\_ fallsIn \_ : Date} \leftrightarrow \texttt{Period}
\end{aligned}
$$

$$
\begin{aligned}
&\forall\texttt{p : Period} \bullet \\
&\quad \texttt{start(p) = first(p)} \wedge \\
&\quad \texttt{end(p) = second(p)} \wedge \\
&\quad \texttt{length(p) = daysDiff(end(p),start(p))} \wedge \\
&\quad \texttt{datesIn(p) = \{d : Date | d fallsIn p\}} \\
&\forall\texttt{d : Date; p : Period} \bullet \\
&\quad \texttt{d fallsIn p} \Leftrightarrow \\
&\qquad \texttt{start(p) isOnOrBefore d isOnOrBefore end(p)}
\end{aligned}
$$

There are several points here that are worth highlighting:

- To develop data type `Period`, we have assumed that imports from `Date_Adt` include the function `daysDiff`, where `daysDiff( d1,d2 )` calculates the number of days separating one date `d1` from another `d2` (the two dates can be in any order).

- `start`, `end`, `length` and `datesIn` are no different in kind to the function variables of the `VanHire` state model. As with relations, functions described axiomatically are usually constants; i.e., the defining predicates, typically involving equalities, uniquely fix which functions the global function names 'stand for' (the next chapter looks at axiomatic function definition in some detail). We could side-step `start` and `end` by using `first` and `second` directly. However, remember that `Period` is being developed in the spirit of abstraction so that a user of `Period` cannot detect how it is modelled.

- The syntax

  $\text{Arg}_1\ \text{Rel}_1\ \text{Arg}_2\ \text{Rel}_2\ \text{Arg}_3\ \ldots$

  where the Rel_i are binary relations, is a permitted abbreviation for

  $\text{Arg}_1\ \text{Rel}_1\ \text{Arg}_2 \wedge \text{Arg}_2\ \text{Rel}_2\ \text{Arg}_3 \wedge \ldots$

`Period` typifies the important process of developing data types to provide support for system specification. The next chapter is largely devoted to this topic.

INITIAL STATE

To complete the formalization of the Van Hire state model, a suitable initial state description is required. When the computerized system is implemented, the real-world business will have been ongoing for some time. The garage management decides that, after acceptance, the changeover strategy to the computerized system will be:

On the agreed start date of changeover, all NEW bookings will be recorded in the computerized system, together with current 'paper' bookings YET TO GO ACTIVE (those scheduled to start from the changeover date onwards). Current ACTIVE bookings will continue to be dealt with 'on paper' until they have ALL passed through the system. From that point onwards, the system will then be fully computerized.

The simplest way for the system to begin in a state required by the above strategy, and be consistent with the domain, is firstly to initialize it to 'empty'. The following schema describes this state, using `dateZero`—a `Date` constant provided by `Date_Adt`—as the initial value for `today`'. Note that this state is consistent with the state invariant of `VanHire`' (as it must be—can you informally argue that this is so?).

```
┌─ InitVanHire ──────────────────────────────────────────────┐
│ VanHire'                                                    │
├─────────────────────────                                    │
│ custom' = ∅; commit' = ∅; hirePeriods' = ∅                  │
│ activeBkngs' = ∅                                            │
│ fleet' = ∅                                                  │
│ vansOnHire' = vansHireable' = ∅                             │
│ activeHires' = ∅                                            │
│ today' = dateZero                                           │
└─────────────────────────────────────────────────────────────┘
```

Next, by various system operations (see Section 6.2 for some examples), the system can be updated to the scheduled changeover date, the actual fleet, and the 'paper' bookings yet to go active; note that vans still on hire at the changeover date must be excluded initially from the hireable vans. The system is then ready 'to go live' as required.

EXERCISE 6.4

1. Do the `start`, `end`, `length` and `datesIn` functions of data type `Period` possess any properties not expressed in their declarations?

2. Give definitions of the following `Period` relations:

    a. `p1 overlaps p2` holds if the two periods `p1` and `p2` overlap, i.e., they have at least one date in common
    b. `disjntPds( sp )` holds if none of the members of the `Period` set `sp` overlap each other.

6.2   SYSTEM OPERATIONS

We will not attempt to specify every conceivable operation that the client might require of the computerized Van Hire system. Instead, we will concentrate on a representative subset which, for convenience, has been divided into two groups: one that covers operations which update the state of the system, and one that covers operations providing information about the current state of the system. In the informal descriptions of operations overleaf, the character '?' denotes an input that will be needed by an operation, and '!' denotes an output it will produce. The general style of predicate description adopted in operation schemas will be to place conjuncts, where possible, in the following order:

i.   preconstraints   ii.   output description
iii. update transition description   iv.   identity transitions.

As there is quite a gap between Chapter 3 and here, a quick review by the reader of material relevant to operation specification in Section 3.2 onwards might be useful.

Some Update Operations

The basic update operations required by the client are fairly obvious:

A1. A customer books a van of a certain class over a specified period:
?   The customer
?   The class of van the customer requires
?   The period of hire the customer requires
!   The booking made.

A2. A customer arrives to pick up a van at the start of a hire period as per some booking the customer has made:
?   The booking involved
?   The van allocated.   — but see also the answer to Exercise 6.6

A3. A customer returns a van she has been hiring:
?   The booking involved.

A4. A customer cancels a booking:
?   The booking involved.

A5. A customer requests alteration, in advance of hiring, of a van class booked:
?   The booking involved
?   The new van class required.

A6. The garage purchases a batch of new vans to add to its existing fleet:
?   The new vans.

A7. One or more vans are deleted from the fleet, e.g., to be sold second-hand:
?   The van(s) involved.

To simplify the operations a little, no charge calculations have been included. Operations A1, A3 and A4 might in practice use some pricing scheme to calculate and output respectively: minimum deposit required plus total charge, excess charge for late return, cancellation fee.

Each of the above operations will include ΔVanHire in its specification as each models some update to the Van Hire system state. We must remember to include an equality for any 'before' and 'after' variable pairs modelling a state component which a given operation leaves unchanged. Some update operations do not affect the Bookings component, or alternatively Vans component, of the state model. In either case, we could adopt the technique used in the Digital Watch specification. For example, if the Vans component does not change, we could write

    ΔVanHire; ΞVans

in the declaration part, thus usefully exploiting the separation of concerns in the state model. The reader should recall from Chapter 3 what the Ξ-abbreviation stands for. In the case of ΞVans, it will be

```
┌─ΞVans ─────────────────────────────────────────────────────────┐
│ Vans; Vans'                                                     │
│ ────────────                                                    │
│ fleet' = fleet                                                  │
│ vansOnHire' = vansOnHire                                        │
│ vansHireable' = vansHireable                                    │
└─────────────────────────────────────────────────────────────────┘
```

A tidier possibility we will adopt is to define our own special 'delta schemas':

$\quad$ ΔVH_XiBookings $\triangleq$ [ΔVanHire; ΞBookings]
$\quad$ ΔVH_XiVans $\triangleq$ [ΔVanHire; ΞVans]

Now we can use just ΔVH_XiBookings or ΔVH_XiVans as appropriate. To get back into the rhythm of operation specification from Chapter 3, we start with one of the simpler examples in the previous list.

OPERATION A7
The following schema has several features worthy of comment, indicated by letter identifiers, including use of a new operator. The operation has an explicit preconstraint to avoid the invalidity of disposing of vans that are currently recorded as being on hire to customers.

```
┌─ DisposeOfVans ────────────────────────────────────────────────┐
│ ΔVH_XiBookings           — the Bookings component does not change│
│ vansToGo? : ℙ VAN                                               │
│ ─────────────                                                   │
│ — preconstraint: vans to be deleted must be part of the fleet but not currently on hire│
│ vansToGo? ⊆ dom fleet \ vansOnHire                              │
│ fleet' = vansToGo? ⩤ fleet                              — (a)    │
│ vansHireable' = vansHireable \ vansToGo?               — (b)    │
│ activeHires' = activeHires                             — (c)    │
│ today' = today                                                  │
└─────────────────────────────────────────────────────────────────┘
```

Conjunct (a) is a simpler, more pleasing way of saying

$\quad$ fleet' = fleet \ { v : vansToGo? • v ↦ fleet(v) }

which captures the 'van deletion update' that occurs to fleet. The new infix operator ⩤ is discussed in the next subsection.

$\quad$ Inclusion of (b) is clearly necessary since some/all of the vans being disposed of might be hireable ones. However, it seems there has been a sin of omission: where is

$\quad$ vansOnHire' = vansOnHire ? $\hfill$ (6.3)

In fact, this is taken care of by conjunct (c). Since, from the before and after state predicates, we have in particular that

$\quad$ vansOnHire = dom activeHires
and $\quad$ vansOnHire' = dom activeHires'

then (6.3) quickly follows from (c) by a simple 'equals for equals' argument. Thus, (6.3) is guaranteed by the state predicates and so its inclusion is unnecessary (though not wrong). This is typical of the way a *derived* component of the state, as a redundant variable like vansOnHire (see page 114) is called, can be handled in operations. A derived component may add materiaily to a state model, but it does not have to lead to more complex operation descriptions as a consequence.

THE RESTRICTION OPERATORS
The operator ◁ belongs to a family of four illustrated in Figure 6.4.

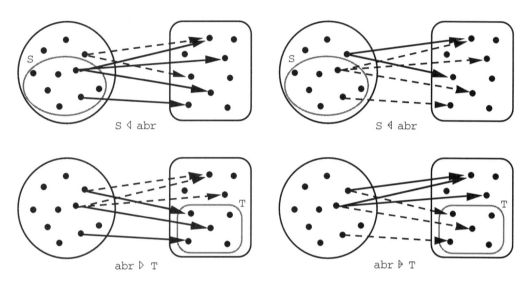

S ◁ abr   S ◁ abr

abr ▷ T   abr ▷ T

Figure 6.4   The four restriction operators.

Each operator provides a way of producing a stronger binary relation (or more partial function) from another by reducing either its domain or range. In the diagram, the solid arrows define the relation calculated by the restriction; the dashed arrows define those maplets in the relation prior to calculation which do not participate in the restricted relation.

More formally, given

$$\text{abr} : X \leftrightarrow Y; \ S : \mathbb{P} \, X$$

then

$$S \triangleleft \text{abr}$$

is the relation obtained by restricting abr's maplets to those whose first co-ordinates lie in the set S. That is,

$$S \triangleleft \text{abr} = \{ x : X; \ y : Y \mid x \in S \land (x \mapsto y) \in \text{abr} \bullet x \mapsto y \}$$

Whereas the narrowing effect of ◁, called *domain restriction*, is achieved by selection, that of the ◀ operator used in DisposeOfVans is subtractive. ◀ is called *domain subtraction/deletion*, or *domain anti-restriction*. Its definition is

$$S \triangleleft\!\!\!\!\!- \text{abr} = \{ x : X; \ y : Y \mid x \notin S \land (x \mapsto y) \in \text{abr} \bullet x \mapsto y \}$$

which is the relation obtained by restricting abr's maplets to those whose first co-ordinates *do not* lie in the set S.

The two other operators in this group, namely *range restriction* ▷ and *range subtraction* ⩥, have an entirely similar effect to ◁ and ⩤, but operate on a relation's range rather than domain. Here is an example application of each operator using variables of the Van Hire model:

— the customers with active bookings
ran(activeBkngs ⩤ custom)

— the number of yet-to-start bookings requesting van class vc?
#{ b : dom(activeBkngs ⩤ commit) | commit(b) = vc? }

— that 'slice' of hirePeriods dealing with bookings for just a single day's hire
hirePeriods ▷ { p : Period | length(p) = 1 }

— the hireable vans that are not heavy-duty
dom(fleet ⩥ { heavyDuty }) ∩ vansHireable

The examples emphasize that since restrictions on relations/functions calculate relations/functions, we can apply all the usual relation operators such as dom and ran to their results. It must not be forgotten that since functions are just a special subclass of the binary relations, any operator on binary relations (domain, range, inversion, image, the four restriction operators) is automatically applicable to functions too.

With such a rich complement of operators for handling relations and functions, there is often more than one sensible way to construct a term. Although conciseness is an indicator of good style, the first priority should always be to construct something that one feels comfortable with, and confident about, in terms of its correctness. That said, some of the above examples can be re-expressed with an increase in conciseness; see the first question of the following exercise.

EXERCISE 6.5

1. Rewrite any of the above four example terms (in a simpler form if possible).

2. Give the values of each of the following terms for the cases stated:

    a. (S ⩤ abr) when S = ∅   b. (S ⩤ abr) when S ∩ (dom abr) = ∅
    c. (abr ▷ T) when T ∩ (ran abr) = ∅   d. (abr ⩥ T) when T = ∅

3. Suppose we have

        DegreeClass ::=
            aegrotat | ord | ordMerit | pass | iii | ii2 | ii1 | first
        fdr : STUDENT ⇸ DegreeClass; compSci : ℙ STUDENT

    where fdr records the degree results obtained by final year students, and compSci are the final year students in Computer Science. Using suitable combinations of the domain, range and restriction operators, construct a term or predicate as appropriate for each of the following:

    a. who obtained which degree class in Computer Science
    b. the number of non-computer science students awarded first degrees
    c. the computer science students who failed to get a ii2 or better
    d. the final year results after the External Examiner has changed to a iii degree the awards of all students in Computer Science who were given a pass degree.

OPERATION A1

One of the checks that the booking operation must make is to ensure there is no nominal overbooking. The predicate required is very close to the 'no overbooking' invariant in schema `VanHire` itself. The latter could have made use of range restriction, as the former does, to produce a slightly tidier predicate (page 130).

```
┌─ MakeBooking ─────────────────────────────────────────────────────┐
│ ΔVH_XiVans                        — the Vans component does not change
│ cst? : CUSTOMER
│ vcl? : VanClass
│ hpd? : Period
│ bkngMade! : BOOKING
├───────────────────────────────────────────────────────────────────
│ — preconstraint: the fleet has vans of requested class
│ vcl? ∈ ran fleet
│ — preconstraint: no nominal overbooking in respect of van class/hire period requested
│ ∀ d : datesIn( hpd? ) •
│   #{ b : dom( commit ▷ { vcl? }) | d fallsIn hirePeriods( b )}
│      < #( fleet ▷ { vcl? })
│ — preconstraint: the requested hire period starts no earlier than today
│ start( hpd? ) isOnOrAfter today
│ — preconstraint: the requested hire period is no longer than the allowed maximum
│ length( hpd? ) ≤ maxHireLen
│
│ bkngMade! ∈ BOOKING \ dom custom
│ custom' = custom ∪ { bkngMade! ↦ cst? }
│ commit' = commit ∪ { bkngMade! ↦ vcl? }
│ hirePeriods' = hirePeriods ∪ { bkngMade! ↦ hpd? }
│ activeHires' = activeHires       — which also takes care of activeBkngs
│ today' = today
└───────────────────────────────────────────────────────────────────┘
```

The first preconstraint is in effect covered by the second: if `vcl? ∉ ran fleet`, then the second reduces to ∀ d : datesIn(hpd?) • $0 < 0$, which is of course false. Including both, however, emphasizes that they are qualitatively different kinds of check. A point to observe in the second preconstraint is that it is unnecessary to write

$$... < \#(\text{dom}(\text{fleet} \triangleright \{ \text{vcl?} \}))$$

to count the `vcl?` vans in the fleet. The term actually used simply counts maplets instead of domain elements, which amounts to the same thing for a function (why?).

An interesting feature of `MakeBooking` concerns `bkngMade!`. Firstly, the fact that `bkngMade!` is an output can be interpreted as the operation generating a booking identifier which then appears, say, on a docket that is printed out. This docket is handed to the customer and confirms the basic details of the booking, payment of deposit, etc. More important, though, is the predicate

$$bkngMade! ∈ BOOKING \setminus \text{dom custom} \tag{6.4}$$

This feature makes the operation's behaviour *non-deterministic* (see also page 50). The specification of `MakeBooking` does not uniquely determine `bkngMade!`, but merely states that it is one which is not currently in use. In practice, the process of design and implementation often reduces/eliminates non-determinism (see Section 9.2). Thus, the booking identifier generation algorithm developed could be such that MakeBooking's implemented behaviour is deterministic. Depending on the representation chosen for BOOKING, the algorithm might choose the 'successor' to the immediately previous booking identifier used, for example. This behaviour would still conform to MakeBooking's specification. The key point of the latter is that it says that a choice takes place, but it does not concern itself with *how* this choice is made. Nor should it.

OPERATION A5
In operation A1, predicate (6.4) plays another important role. It ensures that the choice of bkngMade! does not come from the domain of custom, or equally from the domains of commit or hirePeriods. In turn, this guarantees that each of the three equalities in MakeBooking of the form

$$\text{Variable}' = \text{Variable} \cup \{\text{bkngMade}! \mapsto \text{Expr}\} \tag{6.5}$$

does not contradict the constraint that Variable' must be functional like Variable. Suppose it were the case that bkngMade! might come from the domain of custom. Then the set union on the right-hand side of (6.5) would not be strong enough to ensure functionality, since bkngMade! might contribute to more than one maplet in the maplet set calculated. This would be a specification error.

In operation A5 below, unlike in MakeBooking, the component predicates would not be strong enough to rule out this kind of error. So we must avoid it another way, this time by using a different operator to set union. The new infix operator ⊕ is called *override*.

```
┌─ ChangeVanClass ──────────────────────────────────────────┐
│ ΔVH_XiVans                          — the Vans component does not change
│ bkng? : BOOKING
│ newVcl? : VanClass
├────────────────────────────────────────────────────────────
│ — preconstraint: booking exists but must not have started yet
│ bkng? ∈ dom custom \ activeBkngs
│ — preconstraint: a real van class change is being requested
│ newVcl? ≠ commit( bkng? )
│ — preconstraint: the fleet has vans of requested new class
│ newVcl? ∈ ran fleet
│ — preconstraint: no nominal overbooking for the new van class would result
│ ∀ d : datesIn( hirePeriods( bkng? )) •
│    #{ b : dom( commit ▷ { newVcl? }) | d fallsIn hirePeriods( b )}
│       < #( fleet ▷ { newVcl? })
│
│ commit' = commit ⊕ { bkng? ↦ newVcl? }
│ custom' = custom
│ hirePeriods' = hirePeriods
│ activeHires' = activeHires        — which also takes care of activeBkngs
│ today' = today
└────────────────────────────────────────────────────────────┘
```

Given

  $abr1, abr2 : X \leftrightarrow Y$

then

  $abr1 \oplus abr2 = (dom\ abr2 \lhd abr1) \cup abr2$

which is that relation consisting of abr2 plus those maplets from abr1 whose first co-ordinates are not in abr2's domain. Thus, abr2 'takes precedence over' abr1, whence the name 'override'. For example:

  $\{ b3 \mapsto c1, b8 \mapsto c1, b9 \mapsto c4 \} \oplus \{ b3 \mapsto c2, b3 \mapsto c5, b8 \mapsto c4 \}$
    $= \{ b3 \mapsto c2, b3 \mapsto c5, b8 \mapsto c4, b9 \mapsto c4 \}$

When applied between compatible functions f and g, i.e., functions of the same type $X \nrightarrow Y$, then $f \oplus g$ is also a function which can be understood as follows:

  $x \in dom\ g \Rightarrow (f \oplus g)\ x = g(x)$
  $x \in dom\ f \setminus dom\ g \Rightarrow (f \oplus g)\ x = f(x)$

Clearly, if $x \notin (dom\ f \cup dom\ g)$, then $(f \oplus g)\ x$ will be undefined.

  It is easy to see why override is needed in `ChangeVanClass`. Given

  $bkng? \in dom\ custom \setminus activeBkngs$

then

  $commit' = commit \cup \{ bkng? \mapsto vcl? \}$

would be inconsistent: the right-hand term would produce a BOOKING $\leftrightarrow$ VanClass relation that was not functional. In the analogous transitions in `MakeBooking`, set union *is* sufficient for the reason explained previously. These transitions in operation `MakeBooking` are instances of the first case in the more general property that

  $f \oplus g = f \cup g \Leftrightarrow dom\ g \cap dom\ f = \varnothing \lor g \subseteq f \lor f \subseteq g$

That is, override reduces to set union if and only if either the two functions have disjoint domains or one function is a subset of the other. In either case, of course, it is not wrong to use override; some might prefer this as a matter of style anyway.

  EXERCISE 6.6

  Construct specifications for operations A2, A3, A4 and A6.

Some Observer Operations

There is obviously a large number of ways in which the client might wish to interrogate the system data. The following is just a representative selection, disregarding more mundane queries like 'give the van class reserved by the specified booking'. Each of these operations will require ΞVanHire included in its specification.

B1. List any bookings that are late in completing:
  !   The bookings that are late in completing.
  (Assume this operation is requested after 09.00 on any given day to allow for hirers returning vans by 08.45 for bookings completing on the previous day.)

B2. List customers with multiple bookings, including each booking's identification:
  !   For each customer with multiple bookings, the customer and bookings involved.

B3. List those bookings which request the hiring of a van in excess of k days:
? The positive integer k
! Each booking which requests the hiring of a van in excess of k days.

B4. For each van class give the future bookings requesting that class:
! For each such van class: the future bookings requesting that class.

B5. Provide the total number of new bookings starting on specified date(s) on or after today:
? The specified date(s)
! For each date specified, the total number of new bookings starting on that date.

B6. List the maximum number of vans in a given class which are free to be committed *continuously throughout* a specified period that starts on or after the current date:
? The class involved
? The specified period
! The maximum total number of vans in the given class free to be hired continuously over the specified period.
(Assume no vans in the specified class will be off the road or late being returned.)

B7. Give the current operational status of every van in the fleet: either 'off the road', 'out on hire', or 'free for hire today':
! For every van in the fleet: its operational status.

OPERATION B2

The output here has a more complex type structure compared to outputs in, say, Digital Watch operations, but this is typical of lookups over the state of an information system. As query operations go, B2 represents a fairly simple 'slice' though the system data.

```
┌─ CustsWithMplBkngs ──────────────────────────────────┐
│ ΞVanHire                                              │
│ cambs! : CUSTOMER ⇸ ℙ BOOKING                         │
├───────────────────────────────────────────────────────┤
│ cambs! = { c : ran custom |                           │
│              #( custom ▷ { c }) > 1 • c ↦ ( custom~⦇{ c }⦈) }  │
└───────────────────────────────────────────────────────┘
```

The output is constructed straightforwardly as a set of maplets. The set comprehension takes each customer c in the range of custom who has more than one booking (note use of range restriction), and maps c to the bookings currently associated with c. Here we have taken the opportunity to use inversion and image. Whether this is preferred to

$$c \mapsto \mathrm{dom}(\mathrm{custom} \rhd \{ c \})$$

is really a matter of taste. In abstraction, the output is an unordered set. When implemented, an output like cambs! might well be sorted according to some ordering criteria. To describe the latter in specifications, we need various ordering relations (like isOnOrBefore for Date)—one of the topics of Section 6.3.

OPERATION B6

Compared to B2, the output of operation B6 is very simple (just a natural number), but obtaining it requires inspecting the Van Hire system data in a rather non-trivial way. We need an operation description along the following lines:

```
┌─VanTotalAvlblty──────────────────────────────────┐
│ Ξ VanHire                                         │
│ vcl? : VanClass                                   │
│ hpd? : Period                                     │
│ nfv! : ℕ                                          │
│ ─────────────────────                             │
│ vcl? ∈ ran fleet                                  │
│ start( hpd? ) isOnOrAfter today                   │
│ nfv! = DifficultTermToWrite                       │
└───────────────────────────────────────────────────┘
```

The problem is to construct DifficultTermToWrite: the maximum number of vans in class vcl? that could be hired continuously over the specified period hpd?. Suppose d is some date. The total number of vans in class vcl? *committed* on that date is

$$\#\{ b : dom(commit ▷ \{ vcl? \}) \mid d \text{ fallsIn } hirePeriods(b)\}$$

Now consider *all* dates in the period hpd?. The set

$$\{ d : datesIn(hpd?) \bullet$$
$$\#\{ b : dom(commit ▷ \{ vcl? \}) \mid d \text{ fallsIn } hirePeriods(b)\}\}$$

generates the totals of committed vcl? vans on the different days of hpd?. If we find the maximum such total using the Z-provided function max thus:

$$max(\{ d : datesIn(hpd?) \bullet$$
$$\#\{ b : dom(commit ▷ \{ vcl? \}) \mid d \text{ fallsIn } hirePeriods(b)\}\})$$

this represents the maximum commitment of vcl? vans on any day in hpd?. So

$$\#(fleet ▷ \{ vcl? \}) -$$
$$max(\{ d : datesIn(hpd?) \bullet$$
$$\#\{ b : dom(commit ▷ \{ vcl? \}) \mid d \text{ fallsIn } hirePeriods(b)\}\})$$

gives the number we want under ideal conditions (no vcl? vans off the road or late in being returned). Thus, here is operation B6, along with a new feature:

```
┌─VanTotalAvlblty──────────────────────────────────┐
│ Ξ VanHire                                         │
│ vcl? : VanClass                                   │
│ hpd? : Period                                     │
│ nfv! : ℕ                                          │
│ ─────────────────────                             │
│ vcl? ∈ ran fleet                                  │
│ start( hpd? ) isOnOrAfter today                   │
│ ( let commitTotals ==                             │
│   { d : datesIn( hpd? ) •                          │
│     #{ b : dom( commit ▷{ vcl? })| d fallsIn hirePeriods( b )}} • │
│   nfv! = #( fleet ▷{ vcl? }) - max( commitTotals ) ) │
└───────────────────────────────────────────────────┘
```

The complexity of the calculation looks intimidating, but we do not expect its implementation to be any easier. Note that the output would still be well-defined if the first preconstraint were omitted (what would the output be if vcl? ∉ ran fleet?).

The new construct in `VanTotalAvlblty`, called a *local definition*, has the general form

$$(\ \textbf{let}\ \mathsf{Name}_1\ ==\ \mathsf{Expr}_1;\ \mathsf{Name}_2\ ==\ \mathsf{Expr}_2;\ \dots\ \bullet\ \mathsf{TermOrPredicate}\ )$$

A local definition is like a list of one or more local abbreviation definitions, each with the same role as global ones: avoiding multiple instances of complex terms and/or improving readability. The variables Name_i are local to the definition (which must be bracketed), though their scope does *not* include the Expr_i themselves. The variables will be applied in TermOrPredicate (in our example, a predicate), though we must be careful that each Name_i is not already being used in TermOrPredicate. Preferably, each Name_i should be fresh throughout the entire paragraph in which the local definition occurs. This is safe, and good style anyway.

The partial Z functions `max` and `min` are worth remembering when it comes to calculating respectively the maximum and minimum integer in a set of integers. Some care is needed with infinite sets to avoid undefinedness. For example, the set $\mathbb{N}$ has no maximum, the set $\mathbb{Z}$ no minimum or maximum, etc.

FINAL REMARK ON VAN HIRE

A point over which the reader may be puzzling is this: what is supposed to happen if a preconstraint of an operation is *not* satisfied? In `MakeBooking` on page 138, for example, four things can go wrong: (i) the fleet provides no vans in the requested class; (ii) overbooking would result; (iii) the hire period is illegal (starts too early); (iv) the hire period length exceeds the permitted maximum. The problem is that nothing in `MakeBooking` tells us what happens in these error situations. This kind of omission in a specification might well be unacceptable. Fortunately, there are ways to deal with error handling in specifications, as Section 8.3 explains.

EXERCISE 6.7

Construct specifications for operations B1, B3, B4, B5 and B7.

6.3   MORE ON BINARY RELATIONS AND FUNCTIONS

Additional Properties of Binary Relations

Although there are certain aspects of binary relations and functions that we make little use of in the book, their importance warrants some discussion. Given some *homogeneous* binary relation `hbr`, meaning that `hbr` is a relation *on* some set X (i.e., $\mathsf{hbr}\ :\ \mathsf{X} \leftrightarrow \mathsf{X}$), then `hbr` might possess one or more of these basic properties:

- *reflexivity:* $\forall\, \mathsf{x}\ :\ \mathsf{X} \bullet (\,\mathsf{x} \mapsto \mathsf{x}\,) \in \mathsf{hbr}$
- *symmetry:* $\forall\, \mathsf{x}, \mathsf{y}\ :\ \mathsf{X} \bullet (\,\mathsf{x} \mapsto \mathsf{y}\,) \in \mathsf{hbr} \Rightarrow (\,\mathsf{y} \mapsto \mathsf{x}\,) \in \mathsf{hbr}$
- *transitivity:* $\forall\, \mathsf{x}, \mathsf{y}, \mathsf{z}\ :\ \mathsf{X} \bullet (\,\mathsf{x} \mapsto \mathsf{y}\,) \in \mathsf{hbr} \wedge (\,\mathsf{y} \mapsto \mathsf{z}\,) \in \mathsf{hbr} \Rightarrow (\,\mathsf{x} \mapsto \mathsf{z}\,) \in \mathsf{hbr}$

Sometimes, a relation has the negation of a property, such as *irreflexivity*: `hbr` relates no x to itself. There is also *asymmetry*: if `hbr` relates x to y, it does *not* relate y to x. Asymmetry should be carefully distinguished from the property of *antisymmetry*: if `hbr` relates x to y and also y to x, then it must be that x = y.

There are certain important kinds of homogeneous relation that are distinguished by their possession of particular combinations of the previous properties. Three such kinds are as follows:

- *equivalence relation:*   a relation that is reflexive, symmetric and transitive
- *partial order:*   a relation that is reflexive, antisymmetric and transitive
- *total order:*   a partial order with the extra property:

$$\forall x,y : X \bullet (x \mapsto y) \in \text{hbr} \lor (y \mapsto x) \in \text{hbr}$$

Equality is a simple example of an equivalence relation. The reader should be able to confirm this easily. An example of a partial order which is total is the relation $\leq$ on $\mathbb{Z}$. Let us check this out:

- $x \leq x$ for all $x \in \mathbb{Z}$, so it is reflexive
- if $x \leq y$ and $y \leq z$, then $x \leq z$, so it is transitive
- if $x \leq y$ and $y \leq x$, then this is the case only when $x = y$; so it is antisymmetric.

This confirms $\leq$ as a partial order. However, since either $x \leq y$ or $y \leq x$ for any $x, y \in \mathbb{Z}$, $\leq$ is also a total order.

The definition of partial order given characterizes 'less than or equals' type ordering relations. Another possible approach to the idea of partial ordering is from a 'less than' viewpoint. Here, we would require such a (sometimes called 'strict') partial order to have a different set of properties (irreflexivity, asymmetry and transitivity, in fact).

Consider now a list `list` of items of type X, possibly containing duplicates. Given that the list is `k` elements long, we can think of `list` as the function

$$\text{list} : \mathbb{N} \rightarrow X$$

whose domain is `1..k`; hence also `k = #list`. The domain elements act like 'positional indices' to the range elements. Suppose there is a total order `_ ltOrEq _ : X ↔ X`. Using `ltOrEq`, it is then possible to arrange the elements of `list` into a unique ordering according to the property

$$\forall i,j : 1..\#\text{list} \bullet i \leq j \Rightarrow \text{list}(i) \text{ ltOrEq list}(j)$$

In normal computational parlance, we would say that `list` is 'sorted'. Functions like `list` are actually 'sequences'. Because of their usefulness in formal description, Z gives sequences special treatment. Sequences are discussed in Section 7.3.

Could we define a total ordering over bookings, say, if we wanted to include some notion of 'sorting' into operation descriptions in Van Hire? Only indirectly. Assuming the availability of a generic unary relation `totalOrder` for characterizing homogeneous binary relations that are total orders, we could define

```
_ leq _ : BOOKING ↔ BOOKING

totalOrder( _ leq _ )
```

However, we would have no way of describing what `leq` 'means' since BOOKING is a given set; hence, it has no *a priori* properties or accessible internal structure that we can exploit in definitions. This does not matter, though. The axiomatic description asserts the existence of total order `leq`, and that would be good enough for the specification. Later, we would find a way of implementing `leq`, having chosen a representation for BOOKING. In Section 7.5 of the next chapter, we look at this way of specifying— axiomatic 'property-oriented' description—in more detail. Also, in Section 7.3, we see how to define generic relations and functions of our own (generic `totalOrder` is not part of Z's standard mathematical toolkit, but we can easily define it ourselves).

Even if a homogeneous binary relation hbr does not possess the property of reflexivity or transitivity, say, it is still possible to define a relation 'surrounding' hbr that does have the desired characteristics. For this, we use the idea of *closure*. Closure is like defining a boundary that encloses just those objects in which one is interested and excludes everything else (see also page 14). Two important closures, both calculated by postfix operators, are:

- the *transitive closure* of hbr: hbr^+
- the *reflexive transitive closure* of hbr: hbr^*

hbr^+ comprises hbr *plus* just those extra pairs needed to make a transitive relation. So if hbr^+ contains ($x \mapsto y$) and ($y \mapsto z$), it must also contain ($x \mapsto z$) even if hbr itself does not. Relation hbr^* includes hbr^+ and just those extra pairs that are needed to make a reflexive relation. Thus hbr^* definitely contains ($x \mapsto x$) for all $x \in X$, even if hbr does not. Given the *identity relation* on a set X, defined as

$$id\ X\ ==\ \{\,x : X \bullet x \mapsto x\}$$

it follows that

$$hbr^*\ =\ hbr^+ \cup id\ X$$

Note that these closures are the strongest ('smallest') relations that include hbr as a subset and which possess the desired characteristics. Thus, for example, suppose we have some relation sbr where $hbr \subseteq sbr$. If sbr is transitive, then it must also be that $hbr^+ \subseteq sbr$.

To illustrate these concepts further, suppose we have

```
T ::= u | p | c | s
hbr == {u ↦ p,p ↦ c,c ↦ u}
```

Then, using emboldening to indicate maplets added by the closure operation, we will have

$$hbr^+ = \{u \mapsto p, p \mapsto c, c \mapsto u, \mathbf{u} \mapsto \mathbf{c}, \mathbf{p} \mapsto \mathbf{u}, \mathbf{c} \mapsto \mathbf{p}, \mathbf{u} \mapsto \mathbf{u}, \mathbf{c} \mapsto \mathbf{c}, \mathbf{p} \mapsto \mathbf{p}\}$$
$$hbr^* = hbr^+ \cup \{\mathbf{s} \mapsto \mathbf{s}\}$$

The effect is also illustrated by the graphical diagram in Figure 6.5.

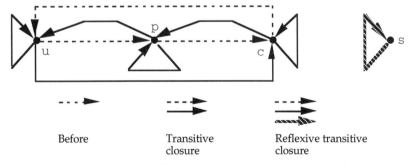

| Before | Transitive closure | Reflexive transitive closure |

Figure 6.5   The effect of closure operations on a binary relation.

In general, hbr^+ adds to hbr just those extra *arcs* (i.e, maplets) such that for every *path* (maplet chain) $x_0 \mapsto x_1 \mapsto \dots x_k$ in hbr, there is also an arc in hbr^+ from each x_i to x_j

in that path for $i < j$. Put another way, in hbr^+ each x_i in an hbr chain can now 'directly reach' every x_j occurring *after* x_i in the same chain. Suppose further that a path is circular, i.e., $x_0 = x_k$. Following through the 'reachability' idea gives two additional features in hbr^+: there will also be an arc from each x_i *to itself* in the path, *plus* for each x_j an arc to each x_i occurring *earlier* than x_j in the path. Finally, hbr^* can be seen as calculating hbr^+ and then adding an arc from every element to itself where this is not present in hbr^+.

The importance of these concepts is that many structures in computing systems, from networks to data structures like trees, are readily modelled as graphs with the appropriate properties. Transitive closure is particularly useful in capturing the idea of reachability in such structures, e.g., which nodes can be reached from some given node in a linked data structure. There is a body of discrete mathematics, *graph theory*, devoted to the subject of graphs, which we have not the space to explore here (terminology like 'path' and 'arc' is graph-theoretic).

EXERCISE 6.8

1. a. Argue that the relation

$$cm3 \;==\; \{\, i,j : \mathbb{N} \mid i \bmod 3 = j \bmod 3 \bullet i \mapsto j \,\}$$

   is an equivalence relation
   b. All equivalence relations have the same general effect on the set over which they are defined. What is this effect? *Hint:* study the effect of $cm3$ on $\mathbb{N}$.

2. Is the relation $\_<\_ : \mathbb{Z} \leftrightarrow \mathbb{Z}$ a partial order? Explain.

3. Consider the homogeneous binary relation $overlaps$ we have defined over $Period$ in Exercise 6.4(2), plus the following:

   $$\begin{array}{|l}
   \_\,joins\,\_ : Period \leftrightarrow Period \\
   \_\,includedIn\,\_ : Period \leftrightarrow Period \\
   \hline
   \forall\, p1,p2 : Period \bullet \\
   \quad (\,p1\ joins\ p2 \;\Leftrightarrow \\
   \qquad end(\,p1\,) = start(\,p2\,) \vee end(\,p2\,) = start(\,p1\,)\,) \wedge \\
   \quad (\,p1\ includedIn\ p2 \;\Leftrightarrow \\
   \qquad start(\,p1\,)\ isOnOrAfter\ start(\,p2\,) \wedge \\
   \qquad end(\,p1\,)\ isOnOrBefore\ end(\,p2\,)\,)
   \end{array}$$

   List the properties that each relation possesses and hence decide whether any of them is an equivalence relation, partial order or total order.

4. The relation: $rel : T \leftrightarrow T$ — for T, see previous page
   is characterized by: $rel = \{\, u \mapsto p, p \mapsto c, c \mapsto s \,\}$

   a. List the properties of rel
   b. Give the members of: i. rel^+
                          ii. rel^*
   What, if anything, is special about rel^*?
   c. Give the members of the *symmetric closure* of rel.

Composition

Suppose we have two relations

abr1 : A ↔ B
abr2 : B ↔ C

Then the *forward composition* of abr1 and abr2, written

abr1 ⨾ abr2

is

{ a : A; c : C | (∃ b : B • (a ↦ b) ∈ abr1 ∧ (b ↦ c) ∈ abr2) • a ↦ c }

For example, using the variables of the Van Hire state model, the term

custom~ ⨾ hirePeriods

constructs a CUSTOMER ↔ Period relation that relates customers to the hire periods they have requested.

If hbr is a homogeneous relation, then it can be composed with itself:

hbr ⨾ hbr
(hbr ⨾ hbr) ⨾ hbr
etc.

which leads to *iteration*: composing a relation with itself k times, which is written

iter k hbr   or   hbr^k

Notice that we do *not* write iter(k , hbr), which would be ill-formed. The reason is because iter is a 'curried' function; see pages 176–179.

Clearly, hbr^2 is the same as hbr ⨾ hbr, and we intend hbr^1 to be just hbr itself; but what of hbr^0? It is mathematically convenient to define this as id X. So we get

hbr^0 = id X
hbr^{k+1} = hbr ⨾ hbr^k = hbr^k ⨾ hbr

for any $k \geq 0$ (note that ⨾ is associative).

There is a strong connection between iteration and the two closures discussed earlier. Firstly, if we join the hbr^k for all $k \in \mathbb{N}_1$, then this makes the transitive closure of hbr. That is,

hbr$^+$ = ⋃ { k : $\mathbb{N}_1$ • hbr^k }

It is perhaps easiest to see that this is so by arguing informally:

- hbr^1 is simply hbr and therefore comprises exactly the maplets of hbr.

- If hbr contains a length-two chain a ↦ b and b ↦ c, then by definition of relational iteration and the operator ⨾ , hbr^2 must contain a ↦ c.

- Similarly, if hbr contains a length-three chain a ↦ b, b ↦ c, and c ↦ d, then hbr^2 will contain a ↦ c and b ↦ d, and hence hbr^3, which is hbr ⨾ hbr^2, must contain a ↦ d.

- This process can be continued for all other k = 4 , 5 , 6… . The result must be a transitive relation constructed from hbr which is the strongest, since the process cannot introduce transitively related pairs that are not derivable from hbr as basis. Thus, the relation calculated is hbr$^+$.

It follows that

$$hbr^* = hbr^+ \cup hbr^0 = \bigcup \{ k : \mathbb{N} \bullet hbr^k \}$$

are equalities which hold for any homogeneous relation hbr.

Since forward composition and iteration are operators on relations, they are applicable to functions. For example, given

$$f : A \twoheadrightarrow B; \; g : B \twoheadrightarrow C$$

then $f \mathbin{\fatsemi} g$ is a function with signature $A \twoheadrightarrow C$. So we can apply it to some $a \in dom\ f$:

$$(f \mathbin{\fatsemi} g)\ a$$

This term yields some value in the set C (the value being defined provided ... what?). In practice, we often write

$$g(\ f(\ a\ ))$$

which calculates the same thing, though the syntax no longer conveys the notion of a single function being applied to its argument. In fact, we can keep syntactic order the same as application order if we use the *backward composition* operator _○_ (which is also applicable to relations in general):

$$(g \circ f)\ a$$

This calculates the same thing as the previous term. In fact,

$$g \circ f = f \mathbin{\fatsemi} g$$

There are a large number of basic laws in the theory of relations. The intention here is not to list all, or even most, of them, but rather to get the reader to obtain a feel for some of the properties of relations and their operators in the final exercise.

EXERCISE 6.9

1. In each partially complete predicate below, replace the question mark(s) with actual symbols so as to make a law. The reader is reminded that the variables appearing in the predicates are implicitly universally quantified. These variables are (for arbitrary sets V, W, X and Y):

$$h : X \leftrightarrow X; \; r : X \leftrightarrow Y$$
$$r1 : V \leftrightarrow W; \; r2 : W \leftrightarrow X; \; r3 : X \leftrightarrow Y$$
$$A, B : \mathbb{P}\, X; \; C : \mathbb{P}\, Y$$
$$f, g : X \twoheadrightarrow Y$$

   a. $A \lhd (B \lhd r) = (A \; ? \; B) \lhd r$
   b. $(r1 \mathbin{\fatsemi} r2) \; ? \; r3 = r1 \; ? \; (r2 \mathbin{\fatsemi} r3)$
   c. $A \; ? \; r = id\ A \mathbin{\fatsemi} r$
   d. $r \; ? \; C = r \mathbin{\fatsemi} id\ C$
   e. $A \lhd r = (X \setminus A) \; ? \; r$
   f. $r \rhd C = r \; ? \; (Y \setminus C)$
   g. $(r1 \mathbin{\fatsemi} r2)^\sim = \; ?^\sim \mathbin{\fatsemi} \; ?^\sim$
   h. $(id\ A)^\sim = \; ?$
   i. $ran(\ r1 \mathbin{\fatsemi} r2\ ) = r2 (\!(\; ? \;)\!)$

j. $r(A) = \text{ran}(A$ **?** $r)$

k. $r(A$ **?** $B) = r(A) \cup r(B)$

l. $h^{i+j} = h^i$ **?** h^j

m. $(h^{?}) = (h^i)^j$

n. f **?** $f = \varnothing$ **?** $f = f$ **?** $\varnothing = f$

2. Given the two functions

$$f == \{ i : \mathbb{N} \bullet i \mapsto i * i \}$$
$$g == \{ i : \mathbb{N} \bullet i \mapsto i \bmod 3 \}$$

calculate the values of the following terms:

a. $(f \mathbin{;} g)\ 5$ b. $(g \mathbin{;} f)\ 5$ c. $(f \mathbin{;} (f \circ g))\ 5$

d. $((f \circ g) \mathbin{;} g))\ 5$ e. $f^2\ 5$ f. $(f^{\sim} \circ f)\ 5$

g. $g^0\ 5$ h. $(f^{\sim})^{\sim}\ 5$ i. $(f^2)^{\sim}\ 16$

SUMMARY OF CHAPTER 6

- The Van Hire case study begun in Chapter 5 is completed by improving the state model and specifying a variety of update and observer operations.

- The application of binary relations and functions, and various operators on these objects, is illustrated in descriptions of states and operations.

- Useful additional theory concerning binary relations and functions is overviewed.

7

SUPPORTING SYSTEM DESCRIPTION: CONSTRUCTING DATA TYPES

Key Topics Z types, mathematical types, data types. Model-oriented data type construction. Schema types, binding formation. Generic specification. Sequences. Axiomatic function description: 'guards', argument structures, inductive definition; lambda abstraction, mu-expressions; curried functions. Free types, data type theories, enrichment, property-oriented specification; inductive properties; abstract syntax, disjoint union types.

7.1 DATA TYPES: AN OVERVIEW

Types, Data Types and Abstraction

As Chapter 6 has shown with `Period`, specification in Z does not necessarily involve just schemas describing states and associated operations. Data types are also fundamental to specification work. Indeed, some Z specifications, like our imagined `Date_Adt` used by the Van Hire specification, might consist solely of data type description and involve no schemas at all. It is essential, therefore, for a specifier to have a thorough grasp of the concepts and techniques associated with data type construction. Unfortunately, discussion of data types can sometimes be confusing because of the loose usage of terminology. What, for example, is the difference (if any) between the following:

type,   mathematical type,   data type,   abstract (data) type?

Since we try to maintain a high degree of consistency in the usage of these terms, it will help to clarify what we mean by them.

In this book, the term *type* is always used in the Z sense. A Z type τ is a certain kind of expression (see below) denoting some set T. The set T is type τ's 'value space', or *carrier* to give the set its proper technical name. Very often, we talk of types and sets interchangeably, which is imprecise; e.g., we might say 'the set $\mathbb{Z}$ is a type', when what we really mean is 'the name $\mathbb{Z}$ is a type that denotes the set of integers'. This kind of imprecision is usually acceptable, unless we have to be especially careful to distinguish between 'types' and 'value spaces'.

What is the 'universe of types' for Z specifications? This is easily answered with a recursive definition. A type is one of the following expressions:

EITHER   The name of a given set
OR   An expression constructed from types, being one of the following three possibilities:
    a. a powerset type $\mathbb{P}\,\tau$
    b. an n-dimensional cartesian product type $\tau_1 \times \tau_2 \times \ldots \tau_n$
    c. a schema type.

A schema type also involves one or more types. We have not encountered schema types yet; they are introduced in Section 7.2.

The preceding definition describes an infinite type hierarchy, whose bottom layer is populated by given sets. Given set names are basic types, and members of a given set are regarded as primitive, having no internal structure of interest. Above this base layer, it is possible to define without limit, using the mechanisms (a), (b) and (c), ever more complex types denoting objects with internal structures of increasing richness.

We use the term *mathematical type* as a convenient way to refer to any general class of mathematical object for which there exists a well-established body of theory, such as sets, tuples, relations, functions, etc. Except for the first two classes of mathematical object, all others are not types in the Z sense, but are modelled in terms of sets and tuples, as previous chapters have shown.

As first indicated in Section 5.5, we use the term 'data type' to mean (the name of) any set over which we construct a collection of useful operations—mainly relations and functions, though sometimes also individual constants of the data type; we use the term 'operation' to cover *all* these possibilities. On this definition of terminology, 'data type' encompasses all the mathematical types defined in Z's toolkit.

To construct a *model-oriented* specification of a data type, we proceed as we did with `Period` in the Van Hire specification. Firstly we model the data type's value space with a suitable set, typically via an abbreviation definition:

DataTypeName == SetModelOfValueSpace

Then, to complete the construction, we describe axiomatically the required collection of operations in terms of SetModelOfValueSpace. Furthermore, providing care is taken with the construction, DataTypeName can be regarded as *abstract* if it can be understood and applied purely through its operations without knowing anything about SetModelOfValueSpace. We were careful to observe this principle when constructing operations for `Period` in Section 6.1.

In certain notations such as some programming languages, data abstraction can be enforced (by encapsulation, see page 19). Although a schema has an enclosing effect of a kind on the ownership of its variables, Z has no built-in mechanism for enforcing data abstraction. However, we postulated in Section 5.5 that it could be provided by a CASE support environment for Z which permits specifications of data types to be imported by other specifications, as we imagined with `Date_Adt`.

Although imposing a veneer of abstraction on `Period` in Van Hire makes it appear externally to be a 'new type', the underlying reality is of course the opposite: `Period` is modelled in terms of `Date`, so it is neither 'new' nor a type in the strict sense. This prompts the question: is it possible to define data types which really are fresh types in their own right? The answer is *yes*, though we can immediately infer two things. Firstly, the approach used cannot be model-oriented; secondly, it must be based on given sets, since given sets provide the only way of introducing fresh basic types into a Z specification. Section 7.5 discusses how we proceed when using the alternative to model-oriented data type specification.

Remark
State-based specifications can also be regarded as data types; there is no essential difference between 'state-space model' plus state-transitional operations and 'value-space model' plus relational/functional operations. So we can view a system-level description like Van Hire or Digital Watch as a (state-based) data type, even though it cannot be used to underpin other specifications in the way that `Date_Adt` can.

Nevertheless, schemas can be used as types, as Section 7.2 explains; and even state models plus their operations can be 'promoted' to contribute like data types to more complex state descriptions (we see this in Chapter 8). Furthermore, any state-based schema specification can be implemented as an abstract 'object' or abstract data type in a programming language that has suitable data abstraction facilities. In this chapter, however, *data type* refers to data types like `Date` and `Period`, i.e., the set-based, non-state variety whose operations are constructed using axiomatic descriptions. It is data types specified in this way which provide general support for the data type infrastructure of other specifications, state-based or otherwise.

Model-oriented Data Type Construction: an Example

As a more extensive illustration of the model-oriented route to data type construction, and to round off the Van Hire scenario of the previous two chapters, we might expect the internals of `Date_Adt` to look something like that given below. Note that specifications which are axiomatic and functional, rather than schema-based, can be much more complex than `Date_Adt`.

$$DaysInWeek ::= mon \mid tue \mid wed \mid thu \mid fri \mid sat \mid sun$$
$$bottomYr == 1753$$
$$Year == \{ y : \mathbb{N} \mid y \geq bottomYr \} \qquad \text{— for convenience}$$

Definitions of relations `ajsn`, `leapYr`, and `isDate` as in Section 4.4, though using `Year` instead of $\mathbb{N}$ where beneficial (see Exercise 7.1(1)).

— Now the actual value-space model:
$$Date == \{ d : 1..31; m : 1..12; y : Year \mid isDate(d,m,y) \}$$

— A useful constant:
$$dateZero == (1,1,bottomYr)$$

— Some useful relations and functions
$$\_ isBefore \_, \_ isOnOrBefore \_ : Date \leftrightarrow Date$$
$$\_ isOnOrAfter \_, \_ isAfter \_ : Date \leftrightarrow Date$$

$eom \_ : \mathbb{P} \, Date$	— now elevated to a `Date` operation
$dayOf : Date \to 1..31$	— projection function
$monthOf : Date \to 1..12$	— projection function
$yearOf : Date \to Year$	— projection function

— makes a date from its arguments:
$$mkDate : (1..31) \times (1..12) \times Year \nrightarrow Date$$

$ordDtInYr : Date \to 1..366$	— yields ordinal position of date in year
$next : Date \to Date$	— yields date immediately following date given
$prev : Date \nrightarrow Date$	— yields date immediately preceding date given
$daysOn : Date \times \mathbb{N} \to Date$	— yields date n days on from date given
$daysOff : Date \times \mathbb{N} \nrightarrow Date$	— yields date n days previous to date given

— yields no. of days separating two dates, the first being no earlier than the second:
$$dtMinus : Date \times Date \nrightarrow \mathbb{N}$$
$$daysDiff : Date \times Date \to \mathbb{N} \qquad \text{— as } dtMinus \text{ but order of dates is immaterial}$$

— creates a set of dates from its arguments analogously to $\_..\_$ for the integers:
$$\_ upto \_ : Date \times Date \to \mathbb{P} \, Date$$

Continued on next page ...

— the earliest/latest date in a non-empty set of dates:

earliest : $\mathbb{P}_1$ Date $\rightarrow$ Date

latest : $\mathbb{P}_1$ Date $\twoheadrightarrow$ Date

— yields the day of the week on which the given date fell/falls:

dayOfWeek : Date $\rightarrow$ DaysInWeek

TheDefiningAxioms   — see subsequent exercises and sections of the text

export DaysInWeek, bottomYr, (leapYr _), (isDate _),

        adt (Date, dateZero, (_ isBefore _), ... etc.)

Like our invented import statement used in Van Hire, an **export** statement defines exactly what the specification exports for other specifications to use. Names enclosed in **adt** (...) are exported as an abstract data type. Other names such as DaysInWeek are exported visibly in terms of their definitions. We would expect the export list to exclude ajsn and Year (not very useful outside of Date_Adt) and dtMinus, which is encompassed by the behaviour of daysDiff. These three objects therefore remain completely hidden within Date_Adt.

The abstraction of data type Date is best appreciated by observing that the declarations of all the operations would remain unchanged if we decided to switch our date model to, say, one analogous to DateVarsDY or DateVarsDD on pages 42–43. What *would* change would be TheDefiningAxioms—the reader might like to investigate after reading further, particularly Section 7.4 which covers axiomatic function description.

EXERCISE 7.1

1. Explain how using the set Year instead of $\mathbb{N}$ would affect the description of the relations indicated on the previous page.

2. Construct predicates defining the four binary relations isBefore, etc., plus a slightly revised eom.

3. Explain in each case why certain functions in Date_Adt are not total.

4. Construct predicates defining the following Date_Adt functions:

    a. dayOf, monthOf and yearOf   b. mkDate.

7.2   BINDINGS AND SCHEMA TYPES

Constructing Sets Involving Bindings

The following model of dates was used in the Digital Watch specification. We have modified its predicate slightly to make use of the isDate relation.

┌─ Date ───┐

dy : 1..31

mn : 1..12

yr : $\mathbb{N}$

---

isDate(dy, mn, yr)
└───┘

Schema `Date` can be thought of as defining a set of bindings (see page 32) described by the term

$$\{\,\mathtt{Date}\,\} \tag{7.1a}$$

which is an abbreviation for the set comprehension

$$\{\,\mathtt{Date} \bullet \theta\,\mathtt{Date}\,\} \tag{7.1b}$$

In the comprehension, the second instance of `Date` is the argument of the *binding formation* operator θ. The operator is being used to create bindings from the variables of `Date`, i.e., bindings of the form

$$\langle\,\mathtt{dy} \Rrightarrow \dots,\ \mathtt{mn} \Rrightarrow \dots,\ \mathtt{yr} \Rrightarrow \dots\,\rangle$$

More generally, we can use θ to generate bindings from schema references in a manner clarified later.

To avoid confusion, it is essential to assimilate fully the application of schema names in a context like set construction. Let SchName be the name of some schema and Decor an arbitrary, possibly empty, decoration. A set comprehension of the schema-text form

$$\{\,\mathsf{SchNameDecor}\mid \mathsf{Constraint}\,\} \tag{7.2}$$

involves the schema reference SchNameDecor in the declaration part of the schema text and Constraint in its predicate part, the latter imposing additional constraints on the variables of SchNameDecor; note that in (7.1a) and (7.1b), the predicate part happens to be empty, i.e., Constraint is just `true`. Recall from page 102 that when the optional '• Term' component of a set comprehension is missing, the set is constructed over the declaration part's *characteristic tuple*. The point is that when a schema reference in a schema text contributes to the characteristic tuple of some construct, *it always contributes a binding*. This is why (7.2) is equal to

$$\{\,\mathsf{SchNameDecor}\mid \mathsf{Constraint} \bullet \theta\,\mathsf{SchNameDecor}\,\}$$

not

$$\{\,\mathsf{SchNameDecorDecs}\mid \mathsf{SchNameDecorPred} \wedge \mathsf{Constraint}\,\}$$

tempting though this may seem if one imagines, *wrongly*, unfolding SchNameDecor into its text. Thus, terms (7.1a/b) above are *not* the same as the comprehension

$$\{\,\mathtt{dy}:\mathtt{1..31};\ \mathtt{mn}:\mathtt{1..12};\ \mathtt{yr}:\mathbb{N}\mid \mathtt{isDate(\,dy,mn,yr\,)}\,\}$$

This term constructs a set of *triples* based on the characteristic tuple (`dy`,`mn`,`yr`); that is, it is the same as the comprehension

$$\{\,\mathtt{dy}:\mathtt{1..31};\ \mathtt{mn}:\mathtt{1..12};\ \mathtt{yr}:\mathbb{N}\mid \mathtt{isDate(\,dy,mn,yr\,)} \bullet \mathtt{(\,dy,mn,yr\,)}\,\}$$

and this is a completely different set to the set of `Date` bindings that the previous terms (7.1a/b) actually construct. Later in Section 7.4, we come across other situations of a similar nature where schema references contribute bindings.

On the other hand, consider a comprehension of the form

$$\{\,\mathsf{SchNameDecor}\mid \mathsf{Constraint} \bullet \mathsf{Term}\,\} \tag{7.3}$$

Now we *can* imagine harmlessly unfolding SchNameDecor to give

$$\{\,\mathsf{SchNameDecorDecs}\mid \mathsf{SchNameDecorPred} \wedge \mathsf{Constraint} \bullet \mathsf{Term}\,\}$$

since, due to the presence of '• Term ', no implicit characteristic tuple construction is involved. So, for example, the (not very useful) comprehension

{ Date • dy * mn + yr }

merely constructs a particular set of positive integers.

For the discussion thus far to be made completely general, note that in forms (7.2) and (7.3), the declaration part could contain other declarations—even further references to schemas. However, the principles described still hold. In particular, the presence of other declarations in (7.2) will enrich the structure of the comprehension's characteristic tuple; but this tuple will still include a θ SchNameDecor component in the appropriate position.

Binding Component Access

Suppose a binding Binding includes a component BndCmpName of type τ. Then the term

Binding . BndCmpName

has type τ and its value is the value of component BndCmpName in the binding Binding. For example, suppose

birth ∈ { Date • θ Date }

then

birth.dy

is the value of component dy in that particular binding birth, and its type is $\mathbb{Z}$. It follows that

⟨ dy ⇒ birth.dy, mn ⇒ birth.mn, yr ⇒ birth.yr ⟩

describes the complete binding which is the value of birth.

Some readers will no doubt find the 'dot' notation for component selection of bindings appealingly reminiscent of field selection of records in certain programming languages. In fact, the analogy is even stronger because schema names can be used to type variables in declarations. Schemas used in this way look very much like 'record types'. Thus, suppose we declare, say,

d : Date   which is short for   d : { Date }   — or d : { Date • θ Date }

Note that the binding denoted by d will satisfy the property of Date. We can now write d.dy, d.mn, etc., for the component values of the Date binding d. In a sense, therefore, we are getting projection 'for free' since the by-name selection of binding components is analogous to using projection functions for positional access of tuple components.

We could in fact use schema Date as the model of the value space of our data type in Date_Adt instead of using the set Date as defined on page 152. There would inevitably be some knock-on effects in other paragraphs, necessitating modification to certain defining predicates. For example, the defining predicate for isBefore would become:

∀ d1,d2 : Date •
  d1 isBefore d2 ⇔
    d1.yr < d2.yr ∨ d1.yr = d2.yr ∧ d1.mn < d2.mn ∨
      d1.yr = d2.yr ∧ d1.mn = d2.mn ∧ d1.dy < d2.dy

This predicate is neater (compare with the answer to Exercise 7.1(2)). The defining axioms of various `Date_Adt` functions would also undergo some modification, mainly involving replacement of certain terms by binding component selection. Note, though, that there would be *no change to the external abstraction as seen by a user of the data type*.

Binding Formation, Decoration and Schema Types

In general, a 'theta-term' with the syntax

    θ SchNameDecor

forms a binding whose components have names which are *the names of the variables of the schema* SchName—that is, Decor does *not* contribute to the naming of the binding's components. However, the types and values of those components *are those of the variables of* SchNameDecor, and these are taken *from the environment in which the theta-term finds itself*. To avoid problematic uses of binding formation, the term θ SchNameDecor should be restricted to situations *where a reference to* SchNameDecor *is in scope*.

An example should make all this clearer. Suppose we write

    θ Date′   (7.4)

in some Z description where the current environment is ENV. We can treat ENV, an association between Z names and elements, just like a binding. Thus, if name Name is known in ENV, we can describe Name's value in ENV as ENV.Name. Returning to (7.4), firstly it would be illegal if any of the names dy′, mn′ or yr′ were not in scope, i.e., not known in ENV. Assuming no such illegality, then the binding formed by (7.4) can be described as

    ⟨ dy ⇒ ENV.dy′, mn ⇒ ENV.mn′, yr ⇒ ENV.yr′ ⟩

The binding's component *names* are derived from `Date`, but their *types* and *values* are derived from *the variable names of* `Date′` in the current environment ENV. Thus, dy′, mn′ and yr′ in ENV might have no connection with dy′, mn′ and yr′ in schema `Date′` itself—they could be other variables with the same names, and possibly different types, that happen to be the ones in scope. If so, this is a 'problematic use' of binding formation referred to at the end of the previous paragraph. Of course, when we write a term such as (7.4), our intention in practice would always be to construct a binding based on the schema `Date′`. In other words, we would write (7.4) only where a reference to, and hence the variables of, schema `Date′` was in scope.

Bindings are values, values have types, and as we have seen, schema names can be used as types. Suppose SchName has components named x1, x2, ...xn with types τ1, τ2, ... τn. Then, assuming a reference to SchNameDecor to be in scope, the type of the binding θ SchNameDecor is the *schema type* described by the expression

    ⟨| x1 : τ1; x2 : τ2; ... xn : τn |⟩   (7.5)

This syntax, like the ⟨ ... ⇒ ... ⟩ syntax for describing bindings themselves, is not used directly in Z paragraphs but is provided as an aid to discussing the various concepts involved.

A consequence of schema types is that, assuming appropriate schema references are in scope, the bindings θ SchName and θ SchNameDecor *have the same type*, irrespective of what Decor actually is. This allows us to write expressions like, say,

    θ Date′ = θ Date   (7.6) which is a shorter and much neater way of writing

$$(\theta \, \texttt{Date}') . \texttt{dy} = (\theta \, \texttt{Date}) . \texttt{dy} \wedge$$
$$(\theta \, \texttt{Date}') . \texttt{mn} = (\theta \, \texttt{Date}) . \texttt{mn} \wedge$$
$$(\theta \, \texttt{Date}') . \texttt{yr} = (\theta \, \texttt{Date}) . \texttt{yr}$$

or, of course, just

$$\texttt{dy}' = \texttt{dy} \wedge \texttt{mn}' = \texttt{mn} \wedge \texttt{yr}' = \texttt{yr}$$

since $(\theta \, \texttt{Date}) . \texttt{Var}$ has the value of $\texttt{Var}$ and $(\theta \, \texttt{Date}') . \texttt{Var}$ has the value of $\texttt{Var}'$. The potential for using equalities like (7.6) in operation schemas should be clear. Examples occur in Chapter 8.

As a further example, given that references to `Date` and `Date'` are in scope, then the following four terms

$\theta \, \texttt{Date}$
$\theta \, \texttt{Date}'$
$\texttt{d}$ — where d has been declared as $\texttt{d} : \texttt{Date}$ (or $\texttt{d} : \texttt{Date}'$)
$\texttt{birth}$ — where $\texttt{birth} \in \{ \, \texttt{Date}' \, \bullet \, \theta \, \texttt{Date}' \, \}$, say

all have type

$$\langle\!\langle \, \texttt{dy} : \mathbb{Z}; \; \texttt{mn} : \mathbb{Z}; \; \texttt{yr} : \mathbb{Z} \, \rangle\!\rangle \tag{7.7}$$

It is important to understand that only the schema's signature contributes to the type and not its name, property or the ordering of its components (compare cartesian product types and tuples). Thus, bindings formed from references to schema `Date`, schema `DateNorm` (i.e., normalised `Date`) or even the schema

```
┌─ Ebuf ───────────────────────────────────┐
│ mn,dy : ℕ; yr : -5..5                     │
│ ─────────────────────────                 │
│ AnyPredicate                              │
└───────────────────────────────────────────┘
```

all have the same schema type (7.7) above. This view of schema types is necessary to prevent the notion of subtype arising, otherwise even two schemas that differed only in their properties would now represent *different* types. This is not the case, and hence Z's simple notion of type is not violated.

The use of schema `Date` in the manufacture of `Date_Adt` would be a simple example of using a schema type. More generally, using schemas as types allows us to build a type hierarchy of record-like structures, particularly in modelling states. This more specialized use of schemas in specification begins to show its value with the description of complex systems, as Chapter 8's case study is intended to illustrate.

EXERCISE 7.2

1. Suppose: $\texttt{Triangle} \;\hat{=}\; [\, \texttt{a,b,c} : \mathbb{N}_1 \mid \texttt{a} + \texttt{b} > \texttt{c} \wedge \texttt{b} + \texttt{c} > \texttt{a} \wedge \texttt{c} + \texttt{a} > \texttt{b}]$

   a. Write out in full '| $\bullet$' form the following set comprehensions:
       i. $\{ \, \texttt{Triangle}' \mid \texttt{rtAngld}(\texttt{a}', \texttt{b}', \texttt{c}') \}$
       ii. $\{ \, \texttt{Triangle}; \; \texttt{d} : \mathbb{N}_1 \}$
       iii. $\{ \, \texttt{Triangle} \mid \texttt{rtAngld}(\texttt{a}, \texttt{b}, \texttt{c}) \, \bullet \, \texttt{a} + \texttt{b} + \texttt{c} \}$

    b. Give the component names and their types of the binding θ `Triangle!` when a reference to `Triangle!` is in scope

    c. What, if anything, is wrong with (θ `Triangle`)′ in an environment containing a reference to `Triangle`′?

    d. Suppose: `TriangleD` ≙ `Triangle`′
    Give the component names of the binding θ `TriangleD`′.

2. Write down the types of:

    a. the constant `dateZero` in `Date_Adt` assuming the schema `Date` model

    b. the binding θ `TriangleD`′ in Question 1(d), where a `TriangleD`′ reference is in scope

    c. the state space of schema `DigitalWatch`

    d. each of the three sets in Question 1(a)

    e. the function `daysOn` in `Date_Adt` assuming the schema `Date` model.

3. Assuming the schema `Date` model for `Date_Adt`, appropriately re-express the definitions of: `dateZero`, `dayOf`, `monthOf`, `yearOf`.

4. Suppose schema `Triangle` in Question (1) is to be used as the basis for constructing a data type. Define the following operations of the data type:

    a. constant `unitTri` modelling the triangle with unit length sides

    b. relation `rtAngld` for characterizing right-angled triangles

    c. function `perimLen` which calculates the length of a triangle's perimeter.

5. If `State` is a state schema, give a definition of Ξ`State` which neither depends on the Δ convention nor requires knowledge of the internals of `State`.

7.3 GENERIC DATA TYPES

Generic Definition

In the case study of the next chapter, we will need a data type for *queues*. The properties and behaviour of a queue—adding an element to the back, removing an element from the front, etc.—are independent of the queue element type, and so we should perhaps construct a specification which reflects this fact. We can do this with a *generic definition*. Z's mathematical toolkit is largely made up of a collection of generic definitions (see Spivey (1992)). This is so because of the need to construct generalized operations over sets, relations, functions, etc.

    To construct a generic data type, we must first begin with a definition of the generalized (i.e., generic) class of object over which the data type operations will be specified. We can still do this with an abbreviation definition, but one that is suitably parametrized. The parameters are in effect type parameters, and it is this parametrization which gives us the generality we are seeking to describe. Here again is the generic binary relation abbreviation:

$$X \leftrightarrow Y \ == \ \mathbb{P}\,(\,X \times Y\,)$$

X and Y are the formal generic parameters; note that they are themselves introduced by the definition and must not be declared elsewhere (e.g., in given set definitions).

In order to declare operations over a generic data type, we use an axiomatic description box which has top and bottom bars, the former being doubled and carrying the name(s) of the generic parameter(s). Here, for example, is the definition of the dom and ran operations:

$$
\begin{array}{|l}
\hline\hline [\,X,Y\,] \\
\hline
\mathrm{dom} : (\,X \leftrightarrow Y\,) \to \mathbb{P}\,X \\
\mathrm{ran} : (\,X \leftrightarrow Y\,) \to \mathbb{P}\,Y \\
\hline
\forall\, \mathrm{abr} : X \leftrightarrow Y\; \bullet \\
\quad \mathrm{dom\ abr} = \{\, x : X;\ y : Y \mid (\,x,y\,) \in \mathrm{abr} \bullet x \,\} \;\wedge \\
\quad \mathrm{ran\ abr} = \{\, x : X;\ y : Y \mid (\,x,y\,) \in \mathrm{abr} \bullet y \,\} \\
\hline
\end{array}
$$

Clearly, the 'meaning' of dom and ran—and of course all the other operations on binary relations—is independent of the types that X and Y might actually stand for. However, although a generic object describes a family of type-related objects, it must be a constant—the predicates of the definition must uniquely fix the object for given values of the generic parameters. Using typical definition structures like 'if and only if' predicates for relations and equational predicates for functions, the specifier is on safe ground.

When a generic name is applied, actual parameters are provided for the formal generic ones and a unique actual object is 'instantiated' (see also page 97). Usually, the actual parameters can be inferred from the syntactic context and can be left implicit. For example, given

isIn : VAN $\leftrightarrow$ VanClass

then in the term

dom isIn

it must be the case that X = VAN and Y = VanClass as there is no other way of providing types for X and Y in the definition of dom which makes the term type-correct. Hence, we do not have to write

dom[VAN, VanClass] isIn

though we could do so if we felt so inclined. Fortunately, there are few practical situations where actual parameters *must* be supplied because the syntactic context is not sufficiently informative to determine how the formal generic parameters should be type-substituted. We will not pursue this aspect further in the text.

Back to our definition problem for queues. A queue is one of the most common forms of structure which we think of as being made up of items maintained in some kind of linear order. Other examples include *lists*, *serial files* of data, and *stacks* where items are 'pushed onto' and 'popped off' the front of the stack structure. Since the need to handle ordered structures like these arises frequently in specification, we require a suitable way of modelling them in Z. For this, another generic mathematical type provided by Z's toolkit, namely *sequences*, is used.

Sequences

THE SEQUENCE MODEL

Informally, we view a sequence as a list of elements which are indexed from 1 onwards. Indexing captures the idea of 'items being set out in order' since the element indexed 1 'comes before' the element indexed 2, etc. Indexing items of type X is in effect associating those items with the numbers 1, 2, etc., which is a straightforward mapping thus:

$$\{\, 1 \mapsto x_1, 2 \mapsto x_2, \ldots \}$$

This is just a function whose left set is $\mathbb{N}$ and right set is X, and which has a domain $1 \ldots k$ where k is the length of the sequence being described. Here we have the basis for modelling our queue data type.

Z has a special notation for sequences, together with an accompanying theory. Here are two sequences that might be useful in `Date_Adt`:

```
daysGoneBy == ⟨ 0,31,59,90,120,151,181,212,243,273,304,334 ⟩
daysUp == ⟨ fri,sat,sun,mon,tue,wed,thu ⟩
```

The first sequence contains, in order, the total number of days that have passed in a non-leap year at the start of each month of the year; the second sequence lists the days of the week forwards starting with Friday. The large-ish angle brackets are used to construct explicit sequence displays (cf. parentheses for displaying tuples and curly brackets for displaying sets). The two abbreviation definitions are short for

> daysGoneBy : seq $\mathbb{N}$
> daysUp : seq DaysInWeek
> ___
> daysGoneBy = ⟨ 0,31,59,90,120,151,181,212,243,273,304,334 ⟩
> daysUp = ⟨ fri,sat,sun,mon,tue,wed,thu ⟩

The declarations tell us that `daysGoneBy` is a 'sequence of natural numbers' variable and `daysUp` a 'sequence of `DaysInWeek`' variable. The symbol `seq` is *not* a type constructor, even though it may look like one. Sequences are a mathematical type modelled as indicated earlier, i.e., as a certain specialization of functions. So sequence `daysGoneBy` can be unwound into a function with domain $1 \ldots 12$ and range in $\mathbb{N}$, which in turn is an object of type $\mathbb{P}\,(\,\mathbb{Z} \times \mathbb{Z}\,)$. Similarly, `daysUp` is an object of type $\mathbb{P}\,(\,\mathbb{Z} \times \text{DaysInWeek}\,)$, being a function with domain $1 \ldots 7$ and range `DaysInWeek`.

As a further example, suppose we have

> she : seq HE

where HE is the set $\{\, u, p, c \,\}$. In the absence of any further constraints, she's value can range over a sequence of HE values of any finite length. Here are some possibilities for the value denoted by she:

$$\langle\,\rangle, \quad \langle u \rangle, \quad \langle u,p,c \rangle, \quad \langle p,u,c \rangle, \quad \langle p,c,p,c,p,u \rangle$$

Each is equivalent respectively to the following functions:

$$\varnothing \quad \{\,1 \mapsto u\} \quad \{\,1 \mapsto u, 2 \mapsto p, 3 \mapsto c\} \quad \{\,1 \mapsto p, 2 \mapsto u, 3 \mapsto c\}$$
$$\{\,1 \mapsto p, 2 \mapsto c, 3 \mapsto p, 4 \mapsto c, 5 \mapsto p, 6 \mapsto u\}$$

Clearly, unlike sets, sequences can include multiple instances of elements.

Although sequences can be of arbitrary length, any given sequence is constructible from a finite number of elements; infinite sequences are not part of standard Z. So the functions which model sequences are finite too, their domain always being $1..k$ for some $k \in \mathbb{N}$. We can express finiteness in functions with a special 'herring bone' symbol $\rightarrowtail\!\!\!\!\rightarrow$. Thus, the generic model for sequences can be described as

$$\mathrm{seq}\ X\ ==\ \{\, f : \mathbb{N} \rightarrowtail\!\!\!\!\rightarrow X \mid \mathrm{dom}\ f = 1..\#f \,\}$$

We also have

$$\mathrm{seq}_1\ X\ ==\ \{\, f : \mathrm{seq}\ X \mid \#f > 0 \,\}$$

for non-empty sequences (compare $\mathbb{P}_1$ and $\mathbb{F}_1$ for non-empty sets), and

$$\mathrm{iseq}\ X\ ==\ \mathrm{seq}\ X \cap (\,\mathbb{N} \rightarrowtail\!\!\!\!\rightarrow X\,)$$

for injective sequences, i.e., where all sequence elements are different. There is even the special 'herring bone' symbol $\rightarrowtail\!\!\!\!\rightarrow$ for finite injections. Both daysGoneBy and daysUp on the previous page are obviously injective.

SEQUENCE OPERATIONS

The main operator for constructing sequences is concatenation $\_\,\widehat{\ }\,\_$; both its arguments must be sequences. Two main selector operations are head, which gives the head element of its sequence argument, and tail, which gives a sequence comprising its sequence argument minus the head element. head and tail are clearly not total: their arguments must be non-empty sequences. Two mirror-image selectors are front (all but the end element) and last (the end element). Here are some examples which also include rev; this is a total operation giving a sequence which is the elements of its argument in reverse order. The examples also make use of certain operations which we have encountered in earlier chapters, and this aspect is commented upon after the examples.

Let   the $== \langle\, u,p,c \,\rangle$
then: $\#(\ \mathrm{the}\,\widehat{\ }\,\mathrm{the}\ ) = 6$
       $\mathrm{dom\ the} = 1..3$
       $\mathrm{ran}(\ \mathrm{the}\,\widehat{\ }\,\mathrm{the}\ ) = \{\, u,p,c \,\}$
       $\mathrm{the}(\,\#\mathrm{the}\ ) = c$
       $\mathrm{head\ the} = u$
       $\mathrm{tail}^3\ \mathrm{the} = \langle\,\rangle$
       $\mathrm{front}(\ \mathrm{the}\,\widehat{\ }\,\mathrm{the}\ ) = \langle\, u,p,c,u,p \,\rangle$
       $\mathrm{last}(\ \mathrm{front}(\ \mathrm{tail\ the}\ )) = p$
       $\mathrm{rev}(\ \mathrm{front}(\ \mathrm{tail}(\,\mathrm{the}\,\widehat{\ }\langle\, u \,\rangle)))) = \langle\, c,p \,\rangle$

Since sequences are just (finite) functions, note how #, dom and ran automatically provide *sequence length*, *sequence index range* and *sequence elements* operations. Also, there is no need for a special operator for *sequence indexing*. To select the ith element of a sequence s, we simply apply s in its capacity as a function to the argument i (though i must be in s's domain $1..\#s$, otherwise the term $s(\,i\,)$ will be undefined).

The following definition of function ordDtInYr in Date_Adt (see page 152) makes use of the daysGoneBy sequence described on the previous page. The simple set model for Date is assumed. Note that from now on, to provide a contrast with earlier chapters, we will adopt a leaner style of parenthesis usage when applying prefix names.

$$\text{ordDtInYr} : \text{Date} \rightarrow 1..366$$

$$
\begin{aligned}
\forall \, d &: \text{Date} \bullet \\
&\text{ordDtInYr } d = \text{daysGoneBy}(\text{monthOf } d) + \text{dayOf } d + \\
&\qquad\qquad\qquad (\textbf{if } \text{leapYr}(\text{yearOf } d) \wedge \text{monthOf } d > 2 \\
&\qquad\qquad\qquad \textbf{then } 1 \\
&\qquad\qquad\qquad \textbf{else } 0)
\end{aligned}
$$

In the definition, a *conditional expression* is used to make appropriate correction for dates in leap years. The general form of a conditional expression is

> if Predicate then Expr1 else Expr2

where Expr1 and Expr2 *must have the same type*. The expression's value is that of Expr1 if Predicate holds, otherwise its value is that of Expr2. The syntactic strength of a conditional expression is very weak. The best policy is always to bracket a conditional expression to avoid syntax errors.

There are more sophisticated ways of interrogating the composition of sequences than just by making use of indexing, head, tail, etc. Suppose we wish to take some, not necessarily contiguous, 'slice' of a sequence. Then we can use the *extraction* operator $\_ 1 \_$ and write

> dSet 1 s

where dSet is a set of indices (i.e., a subset of $\mathbb{N}_1$) defining the elements of sequence s in which we are interested. The result is another sequence made up from those elements of s positioned at the indices in dSet, in the same order as they occur in s. A similar operator is *filtering*:

> s ↾ rSet

where rSet is a subset of the element type of s. This term calculates another sequence from those elements of s which are in rSet, in the same order as they occur in s.

For testing sequence composition, we have three partial orders (see page 144):

> s prefix t
> s suffix t
> s in t

These predicates assert respectively that s is a contiguous part of t from the front, at the back, or anywhere. These three relations, and the previous two operators, are illustrated below:

> Let   hex == $\langle u,p,c,u,p,c,u,p,c \rangle$
> then: $\{1,5,3\} 1 \text{ hex} = \langle u,c,p \rangle$
>   hex ↾ $\{u\} = \langle u,u,u \rangle$
> $\langle u,p \rangle$ prefix hex
> $\neg(\langle u,p \rangle$ suffix hex$)$
> $\langle c,u,p \rangle$ in hex

There exist a number of basic laws that embody the fundamental properties of sequences, some of which can be explored as part of the next exercise.

EXERCISE 7.3

1. Complete the following to make useful laws about sequences, replacing the **?** with appropriate terms. As usual, assume universal quantification of the arbitrary variables used, these being

    $s,t,u : seq\ X$

    a. $(s \frown t) \frown u = ?$ b. $\#(s \frown t) = ?$
    c. $rev(s \frown t) = ?$ d. $rev(rev\ s) = ?$
    e. $s \neq \langle \rangle \Rightarrow (front\ s) \frown \langle last\ s \rangle = ?$
    f. $s \neq \langle \rangle \Rightarrow last(rev\ s) = ?$
    g. $(s \frown t) \upharpoonright v = ?$ h. $\emptyset \upharpoonright s = ?$
    i. $s\ prefix\ t \Leftrightarrow s = ?$ j. $s\ in\ t \Leftrightarrow \exists k : 1..\#t \bullet s = ?$

2. § The answer is given in the next subsection.
   A queue data type is such that:

   - the empty queue is a special queue object
   - an item can be added to the back of a queue (there are no restrictions in queue length)
   - a non-empty queue can be reduced by removing its front item
   - a queue can be interrogated to
     - inspect its first (front) element
     - obtain its length.

   Construct a generic specification of an abstract data type `Queue`.

   Note: with a suitable choice of value-space model, all the axioms can be defined with simple equations.

A Generic Queue Specification

A QUEUE DATA TYPE

Queues are modelled naturally as sequences. Since we want a generic data type which has a single parameter for the queue element type, we can write

$$Queue[E] == seq\ E \tag{7.8}$$

If we wished to exclude queues with multiple entries, we could easily arrange for this by choosing the stronger model `iseq E`. More generally, we can have

$$VarName\ [\ ListOfParams\ ]\ ==\ ExprInvolvingParams$$

as in

$$triple[W,X,Y] == W \times X \times Y$$

In applying `Queue`, we write, say, `Queue[ CUSTOMER ]`, `Queue[ 0..9 ]`, etc. Note that although a generic parameter like `E` in (7.8) behaves as a type parameter, the actual parameter supplied can be any *set*. We comment further on this shortly.

Being generic, we present the axiomatic descriptions of `Queue`'s operations within a suitable generic box. The operations represent just the basic essential manipulations on queues; other operations are added later in Exercise 7.13(1) on page 188.

$$
\begin{array}{l}
\text{emptyq} : \text{Queue}[\,E\,] \\
\text{addq} : E \times \text{Queue}[\,E\,] \rightarrow \text{Queue}[\,E\,] \\
\text{remq} : \text{Queue}[\,E\,] \twoheadrightarrow \text{Queue}[\,E\,] \\
\text{fstq} : \text{Queue}[\,E\,] \twoheadrightarrow E \\
\text{lenq} : \text{Queue}[\,E\,] \rightarrow \mathbb{N}
\end{array}
$$

$$
\begin{array}{l}
\text{emptyq} = \langle\,\rangle \\
\forall\, e : E;\ q : \text{Queue}[\,E\,] \bullet \text{addq}(\,e, q\,) = q ^\frown \langle\, e\,\rangle \\
\text{dom remq} = \text{dom fstq} = \text{seq}_1\, E \\
\forall\, q : \text{dom fstq} \bullet \text{fstq } q = q(\,1\,) \\
\forall\, q : \text{dom remq} \bullet \text{remq } q = \text{tail } q \\
\forall\, q : \text{Queue}[\,E\,] \bullet \text{lenq } q = \#q
\end{array}
$$

The way in which `remq` and `fstq` have been defined deserves some comment. When describing a partial function, we must take care in the defining axioms to characterize the function's domain sufficiently precisely. The above shows one way: we define the domain of a partial function with a 'domain documenting' axiom. It is not always convenient to do this, however, and we are not obliged to do it either. Yet there is a subtle distinction between

$$
\text{dom fstq} = \text{seq}_1\, E \\
\forall\, q : \text{dom fstq} \bullet \text{fstq } q = q(\,1\,)
$$

and describing `fstq` as, say

$$
\forall\, q : \text{Queue}[\,E\,] \mid q \neq \langle\,\rangle \bullet \text{fstq } q = q(\,1\,)
$$

With the second description, all we can say is that it tells us nothing about the behaviour of `fstq` when applied to the empty queue. The first description is explicit about `fstq`'s domain and is thus in a sense 'stronger'. For our purposes, it is sufficient to treat the choice of approach as one of style, rather than anything deeper. We will generally use the former when defining partial functions.

So far, we have skimmed over the issue of generic parameter correspondence. Actual generic parameters must be sets, as in the instantiations:

$$
\text{QueueOfCusts} == \text{Queue}[\,\text{CUSTOMER}\,] \\
\text{QueueOfDigits} == \text{Queue}[\,0\,..\,9\,]
$$

The simple way to understand the parameter correspondence is to imagine that a substitution of each formal generic parameter by the corresponding actual parameter takes place everywhere the former occurs in the generic object's description. Since more than one generic parameter is possible, the substitutions must be viewed as simultaneous as this resolves the (unlikely) situation where an actual parameter involves a name that corresponds to a formal parameter. Thus, in the first instantiation above, we can imagine E in Queue's definition being substituted by CUSTOMER. In fact, we could imagine the substitutions in the above two examples to be akin to, respectively,

$$
E == \text{CUSTOMER} \qquad \text{and} \qquad E == 0\,..\,9
$$

More properly, however, recall that formal generic parameters really stand for types. So, given an actual parameter of type $\mathbb{P}\ \tau$, then the underlying *type* substitution is to replace the corresponding formal generic parameter by τ and add an appropriate constraint to the instantiated object's description. For example, since $0..9$ is of type $\mathbb{P}\ \mathbb{Z}$, the underlying substitution with QueueOfDigits above is to replace E by $\mathbb{Z}$. Thus, we should regard something like

$$\{\, q : \text{seq } \mathbb{Z} \mid \text{ran } q \subseteq 0..9 \,\}$$

as being a better description of the resultant value space which is QueueOfDigits.

GENERIC SCHEMAS
Though less commonly used, schemas can also be generic, as in

```
┌─ QueueObj [ ELEM ]──────────────────────────────┐
│                                                  │
│  q : seq ELEM                                    │
│                                                  │
└──────────────────────────────────────────────────┘
```

which could form the basis of a generalized state model of a 'queue object'. To get an actual queue state space, we would write schema definition paragraphs of the form

$$\text{CustQ} \triangleq \text{QueueObj} [\, \text{CUSTOMER} \,]$$
$$\text{DigitQ} \triangleq \text{QueueObj} [\, 0..9 \,]$$

etc. Operations for QueueObj [ELEM] would be handled similarly. For example:

```
┌─ RemQ [ ELEM ]──────────────────────────────────┐
│  ΔQueueObj [ ELEM ]                              │
│ ────────────────────────                         │
│  q ≠ ⟨ ⟩                                         │
│  q′ = tail q                                     │
└──────────────────────────────────────────────────┘
```

Now we can define

$$\text{RemQCusts} \triangleq \text{RemQ} [\, \text{CUSTOMER} \,]$$
$$\text{RemQDigits} \triangleq \text{RemQ} [\, 0..9 \,]$$

and so on.

However, generic definition can often be emulated well enough by the use of given sets. For example:

```
[ ELEM ]
┌─ QueueObj───────────────────────────────────────┐
│                                                  │
│  q : seq ELEM                                    │
│                                                  │
└──────────────────────────────────────────────────┘
```

Although ELEM is a specific type, it acts rather like a parameter since we need say no more about it; ELEM can eventually be represented in any way we require. For many applications, a given-set approach of this kind will suffice. Generic definitions are more important in the establishment of generalized data types of the axiomatically specified kind, on which this chapter is concentrating.

EXERCISE 7.4

1. Give a generic definition for partial orders (see page 144).

2. § Answers are on the page opposite.
    Construct fully generalized descriptions of the following functions (each can be defined by a single equality; `deleteAll` is slightly tricky):

    a. `countOccs( x,s )` which counts how many times x occurs in sequence s
    b. `elemsOf( s )` which yields the elements of sequence s as a set
    c. `deleteAll( x,s )` which yields the sequence obtained by deleting from sequence s *all* instances of x.

7.4 FUNCTION SPECIFICATION

Simple Axiomatic Description

Functions lie at the heart of the behavioural description of a data type. Since there are many ways of specifying functions axiomatically, it is important for the reader to assimilate the different techniques and be able to choose an appropriate, elegant method in a given circumstance. The simplest technique is to give what is in effect a tabular definition: a predicate comprising equations showing the function's value for each different argument in its domain. Truth table definitions of propositional operators are an example of this approach; see page 61. As a further example, the sequence `daysUp` on page 160 could be more tediously defined as

```
daysUp : seq DaysInWeek

daysUp 1 = fri; daysUp 2 = sat; daysUp 3 = sun
daysUp 4 = mon; daysUp 5 = tue; daysUp 6 = wed
daysUp 7 = thu
```

Defining functions this way, or equivalently as a set of maplets by an extensional definition, is possible only if the function is finite and has a sufficiently small domain.

As Section 6.2 showed, functions are often definable in terms of single equalities:

$$\forall \text{ DeclarationsOf } x1, \ldots xk \bullet$$
$$\text{FunctionName}(x1, \ldots xk) = \text{TermInvolving } x1, \ldots xk$$

One of the simplest examples of this approach occurs when defining projection functions, as in Exercise 7.1(4.a). Here again is the `dayOf` function:

```
dayOf : Date → 1..31

∀d : 1..31; m : 1..12; y : Year | ( d,m,y ) ∈ Date •
  dayOf( d,m,y ) = d
```

Defining projection functions is thus very simple—we need just an equality of the form

$$\text{ProjFnName NTupleOfNames} = \text{KthNameInNTupleOfNames}$$

Note: unless stated otherwise, examples in the text and exercises involving `Date` will assume the simple non-schema set model.

Here are definitions of the functions of Exercise 7.4(2) opposite:

$$
\begin{array}{|l}
\hline
=[\,\text{X}\,]\!=\!\!=\\
\quad \texttt{countOccs} : \text{X} \times \text{seq X} \to \mathbb{N}\\
\quad \texttt{elemsOf} : \text{seq X} \to \mathbb{P}\,\text{X}\\
\quad \texttt{deleteAll} : \text{X} \times \text{seq X} \to \text{seq X}\\
\hline
\quad \forall\, \text{s} : \text{seq X} \bullet \texttt{elemsOf s} = \text{ran s}\\
\quad \forall\, \text{x} : \text{X};\ \text{s} : \text{seq X} \bullet\\
\qquad \texttt{countOccs}(\,\text{x,s}\,) = \#\,(\,\text{s} \triangleright \{\,\text{x}\,\}\,) \wedge\\
\qquad \texttt{deleteAll}(\,\text{x,s}\,) = \text{s} \upharpoonright (\,\text{ran s} \setminus \{\,\text{x}\,\})\\
\hline
\end{array}
$$

Note that `elemsOf` 'loses' any element multiplicity in its sequence argument; also that X would be just as acceptable as ran s in the definition of `deleteAll`, which works by filtering from s all range elements except the x to be deleted. When defining functions axiomatically, it is sufficient to use $\to$ or $\nrightarrow$ in declarations, since other properties such as injectivity, etc., can be inferred from the defining axioms. However, such inferences would involve the application of proof, which we will not pursue.

EXERCISE 7.5

Construct definitions of the following functions:

a. `daysDiff` of `Date_Adt`, assuming the function `dtMinus`. Use a conditional expression

b. `ordDtInYr` of `Date_Adt` via a description simpler than that given on page 162. Again, assume the function `dtMinus`

c. `_ upto _` of `Date_Adt`

d. `delFstOcc( x,s )` which yields the sequence obtained by deleting from sequence s *the first* occurrence of x, if any. Assume the function `fstPosIn( e,t )` which yields the index of the first occurrence of e in the sequence t; if there is no occurrence of e in t, `fstPosIn` yields 0.

Definition by Cases: 'Guards'

Tabular or single equality definition works for many functions, but for other, more complex functions extremely unwieldy term constructions would result. In such situations, a 'case style' of definition is usually appropriate. Here, the function's definition is spread over two or more equalities—the 'cases'—together with additional description accompanying the equalities which characterizes when the different cases are applicable. The form of such a definition typically includes one or more axioms with the following structure:

$\forall$ DeclarationsOf $\text{x1}, \dots \text{xk} \bullet$
$\qquad$ PredicateInvolvingSomeOf $\text{x1}, \dots \text{xk} \Rightarrow$
$\qquad\qquad$ FunctionName$(\,\text{x1}, \dots \text{xk}\,) = $ TermInvolving $\text{x1}, \dots \text{xk}$

The antecedent acts as a case-defining 'guard', i.e., the equality applies only if the antecedent is true. A good illustration of this technique would be defining the `Date_Adt` function `next`. In the definition, we make use of the three `Date` projection functions.

$$
\begin{array}{|l}
\hline
\text{next : Date} \rightarrow \text{Date} \\
\hline
\forall d : \text{Date} \bullet \\
\quad (\text{ eom } d \wedge \text{monthOf } d = 12 \Rightarrow \\
\qquad \text{next } d = \text{mkDate}(1, 1, \text{yearOf } d + 1)) \wedge \\
\quad (\text{ eom } d \wedge \text{monthOf } d < 12 \Rightarrow \\
\qquad \text{next } d = \text{mkDate}(1, \text{monthOf } d + 1, \text{yearOf } d)) \wedge \\
\quad (\neg \text{ eom } d \Rightarrow \\
\qquad \text{next } d = \text{mkDate}(\text{dayOf } d + 1, \text{monthOf } d, \text{yearOf } d))
\end{array}
$$

Actually, a case style of predicate description is nothing new to us. next is just the functional equivalent of operation Add1Day in Digital Watch (see page 46). Note how next's definition makes it independent of the model chosen for Date.

As a further illustration, we could define function delFstOcc of Exercise 7.5(d) in this style and avoid reliance on the function fstPosIn. Notice the importance of declaring s as seq$_1$ X in the second combined axiom.

$$
\begin{array}{|l}
\hline
=[X]= \\
\text{delFstOcc : X} \times \text{seq X} \rightarrow \text{seq X} \\
\hline
\forall e : X; s : \text{seq X} \bullet \\
\quad (s = \langle\rangle \Rightarrow \text{delFstOcc}(e, s) = \langle\rangle) \\
\forall e : X; s : \text{seq}_1 \text{ X} \bullet \\
\quad (e = \text{head } s \Rightarrow \text{delFstOcc}(e, s) = \text{tail } s) \wedge \\
\quad (e \neq \text{head } s \Rightarrow \text{delFstOcc}(e, s) = \\
\qquad\qquad \langle \text{head } s \rangle ^\frown \text{delFstOcc}(e, \text{tail } s))
\end{array}
$$

It is a separate issue whether this description of delFstOcc is in some way either 'better' or 'less desirable' than that given as the answer to Exercise 7.5(d). Some might argue that the above version is more understandable because it is more explicit in an 'operational' kind of way—which leads to the next point ...

It will be noted that one of the equalities in the definition of delFstOcc has the form

FnName (...) = ... FnName (...) ... ...

In many contexts, e.g., a programming environment, this feature is referred to as *recursive* definition. It should be borne in mind, however, that our equalities are merely descriptions in predicate logic. Any such equality, whatever its structure, merely asserts that the pattern of symbols on the left- and right-hand sides are interchangeable.

It is important in any case-style definition that the full extent of a function's desired behaviour is covered. The cases between them must 'close off' the domain of the function; i.e., every object in the intended domain, but no other, must be catered for by one of the cases. Since next and delFstOcc above are total functions, their case definitions must cover *all* elements in their left sets. Informally at least, we can convince ourselves that this is so by inspecting their definitions, especially the antecedents of the guarded equations.

A particular defect we must avoid in case-style definitions is non-uniqueness of two or more of the cases. Suppose in the description of a function f we have

$$\text{Guard1} \implies \text{f Arg} = \text{Term1} \land$$
$$\text{Guard2} \implies \text{f Arg} = \text{Term2}$$

where Guard1 and Guard2 are not sufficiently strong to define disjoint cases. Then the definition is inconsistent unless the two equalities agree—i.e., Term1 = Term2—in each instance when both guards are satisfied. Here is a simple example of inconsistency:

$$k \leq 0 \implies \text{f } k = 0 \land k \geq 0 \implies \text{f } k = 1$$

Unfortunately, when $k = 0$, both antecedents hold and we can infer

$$\text{f } 0 = 0 \land \text{f } 0 = 1$$

which simplifies to the contradiction

$$0 = 1$$

To avoid this kind of problem, it is wise always to check that the different cases being defined impart a unique value to a function for each argument in its domain.

EXERCISE 7.6

1. Give an alternative, guarded case definition for the `Date_Adt` function `daysDiff` (see Exercise 7.5(a)) which circumvents use of a conditional expression.

2. Define the `Date_Adt` function `prev`. The answer to Exercise 3.10(1) will be of considerable help. However, note that `prev` is not total in `Date_Adt`.

3. Construct a guarded case definition of the `Date_Adt` function `dayOfWeek`. This is quite difficult. You need to: (i) make use of `daysDiff`, and the sequence `daysUp` on page 160; (ii) calculate the answer relative to a reference date, such as the fact that 1st January 1993 was a Friday.

4. Construct guarded case-style axioms for `countOccs`, `elemsOf` and `deleteAll` defined on page 167. Do not necessarily expect to use the same operators as appear in the terms of those definitions.

Definition by Cases: Argument Structures

Another case style of definition related to the recursive case style used for `delFstOcc` on the opposite page involves enumerating different argument structures or 'patterns' for a function. For example, instead of writing

$$s = \langle \rangle \implies \text{f}(\text{ s } \dots) = \dots \ \dots$$

we could write more directly and concisely

$$\text{f}(\langle \rangle \ \dots) = \dots \ \dots$$

The case-defining constraint has shifted from being a guarding antecedent to being part of the argument structure itself. In effect, we are using this technique even when we write, say,

$$\text{delFstOcc}(\text{ e}, \text{s }) = \dots \ \dots$$

since we are requiring the actual argument of `delFstOcc` to be matched to the ordered pair structure (e, s).

Here is `delFstOcc`'s axiom, re-expressed using an argument structure approach:

$$\forall\, e : X \bullet \text{delFstOcc}(\,e, \langle\rangle\,) = \langle\rangle$$
$$\forall\, e : X;\ t : \text{seq}\ X \bullet \text{delFstOcc}(\,e, \langle e\rangle ^\frown t\,) = t$$
$$\forall\, e, h : X;\ t : \text{seq}\ X \mid e \neq h \bullet$$
$$\text{delFstOcc}(\,e, \langle h\rangle ^\frown t\,) = \langle h\rangle ^\frown \text{delFstOcc}(\,e, t\,)$$

The first predicate deals with the special case where the argument's second co-ordinate is the empty sequence. The other two predicates together cover the general case where this co-ordinate is any arbitrary non-empty sequence. Note the importance of the $e \neq h$ constraint in the quantifier of the third predicate in order to characterize correctly the case where the element we are looking for is *not* the head of the sequence.

Remark

Since we now have two different sets of defining axioms for `delFstOcc`, the reader might wonder whether we are defining two distinct functions. The answer is *no*. In Z, two functions are distinct if and only if their ordered pair sets are different. The two definitions of `delFstOcc` actually define the same set of $(\,(\,e, s\,), t\,)$ pairs ($e \in X$; $s, t \in \text{seq}\ X$). So the two definitions describe the same function.

Definition based on argument structures is applicable to objects other than just sequences, as the following table shows:

	Special Cases	*General Cases*
Sequences:	$\langle\rangle, \langle x\rangle, \ldots$	$\langle x\rangle ^\frown s,\ s ^\frown \langle x\rangle$
FINITE sets:	$\varnothing, \{\,x\,\}, \ldots$	$\{\,x\,\} \cup X,\ X \cup \{\,x\,\}$
Numbers ($\mathbb{N}$):	$0, 1,\ \ldots$	$\text{succ}\ k$

`succ` is the *successor* function, provided by Z; `succ k` means the same as $k + 1$. The 'special cases' are particular constants; the 'general cases' are term patterns which, given that the variables appearing in them are type-correct and *arbitrary*, therefore cover all remaining possibilities. The table entries are based on what are called the *generators* of the data type, namely

For sequences:	$\langle\rangle$	and	$\_^\frown\_$	— left or right singleton concatenation
For finite sets:	$\varnothing$	and	$\_\cup\_$	— left or right singleton union
For numbers:	0	and	succ	

Generators are so named because, between them, they can generate (terms denoting) precisely the value space of the data type to which they belong. Using the kind of syntactic patterns given in the above table, we can always write down a term which denotes any member of the value space. For example, any sequence can be constructed from $\langle\rangle$ and (if it is non-empty) from $\_^\frown\_$ by concatenating elements together in the right order one at a time either from the front or from the back. Furthermore, a sequence is either empty and so matches $\langle\rangle$, or else non-empty and so can be matched to the term structure $\langle x\rangle ^\frown s$ or $s ^\frown \langle x\rangle$, depending on our choice of generator.

To give a specific illustration, consider the sequence

$$\langle u, p, c\rangle$$

Assuming left singleton concatenation for the generator to be partnered with $\langle\rangle$, this sequence is constructed by the term

$$\langle u \rangle \,\widehat{}\, (\,\langle p \rangle \,\widehat{}\, (\,\langle c \rangle \,\widehat{}\, \langle\,\rangle)))$$

Moreover, this term can be matched to the generalized structure $\langle x \rangle \,\widehat{}\,$ s by identifying u with the arbitrary x and ($\langle p \rangle \,\widehat{}\, (\,\langle c \rangle \,\widehat{}\, \langle\,\rangle))$) with the arbitrary s. Ignoring redundant outer parentheses, we can now recursively apply the same analysis to s—that is, to the term

$$\langle p \rangle \,\widehat{}\, (\,\langle c \rangle \,\widehat{}\, \langle\,\rangle)$$

Matching this term to the arbitrary $\langle x \rangle \,\widehat{}\,$ s is achieved similarly by identifying p with x and ($\langle c \rangle \,\widehat{}\, \langle\,\rangle$) with s. Next, c is identified with x and $\langle\,\rangle$ with s. s now matches the constant generator $\langle\,\rangle$ (so it cannot match the structure $\langle x \rangle \,\widehat{}\,$ s), and there the analysis stops.

A similar recursive analysis could be given if we choose to partner $\langle\,\rangle$ with a right singleton concatenation generator. Which we choose—left or right singleton concatenation—may depend on the function we wish to describe. For example, we would not use the structure s $\,\widehat{}\, \langle x \rangle$ to define delFstOcc since its definition is dependent on viewing a sequence as being made up *from the front*, not from the back. However, either structure would work for a function such as countOccs, since the order in which we count occurrences of an element in a sequence is irrelevant, providing the whole of the sequence is 'visited'.

These considerations apart, what is important is that left or right singleton concatenation enables the structure of any sequence to be viewed *uniquely*. Thus, take $\langle u, p \rangle$. Its structure is

$$\langle u \rangle \,\widehat{}\, (\,\langle p \rangle \,\widehat{}\, \langle\,\rangle) \qquad\qquad \text{— left singleton concatenation}$$
$$(\langle\,\rangle \,\widehat{}\, \langle u \rangle) \,\widehat{}\, \langle p \rangle \qquad\qquad \text{— right singleton concatenation}$$

and there is no other possible analysis. If, however, we used generalized concatenation as a generator, the pattern matching would now be against the arbitrary term s $\,\widehat{}\,$ t (s, t ∈ seq X). For any sequence, multiple matching would now occur, which we should avoid. For example, ways of analysing the sequence $\langle u, p \rangle$ against the term structure s $\,\widehat{}\,$ t would include:

$$\langle u \rangle \,\widehat{}\, (\,\langle p \rangle \,\widehat{}\, \langle\,\rangle), \ (\langle\,\rangle \,\widehat{}\, \langle u \rangle) \,\widehat{}\, \langle p \rangle, \ \langle u, p \rangle \,\widehat{}\, \langle\,\rangle, \ \text{and} \ \langle\,\rangle \,\widehat{}\, \langle u, p \rangle$$

However, since also $\langle\,\rangle \,\widehat{}\, \langle\,\rangle = \langle\,\rangle$, the possible matches would actually be infinite!

Another name for (recursive) case style definition based on argument structures is *inductive definition*. This is because the generators of a data type, on which the description of argument structures depends, are closely connected with a concept called 'induction', which is briefly introduced in Section 7.5. We can construct inductive definitions of functions over finite sets and natural numbers, as well as over sequences. Consider first the term-matching aspect. The number 3, for example, is constructed by the term

succ(succ(succ 0))

which is uniquely matched to the arbitrary term structure succ k (for k ∈ ℕ) by identifying (succ(succ 0)) with the arbitrary k. With sets, finiteness is essential because—assuming left singleton union as the main generator—an infinite set cannot be expressed as a finite term of the form

$$\{x_1\} \cup (\{x_2\} \cup (\ldots \varnothing))$$

Choice of left or right singleton union is immaterial with sets since set union is commutative. However, there is a slight problem with unique matching for sets. Consider matching the set $\{a,b\}$ against the term structure $\{x\} \cup s$. Suppose a is chosen to be identified with the x. Then $\{a,b\}$ can be viewed as either $\{a\} \cup \{b\}$ *or* $\{a\} \cup \{a,b\}$ due to the absorptive property of set union.

The way to handle non-unique term matching with inductive definitions over finite sets is illustrated by nOccBefore specified in the following axiomatic description. nOccBefore(d, s) counts how many dates in the finite date set s occur before the date d. Also defined is the Date_Adt function daysOn(d, n), which yields the date n days on from the date d; making use of the function next defined earlier, we obtain an appealing inductive definition:

$$
\begin{array}{l}
\text{daysOn} : \text{Date} \times \mathbb{N} \to \text{Date} \\
\text{nOccBefore} : \text{Date} \times \mathbb{F}\,\text{Date} \to \mathbb{N} \\
\hline
\forall d : \text{Date} \bullet \text{daysOn}(d, 0) = d \\
\forall d : \text{Date};\ k : \mathbb{N} \bullet \text{daysOn}(d, \text{succ}\ k) = \text{daysOn}(\text{next}\ d, k) \\
\forall d : \text{Date} \bullet \text{nOccBefore}(d, \varnothing) = 0 \\
\forall dt, d : \text{Date};\ sd : \mathbb{F}\,\text{Date} \bullet \\
\quad (d\ \text{isBefore}\ dt \Rightarrow \\
\quad\quad \text{nOccBefore}(dt, \{d\} \cup sd) = 1 + \text{nOccBefore}(dt, sd \setminus \{d\})) \wedge \\
\quad (d\ \text{isOnOrAfter}\ dt \Rightarrow \\
\quad\quad \text{nOccBefore}(dt, \{d\} \cup sd) = \text{nOccBefore}(dt, sd \setminus \{d\}))
\end{array}
$$

With nOccBefore, the term-matching problem mentioned above is overcome by writing $sd \setminus \{d\}$ on the right-hand side of each general case axiom. Thus, if $d \in sd$ in $\{d\} \cup sd$, then d is removed from sd, ensuring it is not 'considered again'; however, if $d \notin sd$, then $sd \setminus \{d\}$ is just sd anyway. Note in recursive general cases how a generator that appears on the left-hand side of the equality is absent on the right—the corresponding terms are such that the right-hand term in some sense denotes a 'simpler' object (sequence, number, set) than the term on the left.

In the definition of daysOn, the right-hand term of the general-case equality increases the date co-ordinate by 1 and decreases the number co-ordinate by 1; i.e., adding $k + 1$ days to date d is the same as adding k days to the next date after d. Observe that, instead of using succ, we could construct a correct description of daysOn by writing k on the left and $k - 1$ on the right provided k was declared as a positive integer.

EXERCISE 7.7

1. Recast the axioms of countOccs, elemsOf and deleteAll (see page 167) using argument structures.

2. Use argument structures to define inductively the following functions:

   a. fact n which calculates the factorial of the natural number n
   b. setDeleteAll(s, t) which calculates (*without* using the ↾ operator) the sequence obtained by deleting *every* occurrence of *all* members of the *finite set* s from the sequence t. *Hint*: make use of deleteAll.

3. Construct defining axioms incorporating recursive general cases for the
   Date_Adt functions:

   a. dtMinus(d1,d2) which gives the number of days separating dates d1
      and d2 (d1 occurs no earlier than d2)
   b. daysOff(d,n) which gives the date n days preceding date d.

   Note that neither of these functions is total. In each definition, make use of
   the function prev (see Exercise 7.6(2)).

Lambda Abstraction

The following generic abbreviation definition is a complete description of countOccs
on page 167 using what is called *lambda abstraction*:

$$\text{countOccs}[X] \;==\; \lambda\, e : X;\; s : \text{seq } X \bullet \#(\, s \rhd \{\,e\,\})$$

The right-hand side is a *lambda-expression*, which has the general form

$$\lambda \text{ SchemaText} \bullet \text{Term}$$

which can be verbalized as 'the function, evaluating to Term, with an argument
structure described by (the characteristic tuple of) SchemaText'.

Since a lambda-expression denotes a function, albeit one that is 'nameless', it can be
used in any appropriate syntactic context where function application is well-formed, as
in the term

$$(\,\lambda\, e : \mathbb{Z};\; s : \text{seq } \mathbb{Z} \bullet \#(\, s \rhd \{\,e\,\}))(\,1, \langle\, 1,2,3,2,1\,\rangle\,) \tag{7.9}$$

Evaluation can be understood to proceed via substitution of the lambda-expression
variables pair-wise by the corresponding co-ordinates of the argument. One can
imagine this process as 'stripping off' the '$\lambda \dots \bullet$' part to leave a fully substituted term.
Thus, with (7.9), e is substituted by 1 and s by $\langle\, 1,2,3,2,1\,\rangle$ to give

$$\#(\,\langle\, 1,2,3,2,1\,\rangle \rhd \{\,1\,\})$$

which is 2.

Those readers familiar with functional programming might be tempted to look upon
Z's lambda-expression facility as a manifestation of what is called 'lambda calculus',
but this is not the case. Defining functions with lambda-expressions is merely the same
as defining functions by sets of maplets; that is:

$$\lambda \text{ SchemaText} \bullet \text{Term} = \{\, \text{SchemaText} \bullet \text{ChrTuple} \mapsto \text{Term} \,\}$$

ChrTuple is the characteristic tuple of the SchemaText's declarations; in the previous
example, this would be (e,s). Thus, the definition

$$\text{countOccs}[X] \;==\; \{\, e : X;\; s : \text{seq } X \bullet (\,e,s\,) \mapsto \#(\, s \rhd \{\,e\,\})\}$$

is equivalent to the definition of countOccs given above.

Mention of characteristic tuples, plus the material of Section 7.2, reminds us to be
careful when schema references are involved. Given the schema Date model for
Date_Adt, a lambda-expression beginning

$$\lambda \text{ Date} \bullet \dots \dots$$

is a function requiring an argument *which is a* Date *binding*. Its set-of-maplets equivalent is thus

$$\{\,\text{Date} \bullet \theta\,\text{Date} \mapsto \dots\}$$

This is *not* the same as a lambda-expression beginning

$$\lambda\, \text{dy} : 1..31;\ \text{mn} : 1..12;\ \text{yr} : \text{Year} \mid \text{isDate}(\,\text{dy},\text{mn},\text{yr}\,) \bullet \dots\dots$$

which requires an argument with the tuple shape (dy, mn, yr) and for which

$$\{\,\text{dy} : 1..31;\ \text{mn} : 1..12;\ \text{yr} : \text{Year} \mid \text{isDate}(\,\text{dy},\text{mn},\text{yr}\,) \bullet$$
$$(\,\text{dy},\text{mn},\text{yr}\,) \mapsto \dots\}$$

would be the set-of-maplets equivalent.

Lambda abstraction provides a neat way of describing component selection of bindings. Consider the following function on Date bindings:

$$\text{project\_dy} : \text{Date} \to 1..31$$

$$\text{project\_dy} = (\,\lambda\,\text{Date} \bullet \text{dy}\,)$$

Then, for example, project_dy birth, which is (λ Date $\bullet$ dy) birth, is the same as birth.dy .

EXERCISE 7.8

1. Recast the definitions of elemsOf and deleteAll (see page 167) using lambda-expressions.

2. Calculate the values of
   a. (λ x : $\mathbb{Z}$ $\bullet$ 0) 13
   b. (λ Date | θ Date isOnOrBefore mkDate(25,12,yr) $\bullet$
      daysDiff(θ Date,mkDate(25,12,yr))) mkDate(5,11,1992)
      What does the lambda-abstracted function do in general?
   c. (λ s1,s2 : seq X $\bullet$
      setDeleteAll(ran s2,s1) ^ (s1 $\upharpoonright$ (ran s2)))
      $(\langle 1,2,3,2,1 \rangle,\langle 2,3,4 \rangle)$
      What does the lambda-abstracted function do in general? See Exercise 7.7(2.b) on page 172 for setDeleteAll.

Mu-expressions

Consider the problem of defining mkDate in Date_Adt when the value-space model is schema Date. We would like to have the axiom:

$$\forall\, d : 1..31;\ m : 1..12;\ y : \text{Year} \mid \text{isDate}(d,m,y) \bullet$$
$$\text{mkDate}(\,d,m,y\,) =$$
      'that Date binding whose dy, mn and yr components have the
      values d, m and y respectively'

However, if you try to construct a term to formalize the right-hand side of the equality, the term seems to elude description. What comes to the rescue is a *mu-expression*, also called a *definite description*. Here is the solution:

$$\text{mkDate} : (1..31) \times (1..12) \times \text{Year} \nrightarrow \text{Date}$$

$$\text{dom mkDate} = \{ d : 1..31; m : 1..12; y : \text{Year} \mid \text{isDate}(d,m,y) \}$$
$$\forall d : 1..31; m : 1..12; y : \text{Year} \mid (d,m,y) \in \text{dom mkDate} \bullet$$
$$\text{mkDate}(d,m,y) =$$
$$(\mu \text{ Date} \mid dy = d \land mn = m \land yr = y)$$

The value of the mu-expression is that unique `Date` binding that satisfies the constraint given, which fairly obviously characterizes the binding we are seeking. With the schema `Date` model there is actually no other way to construct `mkDate` but to use a mu-expression—there is no constructor mechanism in Z for building bindings directly from individual variables; bindings can be constructed only from schema names using the operator θ.

In general, a mu-expression has the form

$$\mu \text{ SchemaText} \left[\bullet \text{ Term} \right] \qquad\qquad \text{— large brackets mean 'optional'}$$

Its value is that of the optional Term if present, using those value(s) of the variable(s) of SchemaText for which the property of SchemaText *uniquely holds*. If ' • Term ' is not present, as in the above example, the value of the mu-expression is just that of the characteristic tuple of SchemaText. Therefore, in `mkDate` above, the mu-expression is short for

$$\mu \text{ Date} \mid dy = d \land mn = m \land yr = y \bullet \theta \text{ Date}$$

Again, as originally discussed in Section 7.2 and reprised in the discussion of lambda-expressions, care is needed when schema references occur in SchemaText. The reader should be clear that

$$\mu \text{ Date} \ldots \ldots$$

and

$$\mu \, dy : 1..31; mn : 1..12; yr : \text{Year} \mid \text{isDate}(dy,mn,yr) \ldots \ldots$$

are quite different in a mu-expression if the ' • Term ' component is absent.

Here is another example, the `Date_Adt` function `earliest`:

$$\text{earliest} : \mathbb{P}_1 \text{ Date} \rightarrow \text{Date}$$

$$\forall sd : \mathbb{P}_1 \text{ Date} \bullet$$
$$\text{earliest } sd =$$
$$(\mu \, d : \text{Date} \mid d \in sd \land (\forall e : sd \bullet d \text{ isOnOrBefore } e))$$

Again, note that d in the mu-expression is unique—it is not just a member of the date set `sd` but the earliest date in that set. What is more, any date set must have an earliest date since dates, by the definition of `Date`, do not precede 1st January of `bottomYr`. The function `latest` can be defined similarly to `earliest`, *but with one important difference*: it cannot be total over $\mathbb{P}_1$ `Date`. This is because dates 'go on forwards for ever', and thus in an infinite set of dates, there exists no 'latest date', i.e., the mu-expression (what will it be?) will be undefined in such cases.

In general, there must be a *unique* collection of values to bind to a mu-expression's variables to make the mu-expression's property true. If this uniqueness criterion is not satisfied, the mu-expression is undefined. For example, we cannot write, say,

$$\text{getAnElem} : \mathbb{P}_1 X \to X \qquad \text{— n.b. the example is inconsistent}$$
$$\forall s : \mathbb{P}_1 X \bullet \text{getAnElem } s = (\mu\, e : X \mid e \in s)$$

in an attempt to construct a function which chooses some element from a non-empty set. Since there is in general more than one choice to be made for e which makes $e \in s$ true, the mu-expression is undefined (except when s happens to be singleton). In this example, the construction fails because the behaviour required of `getAnElem` is non-deterministic—no such function can be constructed. Note, however, that `getAnElem` could be described as an operation on a state, since non-determinism here is not a problem.

One must also be careful not to construct mu-expressions which are undefined in a deeper sense. Consider this example:

$$\text{maxPrimeIn} : \mathbb{P}_1 \mathbb{N}_1 \to \mathbb{N}_1 \qquad \text{— n.b. the example is inconsistent}$$
$$\forall \text{spi} : \mathbb{P}_1 \mathbb{N}_1 \bullet \text{maxPrimeIn spi} =$$
$$(\mu\, k : \text{spi} \mid \text{prime } k \wedge (\forall j : \text{spi} \mid j > k \bullet \neg\, \text{prime } j))$$

The mu-expression attempts to construct 'the largest prime number in a given set of positive integers'. This seems to obey the uniqueness criterion. However, if a positive integer set is infinite, k in the mu-expression cannot exist because there are arbitrarily large primes. The undefinedness here is due to non-existence of the unique object the mu-expression is intended to choose. So `maxPrimeIn` cannot be total as declared—for some sets it is undefined. Our description would be correct if either `maxPrime` was limited to finite sets, i.e., $\mathbb{F}_1 \mathbb{N}_1$, or else declared as partial. This comment also applies to function `latest` mentioned on the previous page.

The general conclusion is that mu-expressions require cautious usage to avoid introducing undefinedness into specifications. As with lambda-expressions, the syntactic strength of mu-expressions is weak. To avoid ambiguities, it is best to play safe and place them in parentheses except in clear-cut circumstances, e.g., when they constitute the whole of the right-hand side of an abbreviation definition.

EXERCISE 7.9

Use mu-expressions to construct the following, except in one case where the mu-expression would be potentially undefined (say why):

a. a function `nextAfterMin` which calculates the integer immediately following the smallest integer in the finite set s
b. (using the schema `VanHire`)
   i. an expression for the latest hire end date of the current bookings
   ii. an expression for the customer with the longest hire period
c. the predicate of function `fstPosIn` (see Exercise 7.5(d) on page 167)
d. the predicate of function `daysOn` (see page 172).
e. a shorter predicate for function `prev` (see Exercise 7.6(2) on page 169).

Curried Definition

Repeated on the next page for convenience is the definition of function `countOccs` given on page 167:

```
┌─[X]────────────────────────────────────────────────────────────┐
│ countOccs : X× seq X → ℕ                                         │
│                                                                  │
├──────────────────────────────────────────────────────────────── │
│ ∀ e : X; s : seq X • countOccs( e,s ) = #( s ▷ {e})              │
└──────────────────────────────────────────────────────────────────┘
```

We will now modify the syntax of the definition, giving the function a different name:

```
┌─[X]────────────────────────────────────────────────────────────┐
│ c_countOccs : X→ seq X→ ℕ                                        │
│                                                                  │
├──────────────────────────────────────────────────────────────── │
│ ∀ e : X; s : seq X • c_countOccs e s = #( s ▷ {e})               │
└──────────────────────────────────────────────────────────────────┘
```

The changes, though small, are significant. Firstly, function arrows are *right-associative*, so the declaration of c_countOccs should be read as

> c_countOccs : X→ (seq X→ ℕ)

c_countOccs is therefore a function requiring an argument of type X which has as its result *another function*; this function is a seq X → ℕ function requiring seq X arguments which calculates values in ℕ. Secondly, the defining equality for c_countOccs has this shape:

> c_countOccs e s = ...

and *not*, as for countOccs, this shape:

> countOccs(e,s) = ...

Clearly, it would be ill-formed to write

> c_countOccs(e,s) = ...

since, unlike countOccs, the argument of c_countOccs is not a (X× seq X) pair but just an X object. In fact, countOccs and c_countOccs, quite apart from their distinct names, are *different* functions, even though their 'overall effect' is apparently the same.

The fact that countOccs and c_countOccs are different functions can be highlighted by using lambda-expression definition. The respective definitions would be

> countOccs [X] == λ e : X; s : seq X • #(s ▷ { e})
> c_countOccs [X] == λ e : X • (λ s : seq X • #(s ▷ {e}))

The nested lambda-expression structure for c_countOccs clearly reveals it to be a λ e : X • ... function (function with an X argument) yielding a λ s : seq X • ... function (function with a seq X argument).

Suppose we want to find the number of times that 0 occurs in the integer list sequin ∈ seq ℤ. Then, using the two functions, we would write the terms

> countOccs(0,sequin)   (7.10)
> c_countOccs 0 sequin   (7.11)

With term (7.10), we can think of this as

> countOccs(0,sequin)
>   = (λ e : ℤ; s : seq ℤ • #(s ▷{ e}))(0,sequin)   — lambda definition
>   = #(sequin ▷{ 0})   — substitution

With term (7.11), it is important to remember that function application *associates to the left*, so the term is effectively

    (c_countOccs 0) sequin

which is of course consistent with c_countOcc's declaration. Again, by simple processes of substitution, etc., we can understand the evaluation of this term in the following way:

    c_countOccs 0 sequin
        = (c_countOccs 0) sequin   — left associative
        = (λ e : ℤ • (λ s : seq ℤ • #(s ▷{ e })) 0) sequin   — lambda definition
        = (λ s : seq ℤ • #(s ▷{ 0 })) sequin   — substitution of e
        = #(sequin ▷{ 0 })   — substitution of s

The first substitution strips off the 'λ e : ℤ •' by replacing e with the argument 0. The result is a function described by λ s : seq ℤ • #(s ▷{ 0 }). This substitution process then occurs again, stripping off the 'λ s : seq ℤ •' by replacing s with the argument sequin to leave the expected result.

Functions defined in the syntactic style of c_countOccs are said to be *curried*, a term derived from the person who devised the technique. Any function can be declared in curried style. Consider the arbitrary function anf. If requiring an argument structure with the familiar tuple shape, its declaration would look like

    anf : X1 × X2 × ... Xn → Y

Alternatively, there are ways of declaring anf with various degrees of 'curriedness' depending on the number of components in its tuple argument. The 'maximally curried' version of anf, mxc_anf say, would have a declaration with the syntax

    mxc_anf : X_1 → X_2 → ... X_n → Y

which, using lambda description, would be a function with the following shape:

    λ x_1 : X_1 • (λ x_2 : X_2 • (...(λ x_n : X_n • TermInvolving $x_1, x_2, ... x_n$) ...))

where TermInvolving calculates a value in the set Y. An application of mxc_anf would look like this (for $a_i ∈ X_i$):

    mxc_anf a_1 a_2 ... a_n

We can imagine the 'mechanics' of the evaluation of this term to proceed as described earlier for c_countOccs. Firstly, mxc_anf is applied to a_1 (stripping off the 'λ x_1 : X_1 •'), which yields a X_2 → ... X_n → Y function. This function is then applied to a_2 (stripping off the 'λ x_2 : X_2 •'), which yields ... and so on. Eventually, we obtain a TermInvolving $a_1, a_2, ... a_n$.

Remark
Note the counterpoint associativity at work here. To make currying work smoothly, the *left* associativity of function application needs to be complemented by the *right* associativity of function arrows.

Currying can be seen as an alternative to tuples for making all functions single-argument. The obvious question is: why prefer to define a function in curried style?

After all, `countOccs` and `c_countOccs` do the same job. The simple answer is: it can be beneficial. By defining `c_countOccs`, we can then also write definitions like

```
countOccsOf0 == c_countOccs 0
countOccsOf1 == c_countOccs 1
```

and so on. `countOccsOf0` is a function that counts zeros in integer lists; similarly, `countOccsOf1` counts ones. All we are doing is making direct use of the fact that, when `c_countOccs` is applied to an argument, it yields a particular function. We saw earlier the function result of `c_countOccs` applied to 0. The lambda-expression

$$\lambda s : seq\ \mathbb{Z} \bullet \#(\ s \rhd \{\ 0\ \})$$

describes that function, and this is what the above name `countOccsOf0` therefore provides an abbreviation for.

In conclusion, we can see that if we needed functions like `countOccsOf0` etc. as well as a general counting function itself, defining curried `c_countOccs` provides us with an easy route to obtaining the more specialized functions. With uncurried `countOccs`, there is no way to derive `countOccsOf0` and `countOccsOf1` from `countOccs` itself—they would have to be declared separately in the usual full form. It follows that by a judicious choice of defining certain functions in curried form, coupled with a careful choice of argument order, we can save ourselves considerable work *and* also increase the elegance of our specification.

In non-trivial specifications where axiomatic, rather than schema-based, description dominates, curried and other kinds of 'higher-order' function are often needed to describe the required operations of the data types involved to a sufficient level of abstraction. The reader could try Bowen (1989) or even Sufrin (1986) for examples of this, though much of the latter might prove too exacting first time round.

EXERCISE 7.10

1. Explain the differences that exist, if any, between the following functions:

    $f1 : A \to B \to C \to D$ $f2 : (A \to B) \to C \to D$
    $f3 : A \to (B \to C) \to D$ $f4 : A \to B \to (C \to D)$

2. Construct curried definitions of the following functions:

    a. `c_delFstOcc` (the curried form of `delFstOcc`, Exercise 7.5(d) on page 167) using a lambda-expression
    b. `repl n s` which maps to a sequence by replicating n times the sequence s (n is a natural number); e.g., `repl 3` $\langle a,b \rangle = \langle a,b,a,b,a,b \rangle$
    c. a function `delFstOccNullSet` that deletes the first instance of the empty set from a list of sets of integers
    d. a function `repl10Times` that replicates any sequence 10 times.

3. Explain how, by making minor changes, one could exploit currying in `Date_Adt` to facilitate definition of the following functions:

    a. a function that creates that date which is Christmas Day of the given year
    b. a function that calculates the date four weeks on from the given date.

7.5 PROPERTY-ORIENTED DATA TYPE SPECIFICATION

Constructing Fresh Data Types

Suppose we wish to introduce a completely fresh type into a Z specification, i.e., one not modelled on (constructed from) other existing types. Our only choice is to base the type we need on a given set. A given set can be introduced directly:

> [NewBasicType]

or it can be 'wrapped up' in a free type definition (e.g., see page 92):

> NewBasicType ::= ... ...

A given set or free type may be entirely sufficient for the purposes of the specification—witness BOOKING, CUSTOMER, VAN and VanClass in Van Hire, for example. However, what do we do if we need to construct something richer, i.e., a data type with various relations, functions, etc.? How to achieve this is not immediately obvious. Since there is no value-space model for NewBasicType, we cannot tackle the problem in model-oriented fashion.

As a first glimpse of the approach needed, consider again VanClass in Van Hire:

> VanClass ::= mini | transit | light | medium | heavyDuty

Imagine that in the Van Hire specification, we needed a $\leq$ relation over van classes to express the idea of 'smaller than or equal to'. Since VanClass is a new type and therefore comes with nothing else 'given' apart from the distinct constants that denote its values, we will have to introduce the desired relation explicitly. All we have available to work with are the constants of VanClass. In that case, we can declare the relation as follows, using a new name to avoid masking out the standard definition of $\leq$:

> _ lessOrEq _ : VanClass ↔ VanClass

Then we attach to the declaration axioms like

> mini lessOrEq transit; transit lessOrEq light
> light lessOrEq medium; medium lessOrEq heavyDuty

Though tedious, we could incorporate sufficient axioms into our description until the meaning of lessOrEq had been completely captured. Note that the four axioms given would be insufficient on their own. Presumably, we would require reflexivity, i.e.:

> vanClass lessOrEq vanClass

for each van class. Transitivity would also be needed, but we cannot infer, say

> mini lessOrEq light

just because of the first two axioms above. That is, we cannot infer from the axioms

> vanClassA lessOrEq vanClassC

simply because we have

> vanClassA lessOrEq vanClassB ∧ vanClassB lessOrEq vanClassC

This would *assume* that lessOrEq is transitive, which we cannot do. Remember that there are no *a priori* properties possessed by VanClass, apart from it comprising five distinct constants. Any additional properties we require `VanClass` to have must all be given to it by axiomatic description.

The approach being illustrated here is what is called *property-oriented* specification. Basically, what this means is that the operations of a data type are described not by axioms directly expressing behaviours over a value-space model (there is no model), but by axioms describing properties that the operation behaviours are required to exhibit. In order to express those properties, we make reference to the various terms which denote values of the data type. With `VanClass`, this is just its five constants. Shortly, we see that there are possibilities other than just constants.

The completion of the definition of `lessOrEq` for `VanClass` is left as part of the next exercise. Here is a further example of property-oriented description:

$$
\begin{array}{l}
[\,\text{T}\,] \\
\hline
\quad \text{c : T} \\
\quad \text{f : T} \rightarrowtail \text{T} \\
\hline
\quad \text{disjoint} \langle \{\,\text{c}\,\}, \text{ran f} \rangle
\end{array}
$$

This introduces a basic type as a given set and associates with it one constant and one total injection, which exhibit the disjointness property stated. Of course, these two Z paragraphs by themselves do not describe a particularly rich or useful new data type. So let us *enrich* the description with some extra functions and properties:

$$
\begin{array}{l}
\quad \text{p : T} \times \text{T} \rightarrow \text{T} \\
\quad \text{t : T} \times \text{T} \rightarrow \text{T} \\
\hline
\quad \forall\, \text{x : T} \bullet \\
\qquad \text{p(x,c) = x} \land \\
\qquad \text{t(x,c) = c} \\
\quad \forall\, \text{x,y : T} \bullet \\
\qquad \text{p(x,f y) = f(p(x,y)) } \land \\
\qquad \text{t(x,f y) = p(t(x,y),x)}
\end{array}
$$

The enrichment has two new functions p and t which 'interact' with the earlier c and f as indicated by the four new axioms.

Despite the extra functions, the reader might still be wondering: of what possible use is data type T and its operations? We could continue the enrichment process as far as we wished. Even so, the description does not look very promising or 'informative'. The point is that if we were considering introducing T into a specification, we would have something in mind for T, i.e., an *interpretation* for the set T and its operations c, f, p and t. What is more, we would, as is the usual practice, choose names other than T, etc. that better suggest the interpretation we wish the data type to have.

EXERCISE 7.11

1. Give a full axiomatic description of the relation `lessOrEq` for data type `VanClass`. You could simply list all necessary `lessOrEq` axioms like those on the previous page. However, a much more concise and elegant description of the relation can be constructed from the four explicit axioms given earlier. (*Hint*: if you get stuck, re-read Section 6.3.)

2. § The answer is discussed below.

Devise an interpretation that 'makes sense' for type T in the text and its operations. That is, think of a set which T might stand for, and then think of some operations over that set which c, f, p and t could stand for and which exhibit the properties expressed by the axioms of T's description. *Hint*: consider a certain subset of the integers.

Our examples lead to the idea of a data type *theory* and its *models*. Data type theories are not new to us. We talk about 'set theory', for example. By this we mean a collection of *laws* (as they are often called) that convey useful properties about sets. A property-oriented axiomatization represents a theory, its basic laws being the axioms we have 'given' to the data type being constructed. A *model* of a data type theory is an interpretation of the theory for which all the theory's axioms are true. Consider VanClass on the previous page. If we make the following interpretation (read ← as 'is given the interpretation'):

VanClass ← 0..4 (i.e., mini ← 0, transit ← 1, light ← 2, ... etc.)
_ lessOrEq _ ← _≤_

then the axioms of VanClass are satisfied (check this). So this interpretation is a model for VanClass. For the data type theory T, if

T ← ℕ
c ← 0
f ← succ
p ← (_+_)
t ← (_*_)

then the axioms of T are satisfied. For example, the first axiom involving operation p becomes (for any two natural numbers x and y)

x + succ y = succ(x + y)

which is true. Thus, ℕ with successor function, addition and multiplication is a model for T.

A theory can have many models, though usually we are interested only in one of them. For example, it is clear that any five-element subset of the integers accompanied by ≤ would do for VanClass. Which ever model we choose can be thought of as deciding upon how to implement VanClass. We return to this idea later. What about T? As a theory for ℕ it is acceptable as far as it goes, but to make it 'more like' its intended model, we should add functions interpreting to subtraction and division, say, and relations interpreting to 'less than', 'less than or equals', etc. In fact, we would need to enrich our T theory substantially.

There is also a deeper question to consider regarding T. The declarations of c and f plus the axiom disjoint ⟨{c}, ran f⟩ tell us that c is a different T object to any produced by f; but are there any other T objects apart from c and the members of ran f, such as those produced by functions p and t? Given the intended interpretation above, we would be inclined to say *no*, but the theory as it stands makes no statement to this effect. We will return to this issue later also.

Our T example shows how we could introduce the natural numbers as a fresh data type into a specification rather than treating them merely as a subset of ℤ. Since this is not something we would want to do very often using the Z notation, the T example is not a particularly realistic example of property-oriented description! More realistic would be, say, a queue data type, for which we earlier constructed a model-oriented description. However, before getting further embroiled in the property-oriented approach, we need to look at free types in more detail.

Free Types Revisited

Free type definition offers no extra descriptive power above and beyond what can be described by given sets and sufficiently rich axioms. However, the main advantage of free type definition is that it can be used to produce more elegant and compact data type constructions than corresponding given-set based description. We will reinforce this point later.

To recap, a free type definition has the general form

NewType   ::=   Alt$_1$ | Alt$_2$ | ... Alt$_n$

where Alt$_1$, Alt$_2$, etc. describe different alternative ways of constructing terms denoting values of the type NewType. In the simplest case, the alternatives are just *constants*, as with VanClass. In the more general case, alternatives can introduce *constructor* functions using the syntax

CnstrFn 《 DomainSet 》

This form means that one way of constructing a value of the type named on the left of the '::=' is to apply the function CnstrFn to an argument from the set DomainSet. Here are two simple examples of free type definitions involving constructor functions:

```
Char ::= ascii《 0..127 》
RoadTransport ::=
    cycle | motorCycle | van《 VanClass 》 | car | coach | bus
```

Thus, terms such as ascii(33) and ascii(64) denote values of type Char, and terms such as cycle and van(medium) denote values of type RoadTransport.

Extended Remark
Unless names had been chosen perversely, type Char above would obviously be intended as some kind of *character* type. Taking cues from what is commonly offered by programming languages, newcomers to Z are sometimes puzzled by the absence of types *real* and *boolean*, as well as *character*. Firstly, type *real*. One problem is that the relationship between the mathematical reals and the real numbers available on an actual computing machine is non-trivial, not least because of the approximate nature of real (i.e., floating point) arithmetic on computers due to rounding errors, etc. In practice, information systems, unless leaning heavily towards the number-crunching variety, can be described with little if any reference to real arithmetic. However, real numbers cannot be ignored, and the interested reader might care to try Valentine (1992) as one proposal for incorporating a theory of reals into standard Z.

A *boolean* type is simply not needed in Z. Firstly, because of Z's syntax, it is always known where a predicate ('boolean expression') is expected in Z constructs. Secondly, the way relations are handled in Z side-steps the need for a boolean type—what would be n-argument 'boolean functions' in other notations are simply n-ary relations in Z.

Finally, where 'boolean variables' are needed, we can simply define an appropriate two-valued free type.

Characters are merely 'concrete marks of representation'. There is no single all-embracing 'universal character set', let alone one with a collection of useful abstract properties to axiomatize. If we need a character type in a specification, we can construct one, as with type `Char` on the previous page. In some cases, a bare given set might be all that is needed. The reader should note, however, that the proposed Z standard (Brien and Nicholls 1992) permits string literals, though their representation is defined to be implementation dependent.

Consider next this example:

$$\texttt{List} ::= \texttt{nil} \mid \texttt{cons} \, \langle\!\langle \, \texttt{X} \times \texttt{List} \, \rangle\!\rangle$$

This definition says that values of type `List` are denoted by the constant `nil` and terms of the form `cons( e,s )`, where `e ∈ X` and `s ∈ List`. Free type definitions can thus be recursive. Moreover, drawing upon earlier terminology introduced on page 170, it turns out that the constants and constructors of a free type are its *generators* too. So, constant `nil` and constructor `cons` together are the generators of type `List`. Recalling other associated material in Section 7.4, we might therefore expect to see operations on `List` defined using argument structures based on its generators. Here, for example, is a function that counts how many items make up a list:

---

lengthOf : List → ℕ

---

lengthOf nil = 0
∀ e : X; s : List • lengthOf(cons(e,s)) = 1 + lengthOf s

It is as though the left-hand sides of the defining equations 'fall out automatically' from the free type definition. Indeed, when constructing functions over (especially recursive) free types, case-style definition over the structure of terms based on the type's generators comes into its own—the different argument structures needed in the defining equalities come directly from inspecting the type's definition. For example, suppose `AFreeType` is defined as

$$\texttt{AFreeType} ::= \texttt{aconst} \mid \texttt{cf1} \, \langle\!\langle \, \texttt{X} \, \rangle\!\rangle \mid \texttt{cf2} \, \langle\!\langle \, (\,\texttt{seq Y}\,) \times \texttt{AFreeType} \, \rangle\!\rangle$$

Then, in defining a total function `someFn` on `AFreeType`, we would expect to see

---

someFn : AFreeType → ...

---

someFn aconst = ...
∀ x : X • someFn(cf1 x) = ...
∀ s : seq Y; e : AFreeType • someFn(cf2(s,e)) = ...

---

as the axiom structures occurring in `someFn`'s definition.

Recursive free types enable us to construct elegant definitions of objects we think of as being 'recursively structured' in some way, as with lists and binary trees. However, we must be careful to avoid writing inconsistent free type definitions. Simplifying considerably, any recursive alternative in the definition of a free type FreeType must define elements of FreeType that are made from 'a finite number of FreeType elements'; in addition, the recursive definition of FreeType must also include at least one nonrecursive alternative. To circumvent a technical discussion well beyond the scope of this book, constructors with domains built from cartesian products, finite functions, finite sets or sequences will cause no problems.

GIVEN PROPERTIES OF FREE TYPE DEFINITIONS
On page 92, the elementary properties implicitly conveyed by a simple free type definition were briefly referred to. We now need to extend this property list to the general case for an arbitrary free type ArbFreeType involving any number of constants and constructors:

$$\text{ArbFreeType} ::= c_1 \mid ... \mid c_k \mid f_1 \langle\!\langle \text{SetExpr}_1 \rangle\!\rangle \mid ... \mid f_n \langle\!\langle \text{SetExpr}_n \rangle\!\rangle$$

Here is the full list of the properties, informally expressed, that are given by such a definition:

- the constants $c_1, ... c_k$ are distinct
- the constructors $f_1, ... f_n$ are total and injective
- the constants and ranges of the constructors are disjoint
- the smallest subset of ArbFreeType containing all the constants and which is closed under the constructors is ArbFreeType itself.

The first three properties together guarantee that no constant is generated by any constructor, no constructor generates duplicates, and no constructor generates an object that any other generator produces. The last property in the list in effect says: the constants and constructors 'exhaust' ArbFreeType, i.e., there are no elements of ArbFreeType not generated by the constants and constructors.

The list of given properties shows what we would have to say if we unwound a free type definition into an explicit property-oriented one based on a given set. If the definition of ArbFreeType comprises constants only, as with VanClass, the above list reduces to the first and fourth property, where the latter can be expressed simply as: ArbFreeType is precisely the set of constants in the definition. Thus, for VanClass:

[VanClass]

mini, transit, light, medium, heavyDuty : VanClass

disjoint $\langle \{ \text{mini} \}, \{ \text{transit} \}, \{ \text{light} \}, \{ \text{medium} \}, \{ \text{heavyDuty} \} \rangle$
VanClass = { mini, transit, light, medium, heavyDuty }

For less trivial definitions like List on the previous page, the equivalent given-set description would be

[List, X]

nil : List
cons : X × List $\rightarrowtail$ List

disjoint $\langle \{ \text{nil} \}, \text{ran cons} \rangle$
InductionPrinciple

The reader need not worry about the exact form of InductionPrinciple, by which we mean the fourth property in the previous list of 'givens'. The axiom has considerable significance as regards proof, so we will not pursue this aspect any further, suffice it to say that this explains the origin of the term 'inductive definition' when describing function behaviour via argument structures. Note that if we enrich the earlier T theory with an InductionPrinciple, this resolves the issue concerning the relationship between the members of T and what its constant and function ranges are capable of providing. We would, of course, get an InductionPrinciple 'for free' if we introduced T using a free type definition instead ... see Question (2) in the exercise which follows.

EXERCISE 7.12

1. Develop further the free type Char (page 183) by defining the following:
   a. the specific characters null and esc which have integer codes 0 and 27 respectively, the upper-case letters (codes 65–90 inclusive), and the digits (codes 48–57 inclusive)
   b. a function ctoi which maps a character to its integer code, and a function nextCh which gives the character that (in some useful sense) immediately follows its character argument
   c. a relation chle which defines a total order ≤ over characters.

2. Consider the given-set based definition of T on page 181:
   a. If, instead, you were introducing T by a free type definition, what free type definition would you write?
   b. Give the axiomatic description that would then need to accompany the free type definition in order to express at least everything that the enriched given-set based definition of T in the text expresses
   c. What properties, if any, would the free type definition provide which the given-set based definition as described does not provide?

A Property-Oriented Queue Description

It should now be clear that free type definition provides a more economical basis for property-oriented description than using explicit given sets. A free type definition will provide the generators needed, with the right properties, and we can quickly turn our attention to constructing the rest of the data type's operations.

Consider the problem of specifying our queue data type in property-oriented mode. Firstly, its generators. A little thought should show that these are the constant emptyq and the constructor addq. We quickly arrive at the recursive definition

$$\text{Queue} ::= \text{emptyq} \mid \text{addq} \langle\!\langle X \times \text{Queue} \rangle\!\rangle$$

Note the limitation that X must be a given set; generic free type definitions are not permitted.

The way to proceed now is to consider how each of the other required queue operations 'interacts' with the generators. For the total operation lenq, this is easy (we omit quantification clutter):

```
lenq emptyq = 0
lenq( addq( e,q ) ) = 1 + lenq q
```

Here is our familiar friend—inductive, case-style definition over term structures based directly on the generators. Sometimes, however, the equational patterns on the left-hand side cannot be quite so simple. This is the case with remq and fstq whose behaviours are more complex to describe.

Consider first remq. Function remq is not total since it is not applicable to emptyq. So we will not have any equality beginning remq emptyq = ... However, singleton and non-singleton queues need to be treated separately, because the effect of remq is different in each case. A singleton queue is made by adding an element to an empty queue; if we remove the first element of this queue, we expect to end up with the empty queue. That is,

> remq(addq(e,emptyq)) = emptyq

However, if the argument of remq is non-singleton, then the effect is more subtle. The simplest arbitrary term structure that represents a non-singleton, non-empty queue is

> addq(e1,addq(e2,q))

so the property we are trying to express will be captured by an equality of the form

> remq(addq(e1,addq(e2,q))) = SomeQueue

To determine SomeQueue, it must be remembered that we wish to view addq as adding to the *back* of a queue. Thus, SomeQueue is the same as if remq had been performed on addq(e2,q) and *then* e1 added:

> addq(e1,remq(addq(e2,q)))

So we end up with a property that is expressed by the rather unappealing equality

> remq(addq(e1,addq(e2,q))) = addq(e1,remq(addq(e2,q)))

The important feature of this axiom is that the term involving remq on the right-hand side is 'simpler than' the term involving remq on the left (see also page 172).

A similar analysis leads to equations for fstq. Parcelling everything together, we get the following description, where we have added explicit information about the domains of the partial functions remq and fstq:

> [X]
> Queue ::= emptyq | addq《 X× Queue 》
>
> ---
>
> remq : Queue ⇸ Queue
> fstq : Queue ⇸ X
> lenq : Queue → ℕ
>
> ---
>
> lenq emptyq = 0
> ∀ e : X; q : Queue •
>   lenq(addq(e,q)) = 1 + lenq q
> dom remq = dom fstq = Queue \ { emptyq}
> ∀ e : X •
>   remq(addq(e,emptyq)) = emptyq ∧
>   fstq(addq(e,emptyq)) = e
> ∀ e1,e2 : X; q : Queue •
>   remq(addq(e1,addq(e2,q))) = addq(e1,remq(addq(e2,q))) ∧
>   fstq(addq(e1,addq(e2,q))) = fstq(addq(e2,q))

The reader should compare this specification with the model-oriented one on page 164, ignoring generics.

EXERCISE 7.13

1. Define the following additional functions over property-oriented `Queue`. Analogues of most of these functions over sequences have occurred in Section 7.3 and could be added to the model-oriented specification on page 164.

   a. `elemsOfq( q )` (yields the elements of a queue as a set)
   b. `delFstOccq( e,q )` (yields the queue obtained by deleting the first occurrence, if any, of element e from queue q)
   c. `quToSeq( q )` (converts a queue to a sequence, preserving element order)
   d. `fstPosInq( e,q )` (yields the positional index of the first occurrence of element e in queue q ; if e is not a member of q, the function returns 0).

2. Use `Queue` above to construct a data type `InjQueue` for 'injective queues'. A queue is injective if all its elements are unique (the definition of `Queue` as it stands does not exclude element duplication).

3. Give a property-oriented specification of a *stack* data type `Stack` with elements of type X. Stack operations are like those for queues, with `push` adding an element to the top of the stack and `pop` removing a stack's top element. Use the `Queue` theory as a guide. The axioms required for `Stack` are fewer and simpler than for `Queue`.

MODEL-ORIENTED OR PROPERTY-ORIENTED?

Arguably, the characteristics of property-oriented specification make it closer to the true spirit of 'being abstract' compared to the model-oriented route—the former enables us to capture the semantics of a data type's operations without reference to any value-space model. For that reason, a property-oriented data type is sometimes referred to as 'syntactic'. Its generators allow us to write term patterns that denote the data type's values; the way we then describe the behaviour of other operations of the data type is via those term patterns. In contrast, a model-oriented data type is sometimes referred to as 'semantic'. The value-space model provides an interpretation for the data type's values, and we define the behaviour of *all* the data type's operations in terms of this model.

It must be emphasized that we are merely lightly brushing over the property-oriented approach. There are many questions to be answered such as: how do we know precisely which axioms to include in a property-oriented specification so that it is sufficient and complete? Also, when we enrich a theory with extra properties to construct a more specialized data type, we have to be careful not to generate meaningless descriptions, e.g., a theory whose axioms are inconsistent. Issues like these go beyond what scope and space constraints permit here.

Some languages such as OBJ (see for example Gallimore *et al*. (1989)) have been designed specifically for property-oriented specification. Since all axioms end up being expressed as equalities, the specification paradigm typified by OBJ is sometimes referred to as *equational* specification, or *algebraic* specification. The reason for the latter name is because an implementation of such a specification—in the sense that our model-oriented `Queue [ X ]` could be an implementation model for the property-oriented `Queue` theory—constitutes an *algebra*. The reader can find out more about algebras by referring to any suitable text on discrete mathematics; alternatively, try Woodcock and Loomes (1988) for a gentle introduction.

The model- and property-oriented paradigms are 'rivals' in the arena of specification; a useful comparison of the different approaches is covered in Cohen *et al.* (1986). Each paradigm has its own strong adherents, its own arguable strengths and weaknesses. Overall, we should perhaps see the two paradigms as complementary, using model-orientation for systems and property-orientation for (some) data types. Though the property-oriented approach is not limited to 'specification in the small' (e.g., see Coleman *et al.* (1987)), many would argue that for even moderately sized—and especially state-based—systems, model-oriented specification has proved in practice to be more suitable and successful.

Apart from Section 7.5, no application of property-oriented specification occurs in this book—a conscious decision to keep to the model-oriented paradigm, which is arguably the one people generally find more accessible. Going from theory to model is the 'purer' development approach; e.g., we construct a `Queue` theory, implement it with a suitable model and then prove that our model satisfies the laws of the theory. Nevertheless, constructing a model-oriented specification and then proving it has the desired properties is intuitively more natural. At least, this is so for state-based systems: a state model plus operations *is closer to the user's view of a system* than any other kind of description. As far as Z itself is concerned, we are free to use it how we want, in any way that seems appropriate to the task at hand.

Further Applications of Free Types

DESCRIBING ABSTRACT SYNTAX

One common use of free types is to describe the *abstract syntax* of constructs, i.e., their underlying syntactic structure ignoring surface features such as punctuation, style, etc., which are present merely to aid humans or machines to recognize the syntax. As a simple example, consider the syntax of an if–statement in some imagined programming language. This statement might have the *concrete* syntax

> **if** Cond **then** Statement
>   **else** Statement
> **end if**

The indentation and alignment, and the surface keywords **if**, etc., provide readability and aid recognition of syntactic structure. The abstract syntax, however, would merely need to express that an **if** statement comprises three parts: a condition and two statements suitably distinguishable as the 'then' and 'else' components.

Imagine defining a type `Statement` for the abstract syntax of programming language statements. We might construct a definition looking like

```
Statement ::= ... | ifStmt《 Cond × Statement × Statement 》 | ...
```

The `ifStmt` constructor handles the disjoint subset of `Statement` which denotes all **if** statements. `Cond` would be another free type:

```
Cond ::= ... | ...                                    — see next exercise
```

and so on. In this way, we can build up free type definitions that model the complete abstract syntax of a language.

As another example of this technique, consider *JSP-trees* (JSP = 'Jackson Structured Programming'; see Cameron (1989)). A JSP-tree is used to represent the structure of sequential algorithms. These algorithms are composed of primitive operations (assignments, input/output operations, etc.) and three standard control structures: *sequence, selection*, and *iteration*.

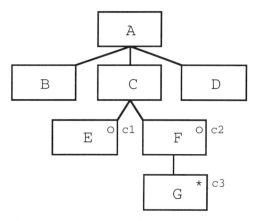

Figure 7.1   An example JSP-tree.

An example JSP-tree is given in Figure 7.1. Primitive operations are leaf nodes. A sequence node, representing instruction sequences (bracketed with **begin** ... **end** where necessary) is a non-leaf node with one or more sibling nodes; e.g., A is the sequence B, C, D. A selection node represents **if** ... **then** ... **elsif** ... **end if** constructs. It is a non-leaf node with two or more sibling nodes, each of which has a '$\circ$' in the top right-hand corner of its box and an annotation describing the (mutually exclusive) condition guarding that alternative in the selection; e.g., C is a selection of E guarded by c1 and F guarded by c2. An iteration node represents **while** ... **do** ... **end do** constructs. It is a non-leaf node with just one sibling node having a '$*$' in the top right-hand corner of its box and an annotation describing the condition controlling the iteration; e.g., F is an iteration of G controlled by the condition c3. Note that: (i) '$\circ$' and '$*$' decorate the components *which are selected/iterated*; (ii) a JSP-tree is never empty and each non-leaf node can be any of the three kinds of structure.

The following free type definition characterizes syntactically (though not necessarily semantically!) well-formed JSP-trees. Assume that types OpId and Cond have already been defined. The generic prefix symbol $\mathbb{F}_2$ is defined for convenience.

```
F₂ X == { s : F X | #s ≥ 2 }
JSPTree ::= op ⟪ OpId ⟫ |
            seqCmp ⟪ OpId × seq JSPTree ⟫ |
            select ⟪ OpId × F₂ ( Cond × JSPTree ) ⟫ |
            iter ⟪ OpId × Cond × JSPTree ⟫
```

The constructors disjointly generate primitive operations, sequences, selections and iterations respectively. Use of a set in the description of the select constructor is sufficient since a selection in a JSP-tree containing two or more instances of the same Cond × JSPTree pair would be ill-formed.

Using the definition of data type JSPTree, we can now write down terms that interpret to particular JSP-trees. For example, assuming that capitalized identifiers represent unique OpId objects and lower-case identifiers represent Cond terms, then the term

```
seqCmp( A, ⟨  op B,
              select( C, {  ( c1,op E ),
                            ( c2,iter( F,c3,op G )) })
              op D ⟩)
```

interprets to the JSP-tree in Figure 7.1.

DISJOINT UNION TYPES
Suppose a programming language allows us to write declarations like

V : **union**(INTEGER , CHARACTER)

Here, **union** is a type constructor (as **array** and **record** would be, say) which enables *disjoint union* types to be constructed. In the example, this would mean that the program variable V is capable of holding a value of either of the two types in the union list. In programs, we can imagine involving a variable like V safely in computations via a special **case** statement which enables us to interrogate the variable and discover at run-time the type of its current value.

To describe union types in Z, a free type definition provides the natural way:

IntOrChar ::= int ⟪ $\mathbb{Z}$ ⟫ | chr ⟪ Char ⟫

The constructors are injections into the domain IntOrChar which is thus the disjoint union of the ranges of the constructors. Example members of IntOrChar are int(0) and, assuming Char as described on page 183, chr(ascii 44). Incidentally, note that there are no constants in the definition of either JSPTree or IntOrChar.

Remark
In a programming language like Pascal, Modula-2, or Ada, disjoint union types are somewhat inadequately and messily realized by so-called 'record variants' (or similar).

EXERCISE 7.14

1. Complete the definition of type Cond on page 189. Assume that conditions are conjunctions, disjunctions, negations, or relational expressions (treat the last of these as basic). Other types needed in your description should simply be assumed.

2. a. Translate the following construct into a JSPTree term; operation identifiers are given as labels.

    ```
    P: while c1 do
       Q: if c2
          then R: while c3 do C end do
          else S: while c3 do D end do
          end if
       end do
    ```

    Make use of the answer to Question 1 (why?).

   b. Interpret the following JSPTree term as an algorithm:

    ```
    select( A,{( c3,iter( B,c2,
      iter( C,c1,op D ))),( c4,op D )})
    ```

3. (Quite hard) Construct definitions of the following:

   a. Functions nNdsInSeq and nNdsInFinSet which count the total number of nodes (i.e., boxes) making up the members of a sequence or finite set, respectively, of JSP-trees. Assume a function nNode which counts the nodes making up a single JSP-tree

   b. The function nNode just mentioned. Make use of functions nNdsInSeq and nNdsInFinSet !

   c. The relation loopFree over JSP-trees, with the obvious interpretation. *Hint*: you will need more than one ⇔-predicate to express loopFree.

4. Define the following:

   a. a type VanClOrChar which is the disjoint union of types VanClass and Char (see page 183 for the latter)

   b. a function convToNat, which converts its VanClOrChar argument to a member of $\mathbb{N}$ thus: VanClass-based terms get mapped according to the interpretation given on page 182, and Char-based terms are mapped to Char 'integer codes'.

SUMMARY OF CHAPTER 7

- The construction of data types in specifications is elaborated upon, contrasting the model-oriented and property-oriented approaches.

- Sequences are introduced, and an in-depth coverage is provided of different techniques for describing functions axiomatically.

- A number of more advanced features of Z are covered, such as: schema types, binding formation, generic specification, lambda- and mu-expressions, recursive free types.

8

THE ONLINE MONITOR:
STRUCTURING A NON-TRIVIAL SPECIFICATION

Key Topics   State modularization: horizontal, vertical. Schema calculus: compatibility, renaming, propositional operators. Error handling, robust specifications. Preconditions: meaning, usages; hiding operator; calculation. Framing, promotion. Sequential composition, piping.

8.1   STATE MODELLING: CHOICES

The Problem Scenario

The case study for this chapter is another system-level problem like Digital Watch and Van Hire. Typically, systems are classified as being 'real time systems' or 'information systems', where the former are distinguished from the latter by their obligation to monitor, respond to, and control their external environment continuously as real-world time ticks by at a rate measured in terms of milliseconds or finer. Often, the only essential difference between two systems is the granularity of time and speed of response required. A safety-critical system such as a medical support system would be a typical real-time system as just described. An online transaction processing system would be required to respond as rapidly as possible to each transaction. In an information system (in the narrower sense), some responses might be required only to the granularity of days, weeks, or even longer. Digital Watch is a fairly coarse-grained 'real-time' system in an almost literal sense. Van Hire is a relatively slow information system, being required to respond to real world events like 'customer makes booking', 'customer returns van', etc. The present case study deals with specifying what might be termed 'systems software'. Part of this software would have to deal with potentially quite rapidly occurring events at the sub-second level.

The case study concerns an organization which runs a computing resource comprising a number of different non-networked machines; see Figure 8.1. The machines are accessible via a large number of remote terminals spread around the organization's premises. Terminal–machine communication is handled by a processor known as Uhura.

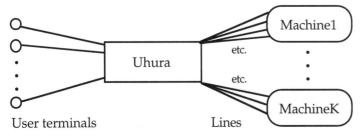

Figure 8.1   Topology of the case-study computing resource.

We are concerned with specifying a new subsystem for Uhura that is to

- keep track of various status data such as the load on each machine
- control which users can get connected to which machine
- manage/monitor connects and disconnects of users

and so on. The relevant aspects of the problem domain are as follows:

- Each machine has a registered set of users; a user can be registered on one or more machines.

- A user is identified by Uhura via a single code which is used to access the whole system, irrespective of machine required.

- Each machine has a certain number of lines between itself and Uhura which limits the load—number of simultaneously connected users—that the machine has to handle (one connected user per line).

- When a user attempts to enter the system to use a machine, the connection is effected if a line is free. If no line is free, the user is placed in a connect queue for that machine. Different maximum lengths are operative for the connect queues of the various machines.

- If all lines to a machine are busy and there is a non-empty queue, then when someone disconnects from that machine, thus freeing a line, the first user in the queue is automatically connected.

- To exert control over potential abuse of resources and system overload, multiple connections to, and queuings for, the same machine by a user are not permitted. Additionally, an automatic disconnect occurs on any allocated line that has been inactive for more than 5 minutes.

All users can

- enter the system to get connected to any machine on which they are registered
- delete themselves from connect queues
- interrogate the availability of any machine.

There are also certain operations restricted to privileged users, e.g., systems staff. These include

- registering new users on, or withdrawing users from, a machine or the whole system
- increasing/decreasing lines to a particular machine
- taking a machine off line, or bringing a machine back on line.

In addition, Uhura issues helpful information—error messages, status data, etc.—to users to inform them of what is going on.

A BRIEF ANALYSIS
Recalling material from the early pages of Chapter 5, one of the essential objectives of the analysis phase, prior to any technical specification in Z, is to scope the domain. We will suppose that the main results of this scoping are as follows:

- The new Uhura subsystem, to be called Online Monitor, is concerned only with managing user registrations and user connections. It will maintain user registrations on the various machines and will know which users are privileged users. It will manage and monitor user connections to each machine and will maintain the connect queues of machines. It will be able to make appropriate preliminary checks when someone attempts to enter the system to get connected to a particular machine.

- Online Monitor is *not* concerned with the management of communication pathways between machines and users at different terminals, all of which is to be carried out by separate Uhura software. Nor is it concerned with actual log-ons and log-offs plus associated password checking, which are host machine activities.

More detailed aspects of the domain will be clarified as the case study unwinds. There is, however, sufficient information available for the reader to tackle the following exercise.

EXERCISE 8.1

§ Two possibilities unfold over the remainder of Section 1.1.
Sketch out a state model for Online Monitor. Include as much declaration and predicate detail as possible.

Specification is full of subtleties and decision-making, even (especially!) during the state modelling stage. Although perhaps not immediately clear how it should be done, we anticipate that the Online Monitor state model will be sufficiently complex to merit dividing it across more than one schema. Providing the division is well-chosen, it should have a beneficial effect on the specification, e.g., it will make it clearer and simplify subsequent operation specification. Digital Watch and Van Hire have already demonstrated that the somewhat clichéd software engineering adage of 'separating concerns' is just as applicable to specifications as it is to, say, software designs, and can be used as a guide to making good specification decisions.

State Model I: a 'Horizontal' Modularization

Using the kind of approach adopted for Van Hire, we could begin by constructing an E–R (entity–relationship) model. It must be stressed that E–R modelling is only one of many domain description techniques. It is certainly *not* always the best choice, irrespective of whether or not its purpose is to 'get a handle on' a Z state model. The technique works best with classic, data-rich information system domains like Van Hire. It works less well the more event-rich a domain is. In an event-rich domain, event sequences can occur which rapidly change the state of the domain, and as a consequence the life-spans of some types of entity and relationships can be very short.

The Online Monitor system is something of a hybrid, its domain basically comprising two main components:

A. one involving machines in the system and the users registered on them
B. another which involves machine access, i.e., user-machine connections and queues.

Sub-domain (B) deals with the event-dominated fast-changing part of the system, the state of which can get updated possibly many times within a second. In comparison, sub-domain (A)—where users are registered, computers get added to/removed from the system, etc.—changes much more slowly. Here, entities (users, machines) and the relationships they enter into are more stable and longer-lived. It is also worth observing that we expect a change in one sub-domain to have little, if any, effect on the other.

Although Online Monitor veers towards event richness, an E–R route to specification is still viable. Without going into a detailed data analysis of the kind presented in Chapter 5 for Van Hire, we might construct the minimal model in Figure 8.2. Note that the set USER pertains to 'system users', i.e., users as recognized by Uhura through their user codes. A 'real world user' could have several user codes, or a user code might be shared by many such users. This complication is not dealt with in the case study.

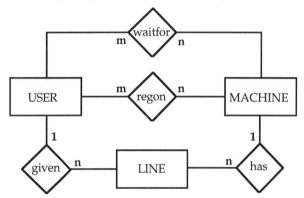

Figure 8.2   Simple E–R model of the Online Monitor's domain.

The model in Figure 8.2 is 'minimal' in the sense that we could not do with fewer entity types and relations, given that the eventual software is to handle not only user registrations on machines but also queues for, and individual line de/allocation to, machines. The model could be easily expanded. For example, regon could be replaced with an entity REGISTRATION. This would break regon into a one(USER)-to-many(REGISTRATION) relationship and a many(REGISTRATION)-to-one(MACHINE) relationship. We would do this if a registration had attributes, e.g., start and finish dates, which the system had to keep track of and provide information about.

Remark
Practical E–R modelling is far richer in notation and scope than is being exploited here and in Van Hire. Our use of simplified E–R diagrams is intended solely to show how they can act as a springboard for fleshing out the nucleus of a meaningful Z state model. It is certainly not being used as a pointer towards some particular kind of (e.g., relational database) implementation, which would run counter to the whole purpose of an abstract Z specification! Nevertheless, the extent to which an envisaged implementation might bias decision-making in specification is a moot point. Indeed, the whole business of interfacing domain modelling techniques to technical specification, and the extent to which implementation concerns influence even these early stages, are fascinating research areas.

Assuming that the E–R model of Figure 8.2 is sufficient, we begin the Z specification by declaring three given sets for the main entity types:

```
[ USER,MACHINE,LINE ]
```

We will impose some realistic size constraints on entity populations via three global variables. As the constraints are something of a side issue, we document them in a separate schema to avoid their being too much of a distraction. The schema plays its role later in the model.

$$\mathtt{maxNoUsers,maxNoMcs,maxNoLines} : \mathbb{N}_1$$

```
┌─ SysConstraints ────────────────────────────────────────────────────┐
│ allUsers : ℙ USER          — registered user population of the whole system
│ olmMcs : ℙ MACHINE         — all machines known to Uhura
│ linePool : ℙ LINE          — pool of lines available from Uhura to machines
│
├──────────────────────
│ #allUsers ≤ maxNoUsers
│ #olmMcs ≤ maxNoMcs
│ #linePool ≤ maxNoLines
└──────────────────────────────────────────────────────────────────────┘
```

Global variables whose values are not uniquely fixed act like 'parameters', imparting *looseness* to a specification. A loose specification in effect describes a *family* of data abstractions, the looseness giving a certain degree of freedom to the implementor.

The division of the domain into two main components on the previous page represents a separation of concerns which it seems natural to carry through into the specification structure. The state component for sub-domain (A), which will be called SysConfig, records all users and machines that Uhura 'knows about'.

$$\mathtt{sysManager} : \mathtt{USER}$$

```
┌─ SysConfig ─────────────────────────────────────────────────────────┐
│ mcsOnline : ℙ MACHINE              — on-line machines
│ maxQLenFor : MACHINE ⇸ ℕ           — max. queue length per machine
│ linesToMcs : LINE ⇸ MACHINE        — the has relationship of Figure 8.2
│ privUsers : ℙ USER                 — privileged users
│ mcRegns : USER ↔ MACHINE           — the regon relationship of Figure 8.2
│
├──────────────────────
│ mcsOnline ⊆ ran linesToMcs ⊆ dom maxQLenFor
│ ran mcRegns = dom maxQLenFor
│ privUsers ⊆ dom mcRegns
│ sysManager ∈ privUsers
│ mcRegns (| { sysManager } |) = ran mcRegns
└──────────────────────────────────────────────────────────────────────┘
```

mcsOnline, privUsers and maxQLenFor are 'attribute variables' as discussed in Section 5.5. The first two typify the 'all entity instances with this particular value for this attribute' variety, whereas maxQLenFor is the more general kind, mapping entity instances to values for the attribute concerned. Note that each machine in the system has a 'maximum queue length' attribute, even if the value is merely 0. Making this attribute a variable quantity allows system staff to 'tweak' load distribution in the system.

Every machine has at least one registered user—a special privileged user called sysManager who is automatically registered on each machine when it first comes into service. The available lines, as uniquely identified by Uhura, can be routed to different machines. It is possible for a machine to have no lines, although it cannot then be on line. For example, all the lines to a machine which is off line for a long period might be temporarily allocated to other machines with spare line capacity. Note that a machine can be on line but inaccessible (e.g., because all lines to it are down). 'Off line' means the machine has been withdrawn for a period of time, e.g., for maintenance.

Sub-domain (B) on page 195 gives rise to the fast-changing part of the state, to be called `SysActivity`. To describe connect queues, the `waiting` component makes use of generic data type `InjQueue` (as on page 164 but enriched along the lines of Exercise 7.13(1,2) on page 188). Thus, we are supposing that a specification `InjQueue_Adt` is being imported into Online Monitor bringing `InjQueue` as an abstract data type, just as we imagined `Date_Adt` was being imported into Van Hire. Several of its operations—`emptyq`, `elemsOfq`, `quToSeq`, etc.—are used in subsequent schemas.

```
┌─ SysActivity ──────────────────────────────────────────────────┐
│ linesUp : LINE ⇸ MACHINE                — working lines to machines
│ cnnctns : LINE ⇸ USER                   — the given relationship of Figure 8.2
│ waiting : MACHINE ⇸ InjQueue [ USER ]   — includes waitfor of Figure 8.2
│ ────────────────────────────────────────────
│ dom cnnctns ⊆ dom linesUp
│ ran linesUp ⊆ dom waiting
│ ∀ m : ran linesUp •
│    linesUp~ ⦇{ m }⦈ ◁ cnnctns ∈ ( LINE ⤖ USER ) ∧
│    ( waiting m ≠ emptyq ⇒ linesUp~ ⦇{ m }⦈ ⊆ dom cnnctns )
│ ∀ ln : dom cnnctns •
│    cnnctns ln ∉ elemsOfq( waiting( linesUp ln ) )
└─────────────────────────────────────────────────────────────────┘
```

The `waiting` component embodies both the waitfor relation of Figure 8.2 and the necessary positional information. Simple translation of waitfor would be inadequate on its own, giving just a many-to-many USER ↔ MACHINE relation. `waiting` is a transformation of `waitfor` into a MACHINE ⇸ ℙ USER function, with ℙ USER strengthened into `InjQueue [ USER ]` to provide the full queue modelling needed.

```
┌─ OnlineMonitor ──────────────────────────────────────────────┐
│ SysConfig; SysActivity; SysConstraints
│ ────────────────────────────────────────────
│ dom mcRegns = allUsers
│ ran mcRegns = olmMcs
│ dom linesToMcs ⊆ linePool
│ linesUp ⊆ linesToMcs
│ dom waiting = mcsOnline
│ ∀ m : mcsOnline •
│    lenq( waiting m ) ≤ maxQLenFor m ∧
│    elemsOfq( waiting m ) ⊆ mcRegns~ ⦇{ m }⦈
│ ∀ ln : dom cnnctns • cnnctns ln ∈ mcRegns~ ⦇{ linesUp ln }⦈
└───────────────────────────────────────────────────────────────┘
```

In the total system state, we are able to describe necessary constraints between the three sub-models, e.g., users must be registered on the machines to which they are connected, etc. Many of the important (and more difficult) aspects of the last two schemas have not been commented upon, but are dealt with in the following exercise.

EXERCISE 8.2

1. Identify any derived (i.e., redundant) components in Online Monitor's state model.

2. Interpret as succinctly as possible in your own words each constraint included in schemas `SysActivity` and `OnlineMonitor`.

3. Answer the following questions, explaining your answer in each case.
   a. If all lines to a machine are down, nobody can be connected to it. Where have we taken care of this constraint?
   b. If not all working lines to a machine are in use, then its connect queue must be empty. Have we failed to include this constraint?
   c. If all working lines to a machine are in use, what is the state of its connect queue according to the model?
   d. Can there be a non-empty connect queue for, but zero connections to, a machine?

4. Specify the operation `WithdrawMc`: a machine is withdrawn permanently from service. Exploiting the fact that certain components of the state model are derived (see Question (1)), construct a schema which provides the minimum amount of detail necessary to constitute a complete description.

OBSERVATIONS ON STATE MODEL I

Model I would be adequate enough to take the Online Monitor specification through to completion. Yet being based on a particular view of the domain involved, it represents only one possible way of abstractly describing the system state. Within its limitations, that view—focusing on entity relationships and attributes—works well enough. Arguably, though, it works better for Van Hire, for reasons briefly aired on page 195. Some of the predicates in the Online Monitor model seem a trifle clumsy; and the description overall has a vague air of, perhaps avoidable, complexity about it.

To see if the model can be improved, we might experiment with Model I, treating it as a 'first shot'. We could keep the basic schema structure as it stands but 'tweak' certain variables, altering declarations to see what effect this has on predicate parts. One way this could be done is to make one of the entity types more dominant in the description. For example, consider this re-arrangement of `SysActivity`:

```
┌─ SysActivity ────────────────────────────────────────────────────┐
│ linesUp : MACHINE ⇸ ℙ LINE            — working lines per machine  │
│ cnnctns : MACHINE ⇸ ( LINE ⤔ USER )   — user connections per machine │
│ waiting : MACHINE ⇸ InjQueue [ USER ] — users waiting on each machine │
│ ─────────────────────────                                          │
│ Predicate                                                          │
│                                                                    │
└────────────────────────────────────────────────────────────────┘
```

It is clear that the description is now oriented much more towards machine entities, treating them almost as the focal point. Of course, care must be taken that the modification maintains integrity with the domain. The alteration may well have effected subtle changes. The precise interpretation of each modified variable and its impact on the schema predicate needs to be carefully determined. You are asked to work this out in the next exercise.

There are other parts of Model I which could be similarly modified to maintain descriptive consistency with the new version of SysActivity. The issue is whether or not we should go down this route. Do we end up with two state models where the superiority of one over the other is at best marginal? Here is a tangential answer: if the suggested modification is followed through to its ultimate conclusion, a state model with a quite different structure to Model I can be constructed. The next section deals with this alternative.

EXERCISE 8.3

1. Carefully describe how the variables in the modified version of SysActivity relate to the variables of the first version. Then construct the new schema's predicate.

2. Describe changes—declarations and predicates—that could be made to the SysConfig component of the Online Monitor state model to keep its orientation in line with the new version of SysActivity.

3. Assuming all the changes addressed by Questions (1) and (2) are effected, rewrite the predicate of the OnlineMonitor schema accordingly.

State Model II (Partial): a 'Vertical' Modularization

So far in this and previous case studies, the approach to system specification has been essentially as follows: (i) construct a model of the *whole* system state; (ii) specify operations over the state model. Simplistic use of a certain data modelling technique has illustrated one way of bridging between problem domains and task (i). Where state models have been split over two or more schemas, this has been driven by appeal to separating concerns. Overall, the resulting specification describes a single state-based data 'object', or family of objects if it is 'loose'.

This approach does not, however, always yield the best specification structure. Sometimes domains are populated by entities which have clearly identifiable rich and interesting properties of their own, both static and dynamic. It may then be better to describe system behaviour at two, possibly more, *hierarchical* levels. Certain facets of behaviour can be described at the full system level, but other facets can be localized to individual entities. This localization at lower levels will reduce the complexity of the model at higher levels and impart what might be termed a 'vertical' structure to the description. The system, as well as being a 'data object' itself, is now described in terms of lower-level data objects which have states and behaviours too.

The Online Monitor domain presents us with the opportunity to exploit this alternative approach. Instead of concentrating on relationships between entities—users, machines, etc.—we focus more on events occurring in the domain and the entities to which they relate. Consider the machines in the Online Monitor system. We can regard each machine as having a number of different attributes whose values events in the domain can change. These attributes include: line capacity, registrations, current connections, connect queue, etc. The following schema translates this attribute list into a model of the monitored state of an individual, arbitrary machine. Note that the term 'attribute' now has a somewhat wider scope than in our E–R models, since it can include non-primitive objects with interesting internal structures which involve other entity types.

```
AvailState ::= online | offline
```

```
┌─ Computer ──────────────────────────────────────────────────┐
│ avlblty : AvailState          — whether machine is on line or not
│ users, priv : ℙ USER          — registered users of the machine
│ allLines, linesUp : ℙ LINE    — lines to machine (all/working)
│ cnnctd : LINE ⤚ USER          — those users currently connected
│ cnnctQu : InjQueue [ USER ]    — users waiting to get connected
│ maxQLen : ℕ                   — maximum queue length
│ ─────────────────────────────
│ sysManager ∈ priv; priv ⊆ users
│ ran cnnctd ∪ elemsOfq cnnctQu ⊆ users
│ ran cnnctd ∩ elemsOfq cnnctQu = ∅
│ dom cnnctd ⊆ linesUp ⊆ allLines
│ lenq cnnctQu ≤ maxQLen
│ cnnctQu ≠ emptyq ⟹ #cnnctd = #linesUp
│ avlblty = online ⟹ allLines ≠ ∅
│ avlblty = offline ⟹ linesUp = ∅ ∧ cnnctQu = emptyq
└──────────────────────────────────────────────────────────────┘
```

The number of variables in the declaration part is on the highish side, although there is no obviously useful way we could split the schema. The plus side is that the types of the variables are simple, as are the various components of the schema's predicate.

A suitable initial state for Computer is dealt with in the next exercise. The reader should be able to correlate most of the features in Computer with those occurring in Model I, especially the modified version of Model I as suggested on pages 199–200. One difference should be noted between Computer and Model I. We have modified the state description in respect of when the machine is off-line. The last invariant of Computer means that if the machine is off line, nobody can be connected to it or waiting for a connection to it. In Model I, this aspect was taken care of differently (how?).

Here are some of the domain events that update or observe the attributes of an individual machine:

- a user is connected to the machine
- a user is queued for the machine
- a user disconnects from the machine
- a user is automatically connected from the head of the machine's connect queue
- the machine goes down, disconnecting/de-queuing all 'attached' users and temporarily inhibiting any re-queuing
- new users are registered on the machine
- the machine is taken off line
- a report of the machine's current state is requested

and so on. Using the Computer model, we can easily specify operations corresponding to these events. As an example, the following schema deals with the last in the list. This is a privileged operation like its two immediate predecessors. Later, we build some error handling into the specification, with privilege checks being made at the system level. Recall that, like lenq, function quToSeq is an operation of the imported abstract data type InjQueue.

```
┌─ReportMcState──────────────────────────────────────────────────┐
│ ΞComputer                                                        │
│ mcStatus! : AvailState                                           │
│ nLinesInUse!,nLinesFree!,nlinesDown!,cnnctQuLen! : ℕ            │
│ connUsers! : ℙ USER                                              │
│ waitUsers! : seq USER                                            │
│ ─────────────────────────────────────────────────────────────  │
│ mcStatus! = avlblty                                              │
│ nLinesInUse! = #cnnctd                                           │
│ nLinesFree! = #linesUp - #cnnctd                                 │
│ nLinesDown! = #allLines - #linesUp                               │
│ connUsers! = ran cnnctd                                          │
│ waitUsers! = quToSeq cnnctQu                                     │
│ cnnctQuLen! = lenq cnnctQu                                       │
└──────────────────────────────────────────────────────────────────┘
```

EXERCISE 8.4

1. Construct a suitable initial state for `Computer`.

2. Construct operation specifications for the other seven events in the previous
    list. Descriptions of the first four are discussed in subsequent sections of the
    chapter.

COMPARING STATE MODELS I AND II
Figure 8.3 generalizes the contrast between state models I and II of Online Monitor.

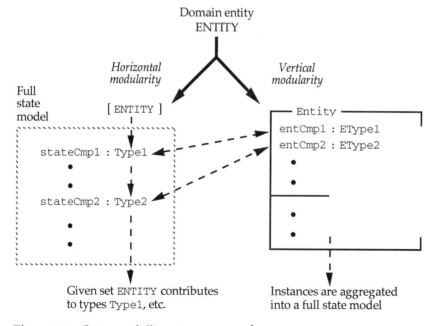

Figure 8.3 State modelling: two approaches.

Taking the left-hand route, as with Van Hire and Model I of Online Monitor, domain entities of a particular type are represented as members of a given set. Entity attributes and relationships in which entities participate are then embodied in variables spread across the state model's schemas. With the right-hand route, the entity type is modelled as a schema which clumps together entity features that would be spread throughout a state model of the horizontal variety. At the component level, a variable which is, say,

> `horizCmp : ENTITY ↔ X`

in a horizontal model would become

> `vertCmp : ℙ X`

in the vertical entity schema; the variable `vertCmp` represents the X objects which that entity instance would be related to in `horizCmp`. The entity schema represents an arbitrary instance of the entity type, which has an identifiable behaviour of its own lying at least one level vertically below the top system-level behaviour.

Horizontal modularity in a Z description tends to arise by emphasizing an entity–relationship/attribute view of the domain, or similar. Vertical modularity arises when a more event-driven, 'object-based' view of the domain is reflected in a Z description (we use the term 'object-based' fairly loosely). Neither view is 'more correct' than the other. Nevertheless, as always, the existence of choices means that decisions have to be made. Certainly, schema `Computer` has some pleasing characteristics. Its object-based resonance with the domain conveys a sense of rightness that is less tangible with Model I, where the 'objectness' of machines is more diffuse. Of course, `Computer` is not a complete state model, but given the information it embodies, it seems likely that the complete state description for Online Monitor will mainly comprise some suitable aggregate of `Computer` instances with relatively few extra constraints. This turns out to be the case, as Section 8.5 shows.

A big advantage of `Computer` concerns operation specification. Despite `Computer` being a partial state model, this does not hamper development of the specification—rather, the opposite. Using `Computer`, we can firstly specify operations on an individual machine (see page 201). This task is inevitably simpler, hence less error prone, than describing the same operations over the more complex, full-state description of Model I. Later, when the complete state model has been constructed, we can 'promote' operations over an individual machine into the full state context without much extra work.

Overall, there is little doubt that Model II is the better choice for Online Monitor, and we will proceed on this basis. However, to develop the Online Monitor specification, we will need to use 'in anger' the schema calculus, a first glimpse of which appeared in Digital Watch (page 50). Thus far in the book, we have really exploited only schema inclusion, which is just a small part of the expressive power available.

EXERCISE 8.5

1. Suppose we attempted a vertical modularization for Online Monitor based on *user* entities. Sketch out a schema that would form the basis of the description. Explain why you think this would be an inferior choice to `Computer`.

2. In what useful way, if any, could vertical, object-based modularity be applied to constructing the Van Hire state model? Develop any ideas through to a tentative schema description.

8.2   SOME LIGHT SCHEMA CALCULUS

Schema Compatibility

The schema calculus enables us to avoid 'monolithic'—i.e., single, large, unstructured—descriptions, which are a sin just as deadly in specification as in design. The various calculus operators allow us to write expressions which combine existing schemas into new, more complex descriptions. However, combining schemas requires some care:

- to avoid ill-formed constructs, the signatures of the schemas must be *type compatible*
- global variables need to be considered to avoid name clashes
- the combination should be meaningful.

Type compatibility means that, if the combining schemas have any common variable in their signatures, that variable must have the same type (though not necessarily the same constraint) in each signature. To illustrate, suppose we have

```
SchemaA ≙ [ a : ℕ; b : 1..8 | a = 63 mod b ]
SchemaB ≙ [ b : ℕ₁; c : Date | b ≤ monthOf c ∧ c isAfter StartOf93 ]
SchemaC ≙ [ b,c : Date; d : ℕ₁ ]
SchemaD ≙ [ b : ℤ; c,d : Date | b < 2 * a ∧ c isOnOrBefore d ]
```

`SchemaA` and `SchemaB` are type compatible: they have one common variable which is b, and b has the same type, namely $\mathbb{Z}$, in both cases; the fact that the variable is constrained differently in each does not matter. However, no other two schemas taken from the first three are type compatible. For example, `SchemaB` and `SchemaC` have two common variables b and c, but the types of the b variables are quite different.

Global variables complicate matters further. `SchemaD` is type compatible with `SchemaB`, and it looks to be type compatible with `SchemaA` also, but there is a snag. `SchemaA` has a variable called a, and `SchemaD` references a *global* variable called a. Clearly, these two variables cannot be merged in any combination of `SchemaA` and `SchemaD`. The best way to avoid this kind of name clash is pragmatic: do not choose the same names for global and local variables. Alternatively, we can combine `SchemaA` and `SchemaD` providing an appropriate change occurs to component names.

Type incompatibility and name clashing between schemas can be overcome via careful use of the *renaming* operation:

```
SchemaName [ NewVar₁ / OldVar₁, NewVar₂ / OldVar₁ ... ]
```

The $OldVar_i$ are distinct variables declared in the text of SchemaName, and the $NewVar_i$ are the fresh names to be consistently substituted throughout the text of SchemaName for the current variables. The $NewVar_i$ do not have to be distinct provided that the components they rename have the same type and hence can be merged, though we would perhaps not require this particular effect very often.

Schema variable renaming is considered to be simultaneous if the rename list is more than one component long. So

```
SchemaA [ b / a, a / b ]
```

causes no problems. Its text is equivalent to

```
[ b : ℕ; a : 1..8 | b = 63 mod a ]
```

The original definition of `SchemaA` stays intact of course.

Using renaming, we can see that something like

SchemaB [x / b]

overcomes SchemaB's incompatibility with SchemaC. Obviously, renaming the clashing component in SchemaC instead would be equally effective. Furthermore, something like

SchemaA [x / a]

overcomes the local/global name clash between SchemaA and SchemaD. Here, only SchemaA can be subjected to the renaming operation. We could *edit* the specification text to change the name of the global variable a instead, but then the entire specification is affected.

EXERCISE 8.6

1. State which pairs of schemas in the following list could not be combined as they stand, and explain why.

$$Vars1 \triangleq [\, c,d,e : 0..9\,]$$
$$Vars2 \triangleq [\, b,x? : Date \mid b \neq x?\,]$$
$$Vars3 \triangleq [\, a : \mathbb{N};\ d : \mathbb{N}_1 \mid d - a = c\,]$$
$$Vars4 \triangleq [\, a,b,x! : \mathbb{Z};\ c' : Date \mid$$
$$a < 0 \wedge b \neq 0 \wedge (\, dayOf\ c' = - a\ mod\ b)\,]$$

2. a. Which incompatible pairs in (1) could be combined via suitable renaming?
   b. Write out the schema text equivalent to the following expression:

   Vars4 [a / b, b / c' , c' / a]

Schema Propositional Operators

The simplest combining operators in the schema calculus are the propositional operators, which have a similar effect on schemas as they have on predicates. In general, we can write

Schema1 Opr Schema2

where Opr is any of the four standard infix propositional connectives, plus other possibilities discussed later. We can think of the text of the combination as comprising:

- A declaration part which is some merge, dependent on Opr, of the declaration parts of the two schemas, with no multiple instances of declarations of common variables.

- An axiom part which is some combination, dependent on Opr, of the predicates of the two schemas. If the constraints in the declarations of a common variable are different, a full merging is achieved by normalization of the common variable. The result is that some extra constraints now occur in the combined predicate that were not present explicitly in the separate schemas.

In the case of an infix propositional operator, the merge of the two declaration parts is accomplished simply by 'joining' them. The axiom part of the combination is essentially

Schema1Pred PropOpr Schema2Pred

subject only to the possible effects of normalization as just described. To illustrate with the schemas on page 204, the text of

SchemaAorB ≙ SchemaA ∨ SchemaB

is equivalent to

[a : ℕ; b : ℤ; c : Date | (a = 63 mod b ∧ 1 ≤ b ≤ 8) ∨
    (b ≥ 1 ∧ b ≤ monthOf c ∧ c isAfter StartOf93)]

Note the effect that has occurred because of the need to normalize b.

SchemaAorB's property is satisfied when either SchemaA's property is, or SchemaB's property is, or both are. More precisely, the bindings which satisfy SchemaAorB are

- either those which satisfy SchemaA when they are restricted to the signature of SchemaA, i.e., by dropping the binding components only in SchemaB
- or those which satisfy SchemaB when they are restricted to the signature of SchemaB, i.e., by dropping the binding components only in SchemaA
- or those which, when appropriately restricted, satisfy both schemas.

Thus, assuming StartOf93 is mkDate(1, 1, 1993), each of the following bindings satisfies SchemaAorB:

β1: ⟨ a ⇛ 0, b ⇛ 7, c ⇛ mkDate(7, 3, 1949) ⟩
β2: ⟨ a ⇛ 7, b ⇛ 5, c ⇛ mkDate(25, 11, 1997) ⟩
β3: ⟨ a ⇛ 7, b ⇛ 8, c ⇛ mkDate(31, 8, 1993) ⟩

If we restrict β1, say, to SchemaA and to SchemaB we get the respective bindings

⟨ a ⇛ 0, b ⇛ 7 ⟩   ⟨ b ⇛ 7, c ⇛ mkDate(7, 3, 1949) ⟩

Although the latter binding does not satisfy SchemaB's property, the former binding satisfies SchemaA's property; so binding β1 satisfies SchemaAorB's property. Bindings β2 and β3 can be similarly checked.

The conjunction of SchemaA and SchemaB, as in

SchemaAandB ≙ SchemaA ∧ SchemaB

has a text equivalent to

[a : ℕ; b : ℤ; c : Date | (a = 63 mod b ∧ 1 ≤ b ≤ 8) ∧
    (b ≥ 1 ∧ b ≤ monthOf c ∧ c isAfter StartOf93)]

The bindings satisfying SchemaAandB are those which satisfy SchemaA when restricted to SchemaA's signature *and* satisfy SchemaB when restricted to SchemaB's signature. The reader should be able to determine that only binding β3 above satisfies SchemaAandB. Note that if we include, say, SchemaB in SchemaA's text:

[a : ℕ; b : 1..8; SchemaB | a = 63 mod b]

the resulting text is the same as for SchemaAandB. In fact, schema inclusion is just a special form of schema conjunction.

Suppose we define

SchemaAandD ≙ SchemaA [x / a] ∧ SchemaD

The text equivalent to SchemaAandD would be

$$[\,x : \mathbb{N};\ b : \mathbb{Z};\ c, d : \text{Date}\ |$$
$$(\,x = 63\ \text{mod}\ b \wedge 1 \le b \le 8\,) \wedge (\,b < 2 * a \wedge c\ \text{isOnOrBefore}\ d\,)\,]$$

We would now have a potential problem on our hands if global a was, say, some value less than 1. The combined schema's property would reduce to `false`, i.e., the binding space { SchemaAandD • θ SchemaAandD } would be empty. This is because there is no binding in which b can satisfy both $1 \le b$ and $b < 2 * a$, given a's assumed value. In practice, we would have little use for schemas with properties that are `false`. The more general point is that although, syntactically, the combination of two or more schemas can be well-formed, semantically the combination might be meaningless. As a more extreme example, we could write a schema expression which combines in some way the schemas VanHire and OnlineMonitor, say. The result would pass a Z syntax checker but it is unlikely to represent a sensible model of anything we can imagine. The onus must rest with specifiers to avoid meaningless combinations.

The schema operators ∧ and ∨ are much more frequently applied than ⇒ or ⇔. However, ¬ has its uses. If we write ¬ Schema, the result has *the same signature* as Schema but a property that is the negation of Schema's property, i.e., ¬ Schema defines that set of bindings which do *not* satisfy Schema. Care is needed in working this out. For example, the text of

¬ SchemaA

is *not*

$$[\,a : \mathbb{N};\ b : 1..8\ |\ \neg (\,a = 63\ \text{mod}\ b\,)\,]$$

The problem is that we have negated only the schema's predicate and not the whole of its property, i.e., we have left out the constraints in the variable declarations. The text actually equivalent to ¬ SchemaA is

$$[\,a : \mathbb{Z};\ b : \mathbb{Z}\ |\ \neg (\,a \ge 0 \wedge 1 \le b \le 8 \wedge a = 63\ \text{mod}\ b\,)\,]$$

In other words, schema negation must be understood in terms of the normalized text of the schema argument. Consider the generalized expression

{ SchemaSig • θ SchemaSig } \ { Schema • θ Schema }

The first set defines the bindings satisfying Schema's signature only (SchemaSig). The second set defines the bindings satisfying Schema's signature *and* property. The difference thus gives us the binding space of ¬ Schema.

To emphasize the care needed with schema negation, consider this example:

SchemaE ≙ [f : X ⇸ Y | #f ≤ max]

Now suppose we define

NotSchemaE ≙ ¬ SchemaE

We might intend this to mean 'some function from X to Y with domain size exceeding max'. If so, we are getting more than we bargained for. Normalizing SchemaE to reveal its full property and then negating, we get this text for NotSchemaE:

$$[\,f : \mathbb{P}(\,X \times Y\,)\ |\ \neg (\#f \le \text{max} \wedge f \in X \nrightarrow Y\,)\,]$$
or $$[\,f : \mathbb{P}(\,X \times Y\,)\ |\ \#f > \text{max} \vee f \notin X \nrightarrow Y\,]$$

NotSchemaE, as well as giving us the function states we want, also gives us states that are not even functional and which may or may not exceed max in terms of size.

EXERCISE 8.7

Given: Vars $\triangleq$ [x,y : $\mathbb{N}$ | x < n ∧ y < m]
Exch $\triangleq$ [ΔVars | x' = y ∧ y' = x]

write out, exploiting usual Z conventions, the texts of

a. Exch ∨ ΞVars
b. ¬ ΔVars
c. Exch [x''/x' , y''/y'] ∧ Exch [x''/x , y''/y]

A Simple Example

In Online Monitor, when a user is disconnected from a machine, i.e., the user logs off or the disconnection is enforced by a time-out, one of two things can happen: either the line that was allocated to the user becomes free for future use or, if the connect queue is non-empty, the line is used immediately to connect the user waiting at the head of the queue. Rather than attempt to describe what happens in a single schema, it is better technique to put the schema calculus to work, decomposing the update into two smaller operations. Thus:

```
AutoCnnctFlag  ::= noAutoCnnct | autoCnnctMade
```

```
┌─ FreeLine ──────────────────────────────────────────────┐
│ ΔComputer
│ ln? : LINE
│ msg! : AutoCnnctFlag
│ ─────────────────────────
│ ln? ∈ dom cnnctd; cnnctQu = emptyq
│ msg! = noAutoCnnct
│ cnnctd' = { ln? } ⩤ cnnctd
│ avlblty' = avlblty; users' = users; priv' = priv
│ allLines' = allLines; linesUp' = linesUp
│ cnnctQu' = cnnctQu; maxQLen' = maxQLen
└──────────────────────────────────────────────────────────┘
```

The output msg! is included to make the operation usefully informative. For the same reason, the second sub-operation below has an additional output acUser!: the user who gets auto-connected.

```
┌─ AutoConnect ───────────────────────────────────────────┐
│ ΔComputer
│ ln? : LINE
│ msg! : AutoCnnctFlag
│ acUser! : USER
│ ─────────────────────────
│ ln? ∈ dom cnnctd; cnnctQu ≠ emptyq
│ msg! = autoCnnctMade; acUser! = fstq cnnctQu
│ cnnctd' = cnnctd ⊕ { ln? ↦ fstq cnnctQu }
│ cnnctQu' = remq cnnctQu
│ avlblty' = avlblty; priv' = priv; allLines' = allLines
│ users' = users; linesUp' = linesUp; maxQLen' = maxQLen
└──────────────────────────────────────────────────────────┘
```

The full operation is then just a disjunction of these two sub-operations:

$$Disconnect \; \hat{=} \; FreeLine \lor AutoConnect$$

`Disconnect` is deterministic since either `FreeLine` or `AutoConnect` will be applicable, but never both (why?). It is important that `msg!` appears in both sub-operations so that its value in `Disconnect` is always meaningful—a situation to be careful of when an output in some way indicates the outcome of a *combination* of sub-operations.

EXERCISE 8.8

1. a. If the output `msg!` was omitted from `AutoConnect`, say, what would its value be in `Disconnect` if `AutoConnect` was the applicable component?
   b. Why is it not necessary for `AutoConnect`'s additional output `acUser!` to be defined in `FreeLine`? What is the value of `acUser!` in `Disconnect` if `FreeLine` is the applicable component?

2. Construct an operation `ChangeLineCap` which alters the line capacity to a machine. Both increases and decreases to lines are possible.

8.3 SPECIFYING EXCEPTION HANDLING

Robust Specification

An operation, unless total, will not be applicable to all possible State × Input? combinations. Loosely, we can think of the applicable start space of *any* operation as the set

$$\{ \, State \times Input? \mid PreConOp \, \}$$

where PreConOp is the overall predicate that accurately subsets the start space to just those bindings for which the operation is applicable, i.e., for which it can produce a valid after state and outputs. PreConOp is called the operation's *precondition*. Typically, non-satisfaction of an implemented operation's precondition would indicate that some kind of exception—error or other atypical event—has occurred.

In Van Hire, many of the operations were definitely not total. In each such operation, preconstraints were included explicitly to assert the way in which the operation's partialness manifested itself. However, the specification said nothing about what was to happen if any of these preconstraints were not satisfied. Does this really matter? The answer is *no* if we are specifying a subsystem which, when implemented, will be guaranteed by its environment to receive only correct inputs. Even if this is not the case, one possible stance to take is simply to leave non-total operations as they are, on the basis that responsibility is now shifted to the implementor to decide what error handling behaviour should be built in.

'Leaving it to the implementor' is not always an acceptable position to take, however. Whether because of contractual obligation or just adopting good practice, we need to know how to specify *robust* systems, i.e., systems where *all* operations are total. There are two issues:

- How do we strengthen specifications with exception-handling descriptions?
- For each operation, how do we know precisely what partialness the operation exhibits, so that we can be sure that all error cases are properly dealt with?

The answer to the second question is that we calculate the operation's precondition (i.e., PreConOp on the previous page). We deal with preconditions and their calculation as a separate topic in Section 8.4.

We will use the operation name template RbOpName to imply 'robust', indicating that the behaviour is total and has been made so by adding error handling to OpName. Consider thus the operation—we will call it RbAttachUser—of a user attempting to get 'attached', i.e., connected or queued, to a machine. Overall, the behaviour we wish to capture is

- perform necessary checks on the user, machine, etc., rejecting the attempted attach if any check fails
- if the attempted attach is ok, connect the user to the machine if there is a working line free, otherwise queue the user
- produce appropriate output informing the user of what has happened.

Obviously, to specify all this in a single schema would result in an excessively large and clumsy structure. Hence, the modularizing capabilities of the schema calculus will be used to split the description of RbAttachUser into smaller, more understandable parts.

Error Case Description

RbAttachUser has an obvious division of behaviour: that which describes successful attachment of the user, and that which describes rejection of the attempted attach because of one or more errors. We will call the latter RejectAttachRqst. Since the relationship between these two components is clearly 'either/or', RbAttachUser can be defined by the paragraph

$$RbAttachUser \;\hat{=}\; AttachUser \lor RejectAttachRqst$$

where the preconstraints of each component are carefully constructed to ensure determinism.

Remark
Our exposition in this chapter is sometimes 'top down'. In practice, of course, definition of both AttachUser and RejectAttachRqst would have to be placed before the defining paragraph for RbAttachUser.

As a first step towards describing RejectAttachRqst, we can identify the checks that need to be made for the attachment to be possible:

a. The machine must be online. Recall that, even if all lines to the machine are down, it can still be online, allowing the user to be queued (if there is room)
b. The user must be registered on the machine
c. There must be room for the user, i.e., the connect queue must be less than its maximum allowed length
d. The user cannot be already attached to the machine, i.e., connected or waiting.

These checks are documented in the following schema. Note that neither ΔComputer nor ΞComputer appears in the schema since we are not specifying an operation. The schema merely expresses four constraints over the Computer state.

```
┌─ CanDoAttach ─────────────────────────────────────────────────┐
│ Computer                                                       │
│ u? : USER                                                      │
│ ├──────────────────────────────┐                              │
│ avlblty = online                                    — check (a)│
│ u? ∈ users                                          — check (b)│
│ lenq cnnctQu < maxQlen                              — check (c)│
│ u? ∉ ran cnnctd ∪ elemsOfq cnnctQu                  — check (d)│
└────────────────────────────────────────────────────────────────┘
```

We will proceed on the basis that `CanDoAttach` accurately and fully characterizes `AttachUser`'s partialness. In Section 8.4, *we prove that this is so*.

Suppose that a different error message is to be produced depending on which of the above individual checks fails. In preparation for this, and various other messaging requirements in Online Monitor, we will introduce the following free type:

```
OLM_Message ::= mcOffline | userNotReg | noAttachRoom |
                    alreadyAttached | connected | queued
```

The first four constants flag error outcomes. The actual form of messages presented at the user interface, e.g., 'user <u?> is already attached', is of no concern to the error-handling descriptions themselves.

Now consider an arbitrary non-total operation Op which we wish to make robust. One general approach is to construct small operation schemas for handling the different error cases, characterized by the negations of the preconstraints identified for Op. Each such schema will have the general form:

```
┌─ ErrorCaseX ──────────────────────────────────────────────────┐
│ ΞOr ΔState                                                     │
│ Inputs?                                                        │
│ FlagVar! : OutcomeFlagType                                     │
│ AnyOtherOutputs!                                               │
│ ├──────────────────────────┐                                  │
│ ¬ SomePreConstraint                                            │
│ FlagVar! = FlagForCaseX                                        │
│ AnyExtraBehaviourForCaseX                                      │
└────────────────────────────────────────────────────────────────┘
```

SomePreConstraint is the check that has failed. The output FlagVar!, often the only output, indicates the nature of the error that has occurred. Mostly, ΞState rather than ΔState will be included since if an applicability error occurs, we usually do not wish the state of the system to change. Also, AnyExtraBehaviourForCaseX is often empty, e.g., the operation simply reports the error that has occurred. Having defined all error case schemas, we can then define

ErrorBehaviourForOp ≙ ErrorCase1 ∨ ErrorCase2 ∨ ...

followed by

RbOp ≙ Op ∨ ErrorBehaviourForOp

Observe again that each ErrorCase schema represents a complete operation.

Using this approach with `RbAttachUser`, the following are two of the four error-case schemas we would construct:

```
┌─McNotAvail──────────────────────────────────────────────┐
│ ΞComputer                                                │
│ attachMes! : OLM_Message                                 │
│ ─────────────────────                                    │
│ avlblty = offline                                        │
│ attachMes! = mcOffline                                   │
└─────────────────────────────────────────────────────────┘
```

```
┌─ IllegalUser────────────────────────────────────────────┐
│ ΞComputer                                                │
│ u? : USER                                                │
│ attachMes! : OLM_Message                                 │
│ ─────────────────────                                    │
│ u? ∉ users                                               │
│ attachMes! = userNotReg                                  │
└─────────────────────────────────────────────────────────┘
```

Eventually we define

$$RejectAttachRqst \; \hat{=} \; McNotAvail \lor IllegalUser \lor \ldots$$

A modification to the above approach is to construct error-case schemas over just the *before* state, i.e., omitting Ξ from the above. Although such schemas do not themselves describe operations, the definition

$$RejectAttachRqst \; \hat{=} \; \Xi Computer \land (McNotAvail \lor IllegalUser \lor \ldots)$$

will constitute an operation. In either approach, the same `attachMes!` flag variable must be used in each of the error-case schemas. With the latter approach, no reference to after states can be incorporated in any of the error case descriptions themselves.

ADDING SOME PRIORITY

The techniques just described work well enough, but there are two associated issues to consider. Firstly, if either error condition `McNotAvail` or `IllegalUser` arises, the other possible errors are immaterial. In fact, if `McNotAvail` applies, check (c) on page 210 is pointless; and if `IllegalUser` applies, check (d) is pointless. So it makes sense to try to give `McNotAvail` and `IllegalUser` higher priority than the rest; that is, if either of these applies, neither of the other two checks are applicable.

Secondly, since `avlblty = offline` and `u? ∉ users?` can both hold, we might ask: which error state is supposed to be flagged in this situation? The same question can be applied in respect of the other two checks. In other words, the disjunction in `RejectAttachRqst`'s definition above is non-deterministic and leaves open which error state is deemed to have arisen in certain circumstances. This could be acceptable; we are in effect saying to the implementor 'you choose which error to report'. However, if this is not acceptable, a slightly more sophisticated approach is needed.

Suppose for `RejectAttachRqst` the checking priority required is (highest first) check (a) to (d) in that order. We keep `McNotAvail` as it is and modify `IllegalUser` thus:

```
┌─ IllegalUser ──────────────────────────────────────────────┐
│ ΞComputer                                                    │
│ u? : USER                                                    │
│ attachMes! : OLM_Message                                     │
├──────────────────────────────                               │
│ avlblty = online; u? ∉ users                                 │
│ attachMes! = userNotReg                                      │
└──────────────────────────────────────────────────────────┘
```

Hence, the disjunction

> McNotAvail ∨ IllegalUser

is not only deterministic but also embodies the desired priority since, if `avlblty = offline`, `IllegalUser` cannot apply, regardless of whether or not `u? ∉ users`. The remaining two error-case definitions to give the stated priority are left as an exercise.

COMPLETING RbAttachUser

Making use of the earlier schema `CanDoAttach` on page 211, `AttachUser` can be decomposed into

> AttachUser ≙ CanDoAttach ∧ EffectAttach

This definition ensures that in

> RbAttachUser ≙ AttachUser ∨ RejectAttachRqst

the choice is deterministic, since all the error conditions tested in the structure of `RejectAttachRqst` will form the disjunction of the negation of each preconstraint checked in `CanDoAttach`.

Attaching a user is a choice between connecting or queuing the user. So there is an obvious decomposition for `EffectAttach`:

> EffectAttach ≙ ConnectUser ∨ QueueUser

The two component schemas are easily dealt with. Here is the first:

```
┌─ ConnectUser ──────────────────────────────────────────────┐
│ ΔComputer                                                    │
│ u? : USER                                                    │
│ attachMes! : OLM_Message                                     │
│ aFreeLn : LINE                                               │
├──────────────────────────────                               │
│ aFreeLn ∈ linesUp \ dom cnnctd                               │
│ attachMes! = connected                                       │
│ cnnctd' = cnnctd ∪ { aFreeLn ↦ u? }                          │
│ avlblty' = avlblty; priv' = priv; users' = users             │
│ allLines' = allLines; linesUp' = linesUp                     │
│ cnnctQu' = cnnctQu; maxQLen' = maxQLen                        │
└──────────────────────────────────────────────────────────┘
```

Note that `ConnectUser` is non-deterministic because `aFreeLn` represents some non-specific choice from a set. The non-determinism is entirely appropriate—so long as the user gets a free line, we do not care which one. Also, `aFreeLn` is neither an input nor an output, being just an internal observation on the `Computer` state. It would be preferable, therefore, if `aFreeLn` was not part of the operation's interface at all. Shortly, we see how this can be arranged.

EXERCISE 8.9

1. Specify the following schemas so that they are consistent with the priority error-handling scenario described in the text for `RejectAttachRqst`:

   a. `NoSpareCpcty` b. `AlreadyInSys`.

2. Modify the definition of `AlreadyInSys` given as the answer to Question (1) so that the user is also informed of whether she is connected or queued, and if queued, the position in the queue. Do not forget what the imported `InjQueue_Adt` brings into Online Monitor.

3. In `ConnectUser` it appears that we have forgotten the vital constraint that there must be at least one free line available—but have we? Explain.

4. Specify the following operations:

   a. `QueueUser` contributing to `EffectAttach`
   b. A robust `LeaveQueue`: a user, queued on some machine, decides to leave the queue. Again, do not forget what the import `InjQueue_Adt` brings.

8.4 PRECONDITIONS

The Meaning of Preconditions

As indicated at the start of Section 8.3, the *precondition* of an operation Op characterizes precisely when Op is applicable. By 'applicable' we mean in the general case that, for some given start state and input(s), a state transition and output(s) exist in accordance with Op's description. Hence, a precondition, which is basically a predicate on the before state and inputs (if any) of an operation, represents a precise description of an operation's partialness.

Let us pursue these important ideas further. We can think of our arbitrary operation Op as having the structure

```
┌─ Op ──────────────────────────────────────────────────────┐
│ ΔState                                                      │
│ Inputs?                                                     │
│ Outputs!                                                    │
├──────────────                                               │
│ OpPred                                                      │
└─────────────────────────────────────────────────────────────┘
```

We make no assumptions about OpPred. In particular, OpPred might or might not contain preconstraints. If no preconstraint is present in OpPred, this does *not* mean Op is necessarily total; see page 49 for a simple example. Equally, even if OpPred does contain preconstraints, from which we infer Op is non-total, this does *not* mean that the preconstraints together represent Op's precondition, which would be a rather dangerous assumption to make.

Since predicates are used to define relations, we can treat Op as a relation defined by OpPred. We can abstract this relation into a binary relation between Op's start space State × Inputs? and result space State × Outputs!. So another way of viewing Op is

$$
\begin{array}{|l}
\_\,\text{Op}\,\_ : \text{State} \times \text{Inputs?} \leftrightarrow \text{State} \times \text{Outputs!} \\
\hline
\forall\, \text{in?} : \text{Inputs?};\ \text{out!} : \text{Outputs?};\ s, s' : \text{State} \bullet \\
\quad (\,s, \text{in?}\,)\ \text{Op}\ (\,s', \text{out!}\,) \Leftrightarrow \text{OpPred}(\,s, \text{in?}, s', \text{out!}\,)
\end{array}
$$

Thus, for a given s and in?, to claim that behaviour is possible according to Op's description is equivalent to asserting that (s , in?) *belongs to* Op's *domain* (remember that we are viewing Op as a binary relation). That is, we are asserting that

$$(s , \text{in?}) \in \text{dom}(\_\,\text{Op}\,\_)$$

where

$$
\begin{aligned}
\text{dom}(\_\,\text{Op}\,\_) = {}& \\
& \{\, s : \text{State}\,;\ \text{in?} : \text{Inputs?}\ | \\
& \quad (\,\exists\, s' : \text{State};\ \text{out!} : \text{Outputs!} \bullet \text{OpPred}(\,s, \text{in?}, s', \text{out!}\,))\,\}
\end{aligned}
\tag{8.1}
$$

Our description of Op's domain follows the general definition of dom given on page 121 (we are simply using here a different but equivalent form of set comprehension).

In fact, of course, Op's domain is just its 'applicability space', whose defining predicate in (8.1) *is therefore its precondition*! It is true that this predicate looks rather unfriendly, but we will deal with that later. For now, let us refer to Op's precondition as PreConOp. We can now write more simply:

$$\text{dom}(\_\,\text{Op}\,\_) = \{\, s : \text{State}\,;\ \text{in?} : \text{Inputs?}\ |\ \text{PreConOp}(\,s, \text{in?}\,)\,\} \tag{8.2}$$

Thus, the satisfaction of PreConOp by some s and in? *guarantees* that Op itself can be satisfied. That is:

$$
\begin{aligned}
\text{PreConOp}(\,s, \text{in?}\,) \Rightarrow {}& \\
& \exists\, s' : \text{State}\,;\ \text{out!} : \text{Outputs!} \bullet \text{OpPred}(\,s, \text{in?}, s', \text{out!}\,)
\end{aligned}
$$

(clearly, the reverse implication also holds). Note that if Op is total, PreConOp is simply true, i.e., (8.1/2) is just the total start space { s : State ; in? : Inputs? }; hence, every (s , in?) in State × Inputs? will be related by Op to at least one (s' , out!) in State × Outputs!. If Op is not total, only some of the (s , in?) will be so related, and PreConOp tells us exactly which ones. See Figure 8.4.

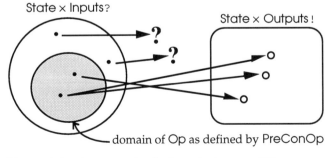

State × Inputs?

State × Outputs!

domain of Op as defined by PreConOp

Figure 8.4 An operation's domain/precondition.

In Z, *precondition* has the precise meaning we have described, i.e., a predicate which defines the domain of an operation when the latter is viewed as a binary relation between start and result spaces. However, 'precondition' is sometimes used more loosely, or even specifically, in the sense of our term *preconstraint*. This is why we have preferred to use the term 'preconstraint' to avoid any confusion with the strict Z meaning of 'precondition'. In our case studies, for clarity we have made a point of always including appropriate preconstraints in non-total operations. However, since we have not done any checking, we cannot safely assume that those preconstraints constitute *actual* preconditions. Fortunately, in Z we can usually calculate an operation's proper precondition in a simplified form, as will shortly be demonstrated.

EXERCISE 8.10

1. Suppose the following are predicates over a state involving $x : \mathbb{Z}$. List them in *decreasing* order of permissiveness. The more (less) permissive, or weaker (stronger), a predicate is, the more (fewer) states will satisfy it.

   $x > 3 \quad x \geq 0 \quad x > 3 \vee x \geq 0 \quad x > 3 \wedge x \geq 0$
   $x > 3 \Rightarrow x \geq 0 \quad x \geq 0 \Rightarrow x > 3$

2. If we described a state-based system axiomatically in terms of relations as shown in the text, how would the difference between deterministic and non-deterministic operations manifest itself, if at all?

3. If the precondition of an operation is `false`, what does this mean?

4. If an operation were applied outside the scope of its precondition, describe what behaviour would result, given a non-robust operation specification. Include relevant comments in your answer in the light of Question (3).

Usages of Preconditions

The main importance of precondition calculation is to obtain a precise description of the applicability of each operation. If an operation's partialness has been left implicit, either wholly or partly, we can calculate its precondition to inform us of its true partialness. Even if we have included all preconstraints we can think of in an operation's specification, the calculation will uncover any errors or omitted cases in our assumptions about the operation's partialness.

Some consider it good technique to include actual preconditions, where they are stronger than `true`, in operation descriptions. At the very least, a recommended practice in the structuring of specification documents is to produce a table showing the calculated preconditions for the non-total operations of the specification. The table, accompanied by the justifying calculations, should be placed between the non-total operation specifications and the total operation specifications. This makes sense because, if a robust system is required, the preconditions define exactly what error checking is needed to construct total operations from the non-total ones. Adopting this ordering of document components clearly aids readability.

Precondition calculation can also uncover defects. For example, a calculated precondition which turns out to be `false` indicates a specification error somewhere, probably a logical inconsistency in the operation description itself. This discovery probably saves us (eventually) grief and money because operations with false preconditions are generally not the sort of animal we should be trying to transform into code. Also, if a precondition calculation unexpectedly breaks down at some point, again some defect in the specification should be suspected, assuming the calculation steps to be correct. The defect could be one of omission—the author once discovered an important constraint to be missing from a state model precisely because a precondition calculation refused to work out as expected.

Applicability and defect checking are however not the sole reasons for precondition calculation. Preconditions also play a vital role in design and implementation, topics which are overviewed in Chapter 9. Preconditions thus feed into the whole development process that ensues after constructing an abstract specification—assuming one is going to continue with a 'formal approach' in later phases.

Precondition Calculation

THE HIDING OPERATOR

Precondition calculation involves another schema operator called schema variable *hiding*. This operator, which occurs in many other situations too, has the syntax

$$\text{Schema} \setminus (v_1, v_2, \dots v_3) \tag{8.3}$$

Here, the v_i must be names of components introduced in the declaration part of Schema. The effect of the operation is to calculate another schema in which the named components are 'hidden'. This does not mean deleting the components, but rather that they are removed from Schema's signature, yet still exert their required role in Schema's predicate. The effect of this is achieved by *existential quantification* of the components to be hidden. That is, expression (8.3) is equivalent to

$$\exists v_1 : T_1; \ v_2 : T_2; \ \dots v_n : T_n \bullet \text{Schema} \tag{8.4}$$

where the T_i are the respective types of the v_i in Schema.

Expression (8.4) looks intimidating, but we can usually simplify it considerably. Firstly, (8.4) is equivalent to removing the declarations of the v_i from Schema's signature and transposing the quantification into its axiom part to scope the *whole* of the predicate there. That is, we apply left-to-right the basic equivalence rule

$$(\exists \text{hide}) \quad \exists x : T \bullet (x : S; \ D \mid P) \equiv D \mid \exists x : S \bullet P \quad [S \subseteq T]$$

We have given the rule an identifier $\exists$hide for easy reference. The rule has been formalized by using D (to stand for declarations—possibly empty), x, T, S and P as 'template' variables to describe the 'effect' of the rule. The right-most part of the rule is a *side condition*, which is an additional proviso that must be satisfied for application of the rule to be valid. Here, the side condition reminds us that x as declared in the schema text must have type T, though it could be further constrained by its declaration.

Other formulations of $\exists$hide are possible, as in:

$$(\exists \text{hide}) \quad \exists x : T \bullet (x : S; \ D \mid P) \equiv D \mid \exists x : T \bullet C \wedge P \quad [S = \{ e : T \mid C \}]$$

Here, the declaration constraint C of the hidden variable is made explicit in the predicate of the schema text result. Whichever formulation is used, the point is that any such constraint *must* be carried over into the right-hand side schema text. A useful variant of $\exists$hide involves schema references:

$$(\exists \text{hide}) \quad \exists \text{SR} \bullet (\text{SR}; \ D \mid P) \equiv D \mid \exists \text{SR} \bullet P$$

Remark

There is a similar hiding rule family involving universal quantification, but in practice this is far less frequently needed.

One common usage of the hiding operator is what might be termed 'operation interface tidying'. Recall from page 213 that operation ConnectUser, contributing to EffectAttach, had a variable aFreeLn declared in its interface where it was not really wanted. We can avoid this by hiding aFreeLn, which thus becomes existentially quantified in ConnectUser. The modified definition

$$\text{EffectAttach} \; \hat{=} \; (\text{ConnectUser} \setminus (\text{aFreeLn})) \vee \text{QueueUser}$$

is what we would prefer to write in practice.

Here is a differently motivated example:

```
┌─ Coeffs ─────────────────────────────────────────────────┐
│ a,b : ℕ                                                    │
└────────────────────────────────────────────────────────────┘
```

```
┌─ Subtract ───────────────────────────────────────────────┐
│ ΔCoeffs                                                    │
│ x? : ℤ                                                     │
│ y! : ℕ                                                     │
│ ─────────────────────────────────                         │
│ a′ = a − x?                                                │
│ y! = a′ + b                                                │
│ b′ = b                                                     │
└────────────────────────────────────────────────────────────┘
```

Suppose we hide in Subtract both after-state variables a′ and b′ and the output y!:

$$\text{Subtract} \setminus (a', b', y!)$$
$$= \quad \text{— by definition of } \setminus$$
$$\exists \, a', b', y! : \mathbb{Z} \bullet \text{Subtract}$$
$$= \quad \text{— unfolding Subtract, i.e., revealing its text}$$
$$\exists \, a', b', y! : \mathbb{Z} \bullet (\Delta \text{Coeffs}; \; x? : \mathbb{Z}; \; y! : \mathbb{N} \mid$$
$$a' = a - x? \wedge y! = a' + b \wedge b' = b)$$
$$= \quad \text{— unfolding Coeffs′ and applying } \exists \text{hide}$$
$$\text{Coeffs}; \; x? : \mathbb{Z} \mid$$
$$\exists \, a', b', y! : \mathbb{N} \bullet a' = a - x? \wedge y! = a' + b \wedge b' = b \qquad (8.5)$$

The variables subjected to hiding have become existentially bound in the schema text predicate, still carrying the declaration constraints they had in Coeffs′. To reveal the constraints after applying ∃hide would mean writing

$$\text{Coeffs}; \; x? : \mathbb{Z} \mid \exists \, a', b', y! : \mathbb{Z} \bullet a' \geq 0 \wedge b' \geq 0 \wedge y! \geq 0 \wedge$$
$$a' = a - x? \wedge y! = a' + b \wedge b' = b$$

Either way, only the before-state and the input remain in the schema text's signature. In fact, it can be seen from (8.1/2) on page 215 that what we have just constructed is the precondition of Subtract. (*Note*: when presenting manipulations on schemas, our style will be to drop square brackets around schema texts, using only parentheses for delimitation where necessary.)

PREDICATE SIMPLIFICATION

To calculate an operation's precondition, we invoke the operator `pre` thus:

pre Op

`pre` is applicable only to operation schemas. The result of the `pre` operator is another schema, though we typically refer to just its predicate as the precondition of Op. A naming convention often used is that `PreOp` names the precondition schema of Op.

Operator `pre` is not very useful if we want to know the details of a precondition. Then we must apply `pre`'s definition, which is: hide all after state variables and outputs in the operation schema. That is,

pre Op ≙ ∃State´; Outputs! • Op

though, clearly, this is just a definition template, so it must get properly instantiated for each precondition we wish to calculate. This definition should come as no surprise, given that from (8.1) and (8.2) on page 215 we have

PreConOp(s, in?) ⟺
    ∃ s´ : State ; out! : Outputs? • OpPred(s, in?, s´, out!)

whence the definition of `pre` above.

One feature of the previous Subtract example is that, despite the operation being simple, the precondition predicate still looks unpleasant and probably not what the reader expects. One general way we can seek to simplify predicates of the form ∃ Decs • Pred is by applying the following rule:

- Let $x : X$ be a variable of Decs in a predicate ∃ Decs • Pred we wish to simplify. We look for an equality in Pred of the form $x = t$, where t is a term that does *not* contain variable x.

- If we are successful in finding such an equality then:
  – we can remove $x : X$ from Decs and drop the equality $x = t$ from Pred ...
  – ... but if the same x occurs elsewhere in Pred, we must substitute each of its instances by t.

This rule, often referred to as the 'one point rule', sounds far worse than it actually is. We can treat it as applying left-to-right the equivalence rule

(onePtRule)   ∃ x : X • P ∧ x = t ≡ P[t / x]   [x ∉ φt; t ∈ X]

There are two side conditions. The first, $x \notin φt$, expresses the fact that x must not occur freely in term t (the 'meta-function' φ calculates the set of all variable names freely occurring in its argument). The second side condition $t ∈ X$ expresses the requirement that t's value must belong to the set X. Both side conditions are 'self-evidently' satisfied in many situations where we want to apply onePtRule, in which case we often do not bother to show that they hold (technically, each requires a proof). However, some care needs to be taken with the second side condition, as our example will demonstrate.

Returning to (8.5) on the previous page, we note the equality $b´ = b$ in the ∃-predicate. Variable $b´$ is bound, and the term to which it is equal does not contain $b´$. Trivially also, b belongs to set ℕ like $b´$. Our onePtRule is thus applicable. Obeying it, we get the following simplification ($b´$ has disappeared altogether from the predicate):

a, b : ℕ; x? : ℤ | ∃ a´, y! : ℕ • a´ = a - x? ∧ y! = a´ + b   (8.6)

It seems we can now apply ∃hide to a′, but we must check that the side conditions of onePtRule hold. Obviously a′ does not occur in a - x?. However, a′ belongs to ℕ, but the most we can guarantee about a - x? is that it belongs to ℤ, given the declarations of a and x?. To 'balance' the sets involved, we need to normalize a′ and rewrite (8.6) as

$$a, b : ℕ;\ x? : ℤ\ |$$
$$\exists a' : ℤ;\ y! : ℕ \bullet a' \geq 0 \wedge a' = a - x? \wedge y! = a' + b \tag{8.7}$$

With a′ and a - x? now in harmony, we can apply onePtRule to give

$$a, b : ℕ;\ x? : ℤ\ |\ \exists y! : ℕ \bullet a - x? \geq 0 \wedge y! = (a - x?) + b$$

Finally, y! can be eliminated by the same mechanism (see exercise) to give

$$a, b : ℕ;\ x? : ℤ\ |\ a - x? \geq 0$$

or

$$a, b : ℕ;\ x? : ℤ\ |\ a \geq x? \tag{8.8}$$

which is as far as we can go.

The derived precondition for Subtract is as expected: we cannot subtract an integer x? from variable a and get a natural number unless $a \geq x?$. We might have included this predicate in Subtract in the first place to make it a more 'honest' description. The calculation would still produce the same result (try it out). Thus, whether Subtract's predicate explicitly includes $a \geq x?$ or not, we are still describing the same behaviour, even though the texts of the two descriptions are not the same.

EXERCISE 8.11

1. Justify the above elimination of y!.

2. Suppose in the definition of Subtract on page 218 we included: $a - x? \geq 9$. Derive its precondition. Is the operation the same as the original Subtract?

3. Consider the following operation on Coeffs (see page 218):

    $$SQRCheck ≙ [\ \Xi Coeffs;\ c? : ℕ;\ e! : ℤ\ |\ e! = b * b - 4 * a * c?\ ]$$

    Show the steps in the calculation of SQRCheck's precondition down to an existentially quantified predicate (*Hint*: careful).

4. Simplify the answer to Question (3) as far as possible, justifying each step.

5. Derive and simplify the precondition of the following operation:

    $$CondInc ≙ [\ \Delta Coeffs\ |\ a' = a + 1 \wedge a' \geq b' \wedge b' = b\ ]$$

A Lengthy and Difficult Example
(This subsection could be omitted on first reading.)

A precondition calculation can uncover 'hidden' constraints, as in the Subtract example. By the same token, it can be used to confirm that our explicit preconstraints constitute the operation's precondition and nothing has been overlooked. Here is an example of the latter. From Section 8.3 (plus page 218), we have

    EffectAttach ≙ (ConnectUser \ (aFreeLn)) ∨ QueueUser
    AttachUser ≙ CanDoAttach ∧ EffectAttach

It follows immediately by substitution of `EffectAttach` that

> `AttachUser =`
> `CanDoAttach` ∧ ((`ConnectUser` \ (`aFreeLn`)) ∨ `QueueUser`)   (8.9)

To calculate the precondition of `AttachUser`, we will need to make use of certain additional properties of the schema calculus. These are:

(sch∧∨dist)   `S1` ∧ (`S2` ∨ `S3`) = (`S1` ∧ `S2`) ∨ (`S1` ∧ `S3`)

(pre∨dist)   pre(`Op1` ∨ `Op2`) = pre `Op1` ∨ pre `Op2`

(sch∧\)   `S1` ∧ (`S2` \ (`Vars`)) =
              (`S1` ∧ `S2`) \ (`Vars`)   [α`S1` ∩ `Vars` = ∅]

(pre\)   pre(`Op` \ (`Vars`)) = (pre `Op`) \ (`Vars`)

The first law states that schema conjunction distributes over schema disjunction. The second law is also a distributive law: pre distributes over operation disjunction. The third law conveys an associative-like interaction between schema conjunction and hiding, providing the side condition holds. This condition requires that the variables declared in the left-hand schema do not occur in the hide list; the meta-function α is similar to φ, giving the names of variables *declared* in a construct. The fourth law describes an interaction between pre and hiding.

Given these rules, we can see that

> pre `AttachUser`
>
>   = — by definition of `AttachUser`
>
> pre(`CanDoAttach` ∧ ((`ConnectUser` \ (`aFreeLn`)) ∨ `QueueUser`))
>
>   = — by law sch∧∨dist
>   pre(`CanDoAttach` ∧ (`ConnectUser` \ (`aFreeLn`)) ∨
>   `CanDoAttach` ∧ `QueueUser`)
>
>   = — by law pre∨dist
>   pre(`CanDoAttach` ∧ (`ConnectUser` \ (`aFreeLn`))) ∨
>   pre(`CanDoAttach` ∧ `QueueUser`)   (8.10)

Furthermore, from the first disjunct in (8.10), we have:

> pre(`CanDoAttach` ∧ (`ConnectUser` \ (`aFreeLn`)))
>
>   = — by law sch∧ \, noting that α`CanDoAttach` ∩ { `aFreeLn` } = ∅
>   pre((`CanDoAttach` ∧ `ConnectUser`) \ (`aFreeLn`))
>
>   = — by law pre \
>   pre(`CanDoAttach` ∧ `ConnectUser`) \ (`aFreeLn`)   (8.11)

Thus, we will begin by calculating pre(`CanDoAttach` ∧ `ConnectUser`).

To reduce clutter, we drop ∧ connectives or else replace them with semicolons. The predicate of `CanDoAttach` is subsumed as `CanDoAttach`[P] since it contains no primed or output variables (our P superscript is used purely to emphasize 'predicate of').

> pre (`CanDoAttach` ∧ `ConnectUser`)
>
>   = — by definition of pre
>   ∃ `Computer′`; `attachMes!` : `OLM_Message` •
>   (`CanDoAttach` ∧ `ConnectUser`)

= — combining schemas by definition of schema ∧; applying ∃hide

$\quad$ Computer; u? : USER; aFreeLn : LINE |
$\qquad$ ∃ Computer′; attachMes! : OLM_Message •
$\qquad\quad$ CanDoAttach^P
$\qquad\quad$ aFreeLn ∈ linesUp \ dom cnnctd
$\qquad\quad$ attachMes! = connected
$\qquad\quad$ cnnctd′ = cnnctd ∪ { aFreeLn ↦ u? }
$\qquad\quad$ avlblty′ = avlblty; users′ = users; priv′ = priv
$\qquad\quad$ allLines′ = allLines; linesUp′ = linesUp
$\qquad\quad$ cnnctQu′ = cnnctQu; maxQLen′ = maxQLen

Even with the short-cuts, there is still an intimidating mass of symbols, which ia fairly typical of precondition calculation in non-trivial specifications. The intimidation is more psychological than real, however.

$\quad$ Firstly, CanDoAttach^P and its immediate successor conjunct can be brought outside the scope of the outer quantifier since neither contains any quantified variables. The basic rule in action here is

$\quad$ (∃scope) $\quad$ ∃ x : X • P ∧ Q ≡ P ∧ ∃ x : X • Q $\quad$ [x ∉ φP]

Secondly, we can see that attachMes! can be immediately eliminated by onePtRule. Also, there are a lot of inviting equalities for primed variables seemingly lined up waiting to come under the axe of onePtRule. However, before using them, we must not forget the predicate lurking subsumed in Computer′, which therefore needs to be unfolded. Putting these preparatory manipulations into effect gives us a schema text that temporarily looks even worse, despite the further notational short-cut of sub-suming the declarations of Computer′:

$\quad$ Computer; u? : USER; aFreeLn : LINE |
$\qquad$ CanDoAttach^P
$\qquad$ aFreeLn ∈ linesUp \ dom cnnctd
$\qquad$ ∃ Computer′^{D} • $\hspace{4cm}$ — declarations of Computer′
$\qquad\quad$ sysManager ∈ priv′; priv′ ⊆ users′
$\qquad\quad$ ran cnnctd′ ∪ elemsOfq cnnctQu′ ⊆ users′
$\qquad\quad$ ran cnnctd′ ∩ elemsOfq cnnctQu′ = ∅
$\qquad\quad$ dom cnnctd′ ⊆ linesUp′ ⊆ allLines′
$\qquad\quad$ lenq cnnctQu′ ≤ maxQLen′
$\qquad\quad$ cnnctQu′ ≠ emptyq ⇒ #cnnctd′ = #linesUp′
$\qquad\quad$ avlblty′ = online ⇒ allLines′ ≠ ∅
$\qquad\quad$ avlblty′ = offline ⇒ linesUp′ = ∅ ∧ cnnctQu′ = emptyq
$\qquad\quad$ cnnctd′ = cnnctd ∪ { aFreeLn ↦ u? }
$\qquad\quad$ avlblty′ = avlblty; users′ = users; priv′ = priv
$\qquad\quad$ allLines′ = allLines; linesUp′ = linesUp
$\qquad\quad$ cnnctQu′ = cnnctQu; maxQLen′ = maxQLen

Except for cnnctd′, applicability of onePtRule to the other primed variables is self-evident, given the equalities involved. We obtain

$\quad$ Computer; u? : USER; aFreeLn : LINE |
$\qquad$ CanDoAttach^P
$\qquad$ aFreeLn ∈ linesUp \ dom cnnctd $\hspace{3cm}$ — continued on next page

$\exists$ cnnctd' : USER $\rightarrowtail$ LINE $\bullet$
  sysManager $\in$ priv; priv $\subseteq$ users   (*)
  ran cnnctd' $\cup$ elemsOfq cnnctQu $\subseteq$ users
  ran cnnctd' $\cap$ elemsOfq cnnctQu $= \emptyset$
  dom cnnctd' $\subseteq$ linesUp $\subseteq$ allLines
  lenq cnnctQu $\le$ maxQLen   (*)
  cnnctQu $\ne$ emptyq $\Rightarrow$ #cnnctd' = #linesUp
  avlblty = online $\Rightarrow$ allLines $\ne \emptyset$ (*)
  avlblty = offline $\Rightarrow$ linesUp $= \emptyset \wedge$ cnnctQu = emptyq   (*)
  cnnctd' = cnnctd $\cup$ { aFreeLn $\mapsto$ u? }

which is a little friendlier, but still not friendly enough.

As regards eliminating cnnctd' with onePtRule, we need to check whether the term cnnctd $\cup$ { aFreeLn $\mapsto$ u? } is functional and injective. Indeed it is, because: (i) the second conjunct after the constraint line '|' ensures that aFreeLn $\notin$ dom cnnctd by properties of sets, thus guaranteeing functionality; (ii) we have u? $\notin$ ran cnnctd from CanDoAttach[P], thus guaranteeing injectivity. So we can also safely eliminate cnnctd' via onePtRule, with four consequential substitutions. At the same time, the conjuncts marked (*) do not involve cnnctd' and are part of the predicate of Computer anyway! So being redundant, they too can be dropped. We obtain

Computer; u? : USER; aFreeLn : LINE |
  CanDoAttach[P]   (1)
  aFreeLn $\in$ linesUp \ dom cnnctd   (2)
  ran(cnnctd $\cup$ { aFreeLn $\mapsto$ u? }) $\cup$ elemsOfq cnnctQu $\subseteq$ users   (3)
  ran(cnnctd $\cup$ { aFreeLn $\mapsto$ u? }) $\cap$ elemsOfq cnnctQu $= \emptyset$ (4)
  dom(cnnctd $\cup$ { aFreeLn $\mapsto$ u? }) $\subseteq$ linesUp $\subseteq$ allLines   (5)
  cnnctQu $\ne$ emptyq $\Rightarrow$ #(cnnctd $\cup$ { aFreeLn $\mapsto$ u? }) = #linesUp   (6)

The individual conjuncts have been indexed for convenience. The existential quantification has at last disappeared, but the predicate still looks quite nasty.

Precondition calculation is often used to confirm one's shrewd assumptions. The fact is that we would suspect that this predicate will simplify much further. Consider (5), which, by the meaning of dom, is the same as

dom cnnctd $\cup$ { aFreeLn } $\subseteq$ linesUp $\subseteq$ allLines   (5')

We already have

dom cnnctd $\subseteq$ linesUp $\subseteq$ allLines

from Computer, and from (2), it immediately follows that

aFreeLn $\in$ linesUp

(if $x \in X \setminus Y$, then certainly $x \in X$). So by properties of sets, these last two predicates guarantee (5'), which means we can discard (5) too! We get

Computer; u? : USER; aFreeLn : LINE |
  CanDoAttach[P]   (1)
  aFreeLn $\in$ linesUp \ dom cnnctd   (2)
  ran(cnnctd $\cup$ { aFreeLn $\mapsto$ u? }) $\cup$ elemsOfq cnnctQu $\subseteq$ users   (3)
  ran(cnnctd $\cup$ { aFreeLn $\mapsto$ u? }) $\cap$ elemsOfq cnnctQu $= \emptyset$ (4)
  cnnctQu $\ne$ emptyq $\Rightarrow$ #(cnnctd $\cup$ { aFreeLn $\mapsto$ u? }) = #linesUp   (6)

In discarding (5), what we have really done is to mobilize another rule which is often very useful in precondition simplification (when applied left to right):

$$(\text{dropRdntCnj}) \quad D \mid P \wedge Q \equiv D \mid P \quad [D \mid P \vdash Q]$$

The side condition can be read as 'Q can be inferred from $D \mid P$' (the symbol $\vdash$ is discussed further in Chapter 9). If we can argue that this is so, then we can drop the Q in $D \mid P \wedge Q$ because it adds 'no further information' to what $D \mid P$ tells us already. We have called the rule dropRdntCnj: drop redundant conjunct. Application of this rule sometimes requires more work than onePtRule. This is because showing that its side condition holds may require a non-trivial argument (i.e., formally, a proof).

It turns out that we can apply dropRdntCnj to (3), (4) and (6) as well, and this is dealt with in the next exercise. The final simplified predicate is thus

```
Computer; u? : USER; aFreeLn : LINE |
    CanDoAttachᴾ
    aFreeLn ∈ linesUp \ dom cnnctd
```

Using this result to continue the equality chain (8.11) on page 221, we get

```
pre( CanDoAttach ∧ ConnectUser ) \ ( aFreeLn )
  = ( Computer; u? : USER; aFreeLn : LINE |
        CanDoAttachᴾ
        aFreeLn ∈ linesUp \ dom cnnctd) \ ( aFreeLn )
  = Computer; u? : USER |
        CanDoAttachᴾ
        ∃ aFreeLn : LINE • aFreeLn ∈ linesUp \ dom cnnctd
  = Computer; u? : USER |
        CanDoAttachᴾ
        linesUp \ dom cnnctd ≠ ∅
```

The second step in this equality chain holds because `aFreeLn` does not occur in CanDoAttachᴾ. The third step holds because `aFreeLn` can exist as a member of the stated set if and only if that set is non-empty; we are applying the set property

$$(\exists x : X \bullet x \in S) \Leftrightarrow S \neq \varnothing$$

A similar calculation will show (see next exercise) that the precondition of CanDoAttach ∧ QueueUser is

```
Computer; u? : USER |
    CanDoAttachᴾ
    linesUp \ dom cnnctd = ∅
```

So from (8.10) on page 221, we see that

```
pre AttachUser
  = ( Computer; u? : USER |
        CanDoAttachᴾ ∧ linesUp \ dom cnnctd ≠ ∅ ) ∨
    ( Computer; u? : USER |
        CanDoAttachᴾ ∧ linesUp \ dom cnnctd = ∅ )
```

cont.

$$= \text{Computer}; u? : \text{USER} \mid$$
$$\quad \text{CanDoAttach}^{P} \wedge \text{linesUp} \setminus \text{dom cnnctd} \neq \varnothing \vee$$
$$\quad \text{CanDoAttach}^{P} \wedge \text{linesUp} \setminus \text{dom cnnctd} = \varnothing$$

$$= \text{Computer}; u? : \text{USER} \mid$$
$$\quad \text{CanDoAttach}^{P} \wedge$$
$$\quad (\text{linesUp} \setminus \text{dom cnnctd} \neq \varnothing \vee \text{linesUp} \setminus \text{dom cnnctd} = \varnothing)$$

$$= \text{Computer}; u? : \text{USER} \mid \text{CanDoAttach}^{P} \wedge \text{true}$$

$$= \text{Computer}; u? : \text{USER} \mid \text{CanDoAttach}^{P}$$

$$= \text{CanDoAttach}$$

So our original prescription for error handling as regards operation `AttachUser` was indeed complete.

The 'heaviness' of the calculation may seem somewhat alarming, but the effort is amply repaid by the important information which the calculation uncovers. Also, there is a definite sense in which once familiarity with the mechanics of precondition calculation has been acquired on difficult examples, the burden of subsequent calculations considerably lessens.

EXERCISE 8.12

1. Justify each of the steps in the immediately preceding equality chain in the text that leads to the precondition of `AttachUser`.

2. Try to show that predicates (3), (4) and (6) on page 223 can be dropped by the dropRdntCnj rule. Dealing with the first two is fairly straightforward, given a simple property of `dom` together with what is subsumed in `Computer` and CanDoAttach^{P}. Dropping (6) is more involved. There is a rule of logic which permits you to deduce $P \Rightarrow Q$ if $\neg P$ holds (Q can be anything you like). So try to deduce $\neg (\text{cnnctQu} \neq \text{emptyq})$. Another rule of logic will be of help here: if $P \Rightarrow Q$ and $\neg Q$ holds, you are permitted to deduce $\neg P$.

3. Calculate the precondition of `CanDoAttach` $\wedge$ `QueueUser`, showing it to be as claimed in the text. See Exercise 8.9(4a) for `QueueUser`. The calculation will proceed in much the same way as the text's example; the simplification is slightly easier.

8.5 SYSTEM-LEVEL STATE MODEL AND BEHAVIOUR

The Full State Model

The Online Monitor system actually comprises many machines, not just one. Using the schema `Computer`, we can construct the full state model with relative ease. This is given on the next page. The given set `MACHINE` is now used to impart unique identification to different 'machine instances' as described by schema `Computer`. The fact that the full state description, coupled with `Computer`, is as simple as it is provides further evidence that vertically structuring the system state on an object-based machine model is the right choice. All globals remain as in Model I of Section 8.1.

```
┌─ OnlineMonitor ─────────────────────────────────────────────┐
│ SysConstraints                                               │
│ mcInsts : MACHINE ⇸ Computer                                 │
│ privUsers : ℙ USER                                           │
│ linesToMcs : ℙ LINE                                          │
├──────────────────────────────────────────────────────────── │
│ olmMcs = dom mcInsts                                         │
│ allUsers = ⋃ {m : olmMcs • (mcInsts m).users}                │
│ privUsers = ⋃ {m : olmMcs • (mcInsts m).priv}                │
│ linesToMcs = ⋃ {m : olmMcs • (mcInsts m).allLines}           │
│ linesToMcs ⊆ linePool                                        │
│ ∀ m1,m2 : olmMcs | m1 ≠ m2 •                                 │
│   (mcInsts m1).allLines ∩ (mcInsts m2).allLines = ∅          │
└──────────────────────────────────────────────────────────────┘
```

Recall that `olmMcs`, `allUsers` and `linePool` come from `SysConstraints`. The two former components, together with `privUsers` and `linesToMcs`, are all derived from the 'Computer instances' variable `mcInsts` (for a comparison with Model I, see schema `OnlineMonitor` on page 198). Variables `privUsers` and `linesToMcs` have been introduced for convenience.

Framing and Promotion

The problem we now face is this. So far, the operations that we have specified—`ReportMcState`, `Disconnect`, `RbAttachUser`, plus others dealt with in exercises such as `ChangeLineCap` and `LeaveQueue`—act only on an individual machine as modelled by `Computer`. We would like a way of elevating them to operations applicable to *any* machine in the Online Monitor system, preferably without any major modification or re-specification. We can achieve this using the techniques of *framing* and *promotion*.

A *frame* describes some part, possibly all, of a state which is accessible for update by an operation. A variable in a frame *may* change, though not necessarily for a given state transition. An operation might not be permitted to change the state of the frame and so can merely observe it. To describe frames and what updating/observing them involves, we construct *framing schemas*. A framing schema in effect represents a 'generalized updating context' within which specific operations can occur. Consider the Online Monitor system. We can define the general nature of an operation on an individual machine in the system, without reference to any particular `Computer` operation itself, by the framing schema φOLM on the opposite page (there are some error-handling issues—we deal with these later). It is a convention adopted by some authors that names of framing schemas begin with the Greek letter φ; we follow this.

Schema φOLM has all the ingredients necessary to describe an operation on one of the `OnlineMonitor` machines as identified by `m?`, but is otherwise completely non-specific. We could of course have written ΔComputer in its declaration part instead of `Computer` and `Computer'`; the latter has been chosen simply to make things clearer. Note that: (i) updates affecting derived variables are taken care of by the equality invariants of `OnlineMonitor`, so references to `olmMcs`, `allUsers`, etc., in φOLM are not necessary; (ii) `linePool` is unaffected by *all* `Computer` operations.

```
┌─ φOLM ─────────────────────────────────────────────────────────────────┐
│                                                                         │
│  ΔOnlineMonitor    — for a (generalized) machine operation on the complete system
│  m? : MACHINE      — this identifies the specific machine involved
│  Computer          — this describes the before-state of the machine instance
│  Computer'         — this describes the after-state of the machine instance
│  ├──────────────────────────────────                                    │
│                                                                         │
│  — obviously the machine must be one that the system knows about:       │
│  m? ∈ olmMcs                                                            │
│  — before the operation, the machine instance is in the state described by Computer:
│  mcInsts m? = θ Computer                                               │
│  — after the operation, the machine instance's state Computer' is (possibly) different:
│  mcInsts' = mcInsts ⊕ { m? ↦ θ Computer' }                            │
│  — linePool is the one OnlineMonitor variable always unaffected in this frame:
│  linePool' = linePool                                                  │
│                                                                         │
└─────────────────────────────────────────────────────────────────────────┘
```

With the framing schema in place, we can now define specific operations on the complete system using our previously specified operations on an individual machine. For example, here is the system-level version of machine-level RbDisconnect, i.e., Disconnect as on pages 208–209 plus some error handling (what would this be?):

$$OLM\_RbDisconnect \triangleq \phi OLM \land RbDisconnect$$

What we have done is *promoted* RbDisconnect to a system-level operation without any rewriting of RbDisconnect itself. The conjunction combines the generalized effect of an update to one of the system's machines as captured by the framing schema with the specific, machine-level update and error checking of RbDisconnect.

As it stands, the definition of OLM_RbDisconnect has one annoying feature: ΔComputer still lurks in its declaration part. We can do better if instead we define the operation thus:

$$OLM\_RbDisconnect \triangleq (\phi OLM \land RbDisconnect) \setminus (\Delta Computer)$$

The hiding operator removes ΔComputer from the promoted operation's signature, existentially quantifying it—that is, the variables of Computer and Computer'—in the predicate part. The result is a tidier description, with ΔOnlineMonitor appearing in the declaration part of the promoted operation, but not ΔComputer, which is what we would expect for a full system operation on OnlineMonitor.

Promoting all the other Computer-level operations would follow the same basic definitional pattern:

$$OLM\_ComputerOp \triangleq (\phi OLM \land ComputerOp) \setminus (\Delta Computer)$$

which itself is a partial instantiation of the more general promotion template

$$PromotedOp \triangleq$$
$$(FramingSchema \land LowerOp) \setminus (StateAndState' VarsOfLowerOp)$$

Actually, the syntax we have used is slightly loose. Strictly, the hiding operator should be given a list of variable names. However, it is a reasonable convention that ΔSchema used in this context is short-hand for a list comprising all primed and unprimed names of the variables declared in Schema. The convention is worthwhile—in our promotion definitions, the list written out explicitly would be 16 names long!

EXERCISE 8.13

1. Explain why, as we would expect, a promoted `ReportMcState` operation (see page 202) will not change the `OnlineMonitor` state.

2. Suppose schema `Buffer` describes the state of a FIFO (first in first out) fixed-length buffer. Operations on the buffer are `AddB`, `RemB`, `FstB` and `LenB`. A system Buffer Manager maintains a number of buffers, which are identified by their start addresses in memory. The system can maintain no more than `maxNoBuff` buffers.

   a. Construct a state schema for Buffer Manager
   b. Define a framing schema for operations on any of the buffers managed by Buffer Manager. Assume error-free conditions
   c. Give some promoted operation definitions, say for `AddB` and `LenB`.

3. Suppose a queue is maintained of `Object` items, `Object` itself being a schema modelling a state over which various operations have been defined. `Object` operations can be applied *only to the object that is first in the queue*. Devise a framing schema for promoting `Object` operations (you will need a queue state model too).

4. Based on the answer to Exercise 8.5(2), give an object-based state model for Van Hire. Sketch out the framing/promotion tactics that would be involved.

5. § The answer is dealt with immediately below.
   a. Outline an approach to defining robust operations over `OnlineMonitor`, whether or not of the promoted variety
   b. Identify and define some operations over `OnlineMonitor` which are additional to promoted operations over `Computer`.

Further Aspects of System-level Description

When `Computer` operations such as `RbDisconnect` and `RbAttachUser` are promoted, they carry whatever error handling is part of their definitions. However, other error handling is needed to deal with exceptions that can be detected only at the `OnlineMonitor` level. Here is each of the main system-level checks that will need to be made, as appropriate, in various circumstances:

- the machine `m?` can be identified
- the user `u?` initiating the operation can be identified
- the line `ln?` specified can be identified.

The first check is at least needed for all promoted operations, as should be obvious from the framing schema φOLM. The second is necessary because many operations require user identification, the third because a few involve line identification. Actually, we need to elaborate the second possibility a bit further: even if the user is known to the system, some operations such as `ReportMcState` and `ChangeLineCap` can be carried out only by privileged users. So we also want to trap an 'ordinary' user attempting to perform a privileged operation.

Firstly, we define the following schemas, given suitable extension of `OLM_Message` on page 211. Although the `m? ∈ olmMcs` check of `MachineOK` occurs in φOLM, having `MachineOK` enables machine identifier checking in non-promotion situations also.

```
MachineOK ≙ [ OnlineMonitor; olmMes! : OLM_Message;
              m? : MACHINE | m? ∈ olmMcs ∧ olmMes! = validData ]
LineOK ≙ [ OnlineMonitor; olmMes! : OLM_Message; ln? : LINE |
           ln? ∈ linePool ∧ olmMes! = validData ]
OrdUserOK ≙ [ OnlineMonitor; olmMes! : OLM_Message; u? : USER |
              u? ∈ allUsers ∧ olmMes! = validData ]
PrivUserOK ≙ [ OnlineMonitor; olmMes! : OLM_Message; u? : USER |
               u? ∈ privUsers ∧ olmMes! = validData ]
BadMachine ≙
  [ ΞOnlineMonitor; olmMes! : OLM_Message; m? : MACHINE |
     m? ∉ olmMcs ∧ olmMes! = mcNotKnown ]
BadLine ≙ [ ΞOnlineMonitor; olmMes! : OLM_Message; ln? : LINE |
            ln? ∉ linePool ∧ olmMes! = lineNotKnown ]
BadUser ≙ [ ΞOnlineMonitor; olmMes! : OLM_Message; u? : USER |
            u? ∉ allUsers ∧ olmMes! = userNotKnown ]
NotPrivUser ≙
  [ ΞOnlineMonitor; olmMes! : OLM_Message; u? : USER |
     u? ∈ allUsers ∧ u? ∉ privUsers ∧ olmMes! = userNotPriv ]
IllicitUser ≙ BadUser ∨ NotPrivUser
```

Now we can specify robust promoted operations. The output olmMes! either flags validData or (non-deterministically in certain cases) some error. For example:

```
RbOLM_RbDisconnect ≙
  ( OLM_RbDisconnect ∧ LineOK ) ∨ BadMachine ∨ BadLine
RbOLM_ReportMcState ≙
  ( OLM_ReportMcState ∧ PrivUserOK ) ∨ BadMachine ∨ IllicitUser
```

With some operations such as RbOLM_RbDisconnect, robustness is spread over the two levels—recognition of a line signalled at the top level does not imply that an error will not be flagged at the lower level. By appropriately inspecting the target machine instance prior to application of an operation (e.g., is line actually owned by target machine?), *all* error handling could be described at the top level. However, our system-level specification would then become unwieldy, and we would begin to negate the usefulness of promotion. By keeping at the Computer level everything that can be handled there, the system-level description is considerably simplified.

Not all the error handling needed for promoted operations is taken care of by BadMachine, etc. Consider the registration of users on machines. At the Computer level, we are concerned only that the users are not already registered on the machine in question. At the system level, if (some of) the users are completely new to the system, we will need to check there is room for them—recall the #allUsers ≤ maxNoUsers size constraint in SysConstraints.

Not all OnlineMonitor operations are promoted Computer ones. RepSysLoad on the next page is an example, which we have supposed is a privileged observation. Note that system-level non-promoted observations like RepSysLoad and its robust version will in general involve access to many machines. System-level non-promoted *update* will relate mainly to adding new machines and deleting existing machines from the system. This is because, apart from changes to the line pool, all other updates are taken care of by the (promoted) Computer operations themselves. Some of the non-promoted OnlineMonitor operations are dealt with in Exercise 8.14.

```
┌─RepSysLoad──────────────────────────────────────────────┐
│ ΞOnlineMonitor                                           │
│ loadPerMc! : MACHINE ⇸ ℕ × ℕ                             │
├──────────────────────                                    │
│ loadPerMc! =                                             │
│   { m : olmMcs | ( mcInsts m ).avlblty = online •        │
│        m ↦ ( # ( mcInsts m ).cnnctd, lenq( mcInsts m ).cnnctQu ) } │
└──────────────────────────────────────────────────────────┘
```

RbRepSysLoad ≙ (RepSysLoad ∧ PrivUserOK) ∨ IllicitUser

A FINAL REMARK

In advanced specification work where a complex system is being defined in terms of a number of subsystems, we will need descriptions that are broken down over a hierarchy of state and operation schemas. The combination of framing and promotion enables operations at a certain level in the specification architecture to be elevated to the next higher level with considerable economy and ease of description. A question to be asked, however, is whether schemas and the schema calculus, despite their express-ive power, are sufficient in themselves as structuring mechanisms for large-scale system specification work. Recent research endeavours by many workers have focused on seeking object-oriented extensions to Z so as to increase its structuring capability via the concepts of *classes* and *inheritance*. This seems an attractive idea, and the interested reader is referred to a useful overview of the issues given by Stepney *et al*. (1992).

EXERCISE 8.14

1. Define a robust operation for deleting a machine from the system (remember the privileged user check).

2. Define a robust operation for adding a new machine to the system (remember the privileged user check). *Hint*: Exercise 8.4(1) should be of help.

3. Define an operation (no error checking) for reporting the status of each mach-ine in the system. 'Machine status' here is defined as 'offline', 'online and quiet, i.e., no activity', 'online and active', 'online and full to capacity'.

8.6 FURTHER SCHEMA OPERATORS

Modelling Sequentiality

Schema operators like ∧ and ∨ are adequate for a large number of situations. However, moving down to the Computer level again, consider the situation where a busy line goes down. Uhura is required to be clever enough to try to re-attach the user involved. This is friendlier than the user getting 'chopped off' the machine and having to seek access again from scratch. It is true that, if there is room to re-attach but no working lines are free, the user will get queued instead of connected; but users at least have the option of dequeuing themselves.

This automatic re-attach scenario has two components:

- `BusyLineDrop`: a busy line goes down
- `ReAttach`:   the user on the dropped line gets re-attached if possible.

There is a definite sense in which `ReAttach` occurs *after* `BusyLineDrop`. In fact, a schema operator exists which conveys the notion of 'first this operation occurs, and then it is followed by this operation'. The operator is called *schema composition*. The symbol is ⨾ and is closely related to relation composition (see page 147). Thus, we can write schema definitions of the form

$$\mathsf{Op1ThenOp2} \;\hat{=}\; \mathsf{Op1} \;\fatsemi\; \mathsf{Op2} \tag{8.12}$$

though it should be appreciated that the resulting schema is 'just another bunch of symbols', not a mechanistic description of operation sequencing as would occur in an algorithm. The ⨾ operator mathematically models the semantics of sequential composition, but that is all.

For our example illustration we will suppress exception handling to avoid unnecessary clutter. Firstly, we specify the two component operations:

```
┌─ BusyLineDrop ───────────────────────────────────────────────┐
│ ΔComputer
│ ln? : LINE
│ usr : USER
│ msg! : OLM_Message
├───────────────────────────────────────────────────────────────
│ ln? ∈ dom cnnctd
│ usr = cnnctd ln?
│ msg! = lineGoneDown              — assume added to type OLM_Message
│ cnnctd' = { ln? } ⩤ cnnctd
│ linesUp' = linesUp \ { ln? }
│ avlblty' = avlblty; priv' = priv; cnnctQu' = cnnctQu
│ users' = users; maxQLen' = maxQLen; allLines' = allLines
└───────────────────────────────────────────────────────────────┘
```

We have chosen to make the malfunctioning line the input rather than the user affected, which seems slightly more natural. The user can be calculated from the line and is treated as an internal observation; later, we hide it. In isolation, `BusyLineDrop` would not need `usr` at all, but we need it here to make the eventual composition work.

The operation of attaching a user has already been dealt with at length in Section 8.3. We can make good re-use of `EffectAttach`, which connects or queues a user. But for one case, all the error checking in `CanDoAttach` on page 211 is unnecessary (why?). The case involved is check (c), since we must ensure there is room for the re-attach. So

$$\mathsf{ReAttach} \;\hat{=}\; [\, \mathsf{EffectAttach} \mid \mathsf{lenq\ cnnctQu} < \mathsf{maxQLen} \,]$$

Remembering that `EffectAttach` has the user u? as input, we define

$$\mathsf{AutoReAttachUser} \;\hat{=}\; (\, \mathsf{BusyLineDrop} \;\fatsemi\; \mathsf{ReAttach}[\, \mathsf{usr}\,/\,\mathsf{u?} \,]\,) \setminus (\, \mathsf{usr} \,)$$

The renaming harmonizes the two sub-operations. The hiding emphasizes that `usr` is regarded as neither an input nor output of the composition, so should not appear in the interface of `AutoReAttachUser`.

In general, given (8.12) on the previous page, where Op1 and Op2 must be operation schemas in accordance with the usual syntactic conventions, the combined schema Op1ThenOp2 is obtained by

- identifying those after-state components of Op1—call them PartOfState1 '—whose plain names (i.e., ignoring the ' decoration) match type-compatible before-state components of Op2—call them PartOfState2
- renaming these matching components in both operations as a common 'intermediate state', say IntState
- conjoining the texts of the two schemas Op1 and Op2, as discussed in Section 8.2
- hiding IntStateVars (the variables of IntState) so that the signature of the combined operation Op1ThenOp2 comprises the before and after states of both operations *except* IntStateVars themselves.

We can get close to a formal definition by translating this description as

$$(\, \text{Op1} \, [\, \text{IntStateVars} \, / \, \text{PartOfState1}\,'\,\text{Vars} \,] \, \wedge$$
$$\text{Op2} \, [\, \text{IntStateVars} \, / \, \text{PartOfState2Vars} \,] \,) \setminus (\, \text{IntStateVars} \,)$$

By renaming the matching after-state components of Op1 and before-state components of Op2 with the same names, they merge in the conjunction; the hiding operator then removes them from the combination's interface. Often, Op1 and Op2 are operations on the *same* state, i.e., IntState is then the *complete* state common to both. Figure 8.5 tries to clarify diagrammatically what is involved in the general case.

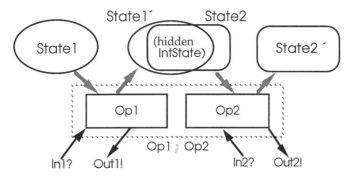

Figure 8.5   Diagrammatic interpretation of sequential composition.

EXERCISE 8.15

Here are two more operations on the `Coeffs` state described on page 218:

```
Incb ≙ [ ΔCoeffs | a' = a ∧ b' = b + 1 ]
Decb ≙ [ ΔCoeffs | a' = a ∧ b' = b - 1 ]
```

1. Simplify the following as much as possible (it is customary to use the same plain names for 'intermediate state' variables but with a different decoration—anything will do such as ' '):

   a. `Incb ⨾ Incb`   b. `Incb ⨾ Decb` (easy after having done (a)).

2. Does the operation: `Decb ⨾ Incb`
   represent the same operation as in Question (1b)? Explain your answer.

Piping

Another useful schema combinator is the schema *piping* operator $\gg$. Given

$$\mathsf{Op1} \gg \mathsf{Op2}$$

then any output in Op1 and type compatible input in Op2 which have the same plain name (i.e., ignoring the ? and ! decorations) are matched. That is, Name! in Op1 becomes matched with Name? in Op2. Similarly to sequential composition, we can describe piping by the expression

$$(\ \mathsf{Op1}\ [\ \mathsf{IOVars}\ /\ \mathsf{IOVars!}\ ]\ \wedge \mathsf{Op2}\ [\ \mathsf{IOVars}\ /\ \mathsf{IOVars?}\ ]\ )\ \backslash\ (\ \mathsf{IOVars}\ )$$

where IOVars represents the names of the undecorated *piped variables* common to Op1 and Op2. The renaming identifies the piped variables in both schemas; after conjunction and merging, the piped variables become hidden.

Piping provides a way of modelling a relationship between two operations where one or more outputs of one operation are to become corresponding inputs of the other. Most often, piping is used to model this data transmission where the two operations are seen as acting more or less independently on separate components of the state. Here is an example.

Suppose the Online Monitor system keeps statistical data concerning users' usage of the various machines on which they are registered. A state fragment suitable for this task could be as follows (an alternative is dealt with in the final exercise of the chapter):

[REGISTRATION]

__ SysUsage _____
regsPerMc : REGISTRATION $\twoheadrightarrow$ MACHINE
regsPerUsr : REGISTRATION $\twoheadrightarrow$ USER
usrUsage : REGISTRATION $\twoheadrightarrow$ $\mathbb{N} \times \mathbb{N}$
_____
dom regsPerMc = dom regsPerUsr = dom usrUsage
$\forall$ r1, r2 : dom regsPerUsr | r1 $\neq$ r2 $\bullet$
   regsPerUsr r1 = regsPerUsr r2 $\Rightarrow$
                          regsPerMc r1 $\neq$ regsPerMc r2

We have introduced a new REGISTRATION entity (see also page 196). Each registration identifies *one* particular user on *one* particular machine. Thus, each machine has many registrations, and so does each user; but a user cannot have multiple registrations on the same machine (second invariant of SysUsage). If the SysUsage state is combined with OnlineMonitor, the predicate will need to express that the MACHINE–USER relationships recorded in the former are consistent with those recorded by mcInsts in the latter. The purpose of SysUsage is to keep a collection of registration records detailing each user's usage of the machine(s) on which she is registered. The usage data per record comprises two quantities:

- the number of times the user has been connected to the machine in question
- the total amount of elapsed time (in seconds, say) the user has been connected to that machine.

These quantities are re-initialized each time certain periodic system-wide management reports from SysUsage are generated.

The following (non-robust) operation performs a cumulative update on the SysUsage component using data relating to the connection of one user. If we assume SysUsage is combined elsewhere with OnlineMonitor to give the complete state model, we would need to modify certain previous operation definitions accordingly. This is dealt with in the final exercise.

```
┌─ UpdateSUData ───────────────────────────────────────────────────┐
│ ΔSysUsage                                                          │
│ mc? : MACHINE                    — machine to which user was connected
│ usr? : USER                      — user involved
│ etc? : ℕ                         — elapsed time of connection
│ r : REGISTRATION                 — registration involved
│ ───────────────────────────────                                   │
│ ( r ↦ mc? ) ∈ regsPerMc                                           │
│ ( r ↦ usr? ) ∈ regsPerUsr                                         │
│ usrUsage' = usrUsage ⊕                                            │
│             { r ↦ (   first( usrUsage r ) + 1,                    │
│                       second( usrUsage r ) + etc?  )}             │
└───────────────────────────────────────────────────────────────────┘
```

Later, the registration r gets hidden.

Where would the inputs for UpdateSUData come from? The obvious answer is Disconnect, or rather its promoted robust version OLM_RbDisconnect which can at least give us the machine involved. To obtain the user usr! and elapsed time etc! from OLM_RbDisconnect, we need to modify suitably the basic Disconnect operation defined on pages 208–209. One way would be to incorporate the extra variables

```
elapsedTime? : ℕ              — the elapsed time for the connection
etc! : ℕ
usr! : USER
```

in each of Disconnect's two sub-operations FreeLine and AutoConnect. We can imagine that the additional input elapsedTime? is provided by separate low-level Uhura software which has access to a clock and monitors connect times on all lines. We also include the extra predicates

```
etc! = elapsedTime?
usr! = cnnctd ln?
```

in each of FreeLine and AutoConnect.

We can now define (ignoring system-level error handling) the following piped combination, which is an operation over the presumed new combined state:

```
mcOut  ≙ [ m?,mc! : MACHINE | mc! = m? ]
FullOLM_RbDisconnect ≙
    ( OLM_RbDisconnect ∧ mcOut ) >> ( UpdateSUData \ ( r ))
```

The effects of the two component operations are independent: OLM_RbDisconnect updates the OnlineMonitor component, UpdateSUData the SysUsage component. In a real system, we can even imagine the two operations being implemented as processes executing asynchronously in parallel, communicating only by a piped data stream.

EXERCISE 8.16

1. Construct the predicate that would be needed when `OnlineMonitor` and `SysUsage` are combined to give the complete system state. Call this state `OLM_SUD`.

2. Describe the changes that would have to be made to the Online Monitor specification as described in Section 8.5 if `OLM_SUD` were the state model.

3. Construct specifications of the following privileged operations on `OLM_SUD`; include appropriate user validation but ignore any error handling needed:

    a. an operation reporting on the system usage so far of user `u?` for each machine on which `u?` is registered
    b. an operation reporting on the system usage so far of machine `m?` for each user registered on that machine
    c. a periodic operation, available only to the system manager, which produces a system-wide report of the usage of the entire system and re-initializes counts for the next accounting period.

    For operation (a) only, show how useful totals could be obtained if Z had 'summation quantification':

    $$\Sigma x : X \mid C(x) \bullet E(x)$$

    This expression calculates the sum of the terms $E(x)$ for all values x satisfying $C(x)$ (if optional $C(x)$ is present). As usual, there is no restriction on X (or C), but $E(x)$ must be of type $\mathbb{Z}$.

4. Construct another description of the `SysUsage` statistics scenario given in the text. *Hint*: consider object-based modularity, framing and promotion.

SUMMARY OF CHAPTER 8

- The main operators of the schema calculus are introduced and their usage—such as building robust specifications and promoting operations—is illustrated within the context of a final 'system software' case study.

- The E–R route to state modelling adopted in the Van Hire case study is contrasted with one that focuses more on an event-driven, object-based view of domains and which leads to hierarchical descriptions of system behaviour.

- Various illustrations and examples demonstrate how modularity coupled with the schema calculus and associated descriptive techniques can be applied to develop and structure a non-trivial system specification.

9

AFTER SPECIFICATION: WHAT ELSE?

Key Topics   Specification validation, verification; sequents, conjectures, theorems; consistency proofs; proofs supporting validity. Design, implementation; data refinement; operation refinement. CASE tools; contractual process model; software engineers, software builders; uptake.

9.1   SPECIFICATION VALIDATION

Validation, Verification and Theorems

The technical phase of developing a software system following a feasibility study, requirements elicitation, problem domain analysis and modelling, etc., begins with construction of an abstract specification. This is a 'functional' (in the broad sense of the word) specification of the system expressed using primarily Z schemas, though possibly supported by data types and their properties (data type theories). However, before launching into activities that might be termed 'design' and 'implementation', it is obviously essential to try to ensure that a specification says 'what it should be saying'. That is, we need to *validate* the specification, which means seeking answers to two broad questions:

a. is the specification 'consistent' in its own right, i.e., is it free of logical defects?
b. does the specification describe the system that the client wants/is expecting to get?

Question (a) is really an *internal* question. It asks: does the specification describe something that can actually be built? Question (b) is an *external* (i.e., client/domain-oriented) question. It asks: are we building the right system?

Back in Chapter 1, a case was argued for why formal methods are important to software engineering—or, perhaps more accurately, why they *are* software engineering. *Verification* was a key issue pinpointed. We can define verification to mean

> *carrying out reasoning tasks which establish that specifications possess certain desirable properties*
>
> (The term *specification* is used here to cover everything from specifications in the current sense, i.e., abstract technical descriptions of artifacts to be built, to coded algorithms.)

One of the great strengths of formal methods is that its mathematical underpinnings provide the most watertight basis for verification at our disposal, namely proof. Indeed, because abstract Z specifications are formal descriptions based on predicate logic, we can reason about them in ways that enable us to: (i) prove they satisfy certain fundamental criteria in respect of point (a) above; (ii) increase our confidence in their validity, i.e., in respect of point (b) above. Notice that according to our definitions of 'validation' and 'verification', acts of the latter can contribute to the former.

We are bound to ask: precisely which properties of a system specification do we therefore seek to establish by proof? The answer splits into several categories. To help discuss them, we make use of the '⊢ notation', first seen in a side condition of a 'reasoning rule' used in the lengthy precondition calculation of Section 8.4 (see page 224). The symbol ⊢ is called 'turnstile', and a construct of the form

    Hyp ⊢ Cnc

is called a *sequent*. Until proven, a sequent represents a *claim* or *conjecture* to the effect that its *conclusion* part Cnc follows—can be deduced/inferred—from its *hypothesis* part Hyp. To verify the conjecture, we construct a strand of reasoning using properties of logic, data types, schemas, etc. which shows that Cnc can indeed by deduced from Hyp. Here is a simple example, being a claim about the Online Monitor specification:

$$\text{Computer} \vdash \text{users} \neq \varnothing \tag{9.1}$$

(see page 201 for Computer). This claim could be read as 'from the Computer schema, we can infer that users ≠ ∅' or more simply 'the users component of Computer is never empty'. Is this the case? The obvious tactic is to look at Computer, particularly its predicate. One component of this predicate is

    sysManager ∈ priv

It therefore follows by a simple property of sets that

    priv ≠ ∅

since, by the previous predicate, priv must consist of at least one element. But the Computer predicate also says

    priv ⊆ users

Hence, by another simple property of sets (if A ⊆ B and A ≠ ∅, then B ≠ ∅)

    users ≠ ∅

which thus establishes claim (9.1).

The above argument, were it formalized in a manner briefly indicated in Section 2.1 (i.e., by the use of inference rules), would be a *proof*. Logical arguments are just informal proofs. Once a sequent has been proven, it becomes a *theorem*. So we have shown sequent (9.1) to be a theorem of the Online Monitor specification, although it is not a particularly useful one. To validate specifications, theorems somewhat deeper than that typified by our example are involved. Many of these theorems come from a standard 'repertoire'. This repertoire has to do with establishing specification *consistency*. Loosely, a consistent Z specification is one that 'can exist' as a mathematical object. More importantly, this means that the specification can then be 'refined' (see Section 9.2) into code. We now discuss the main areas of specification consistency addressable by theorem proving.

Verifying Consistency

CONSISTENCY OF GLOBAL DEFINITIONS

One area where consistency problems can arise concerns free types, as already briefly noted on pages 184–185. If we keep to the guidelines suggested there, our free type definitions will be safe. More generally, it is possible to prove a certain theorem to verify that a given free type 'exists', though this is quite beyond the scope of this text. Interested readers can consult Smith (1992) for further details.

As a simple example of the more general kind of problem to avoid, consider the following axiomatic description (see also page 169):

$$
\begin{array}{|l}
\text{sign} : \mathbb{Z} \to \mathbb{Z} \\
\hline
\forall n : \mathbb{Z} \bullet \\
\quad (n \leq 0 \Rightarrow \text{sign } n = -1) \wedge \\
\quad (n \geq 0 \Rightarrow \text{sign } n = 1)
\end{array}
$$

This description is inconsistent since one consequence of its axiom is that `sign 0 = -1` and `sign 0 = 1`, which contradicts `sign`'s declaration asserting that it belongs to a certain class of function. Formally, checking the consistency of an axiomatic description which is the text GlobalDecs | GlobalPred means establishing the theorem

$\vdash \exists$ GlobalDecs $\bullet$ GlobalPred

In effect, 'there exist values for GlobalDecs which satisfy predicate GlobalPred'. Some theorems, like this one, are written with an empty hypothesis part. Actually, the hypothesis part of a specification thereom is never really empty because it is always taken to include all the data type laws of Z's mathematical toolkit, plus any axiomatic descriptions in the specification text preceding the one under consideration. Preceding descriptions must of course themselves be consistent, otherwise we could prove anything we wanted! It is a property of logic that, from inconsistent hypotheses, anything can be deduced, even 'nonsensical' results such as contradictions.

CONSISTENCY OF STATE MODEL
We need to be sure that the state model is consistent and that the system can start off its life in a sensible state. This check can be expressed as a theorem which has the following general form:

$\vdash \exists$ State' $\bullet$ InitState

which can be extended to

$\vdash \exists$ State'; Inputs? $\bullet$ InitState

if the initial state schema InitState has input variables. In effect: 'there is a state of the general model (and inputs if InitState has any) that satisfies the initial state description'. Proving this theorem not only establishes consistency between State and InitState, but also consistency of State itself in the sense that it describes a non-empty state space, i.e., its predicate does not collapse to `false`.

The argument on pages 51–52 informally verified the claim that

$\vdash \exists$ `DigitalWatch`'; cym? : $\mathbb{N} \bullet$ `InitDigitalWatch` (9.2)

Proving state consistency with a bit more rigour than pages 51–52 is sometimes not all that arduous. One strategy is to unfold the schema references in the sequent and do some rearranging as shown in Section 8.4 for precondition calculation. So, assuming we were setting out to prove (9.2), we could transform its conclusion part by a combination of schema unfolding and application of the $\exists$hide rules (page 217). This would give (eliding top-level $\wedge$'s below $\exists$)

$\vdash \exists\, \mathtt{t'} : 0..1439;\; \mathtt{dy'} : 1..31;\; \mathtt{mn'} : 1..12;\; \mathtt{yr'},\mathtt{cym?} : \mathbb{N} \bullet$

    $\mathtt{yr'} \geq \mathtt{bottomYr}$

    $\mathtt{ajsn(\,mn'\,)} \Rightarrow \mathtt{dy'} \leq 30$

    $\mathtt{mn'} = 2 \Rightarrow \mathtt{dy'} \leq 29$

    $\mathtt{mn'} = 2 \land \neg\, \mathtt{leapYr(\,yr'\,)} \Rightarrow \mathtt{dy'} \leq 28$

    $\mathtt{t'} = 0$

    $\mathtt{dy'} = \mathtt{mn'} = 1$

    $\mathtt{yr'} = \mathtt{cym?}$

Using onePtRule (page 219), the last four equalities can be used to simplify the quantification to give the sequent

$\vdash \exists\, \mathtt{cym?} : \mathbb{N} \bullet$

    $\mathtt{cym?} \geq \mathtt{bottomYr}$

    $\mathtt{ajsn(\,1\,)} \Rightarrow 1 \leq 30$

    $1 = 2 \Rightarrow 1 \leq 29$

    $1 = 2 \land \neg\, \mathtt{leapYr(\,cym?\,)} \Rightarrow \mathtt{cym?} \leq 28$

The three implications are each equivalent to `true` because their antecedents are equivalent to `false` (a basic property of logic), so we can simplify further to

$$\vdash \exists\, \mathtt{cym?} : \mathbb{N} \bullet \mathtt{cym?} \geq \mathtt{bottomYr} \qquad\qquad (9.3)$$

since `P` $\land$ `true` is just `P` (another simple property of logic). By finding a value for `cym?` which makes the following true:

    $\mathtt{cym?} \geq \mathtt{bottomYr}$

it follows that (9.3) holds. Finding such a value is easy here; `bottomYr` itself is good enough. So, since (9.3) is just an equivalent simplification of (9.2), this establishes (9.2).

CONSISTENCY OF OPERATIONS

As with a state schema, we would not want the binding space of an operation schema to be empty because the operation description is inconsistent, its predicate collapsing to `false`. For an operation which is the text OpDecs | OpPred, the consistency theorem is

    $\vdash \exists\, \mathsf{OpDecs} \bullet \mathsf{OpPred}$

In practice, we can check for an operation's consistency by calculating its precondition (see Section 8.4). If the operation is inconsistent, its precondition will be `false`. So a false precondition strongly suggests a defect in the operation description, though it is possible that the cause of the problem lies elsewhere, e.g., with a global variable that is being referenced in the operation.

Supporting Validity

The previous three categories represent the standard repertoire of consistency theorems to prove for any specification. Note how consistency can be *proved*, since the checking involves reasoning about *the formal descriptions alone*. However, consistency proofs on their own are not quite good enough. A specification can be consistent, but it still might not be 'valid' in the more general sense of describing the system that should be built. In other words, the specification could describe something which is implementable, but contains features/properties that are just plainly 'wrong' or are not in accordance with the requirements.

Unlike consistency, validity cannot be 'proved' precisely because it requires reference to the client, domain, and/or requirements. The best we can do in terms of theorem proving is to construct particular conjectures about the specification which, if proven, will add to our conviction that it really is a valid description of the system to be built. Some of these conjectures might still be 'internal', i.e., constructed by the specifiers to increase their confidence in the specification's validity. For example, a collection of operations over a state should be checked for properties that lead us to conclude that they describe the behaviour we think they describe. Consider the Van Hire system. The specification includes `MakeBooking` and `CancelBooking` operations, since this is what the client wants. However, we might raise the following conjecture:

$$\texttt{MakeBooking}\,\fatsemi\,\texttt{CancelBooking} \vdash \Xi\texttt{VanHire} \qquad (9.4)$$

That is, we are claiming that making a booking and then immediately cancelling it should leave the state of the system unchanged. Obviously, we would expect to be able to prove this conjecture. But if we were unable to, this raises a red warning flag. Something must be wrong somewhere, and we should look for bugs in the specification. Note that it is possible for a conjecture like (9.4) to 'fall down', even though each individual schema occurring in it is consistent.

Other conjectures raised might be 'external', i.e., inspired by the client. Obviously, we would like to establish that a state model is a valid abstraction of the reality it is intended to model, and that the operations over the state represent a functionality that the client actually wants. The client can raise questions/issues at a review, say, some of which might be formalizable as conjectures about the specification. These conjectures can then be subjected to proof. For example, the Online Monitor client might ask:

Sometimes there can be no connections to a machine because it is temporarily down for an anticipated short period; but we still want users to be able to queue in readiness for when it becomes available again. Your specification should cater for this. Does it?

Buried just below the surface of this question is a conjecture that can be formalized. It is: 'a machine can be in a state where there are no connections but its connect queue is non-empty'. This can be expressed as the sequent:

$$\vdash \exists\,\texttt{Computer} \bullet \texttt{cnnctd} = \varnothing \wedge \texttt{cnnctQu} \neq \texttt{emptyq} \qquad (9.5)$$

Proving the sequent answers the client's query in the affirmative, which in turn increases confidence in the `Computer` model. In fact, if you answered Exercise 8.2(3d), you were in effect arguing that (9.5) holds for Model I of the Online Monitor state.

Validation techniques applicable to specifications of whatever persuasion include review, constructing prototypes, even specification execution with some development methods. The pay-off with formal specifications is that consistency proofs, and proofs supporting validity, come as a valuable bonus. The standard consistency checks represent *proof obligations*. The word 'obligation' is entirely appropriate, i.e., it behoves us to carry out the required proofs. Proving well-chosen validity-supporting conjectures is also highly desirable. If we do not carry out proofs of these kinds, then: (a) we are not exploiting the full potential of formal notations; (b) we are in danger of letting through to the next development stage a specification that is inconsistent and hence unimplementable, or is defective in some other way, e.g., because it lacks a desired or essential property, or contains an unwanted one.

Nevertheless, we must always keep a clear mind about what can be proved and what cannot. Then we will never be in danger of making false claims about the scope and efficacy of mathematical verification. If a delivered system exhibits functional behaviour that deviates from its specification, it is clearly 'invalid'. Yet, if a delivered system behaves correctly with respect to a thoroughly validated Z specification, but it has a grotesque user interface and/or exhibits inadequate performance, it is hardly likely to be regarded as 'valid' either.

EXERCISE 9.1

1. Prove that the `Computer` state model is consistent, making use of the initial state in the answer to Exercise 8.4(1). Apply the reasoning technique illustrated on page 239 for the Digital Watch state schema, aiming to reduce the sequent's conclusion predicate to just `true`. This approach works well with the suggested initial state since it contains an equality for each `Computer` variable.

2. Using the appropriate consistency theorem stated in the text, prove that operation `Swap` in the following is inconsistent (*Hint*: inconsistency leads to false conclusions).

   ```
   State ≙ [a,b : ℤ | a < b]
   Swap ≙ [ΔState | a' = b ∧ b' = a]
   ```

9.2 DESIGN AND IMPLEMENTATION

Refinement

Once a specification has been validated, design and implementation work can begin. In formal methods, the path from specification to code is more of a continuum of development—more so than suggested by Figure 1.2 on page 11. We can define *design* to be the process of deriving concrete, computer-oriented specifications (though still not containing code) from validated abstract, user-oriented ones to which the former must conform. *Implementation* is the subsequent process which takes a design and transforms it into actual code, again ensuring conformity which is now judged against the design. The general effect of both processes is to increase detail and inelegance in descriptions, and constrain development choices, at the expense of abstraction and simplicity.

It is important to emphasize that not all aspects of design and implementation are formal or formalizable. For example, suppose you have to decide how to organize the Van Hire system data over a small network: is it all held on one server? is it partitioned across more than one machine? if so, which ones? are copies kept? etc. Decision-making of this kind requires software engineering skills and considerations lying outside the formal methods boundary. Thus, we will not be concerned here with physical issues and aspects of software infrastructure, vitally important though they are, e.g., to system performance.

WIDE SPECTRUM?

The abstraction gulf between an abstract Z specification and target code is generally large. This is not always so—consider, for example, implementing the Digital Watch system in software to simulate the passing of time and days. However, a large gulf is the usual reality, and the problem is to find a way of bridging it. The following possibility may at first seem tempting: use a single formal notation that integrates the abstract descriptive power of Z with the concrete 'algorithm formulation power' of a typical modern programming language. Thus, our SuperZ would also include notations enabling us to describe program data structures like arrays and operation imperatives such as assignment, looping, etc. SuperZ would then offer a smooth, seamless transition from abstract specifications to code.

... Or would it? SuperZ would be an exceedingly baroque creation. 'Ordinary' Z is of a complexity that makes it comfortable to handle; it would be a backward step to degrade Z's elegance and impose potential brain overload on its users. The world already has its fair share of unduly complex, unwieldy notations (no names mentioned!). Moreover, the mathematical basis and semantics of SuperZ would shoot up in complexity compared to standard Z. Perhaps most importantly of all, we would be in danger of misusing SuperZ and so defeating the aims of abstract specification. We would be tempted to specify program-oriented solutions to problems before we had even properly understood and described what the problems were.

If one rejects the idea of a single wide-spectrum notation, one must replace it by ways of combining, and smoothly moving between, different notations in a secure manner. In formal methods, this is partly what the process of *refinement* achieves. However, not only does the refinement process get us from Z descriptions to code, it also—and this is a crucial point—enables our development decisions to be verified formally, or even 'correctly calculated'. 'Refinement' is somewhat of a misnomer since proceeding from the relative elegance of abstract specifications to the increased messiness of designs and target code is hardly a refining process, but the term is easier on the ear than the more accurate alternative of 'reification' preferred by some.

We can express the overall refinement scenario as follows:

$$\text{AbsZSpec} \sqsubseteq \text{PLCode} \tag{9.6}$$

The relation $\sqsubseteq$ can be verbalized as 'is refined by'; it was briefly mentioned on pages 9–10. Here, AbsZSpec is the first, most abstract Z specification constructed, and PLCode is the final concrete form of the specification implemented in some chosen programming language (PL). We want sentence (9.6) to be true. This means broadly that:

> Whenever PLCode is applied in circumstances that 'are consistent with' the preconditions of AbsZSpec's operations, the behaviour produced—state-transition and inputs-to-outputs— 'correctly corresponds to' that which AbsZSpec describes in those circumstances.

The intended effect of refinement can be likened to that of 'simulation': a client, expecting a product described by AbsZSpec, actually gets delivered PLCode, but on running PLCode under the conditions described in AbsZSpec, observes behaviour in accordance with AbsZSpec. The client is therefore happy to accept PLCode.

Here is one main approach that can be used to get to PL code from an AbsZSpec. The refinement task is divided into two main phases:

- *Phase I:*   We take AbsZSpec down to a level, call it ConcZSpec, which *is still written in* Z but which is expressed in terms of data types that are suitable for direct translation into PL. This phase, the design phase, is driven by a process called *data refinement*.

- *Phase II:*   We now take ConcZSpec and gradually transform its components into PL constructs until a complete translation into PL algorithms has been obtained. This phase, the implementation phase, is driven by a process called *operation refinement*.

Providing we discharge any necessary proof obligations along the way, we will have arrived at a correct implementation in the sense conveyed by the refinement techniques we use. Recall from page 10 that we require $\sqsubseteq$ to be transitive to make things work:

      if $A \sqsubseteq B$ and $B \sqsubseteq C$ **then** $A \sqsubseteq C$

This property is essential because we do not necessarily accomplish Phase I, and particularly not Phase II, in one go, but by a series of one or more intermediate steps. Figure 9.1 gives a diagrammatic overview of the refinement task.

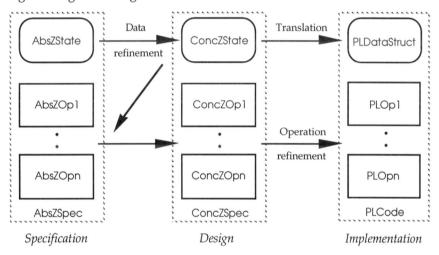

Figure 9.1   A global view of the refinement task.

In some circumstances, it could be that all state components in AbsZSpec can be adequately represented directly as PL data types and data structures, as with the Digital Watch specification. In that case, no data refinement is necessary. Even then, however, certain preliminary refinements to operations might still need to be performed before reaching a stage in the development where actual code begins to emerge.

Data Refinement

The data refinement phase, essentially the process of constructing a concrete data type which simulates an abstract one, can be broken down into two main components:

- The abstract state of AbsZSpec, call it AbsZState, must be 'adequately represented' by concrete types available in PL, i.e., by a concrete state, say ConcZState.

- Each operation AbsZOp over AbsZState must be correctly recast as an operation ConcZOp over ConcZState.

Note that we are giving the general view here for refining a state-based abstract data type. Not all data types that need refining are expressed as state-based models (though they might contribute to such). However, the refinement approach would be similar: construct a set ConcValSp which is a more concrete representation of the abstract value space AbsValSp, and then re-define the various constants, relations and functions to 'have the equivalent behaviour' over ConcValSp. For example, with a data type like `Date` (see Section 7.1), we expect to be able to implement the value space directly, using a record data structure, say. But if `Queue` (see Section 7.3) was going to be implemented as a linked list, we would first need to find a way of describing linked lists in Z; then we would respecify `addq`, `remq`, etc. over this concrete value space.

Space and scope constraints do not permit us to describe data refinement in any great detail, but here is an overview of what is involved using a 'toy' example. The form of data refinement we describe is not the most general form, but it is sufficient for a large number of situations. In the most general form, some of the theorems we subsequently describe would be more complicated.

Suppose we have this abstract state:

$$\mid \texttt{maxSize} : \mathbb{N}$$

```
┌─ NatNumSet ────────────────────────────────────────────────────┐
│ s : ℙ ℕ                                                          │
│─────────────────────────                                        │
│ #s ≤ maxSize                                                     │
└─────────────────────────────────────────────────────────────────┘
```

It has this initial state:

```
┌─ InitNatNumSet ─────────────────────────────────────────────────┐
│ NatNumSet'                                                       │
│─────────────────                                                │
│ s' = ∅                                                           │
└─────────────────────────────────────────────────────────────────┘
```

and one of its operations is

```
┌─ Remove ────────────────────────────────────────────────────────┐
│ ΔNatNumSet                                                       │
│ x? : ℕ                                                           │
│─────────────────                                                │
│ s' = s \ { x? }                                                  │
└─────────────────────────────────────────────────────────────────┘
```

We first note that this operation has a precondition which is

```
true
```

(check this by calculation—see Section 8.4 again!).

We decide to implement the set as an array with an index variable:

```
a : array [ 1..maxSize ] of Natural
nels : 0..maxSize
```

where the first `nels` elements of the array are those in use. Mathematically, our array is simply a sequence with an upper bound on its length. We also wish to keep the array sorted for fast lookup. So our choice of data structuring can be described in Z as

```
┌─ NatNumArray ─────────────────────────────────────────────┐
│ a : seq ℕ                                                  │
│ nels : 0..maxSize                                          │
├───────────────────────────────────────────────────────────┤
│ #a = nels                                                  │
│ ∀ i,j : dom a • i < j ⇒ a(i) < a(j)                        │
└───────────────────────────────────────────────────────────┘
```

Note that the 'sorted' invariant in `NatNumArray` also ensures no duplicates are kept in the array. The concrete initial state is:

```
┌─ InitNatNumArray ─────────────────────────────────────────┐
│ NatNumArray'                                               │
├───────────────────────────────────────────────────────────┤
│ a' = ⟨⟩                                                    │
└───────────────────────────────────────────────────────────┘
```

The abstract `Remove` operation is re-expressed as the concrete operation

```
┌─ RemElem ─────────────────────────────────────────────────┐
│ ΔNatNumArray                                               │
│ x? : ℕ                                                     │
├───────────────────────────────────────────────────────────┤
│ a' = a ↾ (ran a \ {x?})                                    │
└───────────────────────────────────────────────────────────┘
```

This operation also has a precondition which is

```
true
```

Again, check this by calculation (remember that if the elements of a sequence t obey an ordering property, then so will the elements of the sequence $t ↾ X$ for any legitimate X).

The problem now is, how do we know for sure that the design correctly simulates what is abstractly described? We split the verification task into three main checks:

Concrete State Adequacy: *Does the concrete state 'adequately represent' the abstract one?*
There are three facets to answering this question. Firstly, it is not surprising that we require the concrete state to be consistent, just like its abstract partner! So we need to show in general that

$$⊢ ∃ \, ConcState' • InitConcState \tag{9.7}$$

which in our example is

$$⊢ ∃ \, NatNumArray' • InitNatNumArray$$

The proof of this theorem is simple and left to the reader.

Secondly, and simplifying considerably, we need to ask: does every abstract state have at least one concrete representative? One way to determine this is to see if each abstract variable can be derived, or 'retrieved', from the concrete ones by writing down equalities of the form

AbsVar = Expr(ConcVars)

In our example, this is also simple:

s = ran a

We will refer to this predicate as the 'retrieve relation' CARel (concrete-to-abstract relation). It can be documented in a schema that brings together the abstract and concrete states:

```
┌─CARel──────────────────────────────────────────┐
│ NatNumSet                                        │
│ NatNumArray                                      │
│ ─────────────────                                │
│ s = ran a                                        │
└──────────────────────────────────────────────────┘
```

This schema plays a vital role in other theorems. The equality means that CARel is in effect a total function when viewed as 'calculating' the abstract state from the concrete one. Being total means that every concrete state maps to some abstract state. (*Note*: it is this implicit property of the retrieve relation being functional and total which characterizes the fact that we are discussing a simplified form of data refinement.)

Suppose we relaxed the data design a little by removing the 'sorted' invariant from NatNumArray so that array element order was immaterial (we might still sensibly insist that no duplicates were stored in the array). Now the design would include some redundancy—each non-empty, non-singleton set in the abstract state would have more than one concrete representative. For example, the abstract state

$\langle s \Rightarrow \{0,1\} \rangle$

would have two concrete representatives:

$\langle a \Rightarrow \langle 0,1 \rangle, nels \Rightarrow 2 \rangle$
$\langle a \Rightarrow \langle 1,0 \rangle, nels \Rightarrow 2 \rangle$

In general, assuming no duplicates, there would be nels! (factorial nels) concrete representatives for a single abstract state. Such redundancy is harmless and a common consequence of data refinement. Note that it does not compromise the implicit functionality of a retrieve relation like CARel above because the relation expresses a calculation from *concrete to abstract*. In fact, CARel would still hold even if array a were allowed to contain multiple instances of values.

The third and final aspect of checking the concrete state design is to verify that the concrete initial state is correct—it must not describe initial states that have no counterpart in the abstract model. To show this, we prove a theorem of the form

Given the retrieve relation then:
    InitConcState ⊢ InitAbsState   (9.8)

which in effect says 'for each concrete initial state, there is a corresponding abstract one'. In our example, this means proving the sequent (why the ′ decoration?)

Given CARel′ *then:*
    InitNatNumArray ⊢ InitNatNumSet

which is left as an exercise. Note that the retrieve relation now plays a role in the theorem—necessarily so, since to prove the theorem we need to relate two different sets of variables.

The 'direction' of (9.8) is worth noting. In theorems, weaker predicates go on the *right* of the turnstile, just as they go on the right of $\Rightarrow$ in true implications. So (9.8) allows the concrete initial state space to be *narrower* than in the abstract model. Providing every concrete initial state has an abstract counterpart, that is good enough; it is not necessary for every abstract initial state to have a concrete representative. Theorem (9.8) is sufficient to ensure that the implemented system will start off life in a 'sensible' state. If (9.8) were 'the other way round', this would permit some concrete initial states to have *no* abstract counterparts, which is hardly a recipe for guaranteeing that subsequent system behaviour will conform to the abstract specification.

Concrete Operation Applicability: *For each concrete–abstract operation pair, is the former applicable over its state whenever the latter is applicable over its state?*
This check ensures that each concrete operation has an applicability that at least encompasses its abstract partner. To show this requires proving theorems of the form

> *Given the retrieve relation then:*
> pre AbsOp ⊢ pre ConcOp $\qquad\qquad\qquad\qquad\qquad\qquad$ (9.9)

In our example, we need to prove that

> *Given* CARel *then:*
> pre Remove ⊢ pre RemElem

Because the right-hand side is schema text, its declaration part—which will be schema reference NatNumArray and variable x? : $\mathbb{N}$—as well as its predicate must be derivable from the left-hand side. Since CARel acts as an extra hypothesis, we can see that NatNumArray in pre RemElem is provided by CARel. Also, variable x? in pre RemElem is the same as the x? of pre Remove. This means it is valid to re-arrange the sequent by unfolding its left-hand side and writing just the conclusion's *predicate* on the right-hand side of the turnstile. Doing so, we obtain:

> CARel; NatNumSet; x? : $\mathbb{N}$ |
> $\qquad$ true ⊢ true

This sequent is trivially a theorem and so RemElem passes its applicability check. It is worth remembering that a sequent with any of the following simple shapes:

> D | P ⊢ true
> D | P ⊢ P
> D | P∧Q ⊢ P $\qquad\qquad$ —*or* Q

is a theorem. This is because respectively: true trivially holds irrespective of any hypotheses; every predicate is its own inference; and if we have P ∧ Q, then we certainly at least have P (or Q) More generally, a sequent

> D | P ⊢ $Q_1 \wedge \ldots Q_n$

is a theorem provided each Q_i on the right-hand side can be deduced from the left-hand side.

Again, note theorem 'directionality', this time as expressed in (9.9). If (9.9) were 'the other way round', we would be restricting the situations where it is safe to apply the concrete operation, compared to the abstract operation. This in turn would not ensure that all behaviours of which the abstract operation is capable of producing were being simulated in the design. To avoid being unnecessarily restrictive, (9.9) requires concrete preconditions to be at least as liberal as their abstract counterparts. Furthermore, an implementor might see a way of widening the applicability of an operation over a concrete state without compromising the acceptability of the operation's behaviour as seen by the client. Theorem template (9.9) caters for this possibility also.

Concrete Operation Correctness: *For each concrete–abstract operation pair, does the concrete operation, when applied in circumstances conforming to its abstract partner's applicability, produce behaviour which its abstract partner would be capable of producing?*
This sounds the most complicated of the three checks. Theorem-wise, behaviour correctness is assured by proving

$$\text{Given the retrieve relation then:}$$
$$\texttt{pre AbsOp} \wedge \texttt{ConcOp} \vdash \texttt{AbsOp} \tag{9.10}$$

So in our example, we need to show that

$$\text{Given } \Delta\texttt{CARel then:}$$
$$\texttt{pre Remove} \wedge \texttt{RemElem} \vdash \texttt{Remove}$$

You are asked to try to prove this sequent in the next exercise. Note that both `CARel` and `CARel'` are needed since operations involve before and after states.

The composition and 'direction' of (9.10) is also worth comment. Unlike (9.9), this time the reference to the concrete operation appears on the *left* of the turnstile, not the right. Behaviour of a concrete operation cannot somehow 'produce more than' its abstract partner in 'equivalent' circumstances; however, it may be *narrower*, i.e., more deterministic. What is important is that the concrete operation's behaviour, when 'seen through' Δ`CARel`, is behaviour the abstract operation could produce—with a proviso. Since, by (9.9), `ConcOp`'s applicability can be wider than `AbsOp`, we must consider `ConcOp`'s behaviour only when the *abstract* precondition holds. This is why `pre AbsOp` also appears on the left-hand side of the turnstile—we cannot judge `ConcOp`'s behaviour against `AbsOp`'s in situations that do not correspondingly apply to the latter.

Increased determinism in behaviour is a typical consequence of design and implementation decision-making. In Online Monitor, when a user requests a line to a computer, she does not care which one she is given as long as it is working! The fact that the algorithm to do this might always choose the free line with the 'lowest index' is inconsequential. Similarly, if a program to calculate the square root of a number always outputs the positive result, this is quite OK even if its specification stated that either the positive or negative root would be acceptable.

Once the concrete state and each of its operations have passed all these checks, we know the concrete data type to be a correct simulation of the abstract one. Obviously, carrying out data refinement in a strict manner on a non-trivial specification can involve a lot of arduous, symbol-heavy proof work. One of the difficulties in post-specification phases, especially perhaps in operation refinement (see later), is to find an acceptable balance between applying thereom proving in the way refinement methods strictly require against the day-to-day practical realities of cost-effective software engineering. We comment further on this at the end of the chapter.

EXERCISE 9.2

1. Suppose in a data refinement several *abstract* states had the same concrete representative. What do you think this might mean, and what consequences would it have for the form of data refinement discussed in the text?

2. Construct a Z state model corresponding to the program data structure

   `matrix :` **array** `[1..N,1..M]` **of** `INTEGER`

   given that only the first K rows and first L columns of the array are in use at any particular moment (K, or L, or both, can be zero).

3. Prove the correctness theorem for concrete initial state `InitNatNumArray` in the text. First, check that declarations on the right-hand side of the turnstile are provided for on the left. Then unfold the sequent into a D | P ⊢ Q shape to proceed.

4. In the data refinement example of the text, suppose `Remove` was kept as described but `RemElem`'s predicate was modified to include

   `x? ∈ ran a`

   Establish the correctness or otherwise of the refinement.

5. Prove the correctness theorem for operation `RemElem` in the text. The proof is quite tricky (*Hint*: try to 'discover' a guarded equality law for sequences involving the operator ↾ and function `ran` on one side of the equality).

Operation Refinement

Having obtained a validated, fully data-refined specification, the task now is to implement it. By 'fully data-refined', we mean the whole of the state is now expressed at a level of abstraction corresponding to the data structures of the target PL. So the problem is to turn the operation specifications correctly into code. We could, of course, use inspiration to implement algorithms for the operations, then test the algorithms with well-chosen test cases to check that the observed behaviour is consistent with what the concrete specification describes. But the whole point of refinement is to improve on this traditional method and its inherent weaknesses (see Section 1.1). There are two possible approaches:

a. use inspiration to devise algorithms, then verify (by some suitable formal reasoning apparatus) that they conform to the concrete operation specifications
b. gradually transform each concrete operation into an algorithm using rules and checks which guarantee correctness is being maintained in the step-by-step decision-making.

For approach (a) to work, we would need rules that enable us to reason about the behaviour of the constructs used to build PL algorithms, and some way of relating the reasoning back to the concrete Z specification.

A brief moment's thought, however, should suggest that (b) is better than (a). Apart from (b) guaranteeing correctness *as the code emerges*, the main problem with approach (a) lies in conducting *post hoc* correctness proofs. For non-trivial algorithms, this kind of verification is arduous. Far better to refine the algorithm in smallish, comfortably handlable steps, ensuring that each step is correct. In the long run, this approach will be easier for the implementor and is likely to be more cost-effective, due to less defects generated and hence repair work needed.

Approach (b) is generally referred to as *operation refinement*, or *operation decomposition* because of the top-down nature of the process. Note that the term 'operation refinement' is normally used when refinement over the *same* state space is taking place. For operation refinement to work, we will need:

- A toolkit of refinement rules that allow us piecemeal to introduce correct fragments of greater operational detail as expressed by the various constructs of the target PL.

- A way of writing mixed descriptions in this sense: until we have fully refined an operation to code, parts of the operation description (initially none of it) will be described in PL code (the bits already fully refined), and parts of it (initially all of it) will be specification text (the bits still to be refined).

Even then, we are faced with a further decision. Do we

- retain Z (or Z-like) syntax for the specification components during operation refinement, or …
- use a different notation for specification components which is purpose-built for operation refinement?

Both approaches have emerged in the Z community; see Wordsworth (1992) for the former, Morgan (1990) or Woodcock (1992) for the latter. A disadvantage of the latter, referred to as the 'Refinement Calculus', is that, because it uses different notations and conventions to Z, a way is needed of carefully transforming Z specifications into Refinement Calculus specifications (see King (1990)). The advantage is that refinement proceeds more by 'calculation' with a concomitant reduction in the proof obligation burden in certain situations. In fact, the Refinement Calculus also embraces data refinement as well as operation refinement. So, starting with an abstract Z specification, it is possible, after some initial transformation, to use a single refinement system to get down to code.

Typically, in any system of operation refinement, there are rules which permit

- introduction of assignment statements
- introduction of various algorithm structures: sequential composition, selection (multi *if-then* type statements), looping (usually the *while* variety), etc.
- introduction of blocks and local variables
- declaring procedures, with or without parameters.

There will also be many other rules, dependent on the particular refinement system being used, which are concerned with refining specification components in ways that affect the strength of their constituent predicates, the variables they are allowed to access/update, etc. Space constraints permit only a fleeting glimpse of the tip of a small iceberg. Consider again RemElem on page 245. Although this is a data-refined operation, its predicate still looks rather abstract and 'unprogram-like'. Suppose we refine RemElem into RemElem1 opposite This looks far worse, yet it is what we need—it is much more program-oriented! RemElem1 says: if x? is not in the array, nothing changes, but if x? is in the array, it gets removed from its position i, leaving an updated, but still contiguous, sequence:

```
┌─ RemElem1 ─────────────────────────────────────────────────────────┐
│ ΔNatNumArray                                                        │
│ x? : ℕ                                                              │
│ ──────────────────────────────────────────────                     │
│ x? ∉ ran a ⇒                                                        │
│    θ NatNumArray' = θ NatNumArray                                   │
│ x? ∈ ran a ⇒                                                        │
│    ( ∃ i : 1..nels •                                                │
│        a( i ) = x? ∧ a' = ( ( 1..i - 1 )↑a )⌢( ( i + 1..nels )↑a )  ) ∧  │
│    nels' = nels - 1                                                 │
└─────────────────────────────────────────────────────────────────────┘
```

RemElem1 is typical of moving towards code—messy detail increases. But it is perhaps easier to see how RemElem1, rather than RemElem, might be refined into an algorithm looking something like this:

> [*lookFor*(*x?*, *a*, *i*, *found*)]
> **if** ¬ found **then** **skip**
> **elsif** found **then**
>   [*shiftDownOne*(*a*, *i*)]
>   nels := nels - 1
> **end if**

This description is discussed further in the next exercise. The bracketed italics is intended to indicate that the constructs involved are specification components which need to be subjected to further refinement to reach code. We might eventually refine *lookFor*, for example, into an efficient algorithm such as binary search (remember that array a is kept sorted). In fact, most refinement systems take specifications down to algorithms expressed in a *guarded command language*, which is slightly different from the above 'Esperanto' programming language. To find out more about guarded commands etc., consult the references quoted earlier.

EXERCISE 9.3

1. What theorem(s) would you have to prove to verify that RemElem1 is a correct refinement of RemElem (you are relieved from doing any actual proof!).

2. Explain what you perceive to be the relationships between the code/specification mixture above and the predicate of the Z specification of RemElem1.

3. Using NatNumArray in the text, show that BnOp correctly refines AnOp, where:

   > AnOp ≙ [ΔNatNumArray; size! : ℕ |
   >   a ≠ ⟨ ⟩ ∧ size! = nels ∧ ran a' ⊆ ran a]
   > BnOp ≙ [ΔNatNumArray; size! : ℕ |
   >   size! = nels ∧ nels' = 0]

   In what important respects does BnOp differ from AnOp? What do you expect the code derived by refinement from BnOp to look like?

9.3   SOME ISSUES OF PRACTICE

Tools

Any practical method contributing to software engineering needs some kind of CASE support if it is going to be taken up by practitioners in the field. Well-designed, functionally specific toolkits with an appropriate degree of integration between components can

- carry out essential processes that only machines can do really well
- simplify task complexity, organizationally or otherwise
- reduce the chance of making silly mistakes
- aid in the intellectual processes required in software engineering.

For a software development method based on Z, we would expect support in one or more of the following areas: specification construction; theorem proving; refinement. Figure 9.2 outlines an integrated toolkit incorporating all these components.

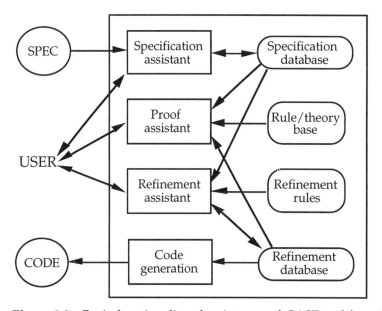

Figure 9.2   Basic functionality of an integrated CASE tool for a 'formal method'.

The specification assistant would function as an editor and as a syntax/type checker, making sure that only syntactically correct specifications were used for further development (isolated fragments apart, all Z paragraphs appearing in this book have been so checked). Obviously, the editor would be dedicated to the Z notation, supplying highly tailored functionality as well as all the expected facilities of a reasonable editor. For example, as well as having a font for all the special characters, we might expect to be able to fold and unfold schema definitions, have a 'goto' facility that takes us directly to a particular schema definition, be able to instantiate a 'schema template' when about to construct a fresh schema, call up an overview of the schema structure of a specification, etc. In an integrated toolkit, the specification assistant would create a specification database—an internal representation of specifications that would be suitable for sharing with other tools applicable later in the development process.

As well as a specification assistant, one would require a proof assistant to help with theorem proving at the abstract specification level and later during refinement. The proof assistant would provide a basic system of logic, plus the various data type theories which make up Z's mathematical toolkit. The proof assistant should have a facility whereby new data type theories could be added into its 'rule base' so that, over a period of time, the tool's library of data types and associated laws would grow. Housekeeping in manual proof construction can be particularly tiresome, and a proof assistant would obviously remove the chance of making mistakes caused simply by dealing with the large volume of symbols sometimes involved. The more subtle errors that arise from invalid deductions due to incorrect use of the logic would also be blocked. For example, in some instances a proof assistant could check that side conditions are being satisfied in application of a rule (see Section 8.4 for examples of rules with side conditions).

Although checking claimed proofs can be automated, proof construction itself cannot be fully automated for proving arbitrary conjectures. However, it is possible to automate proof construction to some extent by building into a proof assistant various tactics that it would try in stock situations, before—whenever necessary—giving up and requesting help from the user. In addition, one could reasonably expect part of the 'slog' of Z precondition calculation/simplification to be automated—it is possible, for example, to automate application of rules like the 'one point rule' (see page 219).

The proof assistant would clearly play a role in refinement, supporting the discharge of proof obligations like proving theorems associated with data refinement. It would be useful to establish and expand a library of standard data refinements. Once the refinement of a data type AbsType into ConcType has been accomplished, there should be no need to have to repeat the exercise, given that the refinement is one that is likely to occur in other projects. As regards operation refinement, the detailed nature of the tool would depend on the 'refinement paradigm' supported. For a refinement method along the lines of Morgan (1990), the refinement assistant would make available the laws of the method, enabling a designer to 'calculate' the code top-down, step by step.

Formal methods, until recent times, have suffered from a lack of tools, which has been one reason (but not the only one) contributing to their slowish uptake in industry. There is now considerable activity on the tool development front. It should not be too long before there is across-the-board support for software development based on application of the Z notation coupled to a standard logic system and refinement method. The reader can find out what has recently been available by inspecting the Z Tools Catalogue (Parker 1991). This publication gives a run-down of tools being developed, what kind of support each tool provides, the tool's availability status (as of 1991), the platform(s) on which the tool can be run (Sun and IBM dominate), etc. The spectrum of support offered by the catalogued tools is quite considerable, some providing only editing, syntax and type checking facilities, for example, whilst others also provide proof obligation generation, proof checking and help with precondition calculation.

Process and People

A question potential users of a formal method might have in mind is the extent to which its application affects (their view of) the life cycle, which is something probably based on the traditional lines of Figure 1.1, page 2. Put another way: does application of formal methods require standard views of the software engineering process to be replaced by a radically different model? The answer is a qualified 'no', although one would expect certain changes at a more detailed process level to take place. One way in which the conventional process might be 'tweaked' in order to derive full benefit from formal methods is as follows. Note that no part of this scenario cuts out tried-and-trusted software engineering practice such as prototyping and reviews; rather it augments it (see the end of Chapter 1 again).

Firstly, we will assume the existence of a client who has commissioned a system and will pay for it. The term 'client' is assumed to be inclusive of 'user' or 'representative(s) of users'. Of the personnel who will develop the software, those directly responsible are split up into

- software engineers
- software builders.

The first group, the *software engineers*, is made up of those who liaise with the client, analyse their requirements and, in particular, draw up a detailed technical specification, the functional component of which will be specified in (say) Z. Software engineers will thus have to be proficient and competent in the application of formal notations for specification, and in the proof techniques needed to reason about such specifications; they will also need excellent communication skills. Their responsibility is not only to validate the specification and ensure that it describes what the client really wants, but also to ensure that the second group of people—*software builders*—actually build what the specification says. In that sense, software engineers are quality assurance champions of clients, and are contracted to ensure that they, the clients, eventually get delivered what they asked for, according to the schedule they agreed.

In a similar way, the software builders, who traditionally might be thought of as 'designers' and 'implementors', are contracted to the software engineers. Their contract is the validated technical specification drawn up by the software engineers. This contract requires them to build software that demonstrably—by proof and testing—conforms to the specification. Note that it is not even necessary for the software builders to belong to the same organization as the software engineers (in some situations, it might even be desirable that they don't, e.g., to avoid conflicts of interest). The builders might belong to a separate company in a company group, or to some completely independent organization. In such a scenario, the specification could be put out to tender. A number of different groups could then submit preliminary designs, with the software engineers having responsibility for selecting and approving the design that will be used. This kind of competitive tendering is possible even within a single organization. In a formal methods context, one can think of a preliminary design as at least comprising a data-refined specification, but possibly also including some highish levels of operation refinement too. Note that submission of preliminary designs might result in adjustment to the abstract specification—subject, of course, to client approval.

Contractual models of the software development process (see Cohen (1989)) such as just described seem to be particularly appropriate for formal methods, given the extent to which, using formality and proof, one can demonstrate that a product definitely conforms to a specification from which it has been derived. A contractual model can even be practised within a single team. For example, instead of regarding the software builders as a homogeneous group of people, some might have primary responsibility for data-refining abstract specifications to concrete form. Others would have the responsibility of carrying out operation refinement from concrete specification down to the detailed algorithm and data structure level. Their contract is with the data refiners and is represented by the concrete specification, which they are required to refine and implement correctly in the target language.

Review techniques like inspections would also play a prominent role, perhaps even more so than in traditional environments. One can envisage the inspection process being carried out by software builders for

- checking data-refined specifications against their abstract counterparts
- checking various levels of refinement
- checking encodings against final refined designs (assuming non-automated code generation).

Additionally, one would expect software engineers to have the right of audit over software builders, their methods and the artifacts that they are generating. Software engineers might even have some power of veto, with the authority to halt production and order a redesign if, say, an unacceptable number of defects was arising.

Uptake

The future for formal methods in general, and Z in particular, looks promising. The discipline is alive, well and kicking. Given the research and development activity occurring, the continuance of its present healthy state looks assured. More companies are becoming actively involved in formal methods, with many links existing between industry and academia. Formal methods have been applied in a variety of areas, including defence, telecommunications, hardware, and aviation. The size of some of the systems developed has been large (~100 K of code). Some software houses offer use of formal methods as one possible development avenue picked from a portfolio of methods they are prepared to undertake, depending on what the client requires.

Z itself has reached a point where it is in the process of being standardized. This reflects the generally held view that Z has been discussed enough and used enough to place it in a position where standardization now makes sense. There will probably be a few minor differences between the official standard and the *de facto* standard of Spivey (1992), though the practical significance of this is likely to be small. There is the associated problem of which refinement paradigm should be used, but this is an issue that is largely decoupled from deciding what the Z notation itself should be. Meanwhile, development continues in other areas with, for example, several groups looking at possible object-oriented extensions to Z (see Stepney *et al.* (1992)). There seems to be a consensus view that the object-oriented avenue is worth exploring.

Despite these healthy vibrations, the rate of uptake of the techniques by industry is perhaps slower than might have been hoped for at this stage. Uptake can partly be seen as a technology transfer problem. Also, the very term 'formal methods' may be off-putting, conjuring up the spectre of needing a higher degree in mathematics to be any good at them. A related problem is aired in Nicholls (1992), namely the differences between the 'strict' and 'liberal' approach, the former being seen as having higher turn-off value. Strictists require that all aspects of a formal method are applied if one wishes to be regarded as a proper member of the club. Liberals take the more pragmatic view that any aspect of formal methods can be applied as and when it is judged to be useful.

On large systems, *fully* formal development is currently too expensive to make sense in the context of a practical risk management strategy. In other words, the reduction in risk of wrongly building the system achievable via a strict approach cannot be justified by the cost involved of applying that approach. Therefore, perhaps what is needed is to promulgate a reasonably liberal 'formal methods culture' which

- emphasizes the need for, and benefits derivable from, abstract specifications
- stresses the importance of deriving concrete specifications which are verified to be adequate designs conforming to their validated abstract specification counterparts
- does not require strict adherence to operation refinement, except in those situations where algorithm correctness is critical.

In particular, it should be stressed that the 'benefits' mentioned in the first point alone are considerable—see the end of Chapter 1 again. At the very least, formalization clarifies, disambiguates, and shows up inconsistencies to produce a watertight precision that is actually quite severe. This severity pays dividends, however, because clients (and developers) can no longer include in specifications questionable features of state or functionality that are risky because they are expressed in some garbled natural language or are poorly understood.

To bring the general theme of this final section back full circle to Chapter 1, the reader could do no better than read Hall (1990) about the 'mythology' that still surrounds formal methods. Our final statement might be that, although it is important to appreciate that formal methods are not a panacea, they are capable of yielding significant cost-effective improvements in quality when used properly on the right projects.

A FINAL EXERCISE

On your next project assignment involving specification work, seek to apply Z to some component of the work, however small. If it is a team assignment that includes design and implementation, adopt some form of contractual model within the team, even if this means your playing different roles at different times. When the project is over, evaluate the contribution that use of Z, and a contractual model if used, made to the quality of work accomplished.

SUMMARY OF CHAPTER 9

- The reader is introduced to theorem proving, specification validation, and the processes of design and implementation as manifested by refinement.
- Issues are discussed concerning the application and uptake of formal methods in practical software engineering environments.

REFERENCES AND BIBLIOGRAPHY

Andrews, A., and Ince, D. (1991). *Practical Formal Methods with VDM*. McGraw-Hill, London.

Bowen, J.P. (1989). POS: formal specification of a UNIX tool. *Software Engineering Journal*, **4**(1), 67–72.

Brien, S., and Nicholls, S. (eds.) (1992). Z Base Standard: Version 1.0. Oxford University Computing Laboratory, 11 Keble Road, Oxford OX1 3QD, UK.

Cameron, J.R. (ed.) (1989). *JSP and JSD: The Jackson Approach to Software Development* (2nd edn.). IEEE Computer Society Press, Washington, DC.

Cohen, B. (1989). Justification of formal methods for system specification. *Software Engineering Journal*, **4**(1), 26–35.

Cohen, B., Harwood, W.T., and Jackson, M.I. (1986). *The Specification of Complex Systems*. Addison-Wesley, Wokingham, UK.

Coleman, D., Gallimore, R.M., and Stavridou, V. (1987). The design of a rewrite rule interpreter from algebraic specifications. *Software Engineering Journal*, **4**(2), 95–104.

Diller, A. (1990). *Z An Introduction to Formal Methods*. Wiley, Chichester, UK.

Gallimore, R.M., Coleman, D., and Stavridou, V. (1989). UMIST OBJ: a language for executable program specifications. *Computer Journal*, **32**(50), 413–421.

Gries, D. (1981). *The Science of Programming*. Springer-Verlag, New York.

Hall, A. (1990). Seven myths of formal methods. *IEEE Software*, September, 11–19.

Harrison, M., and Thimbleby, H. (eds.) (1990) *Formal Methods in Human-Computer Interaction*. Cambridge University Press.

Hayes, I. (1992). VDM and Z: a comparitive case study. *Formal Aspects of Computing*, **4**(1), 76–99.

Hayes, I. (ed.) (1993). *Specification Case Studies* (2nd edn.). Prentice Hall, Englewood Cliffs, NJ.

Hoare, C.A.R. (1985). *Communicating Sequential Processes*. Prentice Hall, Englewood Cliffs, NJ.

Howe, D.R. (1983). *Data Analysis for Data Base Design*. Edward Arnold, London.

Ince, D.C. (1988). *An Introduction to Discrete Mathematics and Formal System Specification*. Clarendon Press, Oxford.

Jones, C.B. (1990). *Systematic Software Development Using VDM* (2nd edn.). Prentice Hall, Englewood Cliffs, NJ.

Jones, C.B., and Shaw, R.C. (1990). *Case Studies in Systematic Software Development*. Prentice Hall, Englewood Cliffs, NJ.

King, S. (1985). Z and the Refinement Calculus. In Bjørner, D., Hoare, C.A.R., and Langmaack, H. (eds), *VDM and Z – Formal Methods in Software Development*, vol. 428 of *Lecture Notes in Computer Science*, Springer-Verlag, pp.164–188.

Lightfoot, D. (1991). *Formal Specification Using Z*. Macmillan, Basingstoke.

Meyer, B. (1985). On formalism in specifications. *IEEE Software*, **2**(1), 6–26.

McMorran, M., and Powell, S. (1993). *Z Guide for Beginners*. Blackwell Scientific, Oxford.

Morgan, C. (1990). *Programming from Specifications*. Prentice Hall, Englewood Cliffs, NJ.

Nicholls, J. (1991). Domains of application for formal methods. In Nicholls, J.E. (ed.), *Z User Workshop, York 1991*, Workshops in Computing, Springer-Verlag, London, pp.145–156.

Parker, C.E. (1991). Z Tools Catalogue. Technical Report ZIP/BAe/90/020. British Aerospace, Warton PR4 1AX, UK.

Potter, B., Sinclair, J., and Till, D. (1991). *An Introduction to Formal Specification and Z*. Prentice Hall, Englewood Cliffs, NJ.

Pressman, R.S. (1992). *Software Engineering. A Practitioner's Approach* (3rd edn.). McGraw-Hill, New York.

Smith, A. (1992). On recursive free types in Z. In Nicholls, J.E. (ed.), *Z User Workshop, York 1991*, Workshops in Computing, Springer-Verlag, London, pp.3–39.

Spivey, M. (1992). *The Z Notation: A Reference Manual* (2nd edn.). Prentice Hall, Englewood Cliffs, NJ.

Stepney, S., Barden, R., and Cooper, D. (1992). A survey of object orientation and Z. *Software Engineering Journal*, **7**(2), 150–160.

Sufrin, B.A. (1986). Formal specification of a display-oriented editor. In Gehani, N. and McGettrick, A.D. (eds.), *Software Specification Techniques*, Addison-Wesley, Wokingham, UK, pp.223–267.

Valentine, S. (1992). Putting numbers into the mathematical toolkit. *Seventh Annual Z User Meeting*, DTI Kingsgate House, London, December.

Woodcock, J., and Loomes, M. (1988). *Software Engineering Mathematics*. Pitman, London.

Woodcock, J. (1992). The rudiments of algorithm refinement. *Computer Journal*, **35**(5), 441–450.

Wordsworth, J.B. (1992). *Software Development with Z: A Practical Approach to Formal Methods in Software Engineering*. Addison-Wesley, Wokingham, UK.

APPENDIX I: GLOSSARY

Abstract data type A data type that can be understood purely through the behaviour of its operations without regard to the representation of its value/state space.

Abstraction The intellectual process by which descriptions of things are constructed so as to exhibit only features that are considered to be essential (at some level, in some context, to some task, etc.) by the 'abstractor'.

Applicable An operation is applicable if the before state and inputs satisfy its precondition.

Axiom A property that is 'given' rather than derived, i.e., semantically, a property that is 'true by definition'.

Calculus Essentially, a system of rules 'for calculating', as in the 'predicate calculus' or 'schema calculus'.

Data refinement (Some prefer 'data reification'.) The process of refining one abstract data type into another whose value/state space is different and in some sense 'less abstract'. See *Refinement*.

Data type A value/state space over which a collection of operations is defined. For a functional data type, 'operation' is taken to encompass constants, relations and functions. For a state-based data type, each operation exhibits state transition as well as input/output behaviour; a description of an initial state is also considered to be part of such a data type.

Data type theory Loosely, a collection of laws that describe interesting and useful general properties exhibited by the data type's operations.

Environment In effect, a binding which records what names denote ('mean') in a Z specification. Each name denotes an 'element', and an element is characterized by a type and value.

Expression An alternative for *Term*. Can also pertain to predicates as in the term 'logical expression', i.e., constructs which have a value of true or false under some interpretation (including assignment of values to any free variables). Note that 'term' is *never* used in the sense of 'logical expression'.

Formal Loosely, 'precise and mathematical'. More strictly, that which pertains to syntax without regard to semantics.

Formal method An inapposite name for: (the liberal view) any approach to software development that at some stage utilizes a mathematically-based notation for specification and/or verification; (the strict view) a way of developing software that begins with an abstract formal specification and then gradually transforms the validated specification into code by various refinement techniques.

Formal system An alphabet and a set of rules for generating certain strings (well formed formulas) using only symbols taken from the alphabet. This basic apparatus has many applications, e.g., proof systems, grammars.

Formula Sometimes used as the (correct) name for any well-formed construct of predicate logic, i.e., a construct involving at least one relation, possibly also any of the propositional operators and quantifiers.

Functional Characterizes behaviour which produces at most one outcome for any 'start case'. Compare *Non-deterministic*.

Functionality Time-independent behaviour; used in a general sense to cover both state-based and functional data types.

Generator The generators of a data type are those of its constants and functions from which all possible (finite) terms can be constructed that denote the values of the data type.

Grammar A formal system which defines the syntax of a language.

Induction principle A certain axiom of a data type theory, the consequence of which is that properties of the data type can be established by proofs with a specialized architecture that is based on the data type's generators (this has not been discussed in the text).

Interpretation An assignment of meanings to the well-formed formulas of a formal system.

Invariant A predicate which characterizes a static property of something that exhibits or undergoes change in some sense, as in 'state invariant'

Law A theorem describing a property of logic or of a data type.

Loose A specification is loose if it does not fix unique values for all its global variables. The given sets of a specification, and those global variables not given unique values, can be thought of as the specification's 'parameters'.

Model (In the general sense) An abstract description. (In a more specific sense) An interpretation for a theory such that all the axioms of the theory are true.

Model-oriented A specification is model-oriented if it bases the description of behaviour on an explicit model of a value/state space. For a state-based data type in Z, the model will be described by a schema defining a set of bindings for the state variables. Compare *Property-oriented*.

Non-deterministic A behaviour is non-deterministic if it has at least one 'start case' for which there is more than one 'result case' (outcome). It follows therefore that non-deterministic behaviour cannot be described using a function.

Operation (In this book) *Either* a particular behaviour of a state-based data type; *or* a constant, relation or function of a functional data type.

Operation decomposition The effect of operation refinement which causes operation descriptions to be broken top-down into (specifications of) sub-operations embedded in the control structures of the target language (this has not been described in the text).

Operation refinement The process of refining one operation into another over the same value/state space; generally occurs after data-refining a specification. See also *Refinement*.

Partial A function/operation is partial if it does not *necessarily* yield a defined outcome for every member of its 'start space'. This holds for *all* functions and operations. Compare *Total*.

Precondition In Z, that predicate which precisely characterizes an operation's 'domain', i.e., those before states/inputs of an operation for which at least one outcome (after state/outputs) exists. Note that this is different to 'precondition' as used in, say, VDM or the Refinement Calculus, i.e., a predicate which the before states/inputs of an operation are required to satisfy but with no guarantee of feasibility (existence of an outcome).

Postcondition The opposite of precondition, i.e., a predicate over the after state/outputs (obtained by hiding the before state/inputs) which precisely characterizes an operation's 'range', i.e., 'what the operation produces' (this has not been described in the text).

Proof A structure which shows that, by using the inference rules and data type laws available, a conjectured conclusion can be derived from the given hypotheses. Informally, a logical argument.

Proof obligation The requirement of a developer to show that a certain description or development decision is consistent or correct, the consistency or correctness being embodied in one or more sequents which have to be proved. Examples: state consistency, data-refined operation applicability.

Proof theory A formal system for conducting reasoning, i.e., inferring (one also says 'deducing') conclusions from hypotheses.

Property In a general sense, just a predicate. More specifically, that attribute which is expressed by the constraint (if any) of a declaration plus an additional predicate (if any) over the variables of the declaration; where there is no constraint and no predicate, the property is just `true`. In an analogous way to relations, one can regard a property as being defined by the set of bindings for which it is true.

Property-oriented A specification is property-oriented if it bases description of behaviour on axioms (typically expressing equational relationships that hold amongst operation behaviours) that require no reference to a value/state space model; hence a property-oriented data type is often expressly referred to as 'abstract'. Compare *Model-oriented*. See also *Theory*.

Refinement A systematic process which, according to certain pre-defined criteria, transforms a description A into another C that is 'no more abstract than' A. C can have wider applicability than A, but when restricted to circumstances corresponding to A's applicability, will produce behaviour that A would correspondingly exhibit but which may be more deterministic. The overall effect is one of C 'simulating' A. Pragmatically, depending on the stage at which it occurs, refinement can be regarded as either an act of design or of implementation.

Relation Syntactically, an n-ary symbol (the relation identifier) which forms a basic predicate when applied to an n-ary argument of the correct type (a single non-tuple value if $n = 1$, otherwise an n-tuple for $n \geq 2$). As an object itself, a relation is defined by the set of those members of its argument's value space for which the resulting predicate (relation applied to argument) is true.

Schema A named combination of a signature and a property.

Sequent A formalization of a claim or conjecture to the effect that a certain conclusion can be inferred from the given hypotheses.

Signature A signature is established by a declaration of one or more variables, each of which is given a name (unique within the signature) and type.

State A 'discrete mode or configuration' in which something can exist. When applied to systems, this is normally used to refer to the information content of a system that persists throughout the system's lifespan; at any given moment, the information content is in a particular state.

State-based That which depends for its description on the concept of state.

State space The complete set of bindings such that each binding respects the signature of some state model and makes the model's property true.

Term A construct of predicate logic built from constants, (free) variables and function applications (which includes all operators, whatever their syntax). If defined, a term has a determinable value that belongs to the value space of the term's type. See also *Expression, Undefined*.

Theorem Strictly, a sequent that has been proved. Also used to describe 'sequent templates' associated with, say, proof obligations, as in the 'state consistency theorem'. Theorems also include the axioms of a formal system or theory.

Theory Formally, an alphabet, a set of axioms expressed in the alphabet and a logical apparatus, such as the predicate calculus with equality. The theory comprises the axioms and all the theorems inferrable from the axioms by the logical apparatus. In a data type theory, the theorems are often referred to as 'laws'.

Total A function/operation is total if its domain—that set of 'start cases' for which it yields a defined outcome—is the *complete* 'start space' over which it acts. Compare *Partial*.

Type An expression with a certain syntax that denotes a value space (the type's 'carrier set'). In Z, a type is either basic, being the name of a given set (which is normally taken to include $\mathbb{Z}$), or is one of the following compound types: powerset type, cartesian product type, schema type. A compound type is built from one or more simpler types (each of which itself can be basic or compound), thus enabling types of any required structural complexity to be defined.

Undefined A predicate or term is undefined when its value cannot be determined. An undefined term can arise for several reasons, e.g., it contains an application of a partial function to an argument which, though type correct, lies outside the function's domain. A predicate is undefined if it contains one or more undefined terms which cause its truth value to be undeterminable.

Well formed formula A construct whose syntax conforms to the formal system (e.g., a grammar) to which it is stated to belong.

APPENDIX II: SOLUTIONS TO EXERCISES

Note that in many cases, e.g., exercises involving schema construction, there is no single correct answer. Thus, many of the solutions presented here should be treated as a guide only.

Chapter 1

1.1 Hopefully, you would implement no algorithm, but instead seek out the person who wrote this 'requirement'! It is completely unclear what the statement means. Such difficulties often arise when using words like 'and' and 'or' in natural language.

1.2 All possible test cases! Thus, if the machine allows n different integers, an array of k elements can hold n^k different array values. So, for arrays of 10 elements or less, the possible array structures total $n^0 + n^1 + n^2 + \dots n^{10}$. If n is of the order of several million, this total is a very large number!

1.3 1. isTheSisterOf, isARelationOf, isAMemberOfTheSameFamilyAs.
  2. $<, \le, =, >, \ge$ (but *not* $\ne$).

Chapter 2

2.1 1. Alphabet (33 symbols): a, b, c, ... z, (,), ¬, ∧, ∨, ⇒, ⇔
    Rules: 26 axiom rules of the form: $\dfrac{}{\lambda}$ (λ is a lower-case letter)   *plus*

$$\frac{P \quad Q}{(P \wedge Q)} \quad \frac{P \quad Q}{(P \vee Q)} \quad \frac{P \quad Q}{(P \Rightarrow Q)} \quad \frac{P \quad Q}{(P \Leftrightarrow Q)} \quad \frac{P}{\neg P} \quad \frac{P}{(P)}$$

  2. a $(a \Rightarrow \neg b)$ $((a \Rightarrow \neg b) \Rightarrow (a \Rightarrow ((\neg \neg c))))$
  3. Taking the wffs in (2) to be indexed 1 . . 3, then wff2 and wff1 match the two antecedent patterns of the given rule; this gives ¬ b. wff3 and wff2 also match; this gives $(a \Rightarrow ((\neg \neg c)))$. But then this latter result and wff1 also match; this gives $((\neg \neg c))$.

2.3 *Discrete*: a, d, f (*NB* real arithmetic is inevitably discrete on a (digital) computer! Do not confuse with the mathematical reals which *are* continuous.)
   Continuous:
   b. Divide plane into a grid of intersecting lines spaced at unit intervals and parallel to x and y axes; the sphere's position can be where any two lines intersect, as given by an (x, y) pair of integer co-ordinates.
   c. As (b): divide air space into three-dimensional blocks with suitable co-ordinate system.
   e. Sample and describe music signal at sufficiently small regular time intervals (though note that keys pressed by pianist's fingers at different moments is discrete).

Chapter 3

3.1 2. The declaration makes v's type $\mathbb{Z}$, but because the subrange $\xi 1 . . \xi 2$ will be 'empty', deciding what values v can denote is not meaningful. We say the declaration is *inconsistent* because it asserts that v is an integer which belongs to the 'empty set', which logically is a contradiction (i.e., false).
  3. It is ill-formed! Remember that the scope of a variable does *not* include the declaration part in which it is defined. Thus, the applications of i and j in the declaration of k are illegal. We would need to declare k : $\mathbb{Z}$ and then add the predicate $i \le k \le j$.

3.2 1. DateVars $\triangleq$ [dy : 1..31; mn : 1..12; yr : $\mathbb{N}$]
    DateVarsNorm $\triangleq$ [dy, mn, yr : $\mathbb{Z}$ | $1 \le dy \le 31 \wedge 1 \le mn \le 12 \wedge yr \ge 0$]

3.3 1. The state spaces of ThreeCntrs and ThreeCntrsNorm are the same, since normalization is just a mathematical transformation. This state space is contained in that of `ThreeCntrsDecs` (three $\mathbb{N}$ variables but no predicate), which is the same state space as that of `ThreeCntrsDecsNorm`. The state space of `ThreeCntrsSig`, which is just three $\mathbb{Z}$ variables, would contain all the others.

2. β1, β2, β5, β6.

3.4 a. hrs'',mins'' : $\mathbb{Z}$ | $0 \leq$ hrs'' $\leq 23 \wedge 0 \leq$ mins'' ≤ 59

   b. c1?,c2?,c3? : $\mathbb{N}$ | c1? $\leq$ n $\wedge$ c3? $\leq$ m $\wedge$ c1? $\leq$ c2? $\leq$ c3?
      Note that n and m are not decorated because they are not declared in `ThreeCntrs`.

3.6 1. The suggested equality would model adding one minute to the time, *but this would not keep the hours value constant* (try out both equalities on a range of time values).

   2.
```
___ResetMin_____
  t,t' : 0..1439
_____
  t' = ( t div 60 ) * 60 + ( t + 59 ) mod 60
```

```
___ResetHr_____
  t,t' : 0..1439
_____
  t' = ( t + 1380 ) mod 1440
```

3.7 1. c1,c2,c3,c1',c2',c3',acv! : $\mathbb{N}$ |
      c1 $\leq$ n $\wedge$ c3 $\leq$ m $\wedge$ c1 $\leq$ c2 $\leq$ c3 $\wedge$ c1' $\leq$ n $\wedge$ c3' $\leq$ m $\wedge$ c1' $\leq$ c2' $\leq$ c3' $\wedge$
      acv! = (c1 + c2 + c3) div 3 $\wedge$ c1' = c1 $\wedge$ c2' = c2 $\wedge$ c3' = c3

   2. Simply replace `Time` and `Time'` in `Add1Min` by `TimeNorm` and `TimeNorm'` respectively. For both `ResetMin` and `ResetHr`, replace the declaration of variables t and t' by `TimeNorm;TimeNorm'`.

3.8 1. Because we want the *changed* time displayed, i.e., *after* another minute has ticked by.

   2. The resulting schema would be *inconsistent* because it would contain
      t' = (t + 1) mod 1440   (from `Add1Min`)
      and   t' = t   (from `TimeOut`)
      Obviously, it is impossible for both equalities to hold at the same time.

   3. `ResetMin` and `ResetHr` also need to include a display behaviour, namely extra hrs! and mins! variables plus two extra equalities in their predicates, just as for `Add1Min`.

3.9 a. yr $\geq$ bottomYr
      $\neg$ leapYr(yr) $\Rightarrow$ doty $\leq$ 365

   b. No predicate is needed

3.10 1.
```
___Sub1Day_____
  Date; Date'
_____
  — The tricky special cases are the first days in months. Firstly, January:
  dy = 1 ∧ mn = 1 ∧ yr = bottomYr            — January 1st, bottomYr
    ⇒ dy' = dy ∧ mn' = mn ∧ yr' = yr
  dy = 1 ∧ mn = 1 ∧ yr ≠ bottomYr            — January 1st, any year but bottomYr
    ⇒ dy' = 31 ∧ mn' = 12 ∧ yr' = yr - 1
  — Now the cases where we have any year, 1st of a month except January:
  dy = 1 ∧ mn = 3 ∧ leapYr( yr )             — March 1st, a leap year
    ⇒ dy' = 29 ∧ mn' = 2 ∧ yr' = yr
  dy = 1 ∧ mn = 3 ∧ ¬ leapYr( yr )           — March 1st, not a leap year
    ⇒ dy' = 28 ∧ mn' = 2 ∧ yr' = yr
  dy = 1 ∧ ajsn( mn - 1 )                    — 1st of May, July, October, or December
    ⇒ dy' = 30 ∧ mn' = mn - 1 ∧ yr' = yr
  dy = 1 ∧ ¬ ajsn( mn - 1 ) ∧ mn ≠ 3 ∧ mn ≠ 1   — all other 1st days
    ⇒ dy' = 31 ∧ mn' = mn - 1 ∧ yr' = yr
  — Finally, any year, any month, and any day except the 1st:
  dy ≠ 1 ⇒ dy' = dy - 1 ∧ mn' = mn ∧ yr' = yr
```

Notes

i. January 1st, `bottomYr` has been dealt with by not changing the state—the easiest solution, partly because it avoids any notion of an 'error condition'.

ii. There is actually a much shorter way of expressing the main group of cases dealing with the 1st of months except January by using the `eom` predicate symbol defined on page 46:

$$dy = 1 \wedge mn \neq 1 \qquad \text{— any year, 1st of a month except January}$$
$$\Rightarrow eom(\, dy'\,, mn'\,, yr'\,) \wedge mn' = mn - 1 \wedge yr' = yr$$

This is sufficient to ensure that the new date is such that dy' represents the end of the previous month, with no change in year.

2. `ResetDateUp` $\triangleq$ [`Add1Day`; `DateOut`]
   `ResetDateDown` $\triangleq$ [`Sub1Day`; `DateOut`]
   (hence the reason for having `DateOut`—it makes life simpler!).

The operations affecting time, i.e., `ResetMin`, `ResetHr`, etc., could be dealt with similarly. We modify `TimeOut`'s predicate on page 41 by removing the equality $t' = t$ and changing the two other occurrences of t to t'. Now we can simply include a reference to `TimeOut` in the declaration parts of `ResetMin` and `ResetHr` to incorporate the idea of the new time being displayed. We could, of course, do the same thing to the simple version of `Add1Min` on page 40, in effect giving us the modified version on page 42.

3.11 1.

$$\begin{array}{|l}
n, m : \mathbb{N} \\
\hline
n \bmod 2 = 1 \\
m \bmod 2 = 1 \\
n \leq m
\end{array}$$

2.

___ResetC1_____
ΔThreeCntrs
_____
$c1' = c3 \bmod (\, c1 + 1\,)$
$c2' = c2$
$c3' = c3$
_____

___CntrDiffs _____
ΞThreeCntrs
$d1!, d2! : \mathbb{N}$
_____
$d1! = c2 - c1$
$d2! = c3 - c2$
_____

3.12 a. *partial*: $c1 < n \wedge c1 < c2$ b. *partial*: $c3 - c2 \geq c2$ c. *total*
d. *partial*: $c1 = c2$ (!)   e. *partial*: $x? \leq n \wedge x? \leq c2 \wedge c2 \leq y? \leq m$
f. impossible: this requires the state to have a component that 'remembers' a certain feature of the system's behaviour; `ThreeCntrs` has no such component
g. *total* (an output capable of signalling at least a 0 or a 1, say, would do).

3.13 ΔDigitalWatch; ΞDate must be included in `ResetMin` and `ResetHr`.
ΔDigitalWatch; ΞTime must be included in `ResetDateUp` and `ResetDateDown`.
Replace ΞDate in `ShowDate` by ΞDigitalWatch

3.14 1.

___OpA _____
ΔThreeCntrs
_____
$c1 < n \wedge c1 < c2$
$c1' = c1 + 1$
$c2' = c2$; $c3' = c3$
_____

___OpB _____
ΔThreeCntrs
_____
$c3 - c2 \geq c2$
$c1' = c1$; $c2' = c2$
$c3' = c3 - c2$
_____

```
  ___OpG _____
  ΞThreeCntrs
  dex! : 0..n - 1
 _____
  dex! = c2 mod c1            — so dex! = 0 means 'yes' and dex! ≠ 0 means 'no'
```

2. OpAorB is *not* deterministic. This is because it is possible for the preconstraints of OpA and OpB to apply at the same time, in which case the behaviour of OpAorB is either that of OpA or that of OpB but the specification does not say which.

3. One possible extra facility is to allow the user to alter the year of a date without (in principle) altering the day and month. In the description of the two operations (one resets upwards, the other downwards), we assume that the watch schedules a year change in between time ticks:

```
  ___ResetYearUp _____
  ΔDigitalWatch
  ΞTime
 _____
  yr' = yr + 1
  — the following avoids producing invalid dates
  dy = 29 ∧ mn = 2                  — incrementing year when February 29th ...
     ⇒ dy' = 1 ∧ mn' = 3           — ... so date changes to March 1st
  ¬ ( dy = 29 ∧ mn = 2 )
     ⇒ dy' = dy ∧ mn' = mn
```

```
  ___ResetYearDown _____
  ΔDigitalWatch
  ΞTime
 _____
  — the following avoids invalid dates with respect to bottomYr
  yr = bottomYr                      — year is bottomYr ...
     ⇒ yr' = yr                      — ... so no change to year
  yr > bottomYr                      — any other year
     ⇒ yr' = yr - 1
  — the following avoids producing invalid dates
  dy = 29 ∧ mn = 2                   — decrementing year when February 29th ...
     ⇒ dy' = 1 ∧ mn' = 3            — ... so date changes to March 1st
  ¬ ( dy = 29 ∧ mn = 2 )
     ⇒ dy' = dy ∧ mn' = mn
```

Assuming the watch has a 'beeping' mechanism, another possible operation is for the watch to give a warning beep every hour, say, according to user preference. For this to work, the state model needs an extra two-valued component which 'remembers' whether beeping is required or not. So we will assume that the Time component of DigitalWatch also incorporates the variable:

    beepState : 0..1   — 0 = beep switched off, 1 = beep switched on

Now we modify Add1Min by adding the following extra variable:

    beepSignal! : 0..1

and these predicates:

    beepState' = beepState
    beepState = 0
       ⇒ beepSignal! = 0
    beepState = 1 ∧ t' mod 60 = 0
       ⇒ beepSignal! = 1
    beepState = 1 ∧ t' mod 60 ≠ 0
       ⇒ beepSignal! = 0

When the output beepSignal! is 0, the watch makes no beep, otherwise it beeps when the time has ticked on to the hour exactly (obviously, one could imagine a more flexible beep facility for the user). We would also need the user operation:

```
___ToggleBeep _____
 ΔDigitalWatch
 ΞDate
 _____
 t' = t
 beepState' = ( beepState + 1 ) mod 2
```

Chapter 4

4.1 1. `(_/_)( (_+_)( -b,`
            `sqrt( (_-_)((_*_)( b,b),(_*_)((_*_)(4,a),c)) )`
        `),(_*_)( 2,a) )`

   2. `eom, i,(_mod_), 31,(_+_), 1, j, bottomYr,(_*_),(_-_)`

4.2 a. binary predicate   b. unary predicate
   c. cannot say (is d in scope? is it integer?)   d. *true*
   e. unary predicate, but there's a catch: we know it to be true because `-3` will always be less than `i`, since `i` is a natural number; in words, '`-3` is less than `i` for any natural number `i`', which foreshadows universal quantification in Section 4.3.

4.3 The proper propositions are: (a), (d), (e), (f), (g), (h). It is irrelevant whether an assertion seems 'ridiculous', as perhaps in (d), (e), (f) and (g). What is important is that it is an assertion of fact whose truth or falsity can be determined. This excludes: (b) which entertains the idea of possibility, (c) which is a question, and (i) which expresses an opinion and involves subjective interpretation of 'revolutionary'.

4.4 1. a. $\neg (P \wedge ((Q \Rightarrow P) \Rightarrow Q))$
       b. $(\neg P \wedge Q \Rightarrow P) \Rightarrow Q$
       c. $\neg P \wedge Q \Rightarrow P \Rightarrow Q$

   2. a. $((((\neg P) \wedge Q) \Rightarrow (P \vee Q)) \Leftrightarrow (\neg P))$
       b. $((P \Rightarrow (Q \wedge (\neg P))) \Leftrightarrow ((\neg Q) \vee P))$

4.5 a. `leapYr( 1992 )`   *true*
   d. `leapYr( 1992 ) ∧ leapYr( 1993 ) ∧ leapYr( 1994 )`   *false*
   e. `leapYr( 1992 ) ∨ leapYr( 1992 )`   *true*
   f. `leapYr( 1993 ) ⇒ ¬ leapYr( 1992 )`   *true*
   g. `leapYr( 1992 ) ⇔ leapYr( 1993 )`   *false*
   h. `¬ ( leapYr( 1900 ) ∨ leapYr( 1901 ) ∨ leapYr( 1902 ) ∨ leapYr( 1903 ))` *true*
      or
      `¬ leapYr( 1900 ) ∧ ¬ leapYr( 1901 ) ∧ ¬ leapYr( 1902 ) ∧ ¬ leapYr( 1903 )`

4.6 1. a. $\neg (P \Leftrightarrow Q)$ b. $\neg (P \wedge Q)$

   2. One operator, call it β, is such that β P is false when P is false and true when P is true, which is just the same as P on its own, i.e., β is the identity operator. Another operator, call it ω, is such that ωP is true regardless of P, which is just `true`; similarly, the other unary operator is just the same as `false`.

4.7 (Answers only partially given.)
   In each case, you begin by constructing a truth table with columns for P and Q, giving four rows altogether. Then:
   - For $\neg P \wedge Q \Rightarrow P$ construct columns for: $\neg P$, $\neg P \wedge Q$ and $\neg P \wedge Q \Rightarrow P$. The column for the last formula should contain both *true* and *false*.
   - For $\neg (Q \Rightarrow P \Rightarrow Q)$ construct columns for: $P \Rightarrow Q$, $Q \Rightarrow P \Rightarrow Q$ and $\neg (Q \Rightarrow P \Rightarrow Q)$. The column for the last formula should consist of just *false*.
   - For $(P \Rightarrow Q) \wedge P \Rightarrow Q$ construct columns for: $P \Rightarrow Q$, $(P \Rightarrow Q) \wedge P$ and $(P \Rightarrow Q) \wedge P \Rightarrow Q$. The column for the last formula should consist of just *true*.

4.8 1. By writing: Tautology ≡ `true`
      By writing: Contradiction ≡ `false`, or ¬ Contradiction ≡ `true`.

2. $\lor$ is a good analogy for $+$, $\neg$ a good analogy for unary $-$; $\land$ for $*$ works sometimes. So:

- Both $\land$ and $\lor$ are commutative, and thus the following equivalences hold:

$$P \land Q \equiv Q \land P \qquad\qquad P \lor Q \equiv Q \lor P$$

- Both $\land$ and $\lor$ are associative, and thus the following equivalences hold:

$$(P \land Q) \land R \equiv P \land (Q \land R) \qquad (P \lor Q) \lor R \equiv P \lor (Q \lor R)$$

- Both $\land$ and $\lor$ distribute over each other (thus the analogy with arithmetic breaks down here), so the following equivalences hold:

$$P \land (Q \lor R) \equiv (P \land Q) \lor (P \land R) \qquad P \lor (Q \land R) \equiv (P \lor Q) \land (P \lor R)$$

- Finally, $\neg$ has the property that: $\qquad \neg \neg P \equiv P$

3. *Note*: references are to the `Date` predicate as given on page 44.
   i. Apply L1 to second conjunct
   ii. Apply L1 to third conjunct and change $\neg(\text{mn} = 2)$ into $\text{mn} \neq 2$
   iii. Apply L1 to fourth conjunct. This gives $\neg(\text{mn} = 2 \land \neg \text{leapYr}(\text{yr})) \lor \text{dy} \leq 28$.
   Now apply L2 to the first disjunct, giving $\neg(\text{mn} = 2) \lor \neg\neg \text{leapYr}(\text{yr}) \dots$.
   Change $\neg(\text{mn} = 2)$ into $\text{mn} \neq 2$, and apply L4 to get rid of the $\neg\neg$.
   This gives the answer. In effect, L3 is also being used: because $\lor$ is associative, we can drop any parentheses around the three disjuncts making up the last conjunct.

   The introductory sentence to the question says 'mainly' because we have used another law (twice) as well as L1–L4 listed in the question. Unlike L1–L4 which are laws of logic, this law can be regarded as the Definition of Not-Equals (i.e., it belongs to the 'theory of equality'). The law in effect states that for any terms `t1` and `t2` of some arbitrary type τ:

   $$\text{t1} \neq \text{t2} \Leftrightarrow \neg(\text{t1} = \text{t2})$$

4. It is wrong because we are mixing together 'unlike' symbols. We need a 'meta *if…then…*' and a 'meta *and*' to express the law as in the question, rather than $\Rightarrow$ and $\land$ which, unlike $\equiv$, are not meta-symbols (unless we overload them to have this usage also, which could be confusing).

4.9   a. $\neg(\exists p : \text{PERSON} \bullet \text{loves}(p, \text{nesta}))$
     b. $\text{loves}(\text{carrie}, \text{bill}) \land (\forall p : \text{PERSON} \bullet p \neq \text{bill} \Rightarrow \neg \text{loves}(\text{carrie}, p))$
     c. $\exists p : \text{PERSON} \bullet \text{loves}(p, \text{bill}) \land \text{loves}(p, \text{carrie})$
     d. $\exists_1 p : \text{PERSON} \bullet \text{loves}(p, \text{bill}) \land p \neq \text{nesta}$
     e. $\forall p : \text{PERSON} \bullet \text{loves}(p, \text{carrie}) \Rightarrow \text{loves}(p, \text{nesta})$
     f. $\forall p : \text{PERSON} \bullet \text{loves}(p, \text{nesta}) \Rightarrow \text{loves}(\text{carrie}, p)$

4.10   1. a. true   b. false   c. true   d. false
     2. a. $\exists p : \text{PERSON} \bullet \forall q : \text{PERSON} \bullet \neg \text{loves}(p, q)$
        b. $\exists p : \text{PERSON} \bullet \exists_1 q : \text{PERSON} \bullet \text{loves}(q, p)$
        c. $\exists p, q : \text{PERSON} \bullet p \neq q \land (\forall r : \text{PERSON} \bullet \text{loves}(r, p) \Leftrightarrow \text{loves}(r, q))$
        d. $\exists p, q, r : \text{PERSON} \bullet p \neq q \land q \neq r \land p \neq r \land$
               $\text{loves}(p, \text{bill}) \land \text{loves}(q, \text{bill}) \land \text{loves}(r, \text{bill})$

     3. a. Everybody `nesta` loves has another lover
        b. Some people love `bill` and nobody else.

4.11   1. a. None   b. `r`   c. `q`   d. `p`,`q` or `r`
     2. a. `R(x,y,z)`
         `Q(x,y)`
         `Q(x,y) prOp2 R(x,y,z)`
         `Qntfr2 y : Y • Q(x,y) prOp2 R(x,y,z)`
         `P(x)`
         `P(x) prOp1 (Qntfr2 y : Y • Q(x,y) prOp2 R(x,y,z))`
       b. `Qntfr1 y : X • P(y) prOp1 (Qntfr2 x : Y • Q(y,x) prOp2 R(y,x,z))`
        This is equivalent to the original predicate since the (safe) renaming of bound variables never has any effect on interpretation.

   c. If the substituting term contains a free variable which is called x or y, that variable will become captured (by Qntfr1 or Qntfr2 respectively). This can be avoided by suitable renaming of the clashing bound variable(s). Note that we must not rename the free variable in the substituting term to overcome the problem, as this *would* change the interpretation.

4.12   1. a. $\forall\,k : \mathbb{Z} \bullet \exists\,x : \mathbb{Z} \mid prime(\,x\,) \bullet x > k$

        b. $\forall\,k : \mathbb{Z} \mid k > 2 \bullet$
$$\neg\,\exists\,x,y,z : \mathbb{Z} \mid x > 0 \wedge y > 0 \wedge z > 0 \bullet$$
$$power(\,x,k\,) + power(\,y,k\,) = power(\,z,k\,)$$

   2. a. $P(\,y\,)$ (the $\exists\,x : X \bullet$ 'has no effect' as x does not occur freely in $P(\,y\,)$)

        b. $\exists\,x : X \bullet P(\,x\,)$ (basically the same reason—make $P(\,y\,)$ of (a) into $\exists\,x : X \bullet P(\,x\,)$)

        c. $P(\,y\,) \wedge Q(\,x\,)$ (ditto; note that $Q(\,x\,)$ is not within scope of the $\exists$)

     The same results apply to $\forall$.

   3. a. $(\,\forall\,x : X \bullet P(\,x\,)) \wedge (\,\forall\,x : X \bullet Q(\,x\,))$

        b. This is *not* equivalent to: $(\,\exists\,x : X \bullet P(\,x\,)) \wedge (\,\exists\,x : X \bullet Q(\,x\,))$

        c. This is *not* equivalent to: $(\,\forall\,x : X \bullet P(\,x\,)) \vee (\,\forall\,x : X \bullet Q(\,x\,))$

        d. $(\,\exists\,x : X \bullet P(\,x\,)) \vee (\,\exists\,x : X \bullet Q(\,x\,))$

     You might be able to invent some meanings for P, Q and X which explain the answers to (b) and (c). For example, let X be $\mathbb{N}$, P be 'is odd' and Q be 'is even'.

4.13   1. Date's predicate in `DigitalWatch` could be written simply as isDate(dy,mn,yr).

   2. a. $\forall\,k : \mathbb{N}_1 \bullet prime(\,k\,) \Leftrightarrow k > 1 \wedge \neg\,(\,\exists\,n : 2..k - 1 \bullet k \bmod n = 0\,)$
        This works even for k = 2 because $\exists$ over an 'empty set' yields false.

        b. $\forall\,i,j : \mathbb{Z} \bullet i < j \Leftrightarrow (\exists\,k : \mathbb{N}_1 \bullet i + k = j\,)$

        c. $\forall\,a,b,c : \mathbb{N}_1 \bullet raTri(\,a,b,c\,) \Leftrightarrow$
$$a * a + b * b = c * c \vee b * b + c * c = a * a \vee c * c + a * a = b * b$$

   3. $leapYr(\,y\,) \Leftrightarrow$ $y \bmod 400 = 0 \vee$
                          $y \bmod 100 \neq 0 \wedge y \bmod 4 = 0$
     $eom(\,d,m,y\,) \Leftrightarrow$ $d = 31 \vee$
                          $d = 30 \wedge ajsn(\,m\,) \vee$
                          $d = 29 \wedge m = 2 \wedge leapYr(\,y\,) \vee$
                          $d = 28 \wedge m = 2 \wedge \neg\,leapYr(\,y\,)$

     Strictly, taken in isolation, an isDate(d,m,y) 'check' should be conjoined to eom's defining predicate, since the definition is meaningless if the triple (d,m,y) does not form a valid date. However, the isDate check becomes redundant when eom is used in various `DigitalWatch` schemas (why?).

4.14   1. $ajsn\_\_ : \mathbb{P}(1..12)$
        $leapYr\_\_ : \mathbb{P}\,\mathbb{N}$
        $isDate\_\_ : \mathbb{P}(1..31 \times 1..12 \times \mathbb{N})$

     For eom, we either have
        $eom\_\_ : \mathbb{P}(1..31 \times 1..12 \times \mathbb{N})$
     if its argument is allowed to be any $1..31 \times 1..12 \times \mathbb{N}$ triple (in which case the definition of eom must contain an isDate check—see above); or we have something like
        $eom\_\_ : \mathbb{P}\,Date$
     where the name Date defines only $1..31 \times 1..12 \times \mathbb{N}$ triples that form valid dates (we do not know yet how to define Date).

   2. a. 4, 6, 9, 11

        b. 1792, 1796, 1804, 1808, 1812

        c. (31,1,1992), (29,2,1992), (31,3,1992), (30,4,1992), (31,5,1992), (30,6,1992)

        d. Empty. One can have 'empty relations'. An empty relation interprets to false for all type-correct arguments.

Chapter 5

5.2   a.   hires : $\mathbb{P}$ (CUSTOMER × VAN); books : $\mathbb{P}$ (CUSTOMER × VANCLASS)
       isin : $\mathbb{P}$ (VAN × VANCLASS)
       This is interpreting the relations in the direction intended by their names.

5.4   1.   The given sets needed would obviously depend on the exact nature of the problem in each case. The answers given are in no way definitive, and a proper domain analysis would be needed to determine exactly what basic types were required.
       a.   [CATALOGITEM , TITLE , RESERVATION , BORROWER]
       b.   [USER , PASSWORD , MACHINE]
       c.   [FLIGHT , TICKET , CUSTOMER , SEAT]

      2.   DegreeClass ::= aegrotat | ord | ordMerit | pass | iii | ii2 | ii1 | first

      3.   [Gender]
           male, female : Gender
           male ≠ female
           $\forall$ g : Gender • g = male ∨ g = female
       We need the first predicate to assert distinctness, the second to assert exhaustion (i.e., there are no other Gender values apart from male and female).

5.5   1.   An adequate model would need to provide at least eight distinct representations, and the model given provides only three: { 0 }, { 1 }, and { 0,1 }

      2.   a.   ∅, { male }, { female }, { male , female }
       b.   The expression attempts to construct a set comprising elements of different types, so is ill-typed and hence illegal.
       c.   Distinctness is not ensured—the variables male and female could still denote the same element.

      3.   32, these being: ∅, 5 singleton sets, 10 sets of 2 elements, 10 sets of 3 elements, 5 sets of 4 elements, and the set VanClass itself (readers familiar with 'Pascal's triangle' will recognize the significance of the number sequence 1, 5, 10, 10, 5, 1). The simple formula 2^k where k is the size of the (finite) set X will yield the number of different sets that can be constructed from the elements of X. This explains the name 'powerset' for the operator $\mathbb{P}$.

5.6   1.   a.   type is not determinable   b. $\mathbb{P}\mathbb{Z}$ c.   ill-typed   d. $\mathbb{P}$ ($\mathbb{P}\mathbb{Z}$)

      2.   a. $\mathbb{P}$ (0..1)   b.   (i) $\mathbb{P}\mathbb{Z}$ (ii) $\mathbb{P}$ ($\mathbb{P}\mathbb{Z}$)   c. $\mathbb{N}, \mathbb{N}_1$: $\mathbb{P}\mathbb{Z}$

      3.   a. $\mathbb{P}$ Vanclass   b. $\mathbb{P}$ Vanclass   c. $\mathbb{P}$ ($\mathbb{P}$ Vanclass)   d. $\mathbb{P}$ ($\mathbb{P}$ Vanclass)
       e.   Vanclass   f. $\mathbb{P}$ ($\mathbb{P}$ ($\mathbb{P}$ Vanclass))   g.   type is not determinable   h.   ill-typed

      4.   — the remaining three doubleton sets (making 6 altogether):
          {{ male },{ female }}, {{ male },{ male , female }},
          {{ female },{ male , female }},
       — the trebleton sets (4 in all):
          { ∅,{ male },{ female }}, { ∅,{ male },{ male , female }},
          { ∅,{ female },{ male , female }}, {{ male },{ female },{ male , female }},
       — and the set $\mathbb{P}$ Gender itself:
          { ∅,{ male },{ female },{ male , female }}
       This makes 16 elements of type $\mathbb{P}$ ($\mathbb{P}$ Gender) altogether; see also the answer to 5.5(3).

      5.   Possible values of s: 1
       Possible values of u: 1
       Possible values of su: ∅, or { 1 }
       Possible values of ssu: ∅, { ∅ }, {{ 1 }}, or { ∅,{ 1 }}
       Possible values of sssu: ∅, { ∅ }, {{ ∅ }}, {{{ 1 }}}, {{ ∅,{ 1 }}},
                                   { ∅,{ ∅ }}, { ∅,{{ 1 }}}, { ∅,{ ∅,{ 1 }}},
                                   {{ ∅ },{{ 1 }}}, {{ ∅ },{ ∅,{ 1 }}}, {{{ 1 }},{ ∅,{ 1 }}},
                                   { ∅,{ ∅ },{{ 1 }}}, {{ ∅ },{{ 1 }},{ ∅,{ 1 }}},
                                   { ∅,{ ∅ },{ ∅,{ 1 }}}, { ∅,{{ 1 }},{ ∅,{ 1 }}}, or
                                   { ∅,{ ∅ },{{ 1 }},{ ∅,{ 1 }}}

5.7 1. Use the set $(0..1) \times (0..1) \times (0..1)$. Each member of this set, a triple, then represents a distinct binary integer in the obvious way.

2. (In order, left to right): $\mathbb{Z}$ $\mathbb{P}\,\mathbb{Z}$ $\mathbb{P}\,\mathbb{Z}$ $\mathbb{Z} \times \mathbb{P}\,\mathbb{Z}$ $\mathbb{P}\,\mathbb{Z}$ $\mathbb{P}\,\mathbb{Z} \times \mathbb{P}\,\mathbb{Z}$
   ill-typed $\mathbb{P}(\mathbb{Z} \times \mathbb{Z})$ ill-typed $\mathbb{P}\,\mathbb{Z} \times (\mathbb{Z} \times \mathbb{Z})$
   $(\mathbb{Z} \times \mathbb{Z}) \times (\mathbb{Z} \times \mathbb{Z})$ $\mathbb{P}(\mathbb{Z} \times \mathbb{P}\,\mathbb{Z} \times (\mathbb{Z} \times \mathbb{Z}) \times \mathbb{P}\,\mathbb{Z})$

5.8 1. $\{n : \mathbb{N} \mid (\exists k : \mathbb{N} \bullet k * k = n)\}$, $\{n : \mathbb{N} \bullet n * n\}$, $\{n,m : \mathbb{N} \mid n = m \bullet n * m\}$

2. a. $\{c : \text{VanClass} \mid c = \text{mini} \lor c = \text{transit} \lor c = \text{light}\}$
   b. $\{i : \mathbb{Z} \mid \text{false}\}$ (any contradiction would suffice for the predicate, e.g., $i \neq i$)
   c. $\{x : \mathbb{N} \bullet (x, x * x)\}$
   d. $\{\text{cbPr} : \text{custom} \mid$
        $(\exists \text{bcPr}: \text{commit} \bullet \text{bcPr} = (\text{first}(\text{cbPr}), \text{heavyDuty})) \bullet \text{first}(\text{cbPr})\}$
   e. $\{n,m : \mathbb{N}_1 \mid n > m \bullet (n * n - m * m, 2 * m * n, n * n + m * m)\}$
   Do not forget the simple but necessary constraint $n > m$ here!

3. a. $\_ \geq \_$
   Example (e) in the text constructs the set of all pairs (n, m) for which n is at least as big as m.
   b. $\mathbb{Z}$ (any integer can be calculated from the product of two others)
   c. fleet   d. $\{-5, -4, -3, -2, 0, 1, 2, 3\}$
   e. $\{n : \mathbb{N}_1 \mid (\exists a, b, c : \mathbb{N}_1 \bullet a * a + b * b = c * c \land n = a * b \,\text{div}\, 2)\}$

5.9 1. $\mathbb{N}_1 \subset \mathbb{N} \subset \mathbb{Z}$

2. a. false   b. false   c. true   d. ill-typed   e. true
   f. cannot tell (depends on T; if T is finite, the predicate is false, otherwise true)

3. $[\text{VanClass}]$

   ---
   mini, transit, light, medium, heavyDuty : VanClass
   ---
   disjoint$\langle\{\text{mini}\}, \{\text{transit}\}, \{\text{light}\}, \{\text{medium}\}, \{\text{heavyDuty}\}\rangle$
   VanClass = $\{\text{mini}, \text{transit}, \text{light}, \text{medium}, \text{heavyDuty}\}$

4. ptn : $\mathbb{P}(\mathbb{P}\,T) \mid$
      $\varnothing \notin \text{ptn} \land$
      $(\forall \text{ss1}, \text{ss2} : \text{ptn} \mid \text{ss1} \neq \text{ss2} \bullet \text{disjoint}\langle \text{ss1}, \text{ss2} \rangle) \land$
      $(\forall e : s \bullet \exists \text{ss} : \text{ptn} \bullet e \in \text{ss}) \land$
      $(\forall \text{ss} : \text{ptn} \bullet \text{ss} \subseteq s)$

5. a. $\text{vansHireable} \subseteq \{\text{vcPr} : \text{fleet} \bullet \text{first}(\text{vcPr})\}$
   b. $\forall \text{cbPr1}, \text{cbPr2} : \text{custom} \mid \text{cbPr1} \neq \text{cbPr2} \bullet$
        $\text{second}(\text{cbPr1}) \neq \text{second}(\text{cbPr2})$
   c. $\{\text{cbPr} : \text{custom} \bullet \text{second}(\text{cbPr})\} = \{\text{bcPr} : \text{commit} \bullet \text{first}(\text{bcPr})\}$
   d. $\text{disjoint}\langle \text{vansHireable}, \{\text{bvPr} : \text{activeHires} \bullet \text{second}(\text{bvPr})\} \rangle$

6. $(\_ < \_) \in \mathbb{P}(\mathbb{Z} \times \mathbb{Z})$
   $(\_ < \_) \subseteq \mathbb{Z} \times \mathbb{Z}$
   $(-1, 0) \in (\_ < \_)$
   $\text{disjoint}\langle \{(0, -1), (0, 0), (1, 0)\}, (\_ < \_) \rangle$
   $\forall i : \mathbb{Z} \bullet (i, i) \notin (\_ < \_)$
   $\{i : \mathbb{Z} \bullet (i, i + 1)\} \subset (\_ < \_)$
   $(\_ < \_) = \{i, k : \mathbb{Z} \mid (\exists j : \mathbb{N}_1 \bullet i + j = k)\}$

5.10 1. All of the bottom diagram except the central portion where the two sets intersect.

2. a. $\text{vansHireable} \cap \text{vansOnHire} = \varnothing \land$
   $\text{vansHireable} \cap \text{vansOffTheRoad} = \varnothing \land$
   $\text{vansOnHire} \cap \text{vansOffTheRoad} = \varnothing$
   The point here is to realize that the first and third conjuncts, say, are insufficient on their own to express the required disjointness property (why?).
   b. $\text{vansHireable} \cup \text{vansOnHire} \cup \text{vansOffTheRoad}$
        $= \{\text{vcPr} : \text{fleet} \bullet \text{first}(\text{vcPr})\}$

3. a. $\mathbb{Z}$ b. $\mathbb{N}_1$ c. $\{0\}$ d. $\varnothing$ e. $\mathbb{Z}$ f. $\mathbb{N}_1$

4. a. 10 (the argument of # simplifies to `Units`)
    b. $\{0,1,4,9\}$
    c. $\varnothing$ (the left-hand operand of $\cap$ simplifies to $\varnothing$)
    d. `Units`
        (the left-hand operand of $\cup$ simplifies to `1..9`, the right-hand operand to $\{0\}$)
    e. $\{n : \mathbb{N} \mid n = 0 \vee n \geq 10\}$
        (the left-hand operand of $\setminus$ simplifies to $\mathbb{N}$, the right-hand operand to `1..9`)

5.11 1. $s1 \cup ((s2 \cap s3) \cap s2)$
        $= s1 \cup (s2 \cap (s2 \cap s3))$ — commutativity of $\cap$
        $= s1 \cup ((s2 \cap s2) \cap s3)$ — associativity of $\cap$
        $= s1 \cup (s2 \cap s3)$ — idempotence of $\cap$

   2. — assuming $S, T : \mathbb{P} \tau$
       $(x \setminus y) \cap y$
       $= \{e : \tau \mid e \in (x \setminus y) \wedge e \in y\}$ — definition of $\cap$
       $= \{e : \tau \mid e \in \{d : \tau \mid d \in x \wedge d \notin y\} \wedge e \in y\}$ — definition of $\setminus$
       $= \{e : \tau \mid e \in \tau \wedge e \in x \wedge e \notin y \wedge e \in y\}$ — equivalence given in question
       $= \{e : \tau \mid e \in \tau \wedge e \in x \wedge \neg(e \in y) \wedge e \in y\}$ — definition of $\notin$
       $= \{e : \tau \mid e \in \tau \wedge e \in x \wedge false\}$ — $\neg P \wedge P \equiv false$
       $= \{e : \tau \mid false\}$ — $P \wedge false \equiv false$
       $= \varnothing$ — definition of $\varnothing$

5.12 1. `fleet` is a many-to-1 relation
          `vanAvlblty` is a many-to-1 relation
          the vans of `fleet` are precisely the vans of `vanAvlblty`

   2. The two `fleet` components are identical in declaration and constraint. The `vansOnHire` and `vansHireable` components of `Vans` are those sets of vans referenced in `vanAvlblty` of `Van1` which are paired with a van status of `onHire` and `free` respectively. The vans referenced in `vanAvlblty` of `Van1` which are paired with a van status of `offTheRoad` are precisely those vans referenced in `fleet` of `Vans` which are not members of `vansOnHire` or `vansHireable`.

   3. Because the value of each variable is derivable from other parts of the state, and so it is not strictly necessary; i.e., its information content is embodied elsewhere in the state anyway. The value of `vansOnHire` is
       $\{bvPr : activeHires \bullet second(bvPr)\}$
       and the value of `activeBkngs` is
       $\{bvPr : activeHires \bullet first(bvPr)\}$

   4. In `Bookings`:
       Remove the declaration of `activeBkngs` and constraint (e).
       In `Vans`:
       Remove the declaration of `vansOnHire`. Change constraint (h) to: `vansHireable` are vans in `fleet`. Remove constraint (i).
       In `VanHire`:
       Replace constraints (k) and (l) with two new constraints:
       • the bookings in `activeHires` come from those handled by any one of the three variables in schema `Bookings`
       • the vans in `activeHires` come from those vans in `fleet` of schema `Vans` which are not vans in `vansHireable` of schema `Vans`.

5.14 1. The constraint has not been omitted—it is taken care of by constraint (o), the 'no overbooking' invariant. If the fleet has 0 vans in some class `c`, then 'no overbooking' ensures in particular that the number of bookings requesting class `c` for any given date cannot exceed 0. Hence, no bookings for class `c` can have been taken!

   2. In `Bookings`:
       b. $\forall bcPr1, bcPr2 : commit \bullet$
           $first(bcPr1) = first(bcPr2) \Rightarrow second(bcPr1) = second(bcPr2)$

An alternative is:

∀ b : BOOKING; c1,c2 : VanClass •
   (b,c1) ∈ commit ∧ (b,c2) ∈ commit ⇒ c1 = c2

c. ∀ bpPr1,bpPr2 : hirePeriods •
   first(bpPr1) = first(bpPr2) ⇒ second(bpPr1) = second(bpPr2)
   … with an alternative similar to that for (b).

d. {cbPr : custom • second(cbPr)} = {bcPr : commit • first(bcPr)}
   = {bpPr : hirePeriods • first(bpPr)}

e. activeBkngs ⊆ {cbPr : custom • second(cbPr)}
   … or either of the other two sets in (d).

f. ∀ p : {bpPr : hirePeriods • second(bpPr)} • length(p) ≤ maxHireLen
   We have assumed a length function defined over Period values.

In Vans:

g. ∀ vcPr1,vcPr2 : fleet •
   first(vcPr1) = first(vcPr2) ⇒ second(vcPr1) = second(vcPr2)
   … with an alternative similar to that for (b) or (c).

h. vansOnHire ∪ vansHireable ⊆ {vcPr : fleet • first(vcPr)}

i. vansOnHire ∩ vansHireable = ∅
   … or we could use disjoint of course.

In VanHire:

j. ∀ bvPr1,bvPr2 : activeHires •
   first(bvPr1) = first(bvPr2) ⇔ second(bvPr1) = second(bvPr2)

k. activeBkngs = {bvPr : activeHires • first(bvPr)}

l. vansOnHire = {bvPr : activeHires • second(bvPr)}

Note how use of bound variables over basic types in (m) and (n) below, rather than directly over the relations of VanHire, avoids use of first and second and makes (m) and (n) easier to express (though there is more than one way to do this).

m. ∀ b : BOOKING • ∀ v : VAN; c : VanClass | (v,c) ∈ fleet •
   (b,v) ∈ activeHires ⇒ (b,c) ∈ commit

n. ∀ b : BOOKING; p : Period | (b,p) ∈ hirePeriods •
   (∃ v : VAN • (b,v) ∈ activeHires) ⇒
     startOf(p) isOnOrBefore today

As well as the Date relation isOnOrBefore, we have assumed a startOf projection function defined over Period values. We could use first instead, of course. In fact, the more meaningfully named startOf would just be first in disguise.

o. One way to express the constraint in words is: *Take any van class c. Then for any date d, the number of bookings reserving class c whose hire periods include d does not exceed the number of vans of class c in the fleet.*

The first main set term below uses intersection to form the set of bookings reserving the arbitrary class c which have hire periods that include the arbitrary date d. The size of this set is compared with that of the number of vans in the fleet of class c, which is the second main set term.

∀ c : VanClass • ∀ d : Date •
#({b : BOOKING | (b,c) ∈ commit} ∩
  {bpPr : hirePeriods | d fallsIn second(bpPr) • first(bpPr)})
≤
#{vcPr : fleet | second(vcPr) = c}

We have assumed a fallsIn relation between Date and Period values.

Chapter 6

6.1 1. obj would be a binary relation between the set W and the set of binary relations of type X ↔ Y (recall that ↔ is right-associative). That is, each ordered pair (a,b) ∈ obj would be such that a ∈ W and b ∈ X ↔ Y, i.e., b would be a set of ordered pairs (c,d) where c ∈ X and d ∈ Y.

2. a. Yes. A (binary) relation is an object of type $\mathbb{P}(X \times Y)$ for some X and Y and hence can be empty, i.e., $\emptyset[X \times Y]$, in which case its domain and range are empty too.
   b. Yes. A maplet ($x \mapsto y$) of either abr1 or abr2 will belong to their union and hence x will belong to the domain of the union. Equally, since x will be in the domain of one or the other relation (or both), it will be in the union of their two domains. The equality is thus true in general.
   c. No. If ($x \mapsto y$) $\in$ abr1 and ($x \mapsto z$) $\in$ abr2 where $y \neq z$, then the two maplets do not belong to the intersection of abr1 and abr2, and hence x *does not necessarily* belong to the domain of this intersection. However, x will belong to the domain of both relations and hence necessarily to the intersection of these domains. So the equality in general is *not* true.
   d. Yes (the explanations are similar).

3. a. dom abr   b. ran abr   c. dom abr   d. ran abr   e. dom abr

4. a. In (i , j) $\in$ divEx, i must be a number greater than 1 that is exactly divisible by a number j lying strictly between i and 1. This rules out i being 1 or any prime. So (informally):
   dom divEx = $\mathbb{N}_1 \setminus (\{1\} \cup$ AllPrimeNos)
   b. In (i , j) $\in$ divEx, j must be a number greater than 1 that divides i exactly. This rules out 1 for j. For every other j > 1, there is a number i greater than j which j exactly divides. So: ran divEx = $\mathbb{N}_1 \setminus \{1\}$.
   c. Of the numbers in 1..9, only 4, 6, 8 and 9 are in the domain of divEx by the following maplet subset:
   $\{4 \mapsto 2, 6 \mapsto 2, 6 \mapsto 3, 8 \mapsto 2, 8 \mapsto 4, 9 \mapsto 3\}$
   So the answer is:
   $\{2, 3, 4\}$
   d. None of $\{5, 13, 19\}$ is in divEx's domain (they are all primes), so the answer is $\emptyset$.
   e. All even numbers greater than 2 are related to 2 by divEx. So the answer is:
   $\{k : \mathbb{N}_1 \mid k > 2 \wedge k \bmod 2 = 0\}$

6.2 1. Relation I is many-to-many.
   Relations II and IV are many-to-1.
   Relations III and V are 1-to-1.
   Relations I′, II′, etc. have the same cardinalities as their undecorated counterparts (the extra constraint of the 'egalitarian variations' does not alter their cardinalities).
   The class of binary relation missing is 1-to-many, i.e., one person can have a desk in many offices but each office is allocated to at most one person (a rather unlikely situation in practice!). For example:
   $\{s2 \mapsto o3, s4 \mapsto o1, s4 \mapsto o2, s4 \mapsto o5\}$

6.3 1. All are functional. In the following, 'total' means its domain is $\mathbb{N}$; 'surjective' or 'bijective' means its range is $\mathbb{N}$:
   a. total; range is $\{0\}$ b. partial (0 not in domain), injective, surjective
   c. total, injective; range is $\mathbb{N}_1$ d. total, injective; range is $\{0, 1, 4, 9, 16, \dots\}$
   e. total, bijective   f. total, surjective.

   2. (a)/(c)/(d): always (note that (d) is the 'most partial' function possible).
   (b): only if the domains of the two functions are disjoint, or one function is a subset of the other.
   (e): only if f is injective—if f is just many-to-1, its inverse will not be functional.

   3. (In order): $\{0\}$, 0..4, 2..6, $\{1, 4, 9, 16, 25\}$, 1..5, 0..2

6.4 1. Different periods can have the same start/end/length, so these functions are not injective; but the starts, ends and lengths of periods cover all possibilities (dates and lengths), so all three functions are surjective. datesIn, however, is injective but not surjective. It is injective because each period is made up of a unique set of dates. It is not surjective since not even all finite sets of dates (let alone infinite date sets) can be generated from periods, e.g., the empty date set, and any date set whose members do not form an unbroken span of days.

2. a.
$$\_\,\text{overlaps}\,\_ : \text{Period} \leftrightarrow \text{Period}$$
$$\forall\, p1, p2 : \text{Period} \bullet$$
$$p1 \text{ overlaps } p2 \Leftrightarrow$$
$$\text{start}(p1) \text{ fallsIn } p2 \lor \text{start}(p2) \text{ fallsIn } p1$$

b.
$$\text{disjntPds}\_ : \mathbb{P}(\mathbb{P}\,\text{Period})$$
$$\forall\, sp : \mathbb{P}\,\text{Period} \bullet$$
$$\text{disjntPds}(sp) \Leftrightarrow$$
$$(\forall\, p1, p2 : sp \mid p1 \neq p2 \bullet \neg(p1 \text{ overlaps } p2))$$

6.5 1. In order:

    $\text{custom}(\!|\,\text{activeBkngs}\,|\!)$

    $\#((\text{activeBkngs} \lhd \text{commit}) \rhd \{\,\text{vc?}\,\})$

    (the third term does not admit any sensible rewriting)

    $\text{dom}((\text{vansHireable} \lhd \text{fleet}) \rhd \{\,\text{heavyDuty}\,\})$

An adjacent pair of domain–range restriction operators exhibits associative properties. For example, the second term above could be rewritten as:

    $\#(\text{activeBkngs} \lhd (\text{commit} \rhd \{\,\text{vc?}\,\}))$

Similarly the fourth term.

2. a. $\varnothing$ b. abr   c. $\varnothing$ d. abr

3. a. $\text{compSci} \lhd \text{fdr}$

   b. $\#((\text{compSci} \lhd \text{fdr}) \rhd \{\,\text{first}\,\})$

   c. $\text{dom}((\text{compSci} \lhd \text{fdr}) \rhd \{\,\text{ii2}, \text{ii1}, \text{first}\,\})$

   d. $(\{\,s : \text{compSci} \mid \text{fdr}(s) = \text{pass}\,\} \lhd \text{fdr})$
       $\cup\,\{\,s : \text{compSci} \mid \text{fdr}(s) = \text{pass} \bullet s \mapsto \text{iii}\,\}$

    Note: this is much more easily expressed using the $\oplus$ operator, or even using a 'let expression'; both are discussed later in the chapter.

6.6 Operation A2:

This is the one operation where we pay a slight 'price' for the coupling between Bookings and Vans via activeHires due to the derived variables activeBkngs and vansOnHire. Without activeBkngs, the Bookings component would not change at all and hence certain equalities involving custom, etc. could be handled more simply (how?). In the operation schema, we have assumed that some external mechanism (e.g., the booking clerk) has selected the van to be allocated to the customer, and so this is an input.

```
___CollectVan _____
ΔVanHire
b? : BOOKING
v? : VAN
_____
b? ∈ dom custom \ activeBkngs      — booking exists but is not yet active
v? ∈ vansHireable                  — selected van is hireable
fleet( v? ) = commit( b? )         — van is of correct class
— the next equality also takes care of updates to activeBkngs and vansOnHire
activeHires' = activeHires ∪ { b? ↦ v? }
vansHireable' = vansHireable \ { v? }
fleet' = fleet
custom' = custom
commit' = commit
hirePeriods' = hirePeriods
today' = today
```

A variation is to replace the second and third conjuncts above with

    $\text{v?} \in \text{dom}((\text{vansHireable} \lhd \text{fleet}) \rhd \{\,\text{commit(b?)}\,\})$ (*)

A slightly different specification can be obtained by imagining that CollectVan itself chooses the van to allocate. In this case, the van the operation chooses is an *output*. In fact, all we need do is change v? to v!. The actual 'choosing' is embodied in (*) (or in the second and third conjuncts in the schema), which simply states that v! is a hireable van of the right class. It does not say which one, or how the choice has been made (nor should it—these are implementation issues). CollectVan in this form is *non-deterministic*.

Operation A3:
- we do not attempt to distinguish between early, on-time and late returns
- return of the van completes the booking, which now 'dies'
- the van is assumed to be roadworthy still, i.e., available for immediate re-hire.

```
┌─ ReturnVan ──────────────────────────────────────────────
│ ΔVanHire
│ b? : BOOKING
├───────────────────────────────────────────────────────────
│ b? ∈ activeBkngs              — booking must be active
│ — the next equality also takes care of updates to activeBkngs and vansOnHire
│ activeHires' = {b?} ⩤ activeHires
│ vansHireable' = vansHireable ∪ {activeHires(b?)}
│ custom' = {b?} ⩤ custom
│ commit' = {b?} ⩤ commit
│ hirePeriods' = {b?} ⩤ hirePeriods
│ fleet' = fleet
│ today' = today
└───────────────────────────────────────────────────────────
```

Operation A4:

```
┌─ CancelBooking ──────────────────────────────────────────
│ ΔVH_XiVans
│ b? : BOOKING
├───────────────────────────────────────────────────────────
│ b? ∈ dom custom \ activeBkngs      — booking exists but is not yet active
│ custom' = {b?} ⩤ custom
│ commit' = {b?} ⩤ commit
│ hirePeriods' = {b?} ⩤ hirePeriods
│ — the next equality also takes care of there being no change to activeBkngs
│ activeHires' = activeHires
│ today' = today
└───────────────────────────────────────────────────────────
```

Operation A6:
All new vans are given a pre-check and so are not immediately hireable.

```
┌─ AcquireNewVans ─────────────────────────────────────────
│ ΔVH_XiBookings
│ newVans? : VAN ⇸ VanClass
├───────────────────────────────────────────────────────────
│ dom newVans? ∩ dom fleet = ∅       — vans really are new
│ fleet' = fleet ∪ newVans?
│ vansHireable' = vansHireable
│ — the next equality also takes care of there being no change to vansOnHire
│ activeHires' = activeHires
│ today' = today
└───────────────────────────────────────────────────────────
```

6.7   Operation B1:

```
┌─ LateCompleters ─────────────────────────────────────────
│ ΞVanHire
│ lateBkngs! : ℙ BOOKING
├───────────────────────────────────────────────────────────
│ lateBkngs! = {b : activeBkngs | end(hirePeriods(b)) isBefore today}
└───────────────────────────────────────────────────────────
```

Operation B3:

```
┌─ InExcessOf ─────────────────────────────────────────────
│ ΞVanHire
│ nDays? : 1..maxHireLen - 1        — no hire period can exceed maxHireLen days
│ bkngs! : ℙ BOOKING
├───────────────────────────────────────────────────────────
│ bkngs! = {b : dom custom | length(hirePeriods(b)) > nDays?}
└───────────────────────────────────────────────────────────
```

Operation B4:

```
__FutureBookings_____
ΞVanHire
fbPerVc! : VanClass ⇸ ℙ BOOKING
──────────────────────────────────────────────────────────
fbPerVc! = { vc : ran fleet •
  vc ↦ {b : commit~⦇{vc}⦈ | start( hirePeriods(b)) isAfter today} }
```

Operation B5:

```
__NewBkngsTotals_____
ΞVanHire
dates? : ℙ Date
ttlPerDt! : Date ⇸ ℕ
──────────────────────────────────────────────────────────
— preconstraint: no date earlier than today is to be considered
∀ d : dates? • d isOnOrAfter today
ttlPerDt! =
  { d : dates? • d ↦ #{b : dom hirePeriods | start(hirePeriods(b)) = d} }
```

... or perhaps more friendly, though deviating slightly from spec. with the extra output:

```
__NewBkngsTotals_____
ΞVanHire
dates? : ℙ Date;
ttlPerDt! : Date ⇸ ℕ; badDates! : ℙ Date
──────────────────────────────────────────────────────────
badDates! = {d : dates? | d isBefore today}
ttlPerDt! =
  { d : ( dates? \ badDates! ) •
      d ↦ #{b : dom hirePeriods | start(hirePeriods(b)) = d} }
```

Operation B7:

```
VanStatus ::= offTheRoad | onHire | freeForHire
__StateOfFleet_____
ΞVanHire
vanStates! : VAN ⇸ VanStatus
──────────────────────────────────────────────────────────
vanStates! =
  {v : vansHireable • v ↦ freeForHire} ∪
  {v : vansOnHire • v ↦ onHire} ∪
  {v : ( dom fleet \ ( vansHireable ∪ vansOnHire)) • v ↦ offTheRoad}
```

6.8 1. a. Given the meaning of cm3, the following must hold: (i , i) ∈ cm3 for any i : ℕ
         (reflexive); (i , j) ∈ cm3 ⇒ (j , i) ∈ cm3 for any i , j : ℕ (symmetric); (i , j) ∈ cm3
         ∧ (j , k) ∈ cm3 ⇒ (i , k) ∈ cm3 for any i , j , k : ℕ (transitive). So cm3 is an equiv-
         alence relation.
     b. cm3 partitions ℕ into three subsets called *equivalence classes*: { 0 , 3 , 6 , 9 ... },
         { 1 , 4 , 7 , 10 , ... } and { 2 , 5 , 8 , 11 , ... }. Each subset contains just those elements that
         are in relation to one another by cm3. All equivalence relations partition the set over
         which they are defined. See Exercise 5.9(4) for the properties of a 'partition'.

      2 _< _ is a partial order in the 'strict' (irreflexive) sense of 'less than' relations. It is
         irreflexive: (i , i) does not belong _ < _, for any integer i; it is *asymmetric*: if (i , j)
         belongs to _< _ then (j , i) does not, for any integers i and j; and it is *transitive*: if
         (i , j) and (j , k) belong to _< _ then so does (i , k), for any integers i , j and k.

      3. • overlaps is reflexive and symmetric, but not transitive
          • joins is irreflexive and symmetric, but not transitive
          • includedIn is reflexive, antisymmetric, and transitive.
         So none are equivalence relations; but includedIn is a partial order in the ≤ sense. Yet,
         for any p , q : Period, it is not necessarily the case that either p includedIn q or
         q includedIn p, so includedIn is not a total order. (An exactly similar relation to
         includedIn is ⊆ for sets.)

4. a.   `rel` is irreflexive and asymmetric
   b. i. $rel^+ = rel \cup \{u \mapsto c, u \mapsto s, p \mapsto s\}$
       ii. $rel^* = rel^+ \cup \{u \mapsto u, p \mapsto p, c \mapsto c, s \mapsto s\}$
            rel^* is a total order over T (check it)
   c.   The symmetric closure of `rel` is $rel \cup \{p \mapsto u, c \mapsto p, s \mapsto c\}$, i.e., the smallest relation containing `rel` that is symmetric.

6.9 1. a. $\cap$ b. $\fatsemi$ in both instances   c. $\triangleleft$ d. $\triangleright$ e. $\triangleleft$ f. $\triangleright$ g. r2 then r1
        h. id A   i. ran r1   j. $\triangleleft$ k. $\cup$ l. $\fatsemi$ m. i * j   n. $\oplus$ (or $\cup$) in all instances

     2. a. 1   b. 4   c. 1   d. 1   e. 625   f. 5   g. 5   h. 25   i. 2

Chapter 7

7.1 1. `Year` would replace $\mathbb{N}$ in the declarations and defining axioms of `leapYr` and `isDate`. As a consequence, the constraint $y \geq 1753$ could be dropped from the defining predicates of both relations since it is part of the definition of `Year`.

     2. $\forall$ d1,d2 : 1..31; m1,m2 : 1..12; y1,y2 : Year |
          (d1,m1,y1) $\in$ Date $\wedge$ (d2,m2,y2) $\in$ Date $\bullet$
          (d1,m1,y1) isBefore (d2,m2,y2) $\Leftrightarrow$ y1 < y2 $\vee$ y1 = y2 $\wedge$ m1 < m2 $\vee$
                                                              y1 = y2 $\wedge$ m1 = m2 $\wedge$ d1 < d2
        $\forall$ d1,d2 : Date $\bullet$ d1 isOnOrBefore d2 $\Leftrightarrow$ d1 isBefore d2 $\vee$ d1 = d2
        $\forall$ d1,d2 : Date $\bullet$ (d1 isOnOrAfter d2 $\Leftrightarrow$ $\neg$ (d1 isBefore d2)) $\wedge$
          (d1 isAfter d2 $\Leftrightarrow$ $\neg$ (d1 isOnOrBefore d2))
        $\forall$ d : 1..31; m : 1..12; y : Year | (d,m,y) $\in$ Date $\bullet$
          eom(d,m,y) $\Leftrightarrow$ d = 31 $\vee$ d = 30 $\wedge$ ajsn(m) $\vee$
                                          d = 29 $\wedge$ m = 2 $\wedge$ leapYr(y) $\vee$
                                          d = 28 $\wedge$ m = 2 $\wedge$ $\neg$ leapYr(y)

   Note that the `isDate` constraint needed to make eom's description meaningful is taken care of by the constraint of the quantification, since eom's declaration now defines it to be a unary relation over the set `Date`.

   3. `mkDate` is not total since not all (d,y,m) combinations make a valid date; `prev` is not total since the `prev` of `dateZero` is undefined; `daysOff` is not total since, if date d is less than k days after `dateZero`, daysOff(d,k) is undefined; `dtMinus` is not total since d1 must be on or after d2 in dtMinus(d1,d2); `latest` is not total because there is no latest date in an infinite set of dates.

   4. a. $\forall$ d : 1..31; m : 1..12; y : Year | (d,m,y) $\in$ Date $\bullet$
              dayOf(d,m,y) = d $\wedge$ monthOf(d,m,y) = m $\wedge$ yearOf(d,m,y) = y
      b. dom mkDate = { d : 1..31; m : 1..12; y : Year | isDate(d,m,y) }
          $\forall$ d : 1..31; m : 1..12; y : Year | (d,m,y) $\in$ dom mkDate $\bullet$
              mkDate(d,m,y) = (d,m,y)

   The `isDate` constraint in the definition of mkDate's domain characterizes the function's partialness. In (a), the same constraint (bound up in Date's definition) scopes the variables in the defining predicate to be consistent with the functions' declarations.

7.2 1. a. i.   { Triangle' | rtAngld(a',b',c') $\bullet$ θ Triangle' }
            ii. { Triangle; d : $\mathbb{N}_1$ $\bullet$ (θ Triangle,d) }
            iii. { Triangle | rtAngld(a,b,c) $\bullet$ a + b + c }
                 though it is harmless if you think of this as expanding into
                 { a,b,c : $\mathbb{N}_1$ |
                     a + b > c $\wedge$ b + c > a $\wedge$ c + a > b $\wedge$ rtAngld(a,b,c) $\bullet$ a + b + c }
      b. The component names are a, b and c (*not* a!, b! and c!); all have type $\mathbb{Z}$.
      c. The in-scope reference to `Triangle'` is irrelevant. The 'term' given is simply not syntactically well-formed and hence is meaningless. Decoration, viewed as an operation, is applicable to schemas, but *not* to bindings!
      d. The definition makes `TriangleD` to be [a',b',c' : $\mathbb{N}_1$ ... etc. ...]. So the component names of θ TriangleD' are a', b' and c'. The ' in the names *come from the names in* TriangleD, *not* from the ' decoration in the binding term itself.

2. a. $\langle dy, mn, yr : \mathbb{Z} \rangle$ b. $\langle a', b', c' : \mathbb{Z} \rangle$ c. $\mathbb{P}\langle t, dy, mn, yr : \mathbb{Z} \rangle$
   d. i) $\mathbb{P}\langle a, b, c : \mathbb{Z} \rangle$ ii) $\mathbb{P}(\langle a, b, c : \mathbb{Z} \rangle \times \mathbb{Z})$ iii) $\mathbb{P}\mathbb{Z}$
   e. $\mathbb{P}((\langle dy, mn, yr : \mathbb{Z} \rangle \times \mathbb{Z}) \times \langle dy, mn, yr : \mathbb{Z} \rangle)$

3. You cannot construct an abbreviation definition for `dateZero` in terms of what the text has so far discussed. So a full axiomatic description is needed:

   | dateZero : Date
   |_____
   | dateZero.dy = 1 ∧ dateZero.mn = 1 ∧ dateZero.yr = bottomYr

   The defining axioms of the three functions would become:

   | ∀ d : Date •
   | dayOf d = d.dy ∧ monthOf d = d.mn ∧ yearOf d = d.yr

   which is more pleasing.

4. | unitTri : Triangle
   | rtAngld _ : $\mathbb{P}$ Triangle
   | perimLen : Triangle → $\mathbb{N}_1$
   |_____
   | unitTri.a = unitTri.b = unitTri.c = 1
   | ∀ t : Triangle •
   | (rtAngld t ⇔   t.a * t.a = t.b * t.b + t.c * t.c ∨
   | t.b * t.b = t.c * t.c + t.a * t.a ∨
   | t.c * t.c = t.a * t.a + t.b * t.b) ∧
   | (perimLen t = t.a + t.b + t.c)

5. ΞState ≙ [State; State' | θ State' = θ State]

7.3 1. a. $s \frown (t \frown u)$ b. #s + #t   c. $(\text{rev } t) \frown (\text{rev } s)$ d. s   e. s
     f. head s   g. $(s \upharpoonright V) \frown (t \upharpoonright V)$ h. $\langle \rangle$ i. $(1..\#s) \upharpoonright t$
     j. $(k..k + \#s - 1) \upharpoonright t$

7.4 1. Recall that a partial order is a homogeneous binary relation that is reflexive, anti-symmetric and transitive.
     partOrd[X] == { hbr : X ↔ X | (∀ x : X • (x,x) ∈ hbr) ∧
                                        (∀ x,y : X •
                                          (x,y) ∈ hbr ∧ (y,x) ∈ hbr ⇒ x = y) ∧
                                        (∀ x,y,z : X •
                                          (x,y) ∈ hbr ∧ (y,z) ∈ hbr ⇒ (x,z) ∈ hbr) }

7.5 Note that definitions (a–c) hold regardless of the `Date` model used.
     a. | daysDiff : Date × Date → $\mathbb{N}$
        |_____
        | ∀ d1, d2 : Date •
        | daysDiff(d1, d2) = (**if** d1 isBefore d2
        | **then** dtMinus(d2, d1) **else** dtMinus(d1, d2))

     b. | ordDtInYr : Date → (1..366)
        |_____
        | ∀ d : Date • ordDtInYr d = dtMinus(d, mkDate(1, 1, yearOf d)) + 1

     c. | _ upto _ : Date × Date → $\mathbb{P}$ Date
        |_____
        | ∀ d1, d2 : Date •
        | d1 upto d2 = { d : Date | d1 isOnOrBefore d isOnOrBefore d2 }

     d. |═══[X]═══
        | delFstOcc : X × seq X → seq X
        |_____
        | ∀ x : X; s : seq X •
        | delFstOcc(x, s) = ((1..#s) \ { fstPosIn(x, s)}) ↾ s

7.6 1. | daysDiff : Date × Date → $\mathbb{N}$
        |_____
        | ∀ d1, d2 : Date •
        | (d1 isBefore d2 ⇒ daysDiff(d1, d2) = dtMinus(d2, d1)) ∧
        | (d1 isOnOrAfter d2 ⇒ daysDiff(d1, d2) = dtMinus(d1, d2))

2. Sub1Day in DigitalWatch was defined to be total; prev here is not total. We have to use the 'long-winded' analogue to Sub1Day's description. There is a way of writing a shorter description for prev, but we do not know how to do this yet (see Exercise 7.9(e)). Note the independence of prev's definition from any Date model.

$$
\begin{array}{|l}
\hline
\text{prev} : \text{Date} \nrightarrow \text{Date} \\
\hline
\text{dom prev} = \text{Date} \setminus \{ \text{dateZero} \} \\
\forall \, dt : \text{dom prev} \bullet \\
\quad (\; \textbf{let} \;\; d == \text{dayOf } dt; \; m == \text{monthOf } dt; \; y == \text{yearOf } dt \bullet \\
\quad\quad (\, d = 1 \land m = 1 \Rightarrow \text{prev } dt = \text{mkDate}(\, 31, 12, y - 1 \,)\,) \hfill \land \\
\quad\quad (\, d = 1 \land m = 3 \land \text{leapYr } y \Rightarrow \text{prev } dt = \text{mkDate}(\, 29, 2, y \,)\,) \hfill \land \\
\quad\quad (\, d = 1 \land m = 3 \land \neg\, \text{leapYr } y \Rightarrow \text{prev } dt = \text{mkDate}(\, 28, 2, y \,)\,) \hfill \land \\
\quad\quad (\, d = 1 \land \text{ajsn}(\, m - 1 \,) \Rightarrow \text{prev } dt = \text{mkDate}(\, 30, m - 1, y \,)\,) \hfill \land \\
\quad\quad (\, d = 1 \land m \notin \{1,3\} \land \neg\, \text{ajsn}(\, m - 1 \,) \Rightarrow \text{prev } dt = \text{mkDate}(\, 31, m - 1, y \,)\,) \hfill \land \\
\quad\quad (\, d \neq 1 \Rightarrow \text{prev } dt = \text{mkDate}(\, d - 1, m, y \,)\,)\;) \\
\end{array}
$$

3. The definition uses the reference date 1st January 1993, which fell on a Friday (which is basically why daysUp was defined to start with Friday). We do a suitable subtraction between the date in question and the reference date, perform modulo 7 arithmetic which depends on which date is the earlier (if either), using the result to calculate an index to daysUp which gives the day in question. Use of a **let** expression adds a touch of tidiness to the definition.

Jan1st1993 == mkDate(1,1,1993)

$$
\begin{array}{|l}
\hline
\text{dayOfWeek} : \text{Date} \rightarrow \text{DaysInWeek} \\
\hline
\forall \, d : \text{Date} \bullet \\
\quad (\; \textbf{let} \;\; nDays == \text{daysDiff}(\, d, \text{Jan1st1993} \,) \bullet \\
\quad\quad (\, d \; \text{isBefore } \text{Jan1st1993} \Rightarrow \\
\quad\quad\quad \text{dayOfWeek } d = \text{daysUp}(\, 7 - ((\, nDays + 6 \,) \bmod 7 \,))\,) \land \\
\quad\quad (\, d \; \text{isOnOrAfter } \text{Jan1st1993} \Rightarrow \\
\quad\quad\quad \text{dayOfWeek } d = \text{daysUp}(\, nDays \bmod 7 + 1 \,))\;) \\
\end{array}
$$

4.
$$
\begin{array}{|l}
\hline
\forall \, e : X; \; s : \text{seq } X \bullet s = \langle\rangle \Rightarrow \text{countOccs}(\, e, s \,) = 0 \\
\forall \, e : X; \; t : \text{seq}_1 X \bullet \\
\quad (\, e = \text{head } t \Rightarrow \text{countOccs}(\, e, t \,) = 1 + \text{countOccs}(\, e, \text{tail } t \,)\,) \land \\
\quad (\, e \neq \text{head } t \Rightarrow \text{countOccs}(\, e, t \,) = \text{countOccs}(\, e, \text{tail } t \,)\,) \\
\\
\forall \, s : \text{seq } X \bullet \\
\quad (\, s = \langle\rangle \Rightarrow \text{elemsOf } s = \emptyset \,) \land \\
\quad (\, s \neq \langle\rangle \Rightarrow \text{elemsOf } s = \{ \text{head } s \} \cup \text{elemsOf}(\, \text{tail } s \,)\,) \\
\forall \, e : X; \; s : \text{seq } X \bullet s = \langle\rangle \Rightarrow \text{deleteAll}(\, e, s \,) = \langle\rangle \\
\forall \, e : X; \; t : \text{seq}_1 X \bullet \\
\quad (\, e = \text{head } t \Rightarrow \text{deleteAll}(\, e, t \,) = \text{deleteAll}(\, e, \text{tail } t \,)\,) \land \\
\quad (\, e \neq \text{head } t \Rightarrow \\
\quad\quad \text{deleteAll}(\, e, t \,) = \langle\, \text{head } t \,\rangle \frown \text{deleteAll}(\, e, \text{tail } t \,)\,) \\
\hline
\end{array}
$$

7.7

1.
$$
\begin{array}{|l}
\hline
\forall \, e : X \bullet \text{countOccs}(\, e, \langle\rangle \,) = 0 \\
\forall \, e : X; \; s : \text{seq } X \bullet \text{countOccs}(\, e, \langle\, e \,\rangle \frown s \,) = 1 + \text{countOccs}(\, e, s \,) \\
\forall \, e, h : X; \; s : \text{seq } X \mid e \neq h \bullet \text{countOccs}(\, e, \langle\, h \,\rangle \frown s \,) = \text{countOccs}(\, e, s \,) \\
\\
\text{elemsOf } \langle\rangle = \emptyset \\
\forall \, e : X; \; s : \text{seq } X \bullet \text{elemsOf}(\langle\, e \,\rangle \frown s \,) = \{ e \} \cup \text{elemsOf } s \\
\\
\forall \, e : X \bullet \text{deleteAll}(\, e, \langle\rangle \,) = \langle\rangle \\
\forall \, e : X; \; s : \text{seq } X \bullet \text{deleteAll}(\, e, \langle\, e \,\rangle \frown s \,) = \text{deleteAll}(\, e, s \,) \\
\forall \, e, h : X; \; s : \text{seq } X \mid e \neq h \bullet \\
\quad \text{deleteAll}(\, e, \langle\, h \,\rangle \frown s \,) = \langle h \rangle \frown \text{deleteAll}(\, e, s \,) \\
\hline
\end{array}
$$

2. a.
$$
\begin{array}{|l}
\hline
\text{fact} : \mathbb{N} \rightarrow \mathbb{N} \\
\hline
\text{fact } 0 = 1 \\
\forall \, k : \mathbb{N} \bullet \text{fact}(\, \text{succ } k \,) = \text{succ } k * \text{fact } k \\
\hline
\end{array}
$$

b.
$$
setDeleteAll : \mathbb{F}\, X \times seq\, X \to seq\, X
$$

$\forall\, t : seq\, X \bullet setDeleteAll(\varnothing, t) = t$

$\forall\, e : X;\ s : \mathbb{F}\, X;\ t : seq\, X \bullet$
  $setDeleteAll(\{e\} \cup s, t) = setDeleteAll(\ s \setminus \{e\}, deleteAll(e, t)\ )$

3. a.
$$
dom\ dtMinus = \{\, d1, d2 : Date \mid d1\ isOnOrAfter\ d2\,\}
$$

$\forall\, d : Date \bullet dtMinus(d, d) = 0$

$\forall\, d1, d2 : Date \mid d1\ isAfter\ d2 \bullet$
  $dtMinus(d1, d2) = 1 + dtMinus(\ prev\ d1, d2\ )$

b.
$$
dom\ daysOff = \{\, d : Date;\ k : \mathbb{N} \mid dtMinus(d, dateZero) \geq k\,\}
$$

$\forall\, d : Date \bullet daysOff(d, 0) = d$

— note the importance of k being a positive integer in the following:

$\forall\, d : Date;\ k : \mathbb{N}_1 \mid (d, k) \in dom\ daysOff \bullet$
  $daysOff(d, k) = daysOff(\ prev\ d, k - 1\ )$

7.8   1. $elemsOf[\,X\,] == \lambda\, s : seq\, X \bullet ran\ s$
$deleteAll[\,X\,] == \lambda\, x : X; s : seq\, X \bullet s \upharpoonright ((\ ran\ s\ ) \setminus \{\, x\,\})$

2. a.   0
   b.   50
       Calculates the number of days between Christmas day and the given earlier date (in the same year).
   c. $\langle\, 1, 1, 2, 3, 2\, \rangle$ (which comes from $\langle\, 1, 1\, \rangle \,^\frown\, \langle\, 2, 3, 2\, \rangle$)
       Rearranges the elements of a sequence s1 such that those of its elements not appearing in a sequence s2 move (in order) to the front and those which are in s2 move (in order) to the back.

7.9   a.
$$
nextAfterMin : \mathbb{F}_1 \mathbb{Z} \to \mathbb{Z}
$$

$\forall\, s : \mathbb{F}_1 \mathbb{Z} \bullet nextAfterMin\ s = (\mu\, k : s \mid (\forall\, e : s \bullet k \leq e) \bullet succ\ k)$

b. i. $\mu\, d : end (\!|\ ran\ hirePeriods\ |\!) \mid$
          $(\forall\, c : end (\!|\ ran\ hirePeriods\ |\!) \bullet c\ isOnOrBefore\ d)$
   ii.   not defined—there could be many customers with the same, longest hire period

c.
$\forall\, e : X;\ s : seq\, X \bullet$
  $(e \in ran\ s \Rightarrow$
  $\quad fstPosIn(e, s) = (\mu\, i : 1 .. \#s \mid s(i) = e \wedge e \notin ran((1 .. i - 1) \mathbin{1} s))) \wedge$
  $(e \notin ran\ s \Rightarrow fstPosIn(e, s) = 0)$

d.
$\forall\, d : Date; k : \mathbb{N} \bullet$
  $daysOn(d, k) = (\mu\, e : Date \mid e\ isOnOrAfter\ d \wedge dtMinus(e, d) = k)$

e.
$dom\ prev = Date \setminus \{\, dateZero\,\}$
$\forall\, dt : dom\ prev \bullet$
  (**let** $d == dayOf\ dt;\ m == monthOf\ dt;\ y == yearOf\ dt \bullet$
  $(d = 1 \wedge m = 1 \Rightarrow prev\ dt = mkDate(\ 31, 12, y - 1\ )) \wedge$
  $(d = 1 \wedge m \neq 1 \Rightarrow$
  $\quad prev\ dt = (\mu\, e : Date \mid monthOf\ e = m - 1 \wedge yearOf\ e = y \wedge eom\ e\ )) \wedge$
  $(d \neq 1 \Rightarrow prev\ dt = mkDate(d - 1, m, y)))$

7.10   1.   f1 maps A elements to $(\ B \to (C \to D)\ )$ functions
       f2 maps $(A \to B)$ functions to $(C \to D)$ functions
       f3 maps A elements to $((\ B \to C\ ) \to D)$ functions
       f4 is the same as f1.

2. a.
$$
\underline{\qquad[\,X\,]\qquad}
$$

$c\_delFstOcc : X \to seq\, X \to seq\, X$

$c\_delFstOcc =$
  $(\lambda\, e : X \bullet (\lambda\, s : seq\, X \bullet ((\ 1 .. \#s\ ) \setminus \{\, fstPosIn(e, s)\,\}) \mathbin{1} s))$

b.
$$\underline{\qquad}[X]\underline{\qquad\qquad\qquad\qquad\qquad\qquad}$$

repl : $\mathbb{N} \to$ seq X $\to$ seq X

$\forall$ s : seq X $\bullet$ repl 0 s = $\langle\ \rangle$
$\forall$ k : $\mathbb{N}$; s : seq X $\bullet$ repl (succ k) s = s $^\frown$ (repl k s)

c. delFstOccNullSet == c_delFstOcc $\varnothing[\mathbb{Z}]$
The parameter for $\varnothing$ is essential, otherwise the context is insufficiently strong to determine that $\varnothing$ is intended to be of type $\mathbb{P}\mathbb{Z}$ (or, indeed, any type).

d. repl10Times == repl 10

3. a. Declare mkDate in full curried form (mkDate : 1..31 $\to$ 1..12 $\to$ Year $\to$ Date plus minor change to axiom: mkDate d m y = ...). The function required is then calculated by the term

   mkDate 25 12

b. Declare daysOn in full curried form but with the argument order reversed (daysOn : $\mathbb{N} \to$ Date $\to$ Date plus minor change to axiom: daysOn k d = ...). The function required is then calculated by the term

   daysOn 28

This example illustrates how the need to apply a curried function in particular anticipated ways to calculate other functions may affect the argument order chosen for the parent function.

7.11 1. The simple solution is to apply reflexive transitive closure to a 'sub-relation' comprising the four maplets involved in the four axioms on page 180.

vclMaplets : $\mathbb{P}($ VanClass $\times$ VanClass $)$
_ lessOrEq _ : VanClass $\leftrightarrow$ VanClass

vclMaplets = { mini $\mapsto$ transit, transit $\mapsto$ light,
           light $\mapsto$ medium, medium $\mapsto$ heavyDuty }
(_ lessOrEq _) = vclMaplets*

7.12 1. a. null == ascii 0
        esc == ascii 27
        upLetters == { k : 65..90 $\bullet$ ascii k }
        digits == { k : 48..57 $\bullet$ ascii k }

b.
ctoi : Char $\to$ 0..127
nextCh : Char $\twoheadrightarrow$ Char

$\forall$ k : 0..127 $\bullet$ ctoi(ascii k) = k
dom nextCh = Char \ { ascii 127 }
$\forall$ j : 0..126 $\bullet$ nextCh(ascii j) = ascii(j + 1)

c.
_ chle _ : Char $\leftrightarrow$ Char

$\forall$ k1, k2 : 0..127 $\bullet$ (ascii k1) chle (ascii k2) $\Leftrightarrow$ k1 $\le$ k2

2. a. T ::= c | f$\langle\!\langle$ T $\rangle\!\rangle$
b. Everything in the enriched given-set based description would be needed *except*:
   • given set [T]
   • declarations of c and f and accompanying predicate, all of which (a) takes care of
c. An induction principle over T

7.13 1. a.
elemsOfq : Queue $\to$ $\mathbb{P}$ X

elemsOfq emptyq = $\varnothing$
$\forall$ e : X; q : Queue $\bullet$
   elemsOfq(addq(e, q)) = { e } $\cup$ elemsOfq q

b.
delFstOccq : X $\times$ Queue $\to$ Queue

$\forall$ e : X $\bullet$ delFstOccq(e, emptyq) = emptyq
$\forall$ e : X; q : Queue $\bullet$ delFstOccq(e, addq(e, q)) = q
$\forall$ e1, e2 : X; q : Queue | e1 $\ne$ e2 $\bullet$
   delFstOccq(e1, addq(e2, q)) = addq(e2, delFstOccq(e1, q))

c.

$$\text{quToSeq} : \text{Queue} \to \text{seq } X$$

$$\text{quToSeq emptyq} = \langle\,\rangle$$
$$\forall e : X; q : \text{Queue} \bullet \text{quToSeq}(\text{addq}(e,q)) = \langle e\rangle \,\widehat{}\, \text{quToSeq } q$$

d. This is slightly tricky 'from scratch', i.e., if we avoid use of other Queue functions and attempt to construct a definition of fstPosInq based on generator term structures as in (a), (b) and (c). The problem is not knowing 'in advance' whether the element being searched for is in the queue or not. The solution below uses an auxiliary function findPos that 'carries a number around with it' as shown by its defining predicates. fstPosInq is then defined in terms of findPos, which 'shields' the positional information from the interface of fstPosInq.

$$\text{fstPosInq} : X \times \text{Queue} \to \mathbb{N}$$
$$\text{findPos} : X \times \text{Queue} \times \mathbb{N} \to \mathbb{N}$$

$$\forall e : X; q : \text{Queue} \bullet \text{fstPosInq}(e,q) = \text{findPos}(e,q,1)$$
$$\forall e : X; q : \text{Queue}; k : \mathbb{N} \bullet \text{findPos}(e, \text{emptyq}, k) = 0$$
$$\forall e1, e2 : X; q : \text{Queue}; k : \mathbb{N} \bullet$$
$$(e1 = e2 \Rightarrow \text{findPos}(e1, \text{addq}(e2,q), k) = k) \wedge$$
$$(e1 \neq e2 \Rightarrow \text{findPos}(e1, \text{addq}(e2,q), k) = \text{findPos}(e1, q, k+1))$$

2. The simplest way would be to keep (property-oriented) Queue and define InjQueue as a subset of Queue with the required injective property, which can be expressed as a unary relation over Queue thus:

$$\text{injQ}\_ : \mathbb{P}\,\text{Queue}$$

$$\text{injQ emptyq}$$
$$\forall e : X; q : \text{Queue} \bullet$$
$$\quad \text{injQ}(\text{addq}(e,q)) \Leftrightarrow e \notin \text{elemsOfq } q \wedge \text{injQ } q$$

Now it is easy to define
$$\text{InjQueue} == \{\, q : \text{Queue} \mid \text{injQ } q \,\}$$
and all the Queue operations still apply to InjQueue.

3. $[X]$
$$\text{Stack} ::= \text{emptySt} \mid \text{push}\langle\!\langle X \times \text{Stack} \rangle\!\rangle$$

$$\text{pop} : \text{Stack} \twoheadrightarrow \text{Stack}$$
$$\text{topSt} : \text{Stack} \twoheadrightarrow X$$
$$\text{lenSt} : \text{Stack} \to \mathbb{N}$$

$$\text{lenSt emptySt} = 0$$
$$\forall e : X; s : \text{Stack} \bullet \text{lenSt}(\text{push}(e,s)) = 1 + \text{lenSt } s$$
$$\text{dom pop} = \text{dom topSt} = \text{Stack} \setminus \{\text{emptySt}\}$$
$$\forall e : X; s : \text{Stack} \bullet$$
$$\quad \text{pop}(\text{push}(e,s)) = s \wedge$$
$$\quad \text{topSt}(\text{push}(e,s)) = e$$

7.14 1. Cond ::=
relE$\langle\!\langle$ RelExpr $\rangle\!\rangle$ | conj$\langle\!\langle$ Cond $\times$ Cond $\rangle\!\rangle$ | disj$\langle\!\langle$ Cond $\times$ Cond $\rangle\!\rangle$ | neg$\langle\!\langle$ Cond $\rangle\!\rangle$
We have assumed the type RelExpr for relational expressions. Constructor names are of course purely our choice.

2. a. iter(P, c1, select(Q, { (c2, iter(R, c3, op C)),
(neg c2, iter(S, c3, op D)) }))
Note the relevance of Question (1)—we need to express the guard for the **else** part of the selection, and this is the negation of the guard for the **then** part.

b. A: **if** c3
then B: **while** c2 **do**
C: **while** c1 **do** D **end do**
end do
elsif c4
then D
end if

3. For convenience, the definitions of nNode and loopFree have been combined and spread over the last four 'for alls'. Note that the definitional relationship between nNdsInSeq and nNode is 'mutually recursive'; similarly for nNdsInFinSet.

$$nNdsInSeq : seq\ JSPTree \rightarrow \mathbb{N}$$
$$nNdsInFinSet : \mathbb{F}\ JSPTree \rightarrow \mathbb{N}$$
$$nNode : JSPTree \rightarrow \mathbb{N}$$
$$loopFree\_ : \mathbb{P}\ JSPTree$$

$$nNdsInSeq\ \langle\ \rangle = 0$$
$$\forall jt : JSPTree;\ sqjt : seq\ JSPTree \bullet$$
$$\quad nNdsInSeq(\langle\ jt\ \rangle \frown sqjt) = nNode\ jt + nNdsInSeq\ sqjt$$

$$nNdsInFinSet\ \varnothing = 0$$
$$\forall jt : JSPTree;\ setjt : \mathbb{F}\ JSPTree \bullet$$
$$\quad nNdsInFinSet(\{jt\} \cup setjt) = nNode\ jt + nNdsInFinSet(setjt \setminus \{jt\})$$

$$\forall oId : OperationId \bullet$$
$$\quad nNode(op\ oId) = 1 \wedge loopFree(op\ oId)$$

$$\forall oId : OperationId;\ sqjt : seq\ JSPTree \bullet$$
$$\quad nNode(seqCmp(oId, sqjt)) = 1 + nNdsInSeq\ sqjt \wedge$$
$$\quad (\ loopFree(seqCmp(oId, sqjt)) \Leftrightarrow$$
$$\quad\quad (\ \forall i : 1..\#sqjt \bullet loopFree(sqjt(i))\ )\ )$$

$$\forall oId : OperationId;\ setcjt : \mathbb{F}_2(Cond \times JSPTree) \bullet$$
$$\quad nNode(select(oId, setcjt)) = 1 + nNdsInFinSet(second(\!|\ setcjt\ |\!)) \wedge$$
$$\quad (\ loopFree(select(oId, setcjt)) \Leftrightarrow$$
$$\quad\quad (\ \forall cjt : setcjt \bullet loopFree(second\ cjt)\ )\ )$$

$$\forall oId : OperationId;\ cnd : Cond;\ jt : JSPTree \bullet$$
$$\quad nNode(iter(oId, cnd, jt)) = 1 + nNode\ jt \wedge$$
$$\quad \neg loopFree(iter(oId, cnd, jt))$$

4. a. $VanClOrChar ::= vcInj\langle\!\langle\ VanClass\ \rangle\!\rangle\ |\ chInj\langle\!\langle\ Char\ \rangle\!\rangle$

  b.
$$convToNat : VanClOrChar \rightarrow \mathbb{N}$$

$$convToNat(vcInj\ mini) = 0$$
$$convToNat(vcInj\ transit) = 1$$
$$convToNat(vcInj\ light) = 2$$
$$convToNat(vcInj\ medium) = 3$$
$$convToNat(vcInj\ heavyDuty) = 4$$
$$\forall i : 0..127 \bullet convToNat(chInj(ascii\ i)) = i$$

Chapter 8

8.2 1. allUsers (calculated by dom mcRegns) and olmMcs (calculated by ran mcRegns) in SysConstraints; mcsOnline (calculated by dom waiting) in OnlineMonitor.

  2. (SysActivity)
  - lines allocated to users are working lines
  - machines with working lines have connect queues
  - for every machine with working lines
    - each line allocated can be allocated to only one user
    (note how this has been expressed in the schema—the cnnctns function is domain-restricted to the working lines of the machine and the resulting (possibly narrower) function is asserted to be one-one)
    - if its connect queue is not empty, all its working lines must be allocated
  - for every line allocated to a user
    - the user cannot be in the connect queue of the machine owning the line

  (OnlineMonitor)
  - the users known to Uhura are those registered on one or more machines
  - the machines known to Uhura are those having user registrations

- the lines going to machines come from Uhura's overall line pool
- the working lines to each machine are a subset of the overall lines to each machine
- the machines with connect queues are precisely those which are on line
- for every on-line machine
  - its connect queue does not exceed the maximum permitted length
  - users in the connect queue are registered on the machine
- for every line allocated to a user
  - the user is registered on the machine which owns the line

3. a. In the first conjunct of `SysActivity`. The interpretation is that lines allocated to users (dom cnnctns) come only from working lines (dom linesUp). So if all lines to a machine are down, none of those lines appear in dom linesUp (which will be ∅) and hence nobody can be connected to the machine.

   b. No. It is taken care of by the implication in the first quantification in `SysActivity`. If its consequent is false (not all working lines are allocated), then so is its antecedent, i.e., waiting m ≠ emptyq is false—the connect queue *is* empty (if $P \Rightarrow Q$, then equivalently $\neg Q \Rightarrow \neg P$).

   c. (This involves the same predicate component as in (b).) We can deduce nothing about the state of the connect queue in this circumstance, nor should we be able to—if all lines are in use, the queue could be empty or not empty. Remember that if Q is true in $P \Rightarrow Q$, P can be true or false.

   d. Yes. In `SysActivity`, the machines with working lines are just a subset of the machines with connect queues (and in `OnlineMonitor`, the machines with connect queues are those which are on line). So, a machine can have no working lines, hence zero connections, but it can still have a connect queue. Moreover, its connect queue can be in any permitted state, which includes non-empty. Note that this is in accord with reality—there could be users waiting to use a machine whose lines are all temporarily unavailable.

4.
```
┌─ WithdrawMc ──────────────────────────────────────────
│ ΔOnlineMonitor; m? : MACHINE
├───────────────────────────────────────────────────────
│ m? ∈ olmMcs \ mcsOnline
│ linePool' = linePool
│ maxQLenFor' = { m? } ⩤ maxQLenFor
│ linesToMcs' = linesToMcs ⩥ { m? }
│ privUsers' = privUsers \ ( allUsers \ allUsers' )
│ mcRegns' = mcRegns ⩥ { m? }
│ θ SysActivity' = θ SysActivity
└───────────────────────────────────────────────────────
```

The preconstraint makes the reasonable restriction that the machine to be withdrawn cannot be on line. Note that no explicit updates to the three derived components allUsers, olmMcs and mcsOnline are described in `WithdrawMc`. This is because the required updates can be inferred, as follows:

- The possible update to derived component allUsers is taken care of by the sixth conjunct above and the equality in `OnlineMonitor` involving allUsers.

- The fact that derived component olmMcs must lose m? is taken care of by the sixth conjunct above and the equality in `OnlineMonitor` involving olmMcs.

- The fact that derived component mcsOnline remains unchanged is taken care of by: (a) the last conjunct above, which therefore means in particular that waiting does not change (waiting is a variable of `SysActivity`); (b) the equality in the `OnlineMonitor` schema involving mcsOnline.

Note: the tricky explicit update to describe is on privUsers, which *could* change state; basically, if allUsers 'loses' any users as a result of the operation, any of those users which were privileged must be 'lost' from privUsers.

8.3 1. Variable waiting is unchanged. New variable linesUp is a transformation of linesUp in the first version of `SysActivity`. The latter has been inverted and the range made ℙ LINE to keep the variable a function. New variable cnnctns in effect has been obtained by partitioning the first version across each machine. This has enabled the required injectivity of lines-to-users for each machine to be expressed directly in the declaration of cnnctns, rather than as a (somewhat clumsy) predicate.

With both linesUp and cnnctns, however, there is a potential subtle difference between the new and old versions. In the new version of SysActivity, the fact that some machines may have no working lines can be dealt with differently: we can include them in the domain of linesUp and map them to the empty LINE set. Note that doing this would impinge on the relationship of cnnctns with the other two variables of SysActivity. It would also be possible to treat cnnctns in the same way as suggested for linesUp (machines with no connections mapping to the empty LINE ↛ USER function).

Clearly, care is needed with the predicate of new SysActivity to get the precise interpretation we want. If we wish the roles of the variables of new SysActivity to correspond as closely as possible to the first version, a constraint will be needed to exclude the empty LINE set from the range of linesUp and the empty LINE ↛ USER function from the range of cnnctns. However, altering the roles of linesUp and cnnctns as indicated in the previous paragraph is more consistent with changing the state model to focus on machine entities. In that case, the simplest consistent decision which ties the three variables of new SysActivity together is to require that their domains are equal. Thus, either a machine is recorded as having a set of working lines (possibly empty) *and* a set of user connections (possibly empty) *and* a connect queue (possibly empty too), or it has none of these. We get:

```
___ SysActivity _____
  linesUp : MACHINE ↛ ℙ LINE
  cnnctns : MACHINE ↛ ( LINE ↣ USER )
  waiting : MACHINE ↛ InjQueue[ USER ]
 _____
  dom linesUp = dom cnnctns = dom waiting
  ∀ m : dom cnnctns •
    dom( cnnctns m ) ⊆ linesUp m ∧
    ran( cnnctns m ) ∩ elemsOfq( waiting m ) = ∅ ∧
    ( waiting m ≠ emptyq ⇒ #( cnnctns m ) = #( linesUp m ))
```

2. We could alter SysConfig as below. Note the changes to predicates and declarations.

```
___ SysConfig _____
  mcsOnline : ℙ MACHINE
  maxQLenFor : MACHINE ↛ ℕ
  linesToMcs : MACHINE ↛ ℙ LINE      — consistent with new SysActivity (*)
  privUsers : ℙ USER
  mcRegns : MACHINE ↛ ℙ USER         — consistent with new SysActivity
 _____
  mcsOnline ⊆ dom linesToMcs = dom maxQLenFor   — note the = (not ⊆ – why?)
  dom mcRegns = dom maxQLenFor
  privUsers ⊆ ∪( ran mcRegns )
  sysManager ∈ privUsers
  ∀ m : dom mcRegns • sysManager ∈ mcRegns m
  ∀ m1 , m2 : dom linesToMcs | m1 ≠ m2 •    — now required because of (*) above …
    linesToMcs m1 ∩ linesToMcs m2 = ∅      — … no line sharing between machines
```

3.
```
___ OnlineMonitor _____
  SysConfig; SysActivity; SysConstraints
 _____
  ∪( ran mcRegns ) = allUsers
  dom mcRegns = olmMcs
  ∪( ran linesToMcs ) ⊆ linePool
  mcsOnline = dom waiting
  ∀ m : mcsOnline •
    linesUp m ⊆ linesToMcs m ∧
    lenq( waiting m ) ≤ maxQLenFor m ∧
    ran( cnnctns m ) ∪ elemsOfq( waiting m ) ⊆ mcRegns m
```

8.4 1. Remember that `sysManager` is registered on any machine brought into service.

```
┌─── InitComputer ─────────────────────────────────────────────
│ Computer′
├───────────────────────────────────────────────────────────
│ avlblty′ = offline
│ users′ = priv′ = { sysManager }
│ allLines′ = linesUp′ = Ø
│ cnnctd′ = Ø
│ cnnctQu′ = emptyq
│ maxQLen′ = 0
└───────────────────────────────────────────────────────────
```

2. (Recall that the first four operations on page 201 are dealt with elsewhere in the text.) In the first operation below, remember that a machine which is down does not mean it is no longer on-line—'availability' refers to 'on/off-linedness', *not* 'up/down-ness'; thus, its availability attribute does *not* change. Note how (re)queuing is inhibited—by setting the maximum queue length parameter to 0.

```
┌─── McGoesDown ───────────────────────────────────────────────
│ ΔComputer
├───────────────────────────────────────────────────────────
│ — the second conjunct is not strictly necessary (why?):
│ linesUp′ = Ø;  cnnctd′ = Ø;  cnnctQu′ = emptyq;  maxQLen′ = 0
│ avlblty′ = avlblty;  users′ = users
│ priv′ = priv;  allLines′ = allLines
└───────────────────────────────────────────────────────────
```

In the next operation, we need to know who are new privileged users, if any:

```
┌─── RegNewUsers ──────────────────────────────────────────────
│ ΔComputer
│ newUsers? : ℙ₁ USER          — all new users
│ newPrivUsers? : ℙ USER        — those new users who are privileged
├───────────────────────────────────────────────────────────
│ newPrivUsers? ⊆ newUsers?
│ newUsers? ∩ users = Ø
│ users′ = users ∪ newUsers?
│ priv′ = priv ∪ newPrivUsers?
│ avlblty′ = avlblty;  allLines′ = allLines;  linesUp′ = linesUp
│ cnnctd′ = cnnctd;  cnnctQu′ = cnnctQu;  maxQLen′ = maxQLen
└───────────────────────────────────────────────────────────
```

In the final operation, we have written the minimum description needed. All state components not mentioned have after states consequential on the `Computer′` predicate (work out how).

```
┌─── McGoesOffline ────────────────────────────────────────────
│ ΔComputer
├───────────────────────────────────────────────────────────
│ — we make the reasonable constraint that no user is attached to the machine
│ cnnctd = Ø;  cnnctQu = emptyq
│ avlblty′ = offline;  users′ = users;  priv′ = priv
│ allLines′ = allLines;  maxQLen′ = maxQLen
└───────────────────────────────────────────────────────────
```

8.5 1. UserStatus ::= ordinary | privileged

```
┌─── User ─────────────────────────────────────────────────────
│ status : UserStatus
│ regMcs : ℙ₁ MACHINE          — machine(s) on which user is registered (at least one)
│ cnnctd : MACHINE ⤚ LINE      — machine(s) to which user is currently connected
│ waiting : MACHINE ⇸ ℕ₁       — machine(s) for which user is currently queued …
│                              — … plus position in queue …
├───────────────────────────────────────────────────────────
│ dom cnnctd ∪ dom waiting ⊆ regMcs
│ dom cnnctd ∩ dom waiting = Ø
└───────────────────────────────────────────────────────────
```

This is fine as far as it can go, but it should be clear that a full state model, incorporating many User instances, would require quite a complex predicate, particularly as regards attributes and relations pertaining to machines. Consider, for example, the problem of asserting consistency of composition of connect queues or user line allocations conveyed by the User instances!

2. One could base the state model structure partly on booking entities:

BkngStatus ::= toStart | active

```
┌─── BookingRec ──────────────────────────────
│ cstmr : CUSTOMER
│ vcl : VanClass
│ datePr : Period
│ status : BkngStatus
│ vanAlloc : VAN
│ ────────────────────────────
│ length datePr ≤ maxHireLen
└──────────────────────────────────────────────
```

8.6 1. Vars1/Vars3 (c in the former clashes with global c in the latter)
Vars2/Vars4 (b incompatible)
(remember that x? and c are, respectively, different names to x! and c')

2. a. Any such pair (suitable renaming can side-step any type/name incompatiblity)
   b. $[c',a,x! : \mathbb{Z}; b : \text{Date} \mid c' < 0 \wedge a \neq 0 \wedge (\text{dayOf } b = -c' \bmod a)]$

8.7 a. $[\Delta\text{Vars} \mid (x' = y \wedge y' = x) \vee (x' = x \wedge y' = y)]$

b. $[x,y : \mathbb{Z}; x',y' : \mathbb{Z} \mid \neg(x \geq 0 \wedge y \geq 0 \wedge x < n \wedge y < m \wedge$
$\qquad\qquad\qquad\qquad x' \geq 0 \wedge y' \geq 0 \wedge x' < n \wedge y' < m)]$ which is …
$[x,y,x',y' : \mathbb{Z} \mid \neg(0 \leq x < n \wedge 0 \leq y < m \wedge 0 \leq x' < n \wedge 0 \leq y' < m)]$

c. $[x,y : \mathbb{N}; x'',y'' : \mathbb{N}; x',y' : \mathbb{N} \mid$
$\quad x < n \wedge y < m \wedge x'' < n \wedge y'' < m \wedge x' < n \wedge y' < m \wedge$
$\quad x'' = y \wedge y'' = x \wedge x' = y'' \wedge y' = x'']$ which is …
$[\Delta\text{Vars}; \text{Vars}'' \mid x'' = y \wedge y'' = x \wedge x' = y'' \wedge y' = x'']$

8.8 1. a. Either noAutoCnnct or autoCnnctMade, but we could not say which.
   b. Because acUser! is a subsidiary output of just AutoConnect and is not indicative of the outcome of *the combination* of FreeLine and AutoConnect. If FreeLine is applicable, acUser! in Disconnect is some arbitrary member of the set USER, which is harmless because acUser! is of no significance in this case.

2. LineChange ::= add | delete

```
┌─── LineCapInc ──────────────────────────────────────
│ ΔComputer
│ lc? : LineChange; lns? : ℙ₁LINE
│ ──────────────────────────────────────────────
│ lc? = add; avlblty = offline        — assume machine must be off line
│ lns? ∩ allLines = ∅                  — must be adding completely fresh lines
│ allLines' = allLines ∪ lns?
│ avlblty' = avlblty; users' = users; priv' = priv
│ linesUp' = linesUp; cnnctd' = cnnctd
│ cnnctQu' = cnnctQu; maxQLen' = maxQLen
└──────────────────────────────────────────────────────
```

```
┌─── LineCapDec ──────────────────────────────────────
│ ΔComputer
│ lc? : LineChange; lns? : ℙ₁LINE
│ ──────────────────────────────────────────────
│ lc? = delete; avlblty = offline      — assume machine must be off line
│ lns? ⊆ allLines                       — must be removing lines owned by m/c
│ allLines' = allLines \ lns?
│ avlblty' = avlblty; users' = users; priv' = priv
│ linesUp' = linesUp; cnnctd' = cnnctd
│ cnnctQu' = cnnctQu; maxQlen' = maxQLen
└──────────────────────────────────────────────────────
```

ChangeLineCap ≙ LineCapInc ∨ LineCapDec

8.9 1.

```
┌─── NoSpareCpcty ──────────────────────────────────────
│ ΞComputer
│ u? : USER
│ attachMes! : OLM_Message
│ ───────────────────────────────
│ avlblty = online; u? ∈ users
│ lenq cnnctQu = maxQLen
│ attachMes! = noAttachRoom
└────────────────────────────────────────────────────────
```

```
┌─── AlreadyInSys ──────────────────────────────────────
│ ΞComputer
│ u? : USER
│ attachMes! : OLM_Message
│ ───────────────────────────────
│ avlblty = online; u? ∈ users;  lenq cnnctQu < maxQLen
│ u? ∈ ran cnnctd ∪ elemsOfq cnnctQu
│ attachMes! = alreadyAttached
└────────────────────────────────────────────────────────
```

2. Define the following extra schemas:

```
┌─── Pass3Checks ───────────────────────────────────────
│ ΞComputer
│ u? : USER
│ ───────────────────────────────
│ avlblty = online; u? ∈ users;  lenq cnnctQu < maxQLen
└────────────────────────────────────────────────────────
```

```
┌─── AlreadyInQueue ────────────────────────────────────
│ ΞComputer
│ u? : USER
│ attachMes! : OLM_Message
│ pique! : ℕ₁
│ ───────────────────────────────
│ u? ∈ elemsOfq cnnctQu
│ attachMes! = alreadyQueued        — assume added to OLM_Message
│ pique! = posInq(u?, cnnctQu)
└────────────────────────────────────────────────────────
```

```
┌─── AlreadyOnline ─────────────────────────────────────
│ ΞComputer
│ u? : USER
│ attachMes! : OLM_Message
│ ───────────────────────────────
│ u? ∈ ran cnnctd
│ attachMes! = alreadyCnnctd        — assume added to OLM_Message
└────────────────────────────────────────────────────────
```

Then define:

AlreadyInSys ≙ Pass3Checks ∧ (AlreadyInQueue ∨ AlreadyOnline)

3. No. The requirement is implicit. The assertion of membership for aFreeLn can hold if and only if the set linesUp \ dom cnnctd is non-empty, i.e., there is at least one free working line.

4. a.

```
┌─── QueueUser ─────────────────────────────────────────
│ ΔComputer
│ u? : USER
│ attachMes! : OLM_Message
│ ───────────────────────────────
│ linesUp \ dom cnnctd = ∅
│ attachMes! = queued
│ cnnctQu' = addq(u?, cnnctQu)
│ avlblty' = avlblty; users' = users; priv' = priv
│ allLines' = allLines; linesUp' = linesUp
│ cnnctd' = cnnctd; maxQLen' = maxQLen
└────────────────────────────────────────────────────────
```

b.

```
┌──LeaveQueue ────────────────────────────────────────────
│ ΔComputer
│ u? : USER
│ attachMes! : OLM_Message
├──────────────────────────────────────────────────────────
│ u? ∈ elemsOfq cnnctQu
│ cnnctQu' = delFstOccq(u?,cnnctQu)
│ attachMes! = dequeued                — assume added to OLM_Message
│ avlblty' = avlblty; users' = users; priv' = priv
│ allLines' = allLines; linesUp' = linesUp
│ cnnctd' = cnnctd; maxQLen' = maxQLen
└──────────────────────────────────────────────────────────
```

```
┌──BadLeaveQuReq ─────────────────────────────────────────
│ ΞComputer
│ u? : USER
│ attachMes! : OLM_Message
├──────────────────────────────────────────────────────────
│ u? ∉ elemsOfq cnnctQu
│ attachMes! = notInQueue               — assume added to OLM_Message
└──────────────────────────────────────────────────────────
```

RbLeaveQueue ≙ LeaveQueue ∨ BadLeaveQuReq

8.10 1. $x > 3 \Rightarrow x \geq 0$ $x \geq 0 \Rightarrow x > 3$ $(x \geq 0, x > 3 \vee x \geq 0)$ $(x > 3, x > 3 \wedge x \geq 0)$
The first predicate is satisfied by all possible states of x—if the antecedent is true, so is the consequent (if the antecedent is false, the latter is irrelevant); so the predicate is effectively just `true`. The second is satisfied by all states of x except 0, 1, 2 and 3 (these four cases make the antecedent true but the consequent false). The next two are satisfied when $x \geq 0$, the last two only when $x > 3$. It is worth noting that conjunct addition and disjunct deletion in general strengthen predicates, whereas conjunct deletion and disjunct addition in general have a weakening effect.

2. A deterministic operation has only one possible outcome for any start space binding that satisfies the operation's precondition. This is functional behaviour. So deterministic operations on a state could be expressed axiomatically as functions.

3. Its applicable start space (domain) is $\emptyset$, i.e., there are no start-space bindings for which the operation predicate is satisfiable. We call such an operation *infeasible*. In fact, it is the pathological case of (4) …

4. If a (non-robust) operation is applied outside its precondition, its specification does not say what happens. This means that the operation can do anything. It might produce some coherent after-state, but it does not have to—it can perform arbitrary manipulations and updates. Hence, for an operation whose precondition is `false`, the practical consequence is that we can implement it in any way we like!

8.11 1. The elimination of $y!$ is justified because the term $(a - x?) + b$: (i) does not contain an occurrence of $y!$; (ii) is a member of $\mathbb{N}$ (like $y!$), which is ensured by the declaration of b and the constraint $a - x? \geq 0$.

2. The calculation is the same as on pages 218–220, except that $a - x? \geq 9$ will explicitly appear in each step (after the ' | '). In step (8.8), the constraint will end up as
… | $a - x? \geq 9 \wedge a - x? \geq 0$
which is just $a - x? \geq 9$. This is the precondition.
The two operations cannot be the same since their preconditions are different.

3. `pre SQRCheck`
$= \exists a',b',e! : \mathbb{Z} \bullet$ SQRCheck
$= \exists a',b',e! : \mathbb{Z} \bullet (\Xi$Coeffs; $c? : \mathbb{N}$; $e! : \mathbb{Z} | e! = b * b - 4 * a * c?)$
$=$ Coeffs; $c? : \mathbb{N} |$
$\exists a',b' : \mathbb{N}$; $e! : \mathbb{Z} \bullet e! = b * b - 4 * a * c? \wedge a' = a \wedge b' = b$
The important point is not to forget the equality predicates (or alternatively θ Coeffs' = θ Coeffs) subsumed in ΞCoeffs, which now become revealed when the after-state variables (with $e!$) are removed from the declaration part and existentially quantified in the predicate.

4. Each $\exists$-quantified variable x in (3) obeys the simplification criteria: it is equal to some term ξ which does not contain x and which is a member of the same set as x. The net result is that the whole $\exists$-predicate 'disappears', i.e. the precondition of SQRCheck is just true (as would be expected).

5. pre CondInc
   $= \exists\,a',b' : \mathbb{Z} \bullet CondInc$
   $= \exists\,a',b' : \mathbb{Z} \bullet (\Delta Coeffs \mid a' = a + 1 \wedge a' \geq b' \wedge b' = b)$
   $= Coeffs \mid \exists\,a',b' : \mathbb{N} \bullet a' = a + 1 \wedge a' \geq b' \wedge b' = b$
   Inspection shows that the simplification criteria apply to the a' equality and b' equality. Performing the simplification, we get
   $Coeffs \mid a + 1 \geq b$

8.12   1. Equality 1: by substitution of precondition calculations in (8.10) on page 221
   Equality 2: by combining the two schema texts according to schema disjunction
   Equality 3: by the property of predicate logic: $P \wedge Q1 \vee P \wedge Q2 \equiv P \wedge (Q1 \vee Q2)$
   Equality 4: $a \neq b \Leftrightarrow \neg (a = b)$, plus the property of predicate logic: $\neg P \vee P \equiv$ true
   Equality 5: by the property of predicate logic: $P \wedge$ true $\equiv P$
   Equality 6: by the definition of CanDoAttach, and folding.

  2. • By properties of ran, predicate (3) simplifies equivalently to
   a. ran cnnctd $\cup$ { u? } $\cup$ elemsOfq cnnctQu $\subseteq$ users
   or of course (commutativity of $\cup$)
   b. { u? } $\cup$ ran cnnctd $\cup$ elemsOfq cnnctQu $\subseteq$ users
   This must hold by properties of sets because we have
   c. ran cnnctd $\cup$ elemsOfq cnnctQu $\subseteq$ users
   from Computer and u? $\in$ users from CanDoAttach, hence that { u? } $\subseteq$ users. This together with (c) gives (b), since $A \subseteq C \wedge B \subseteq C \Leftrightarrow A \cup B \subseteq C$. So (b), hence (a), hence (3) is redundant and can be dropped by dropRdntCnj.

   • By properties of ran, predicate (4) simplifies equivalently to
   a. (ran cnnctd $\cup$ { u? }) $\cap$ elemsOfq cnnctQu $= \varnothing$
   or (since $(A \cup B) \cap C = \varnothing \Leftrightarrow A \cap C = \varnothing \wedge B \cap C = \varnothing$)
   b. ran cnnctd $\cap$ elemsOfq cnnctQu $= \varnothing \wedge$
      { u? } $\cap$ elemsOfq cnnctQu $= \varnothing$
   This must hold because we have the first conjunct from Computer and the second follows because we have
      u? $\notin$ ran cnnctd $\cup$ elemsOfq cnnctQu
   from CanDoAttach, which means in particular that u? $\notin$ elemsOfq cnnctQu, i.e., { u? } $\cap$ elemsOfq cnnctQu $= \varnothing$, since $e \notin X \Leftrightarrow \{ e \} \cap X = \varnothing$. So (b), hence (a), hence (4) is redundant and can be dropped by dropRdntCnj.

   • Predicate (2) on page 223 is: aFreeLn $\in$ linesUp \ dom cnnctd
   which can hold *iff* the right-hand argument of $\in$ is non-empty, i.e.:
   a. linesUp \ dom cnnctd $\neq \varnothing$
   Now, from Computer, we have dom cnnctd $\subseteq$ linesUp, which means that, by properties of sets $(A \setminus B \neq \varnothing \wedge B \subseteq C \Leftrightarrow B \subset C)$, (a) can hold *iff*
   b. dom cnnctd $\subset$ linesUp
   We also have from Computer
   c. cnnctQu $\neq$ emptyq $\Rightarrow$ #cnnctd $=$ #linesUp
   Moreover, since cnnctd is a function, it follows that
   d. #cnnctd $=$ #(dom cnnctd)
   which by substituting equals for equals in (c) gives
   e. cnnctQu $\neq$ emptyq $\Rightarrow$ #(dom cnnctd) $=$ #linesUp
   But dom cnnctd $\subseteq$ linesUp from Computer means that (e)'s consequent can hold *iff*
   f. dom cnnctd $=$ linesUp
   which means that we can re-express (e) as
   g. cnnctQu $\neq$ emptyq $\Rightarrow$ dom cnnctd $=$ linesUp
   However, (b) contradicts the consequent of (g), which means that we can invoke the second rule of logic quoted in the question to infer
   h. $\neg$ (cnnctQu $\neq$ emptyq)

Hence from (h) and the first rule of logic quoted in the question, we can infer

i. $\mathtt{cnnctQu} \neq \mathtt{emptyq} \Rightarrow \mathtt{P}$

where $\mathtt{P}$ can be anything we like. So it can be $\#(\mathtt{cnnctd} \cup \{\mathtt{aFreeLn} \mapsto \mathtt{u?}\})$, which makes (i) into predicate (6) on page 223! So predicate (6) is inferrable from other information and so too can be dropped by dropRdntCnj.

3. pre ($\mathtt{CanDoAttach} \wedge \mathtt{QueueUser}$)

$=\ \exists\ \mathtt{Computer'};\ \mathtt{attachMes!}:\mathtt{OLM\_Message}\bullet(\mathtt{CanDoAttach} \wedge \mathtt{QueueUser})$

$=\ \mathtt{Computer};\ \mathtt{u?}:\mathtt{USER}\ |$
    $\exists\ \mathtt{Computer'};\ \mathtt{attachMes!}:\mathtt{OLM\_Message}\bullet$
        $\mathtt{CanDoAttach}^{\mathrm{P}}$
        $\mathtt{linesUp}\setminus\mathtt{dom\ cnnctd}=\varnothing$
        $\mathtt{cnnctQu'}=\mathtt{addq(\,u?,cnnctQu\,)}$
        $\mathtt{attachMes!}=\mathtt{queued}$
        $\mathtt{avlblty'}=\mathtt{avlblty};\ \mathtt{users'}=\mathtt{users};\ \mathtt{priv'}=\mathtt{priv}$
        $\mathtt{allLines'}=\mathtt{allLines};\ \mathtt{linesUp'}=\mathtt{linesUp}$
        $\mathtt{cnnctd'}=\mathtt{cnnctd};\ \mathtt{maxQLen'}=\mathtt{maxQLen}$

$=\ $— by unfolding $\mathtt{Computer'}$ and applying $\exists$Scope
    $\mathtt{Computer};\ \mathtt{u?}:\mathtt{USER}\ |$
        $\mathtt{CanDoAttach}^{\mathrm{P}}$
        $\mathtt{linesUp}\setminus\mathtt{dom\ cnnctd}=\varnothing$
        $\exists\ \mathtt{Computer'}^{\mathrm{D}};\ \mathtt{attachMes!}:\mathtt{OLM\_Message}\bullet$
            $\mathtt{sysManager}\in\mathtt{priv'};\ \mathtt{priv'}\subseteq\mathtt{users'}$
            $\mathtt{ran\ cnnctd'}\cup\mathtt{elemsOfq\ cnnctQu'}\subseteq\mathtt{users'}$
            $\mathtt{ran\ cnnctd'}\cap\mathtt{elemsOfq\ cnnctQu'}=\varnothing$
            $\mathtt{dom\ cnnctd'}\subseteq\mathtt{linesUp'}\subseteq\mathtt{allLines'}$
            $\mathtt{lenq\ cnnctQu'}\leq\mathtt{maxQLen'}$
            $\mathtt{cnnctQu'}\neq\mathtt{emptyq}\Rightarrow\#\mathtt{cnnctd'}=\#\mathtt{linesUp'}$
            $\mathtt{avlblty'}=\mathtt{online}\Rightarrow\mathtt{allLines'}\neq\varnothing$
            $\mathtt{avlblty'}=\mathtt{offline}\Rightarrow\mathtt{linesUp'}=\varnothing\wedge\mathtt{cnnctQu'}=\mathtt{emptyq}$
            $\mathtt{cnnctQu'}=\mathtt{addq(\,u?,cnnctQu\,)}$
            $\mathtt{attachMes!}=\mathtt{queued}$
            $\mathtt{avlblty'}=\mathtt{avlblty};\ \mathtt{users'}=\mathtt{users};\ \mathtt{priv'}=\mathtt{priv}$
            $\mathtt{allLines'}=\mathtt{allLines};\ \mathtt{linesUp'}=\mathtt{linesUp}$
            $\mathtt{cnnctd'}=\mathtt{cnnctd};\ \mathtt{maxQLen'}=\mathtt{maxQLen}$

$=\ $— by onePtRule on: $\mathtt{cnnctQu'},\mathtt{attachMes!},\mathtt{avlblty'},\mathtt{users'},\mathtt{priv'},$
                    $\mathtt{allLines'},\mathtt{linesUp'},\mathtt{cnnctd'},\mathtt{maxQLen'}$
    $\mathtt{Computer};\ \mathtt{u?}:\mathtt{USER}\ |$
        $\mathtt{CanDoAttach}^{\mathrm{P}}$

$\mathtt{linesUp}\setminus\mathtt{dom\ cnnctd}=\varnothing$	(a)
$\mathtt{sysManager}\in\mathtt{priv};\ \mathtt{priv}\subseteq\mathtt{users}$	(*)
$\mathtt{ran\ cnnctd}\cup\mathtt{elemsOfq(\,addq(\,u?,cnnctQu\,)\,)}\subseteq\mathtt{users}$	(b)
$\mathtt{ran\ cnnctd}\cap\mathtt{elemsOfq(\,addq(\,u?,cnnctQu\,)\,)}=\varnothing$	(c)
$\mathtt{dom\ cnnctd}\subseteq\mathtt{linesUp}\subseteq\mathtt{allLines}$	(*)
$\mathtt{lenq(\,addq(\,u?,cnnctQu\,)\,)}\leq\mathtt{maxQLen}$	(d)
$\mathtt{addq(\,u?,cnnctQu\,)}\neq\mathtt{emptyq}\Rightarrow\#\mathtt{cnnctd}=\#\mathtt{linesUp}$	(e)
$\mathtt{avlblty}=\mathtt{online}\Rightarrow\mathtt{allLines}\neq\varnothing$	(*)
$\mathtt{avlblty}=\mathtt{offline}\Rightarrow\mathtt{linesUp}=\varnothing\wedge\mathtt{addq(\,u?,cnnctQu\,)}=\mathtt{emptyq}$	(f)

Those conjuncts marked (*) can be dropped immediately as they are part of $\mathtt{Computer}$. Using dropRdntCnj, the following can also be discarded:

- (d) because, by properties of $<$ and $\leq$, (d) follows from $\mathtt{lenq\ cnnctQu}<\mathtt{maxQLen}$ in $\mathtt{CanDoAttach}$ and $\mathtt{lenq(\,addq(\,u?,cnnctQu\,)\,)}=1+\mathtt{lenq\ cnnctQu}$ (property of $\mathtt{lenq}$)

- (e) since its consequent holds thus: (a) and $\mathtt{dom\ cnnctd}\subseteq\mathtt{linesUp}$ from $\mathtt{Computer}$ together (by sets) give $\mathtt{dom\ cnnctd}=\mathtt{linesUp}$; so $\#(\mathtt{dom\ cnnctd})=\#\mathtt{linesUp}$, hence $\#\mathtt{cnnctd}=\#\mathtt{linesUp}$ ($\mathtt{cnnctd}$ is a function). Hence, (e) itself follows by the following rule of logic: if $\mathtt{Q}$ holds, $\mathtt{P}\Rightarrow\mathtt{Q}$ can be inferred ($\mathtt{P}$ can be anything)

- (f) because its antecedent is false by `avlblty = online` in `CanDoAttach`. The rule used here is that if P holds, $\neg P \Rightarrow Q$ can be inferred (Q can be anything).

We are left with

> Computer; u? : USER |
>   CanDoAttach^P
>   linesUp \ dom cnnctd = ∅   (a)
>   ran cnnctd ∪ elemsOfq(addq(u?, cnnctQu)) ⊆ users   (b)
>   ran cnnctd ∩ elemsOfq(addq(u?, cnnctQu)) = ∅   (c)

A property of `elemsOfq` is that

i.   elemsOfq(addq(u?, cnnctQu)) = { u? } ∪ elemsOfq cnnctQu

From `Computer`, we have

ii.   ran cnnctd ∪ elemsOfq cnnctQu ⊆ users
iii. ran cnnctd ∩ elemsOfq cnnctQu = ∅

From `CanDoAttach`, we have

iv. u? ∈ users
v.   u? ∉ ran cnnctd ∪ elemsOfq cnnctQu

By properties of sets and set operations, (b) follows from (i), (ii) and (iv), and (c) follows from (i), (iii) and (v). So (b) and (c) can also be discarded by dropRdntCnj. This leaves

> Computer; u? : USER |
>   CanDoAttach^P ∧ linesUp \ dom cnnctd = ∅

8.13   1. Since `ReportMcState` includes ΞComputer, this means that the 'instance bindings' θ Computer and θ Computer' in the framing schema φOLM will be equal. So there is no change of state to `OnlineMonitor` in the promoted version of `ReportMcState`.

    2. [ADDR]
     maxNoBuff : $\mathbb{N}_1$
     BufferManager ≙ [buffs : ADDR ⇸ Buffer | #buffs ≤ maxNoBuff]

> ___φBM_____
> ΔBufferManger
> ΔBuffer
> startAddr? : ADDR
> _____
> startAddr? ∈ dom buffs
> buffs startAddr? = θ Buffer
> buffs' = buffs ⊕ { startAddr? ↦ θ Buffer' }

    BM_AddB ≙ (φBM ∧ AddB) \ (ΔBuffer)
    BM_LenB ≙ (φBM ∧ LenB) \ (ΔBuffer)

    3. Assuming the state was something like

> QueueOfObj ≙ [objQu : seq Object]

    then the framing schema would be

> ___φQO_____
> ΔQueueOfObj
> ΔObject
> _____
> #objQu > 0
> objQu(1) = θ Object
> objQu' = objQu ⊕ { 1 ↦ θ Object' }

    4. The full system state would be something like schema `VanHire` on the next page. This schema is followed by a framing schema φVH. Note that `today` in this frame never changes, and that the schema says nothing explicit about the `Vans` component, for reasons which are explained below it (`activeBkngs` in `VanHire` is the same derived component that in the state model of Chapters 5/6 resided in subschema `Bookings`).

```
___VanHire_____
Vans                                    — as was in VanHire
bkngs : BOOKING ⇸ BookingRec            — see answer to Exercise 8.5(2)
activeBkngs : ℙ BOOKING
today : Date
_____
activeBkngs = { b : dom bkngs | ( bkngs b ).status = active }
vansOnHire = { b : activeBkngs • ( bkngs b ).vanAlloc }
∀ b : activeBkngs •
   fleet(( bkngs b ).vanAlloc ) = ( bkngs b ).vcl ∧
   startOf(( bkngs b ).datePr ) isOnOrBefore today
∀ c : VanClass • ∀ d : Date •
   #{ b : dom bkngs |
         ( bkngs b ).vcl = c ∧ d fallsIn ( bkngs b ).datePr }
     ≤
   #( fleet~⦇{ c }⦈)
```

```
___φVH_____
ΔVanHire
ΔBookingRec
b? : BOOKING
_____
b? ∈ dom bkngs
bkngs b? = θ BookingRec
bkngs' = bkngs ⊕ { b? ↦ θ BookingRec' }
today' = today
```

The reason for φVH's predicate not mentioning any variables of Vans explicitly is that it is possible to identify two kinds of promotion, described below, for BookingRec operations: one for operations OpBR1 where an update, say OpDV, on component Vans is involved; and one for those operations OpBR2 which have no effect on Vans. Most BookingRec operations would fall in the latter category; an example which would not is CollectVan (page 274), since allocation of a van (to some booking) is involved. Here, the OpDV component would describe the specific update on Vans that is also required (which is that vansHireable loses the van allocated).

$$VH\_OpBR1 ≙ (φVH ∧ OpBR1 ∧ OpDV) \setminus (ΔBookingRec)$$
$$VH\_OpBR2 ≙ (φVH ∧ OpBR2 ∧ ΞVans) \setminus (ΔBookingRec)$$

8.14 1. We assume that a machine can be deleted (by a privileged user) only if it is off line.

```
___DeleteMc_____
ΔOnlineMonitor
m? : MACHINE
_____
( mcInsts m? ).avlblty = offline   — m? ∈ olmMcs is in MachineOK below
mcInsts' = { m? } ◁̸ mcInsts
linePool' = linePool       — recall: most variables in OnlineMonitor are derived
```

For data checking and error handling, we will use various schemas on page 229, plus:

```
___McStillOnline_____
ΞOnlineMonitor
m? : MACHINE
olmMes! : OLM_Message
_____
m? ∈ olmMcs
( mcInsts m? ).avlblty ≠ offline
olmMes! = mcNotOffline      — assume added to OLM_Message
```

Then:

$$RbDeleteMc ≙ (DeleteMc ∧ PrivUserOK ∧ MachineOK) ∨$$
$$IllicitUser ∨ BadMachine ∨ McStillOnline$$

which either flags validData (the delete is effected) or some error message.

2. We make use of `InitComputer` in the answer to Exercise 8.4(1), page 286:

```
┌─── AddMachine ──────────────────────────────────────────────────────────────
│ ΔOnlineMonitor
│ m? : MACHINE            — an input here, but we could make the operation choose the identifier
│ InitComputer                              — the new 'machine instance' being added
├───────────────────────────────────────────────────────────────────────────
│ m? ∉ olmMcs                               — the machine identifier must be new
│ #olmMcs < maxNoMcs                        — there must be 'room' for the new machine
│ mcInsts' = mcInsts ⊕ { m? ↦ θ InitComputer }
│ linePool' = linePool                      — see comment in DeleteMc on previous page
```

We will need two more error-handling operations (here given a touch of priority):

```
┌─── McIdNotNew ──────────────────────────────────────────────────────────────
│ ΞOnlineMonitor
│ m? : MACHINE
│ olmMes! : OLM_Message
├───────────────────────────────────────────────────────────────────────────
│ m? ∈ olmMcs
│ olmMes! = notNewMcId                      — assume added to OLM_Message
```

```
┌─── NoRoomForNewMc ──────────────────────────────────────────────────────────
│ ΞOnlineMonitor
│ m? : MACHINE
│ olmMes! : OLM_Message
├───────────────────────────────────────────────────────────────────────────
│ m? ∉ olmMcs
│ #olmMcs = maxNoMcs
│ olmMes! = sysAtMcLimit                    — assume added to OLM_Message
```

Using `PrivUserOK` on page 229, we can now define the full robust operation, hiding `InitComputer` at the same time:

$$RbAddMachine \hat{=} ((AddMachine \setminus (InitComputer)) \wedge PrivUserOK) \vee$$
$$IllicitUser \vee McIdNotNew \vee NoRoomForNewMc$$

3. `McStatus ::= unavailable | quiet | active | full`

```
┌─── McStatusRprt ────────────────────────────────────────────────────────────
│ ΞOnlineMonitor
│ mcStates! : MACHINE ⇸ McStatus
├───────────────────────────────────────────────────────────────────────────
│ mcStates! =
│   { mIdr : dom mcInsts | ( mcInsts mIdr ).avlblty = offline •
│       mIdr ↦ unavailable } ∪
│   { mIdr : dom mcInsts | ( let m == mcInsts mIdr •
│         m.avlblty = online ∧ m.cnnctd = ∅ ∧ m.cnnctQu = emptyq ) •
│       mIdr ↦ quiet } ∪
│   { mIdr : dom mcInsts | ( let m == mcInsts mIdr •
│         ran m.cnnctd ∪ elemsOfq m.cnnctQu ≠ ∅ ) •
│       mIdr ↦ ( if lenq( mcInsts mIdr ).cnnctQu < ( mcInsts mIdr ).maxQLen
│                 then active else full )}
```

8.15 1. a. `Incb ⨾ Incb`

$$= (Incb[a''/a',b''/b'] \wedge Incb[a''/a,b''/b]) \setminus (a'',b'')$$
$$= ((Coeffs; Coeffs'' | a'' = a \wedge b'' = b + 1)$$
$$\wedge (Coeffs''; Coeffs' | a' = a'' \wedge b' = b'' + 1)) \setminus (a'',b'')$$
$$= (Coeffs; Coeffs''; Coeffs' |$$
$$a'' = a \wedge b'' = b + 1 \wedge a' = a'' \wedge b' = b'' + 1) \setminus (a'',b'')$$
$$= \exists a'',b'' : \mathbb{Z} • (Coeffs; Coeffs''; Coeffs' |$$
$$a'' = a \wedge b'' = b + 1 \wedge a' = a'' \wedge b' = b'' + 1)$$
$$= Coeffs; Coeffs' |$$
$$\exists a'',b'' : \mathbb{N} • a'' = a \wedge b'' = b + 1 \wedge a' = a'' \wedge b' = b'' + 1$$

— using the first two equalities for simplification purposes via onePtRule

$=$ Coeffs; Coeffs' | a' = a ∧ b' = (b + 1) + 1   (*)

$=$ Coeffs; Coeffs' | a' = a ∧ b' = b + 2

b. This is identical to (a) except that we have b'' - 1 instead of b'' + 1 in the various predicates. So, omitting the detail, and starting from step (*), we have

Incb ⨾ Decb

$=$ Coeffs; Coeffs' | a' = a ∧ b' = (b + 1) - 1

$=$ Coeffs; Coeffs' | a' = a ∧ b' = b

$=$ ΞCoeffs

which is what we would expect.

2. No. The operation of (1b) is total—its precondition is `true` (check this!). Decb ⨾ Incb is non-total because the effect of Decb is defined only if b ≥ 1 (which is the combined operation's precondition; again, check this). Decb in (1b) is always applicable because it 'follows' Incb whose effect guarantees a state where b > 0, and hence that b ≥ 1.

8.16 1. The full state model would be

```
┌─OLM_SUD────────────────────────────────────────
│ OnlineMonitor; SysUsage
├────────────────────────────────────────────────
│ ran regsPerMc = olmMcs
│ ∀ m : olmMcs •
│    regsPerUsr ⦇ regsPerMc~⦇{ m }⦈ ⦈ = ( mcInsts m ).users
└────────────────────────────────────────────────
```

2. System-level non-promoted operations would now include Δ or ΞOLM_SUD instead of Δ or ΞOnlineMonitor as appropriate. In each such operation affecting only the OnlineMonitor component, we would incorporate

θ SysUsage' = θ SysUsage

into its predicate part. For promoting the majority of Computer operations, we could define a new framing schema over ΔOLM_SUD which is essentially just a combination of φOLM and the above equality. Note that it is important to retain φOLM for a Computer operation like RbDisconnect on page 234, which is handled differently.

3. In (a)–(c), we have used schema inclusion to incorporate the required user checks.

a. u? is the user whose registrations are being inspected, so u? in PrivUserOK must be renamed to avoid a clash.

```
┌─OlmUserUsage──────────────────────────────────
│ ΞOLM_SUD; PrivUserOK [ pusr?/u? ]
│ u? : USER
│ usage! : MACHINE ⇸ ℕ × ℕ
│ totConns!,totCnnTime : ℕ
├────────────────────────────────────────────────
│ u? ∈ allUsers
│ usage! = { r : dom( regsPerUsr ▷ { u? }) • regsPerMc r ↦ usrUsage r }
│ totConns! = ( Σ r : dom( regsPerUsr ▷ { u? }) • first( usrUsage r ))
│ totCnnTime! = ( Σ r : dom( regsPerUsr ▷ { u? }) • second( usrUsage r ))
└────────────────────────────────────────────────
```

Similar summation expressions/outputs could be included in (b) and (c).

b.
```
┌─OlmMcUsage────────────────────────────────────
│ ΞOLM_SUD; PrivUserOK
│ m? : MACHINE
│ usage! : USER ⇸ ℕ × ℕ
├────────────────────────────────────────────────
│ m? ∈ olmMcs
│ usage! = { r : dom( regsPerMc ▷ { m? }) • regsPerUsr r ↦ usrUsage r }
└────────────────────────────────────────────────
```

c. Keeping with the simple error-checking scheme of page 229, we might define:

SysManagerOK ≙ [pusr? : USER; olmMes! : OLM_Message |
                    pusr? = sysManager ∧ olmMes! = validData]

Then:

```
┌─ OlmUsagePMRep ──────────────────────────────────────────
│ ΔOLM_SUD
│ SysManagerOK
│ usage! : MACHINE ⇸ ( USER ⇸ ℕ × ℕ )
├──────────────────────────────────────────────────────────
│ usage! = { m : ran regsPerMc •
│              m ↦ { r : regsPerMc~⦇{ m }⦈ • regsPerUsr r ↦ usrUsage r } }
│ θ OnlineMonitor' = θ OnlineMonitor
│ regsPerMc' = regsPerMc
│ regsPerUsr' = regsPerUsr
│ ran usrUsage' = { ( 0,0 ) }
└──────────────────────────────────────────────────────────
```

The domain of usrUsage' is fixed to be that of usrUsage by the first invariant of
SysUsage and the third and fourth equalities above.

4. A possibly better (and more natural) approach to SysUsage would be to define a user
registration record using a schema which would clump together all attributes of a
registration. For example:

```
┌─ OverallUsage ───────────────────────────────────────────
│ — accumulating 'lifespan of registration' data
│ totNConns : ℕ
│ totConnTm, totCpuTm : ℕ
├──────────────────────────────────────────────────────────
│ totCpuTm ≤ totConnTm
└──────────────────────────────────────────────────────────
```

```
┌─ PeriodUsage ────────────────────────────────────────────
│ — periodic data accumulated since last management report was requested
│ nConns : ℕ
│ connTm, cpuTm : ℕ
├──────────────────────────────────────────────────────────
│ cpuTm ≤ connTm
└──────────────────────────────────────────────────────────
```

```
┌─ Registration ───────────────────────────────────────────
│ usr : USER
│ mc : MACHINE
│ cd : Date                                        — date created
│ OverallUsage
│ PeriodUsage
├──────────────────────────────────────────────────────────
│ nConns ≤ totNConns
│ cpuTm ≤ totCpuTm
│ connTm ≤ totConnTm
└──────────────────────────────────────────────────────────
```

This approach makes it easy to include any number of different attributes in the make-
up of a user registration record and define operations such as

```
┌─ UpdateConnData ─────────────────────────────────────────
│ ΔRegistration
│ etc?, tcpu? : ℕ
├──────────────────────────────────────────────────────────
│ usr' = usr; mc' = mc; cd' = cd
│ connTm' = connTm + etc?; totConnTm' = totConnTm + etc?
│ cpuTm' = cpuTm + tcpu?; totCpuTm' = totCpuTm + tcpu?
│ nConns' = nConns + 1; totNConns' = totNConns + 1
└──────────────────────────────────────────────────────────
```

When promoted, this operation would be akin to UpdateSUData on page 234. Here, we
have also included tcpu?, the target machine CPU time used during the connection
(which we can imagine is also sourced by RbDisconnect via some eventual piping).

Now comes the SysUsage component. Since the usr and mc attributes uniquely
identify registrations, it would be sufficient to have

```
┌─ SysUsage ───────────────────────────────────────────────
│ regRecs : ℙ Registration
├──────────────────────────────────────────────────────────
│ ∀ r1, r2 : regRecs | r1 ≠ r2 • r1.usr ≠ r2.usr ∨ r1.mc ≠ r2.mc
└──────────────────────────────────────────────────────────
```

This would be followed (eventually—the OLM_SUD predicate in the answer to Question (1) would have to be modified) by some framing and promotion. Note the variation on framing due to the form taken by the Registration aggregate involved (just a set).

$$
\begin{array}{|l}
\underline{\quad \phi\text{SUD}\underline{\hspace{5.5cm}}} \\
\Delta\text{OLM\_SUD} \\
\Delta\text{Registration} \\
\text{u? : USER} \\
\text{m? : MACHINE} \\
\hline
\text{usr = u?; mc = m?} \\
\theta\,\text{Registration} \in \text{regRecs} \\
\text{regRecs'} = (\text{regRecs} \setminus \{\theta\,\text{Registration}\}) \cup \{\theta\,\text{Registration'}\} \\
\theta\,\text{OnlineMonitor'} = \theta\,\text{OnlineMonitor} \\
\end{array}
$$

SUD_UpdateConnData ≙ (φSUD ∧ UpdateConnData) \ (ΔRegistration) etc., with robust versions checking that the registration exists.

Chapter 9

(We adopt our usual short cuts in presentation where appropriate: use of indentation and elision of ∧.)

9.1   1. We need to prove the theorem:

⊢ ∃ Computer' • InitComputer

— which is, by unfolding Computer' and InitComputer

⊢ ∃ Computer'^{D} •

    sysManager ∈ priv'; priv' ⊆ users'
    ran cnnctd' ∪ elemsOfq cnnctQu' ⊆ users'
    ran cnnctd' ∩ elemsOfq cnnctQu' = ∅
    dom cnnctd' ⊆ linesUp' ⊆ allLines'
    lenq cnnctQu' ≤ maxQLen'
    cnnctQu' ≠ emptyq ⇒ #cnnctd' = #linesUp'
    avlblty' = online ⇒ allLines' ≠ ∅
    avlblty' = offline ⇒ linesUp' = ∅ ∧ cnnctQu' = emptyq
    avlblty' = offline
    users' = priv' = { sysManager }
    allLines' = linesUp' = ∅
    cnnctd' = ∅
    cnnctQu' = emptyq
    maxQLen' = 0

— which is, by onePtRule on: avlblty', users', priv', allLines',
                              linesUp', cnnctd', cnnctQu', maxQLen'

⊢ sysManager ∈ { sysManager }; { sysManager } ⊆ { sysManager }
    ran ∅ ∪ elemsOfq emptyq ⊆ { sysManager }
    ran ∅ ∩ elemsOfq emptyq = ∅
    dom ∅ ⊆ ∅ ⊆ ∅
    lenq emptyq ≤ 0
    emptyq ≠ emptyq ⇒ #∅ = #∅
    offline = online ⇒ ∅ ≠ ∅
    offline = offline ⇒ ∅ = ∅ ∧ emptyq = emptyq

— which is, by properties of dom, ran and InjQueue

⊢ sysManager ∈ { sysManager }; { sysManager } ⊆ { sysManager }
    ∅ ∪ ∅ ⊆ { sysManager }
    ∅ ∩ ∅ = ∅
    ∅ ⊆ ∅ ⊆ ∅
    0 ≤ 0
    emptyq ≠ emptyq ⇒ #∅ = #∅
    offline = online ⇒ ∅ ≠ ∅
    offline = offline ⇒ ∅ = ∅ ∧ emptyq = emptyq

The first five conjuncts are trivially equivalent to `true` by simple properties of sets. $0 \leq 0$ is also trivially equivalent to `true`. The last three implications simplify to `true`, the first two because the antecedent is equivalent to `false`, the last because both antecedent and consequent are equivalent to `true`. So the original sequent simplifies to just

$\vdash$ `true`

which means it is a theorem.

2. The consistency theorem for the operation would be:

$\vdash \exists \Delta$`State` $\bullet$ `Swap`
— which is, by unfolding Δ`State` and `Swap`
$\vdash \exists a,b,a',b' : \mathbb{Z} \bullet a < b \land a' < b' \land a' = b \land b' = a$
— which is, by onePtRule on: a', b'
$\vdash \exists a,b : \mathbb{Z} \bullet a < b \land b < a$
— which is, by properties of $\mathbb{Z}$
$\vdash \exists a,b : \mathbb{Z} \bullet a < b \land \neg (a < b)$
— which is, by a simple property of logic
$\vdash \exists a,b : \mathbb{Z} \bullet$ `false`
— which is, by a simple property of logic
$\vdash$ `false`

which means the sequent predicate is a contradiction, hence that `Swap` is inconsistent.

9.2
1. Put simply, it would suggest that the 'abstract' state was in fact less abstract than the concrete state (there is a feature of state models known as 'implementation bias' which means that some states are 'indistinguishable' as far as the operations defined over them are concerned). This is not wrong, and is allowed in the more general form of data refinement. The consequence is that the retrieve relation would now be 1-to-many, i.e., not functional, and some of the associated theorems (in fact (9.8) and (9.10) on pages 246 and 248) would be more complicated.

2. We model the two-dimensional array as a sequence of sequences:

N,M : $\mathbb{N}_1$
DataStruct $\hat{=}$ [matrix : seq(seq $\mathbb{Z}$); K,L : $\mathbb{N}$ |
$\qquad$ K $\leq$ N $\land$ L $\leq$ M $\land$ (K $=$ 0 $\Leftrightarrow$ L $=$ 0) $\land$
$\qquad$ #matrix $=$ K $\land$ ($\forall$ i : 1..K $\bullet$ #(matrix i) $=$ L)]

Note that if there are zero rows in use, then there must be zero columns in use, and vice versa.

3. We need to prove
Given CARel' then:
$\qquad$ InitNatNumArray $\vdash$ InitNatNumSet
The declarative part of the right-hand side schema text is just NatNumSet', which is provided by CARel' on the left. So we can unfold the sequent into
$\qquad$ CARel'; NatNumArray' |
$\qquad\quad$ a' $= \langle \rangle \vdash$ s' $= \varnothing$
which holds because we have a' $= \langle \rangle$ on the left and s' $=$ ran a' in CARel'. Hence, by substitution, s' $=$ ran $\langle \rangle$, and s' $= \varnothing$ immediately follows.

4. Considering first applicability, we address the sequent
Given CARel then:
$\qquad$ pre Remove $\vdash$ pre RemElem
As in Question (3), the declarations of the right-hand part of the sequent are provided on the left. Unfolding and substituting the precondition calculations (not shown) gives
$\qquad$ CARel; NatNumSet; x? : $\mathbb{N}$ |
$\qquad\quad$ true $\vdash$ x? $\in$ ran a
But this cannot be a theorem since there is nothing in CARel and/or NatNumSet that enables us to deduce the conclusion predicate x? $\in$ ran a (obviously the declaration x? : $\mathbb{N}$ and the predicate true do not help). So the applicability theorem does not hold and hence the refinement is invalid. Consideration of the correctness theorem thus becomes irrelevant.

5. The correctness theorem for `RemElem` is

Given ΔCARel then:

pre Remove ∧ RemElem ⊢ Remove

All the declarative part of the right-hand side is provided by the left-hand side. So substituting the precondition calculation, unfolding, rearranging, etc. gives

ΔCARel; NatNumSet; ΔNatNumArray; x? : ℕ|

true

a′ = a↾(ran a \ { x? })

⊢

s′ = s \ { x? }

This looks awkward to prove. We need to utilize some properties of sequences to try to transform the hypothesis equality into the conclusion equality. Firstly, from the hypothesis equality, it must follow that

ran a′ = ran(a↾(ran a \ { x? }))   (1)

Consider the right-hand side which has the form ran(s ↾ X). Suppose X ⊆ ran s; then ran(s↾ X) is just X itself since all and only elements of X must end up in s↾ X! Expressing this property more formally:

X ⊆ ran s ⇒ ran(s↾ X) = X   (2)

(Strictly, we should prove this 'lemma', a lemma being a useful side-theorem in a larger proof.) Now, clearly by simple properties of sets,

ran a \ { x? } ⊆ ran a

The antecedent guarding the equality in lemma (2) thus holds in (1). So we can use this equality to transform the right-hand side of (1) to give

ran a′ = ran a \ { x? }

Now the conclusion of the sequent immediately follows because of the equalities s = ran a and s′ = ran a′ in ΔCARel.

So the correctness theorem holds for `RemElem`. The example illustrates the point that, often in the proof of a theorem, side theorems need to be established to act as 'stepping stones' in the construction of the overall proof.

9.3 1. No data refinement is involved since the two operations are over the same state space. Hence no retrieve relation is involved in the expression of the applicability and correctness theorems, which are thus simply:

pre AddElem ⊢ pre AddElem1   — applicability
pre AddElem ∧ AddElem1 ⊢ AddElem   — correctness

2. The overall **if** structure of the code has the form

if P **then** S1 **elsif** not P **then** S2 **end if**

which is derived from refining into code an operation specification whose predicate is basically

P ⇒ Q1 ∧ ¬ P ⇒ Q2

where S1/S2 are the components which the predicate parts Q1/Q2 'give rise to'. The component

[*lookFor(x?, a, i, found)*]

is associated with the predicates x? ∉ ran a and x? ∈ ran a via the (boolean) variable found, but involves an extra variable i which is used to index the position at which x? has been found in a (if it has been found). The instruction

skip

'does nothing' and hence corresponds to refining into code a 'leaving the state unchanged' effect, as expressed in a predicate like θ NatNumArray′ = θ NatNumArray. The component

[*shiftDownOne(a, i)*]

is connected with the existentially quantified predicate, whose i is in effect the value of i obtained by *lookFor* (when x? is in a). *shiftDownOne* moves the elements in positions i + 1 .. #a successively down one, thus geting rid of x?. This is strongly related to the equality in the quantification where a is split into a prefix and suffix that omits x? in position i, and which are then concatenated to give the updated array. The instruction

nels := nels − 1

is obviously derived from the predicate nels′ = nels − 1.

3. The two operations are over the same state space, so we merely need to prove
   a. pre AnOp ⊢ pre BnOp
   b. pre AnOp ∧ BnOp ⊢ AnOp
   Precondition calculations (not given) will yield
       pre AnOp is: NatNumArray; x? : ℕ | a ≠ ⟨ ⟩
       pre BnOp is: NatNumArray; x? : ℕ | true
   Therefore, the applicability theorem (a) unfolds into
       NatNumArray;x? : ℕ |
           a ≠ ⟨ ⟩ ⊢ true
   which trivially holds. (b) is (after unfolding, rearrangement, etc.)
       ΔNatNumArray; size! : ℕ |
           a ≠ ⟨ ⟩ ∧ size! = nels ∧ nels′ = 0
           ⊢
           a ≠ ⟨ ⟩ ∧ size! = nels ∧ ran a′ ⊆ ran a
   The first and second conjuncts of the conclusion trivially follow from the first and
   second conjuncts of the hypothesis. The third conjunct of the conclusion follows from
   the third conjunct of the hypothesis. This is because nels′ = 0 must mean, by
   #a′ = nels′ in the predicate of NatNumArray′, that #a′ = 0 and hence that
       a′ = ⟨ ⟩
   or that
       ran a′ = ∅
   Now ∅ ⊆ X for any X, so
       ∅ ⊆ ran a
   Hence, by substitution,
       ran a′ ⊆ ran a
   So the correctness theorem also holds, which completes the proof.
       BnOp has a more liberal precondition than AnOp, but its behaviour is narrower. In
   fact, BnOp's behaviour is deterministic whereas AnOp's is not—the latter permits a
   range of outcomes for a′ but for the former there is only one possibility, namely ⟨ ⟩.

INDEX OF NOTATION

The following index places the various symbols and special characters of Z into pragmatic groupings for ease of reference. A few symbols have entries in more than one section. Underscores have been used to indicate the arity/syntax of relations and operators where this is considered useful. Entries marked † are not used directly in Z paragraphs (schemas, axiomatic descriptions, etc.). Numbers on the right are page references. Page references identify the first useful point(s) in the main text where the items appear. A page reference which is '—' indicates that the particular (usage of the) item was not covered or illustrated in the text. The index covers virtually the whole of Z. The one significant omission is anything to do with *bags*, the only Z facility not covered in the text.

Remark
For authoritative (though not entirely compatible) descriptions of Z syntax, consult

- Spivey (1992):   the recognized *de facto* standard, which this book follows because of its established status and accessibility in the public domain.
- Brien and Nicholls (1992):   the proposed BSI (British Standards Institute) standard, available from ZIP Standards Secretary, Oxford University PRG.

General Separators

,	(Comma) Separator for items in various kinds of list (no page refs. given)	
;	Declaration separator	31
	Top-level conjunctive separator in predicates of 'box' displays	60
:	Namelist–set expression separator in a declaration	27
|	Declaration–constraint separator in schema text	30
	Separator of alternatives in free type definitions	92
•	Separation of schema text from predicates / terms	66 / 103
	Separator in local definitions	142

Symbols Involving =

=	Equality relation	37
≠	Inequality relation	64
==	Abbreviation definition: as a paragraph / in local definitions	117 / 142
≙	Schema definition	31
::=	Free type definition	92

Bracketing

(...)	General delimitation / Tuple display	77 / (76) 99
[...]	Schema text delimitation / Given set definition	31 / 91
	Generic formal or actual parameter list / Variable renaming	163 / 204
{ ... }	Set display (extensional definition) / Set comprehension	94 / 102
⟨ ... ⟩	Sequence display / Binding display†	(105) 160 / 32
⟪ ... ⟫	Free type constructor domain	183
_⦇_⦈	Relational image operator	122
⦉ ... ⦊	Schema type†	156

Open-face Letters

$\mathbb{P}$ _	Powerset constructor: all sets that are subsets of ...	(77) 96
$\mathbb{P}_1$ _	All non-empty subsets of ...	153
$\mathbb{F}$ _	All finite subsets of ...	98
$\mathbb{F}_1$ _	All non-empty finite subsets of ...	161
$\mathbb{Z}$	The integers	29
$\mathbb{N}$	The natural numbers (zero or any greater integer)	29
$\mathbb{N}_1$	The strictly positive integers	29

Postfix Symbols and Trailing Characters

Alphanumeric Identifiers

Miscellaneous

Prefix generic symbols ($\mathbb{P}$, seq, etc.) bind to the *left* and more tightly than the nine 'function arrows' and $\leftrightarrow$ which all bind to the *right*. All operators/functions bind more tightly than relations which bind more tightly than $\wedge$, $\vee$, etc. Prefix and postfix operators/functions bind to the *left* (postfix tighter than prefix) and more tightly than their infix cousins. The latter have the following relative priorities (increasing to the *right*, with equal-priority symbols in parentheses):

$$\mapsto \quad .. \quad \left(+, -, \cup, \setminus, ^{\frown} \right) \quad \left(\star, \text{div}, \text{mod}, \cap, \mathbb{1}, \restriction, _{\circ}^{\circ}, \circ \right) \quad \oplus \quad \left(\triangleleft, \triangleright, \triangleleft\!\!\!-, \triangleright\!\!\!- \right)$$

SUBJECT INDEX